Volume 6

Ema Toyama

**Translated and adapted by
Alethea Nibley and Athena Nibley**

Lettered by Paige Pumphrey

Character

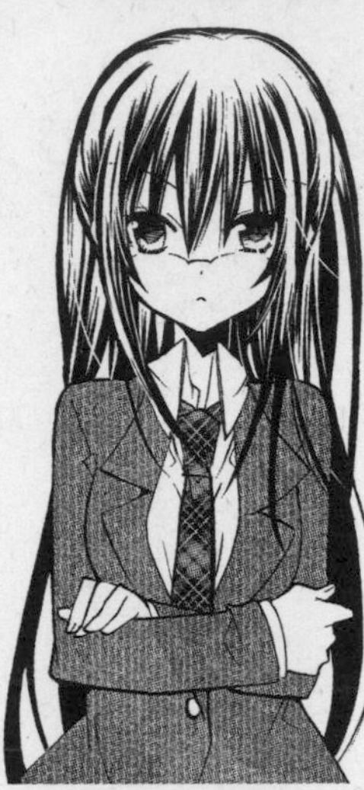

Yukina Himuro

A third-year junior high student who strikes terror in the hearts of all around her with her piercing gaze, feared as the "Absolute Zero Snow Woman." Only Akira knows that she is also the popular cell phone novelist Yupina.

Shigure Kitami

The ever-popular, yet black-hearted, student body president. He made a game of charming all the girls and making them confess their love to him, then writing it all down in his student notebook, but Yukina discovered his secret!

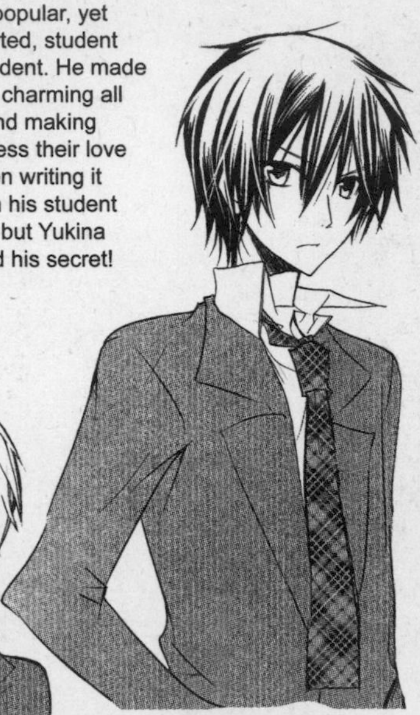

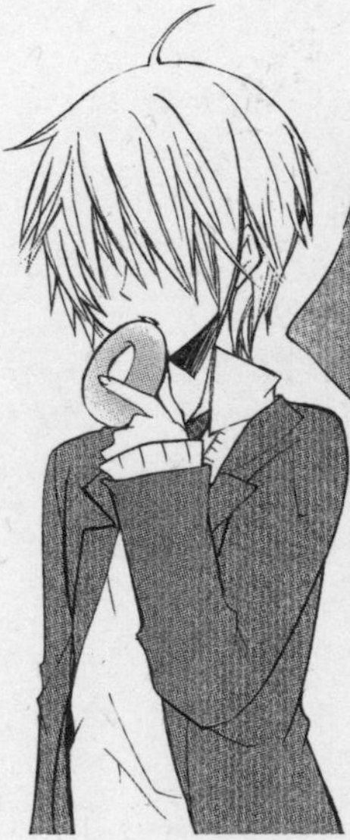

Akira Shimotsuki

Yukina's cousin and fellow student. He loves to eat. As Yukina's confidant, he can always be found nearby, watching over her. There's a good-looking face hiding behind that hair.

ne!

It is time for love.
Secret cell phone novelist vs. the most popular boy in school.
A mission of love for absolute servitude.

Mami Mizuno

A childhood friend of Shigure's. A sickly girl, she had been taking time off from school, but now she has returned. The teachers love her, and she's very popular with the boys. She's a beautiful young girl who always wears a smile, but....

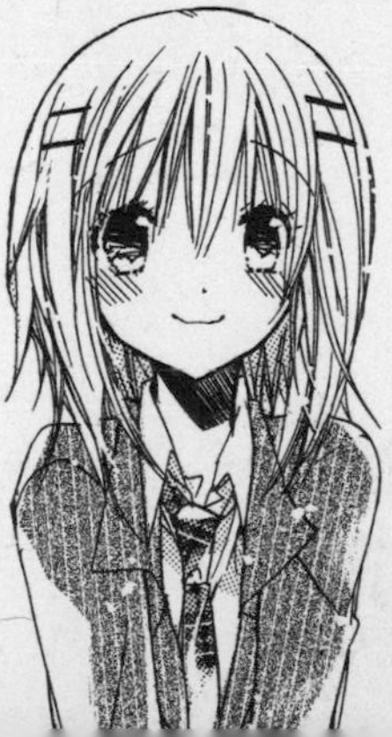

Story

Yukina has been blackmailing Shigure into helping her experience romance, but after Akira's confession of love and the appearance of Mami, she is only more confused... Now Akira has discovered the secret of the girl who has been tormenting Yukina. How will the relationships change between the four!?

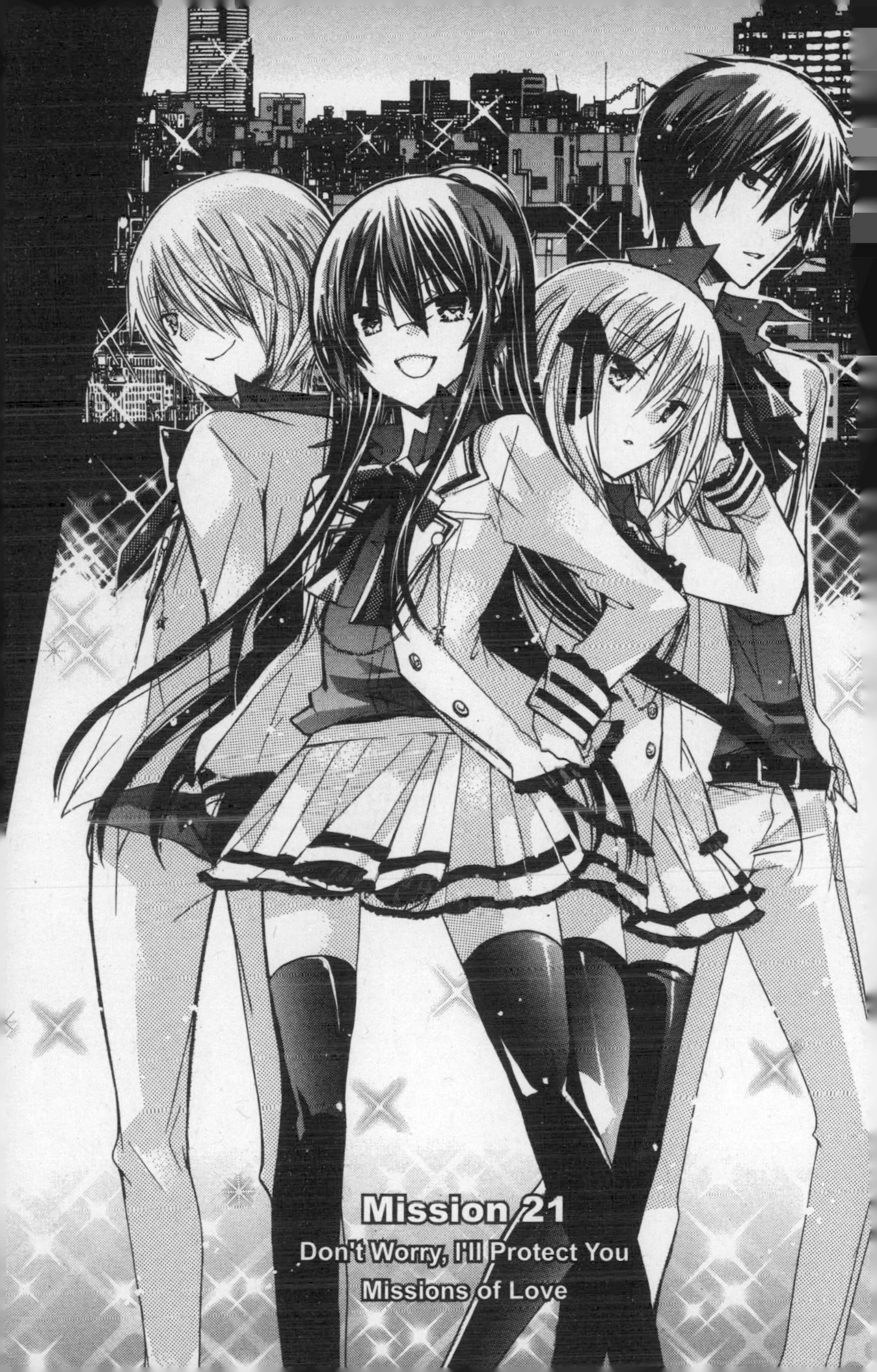

Mission 21

Don't Worry, I'll Protect You

Missions of Love

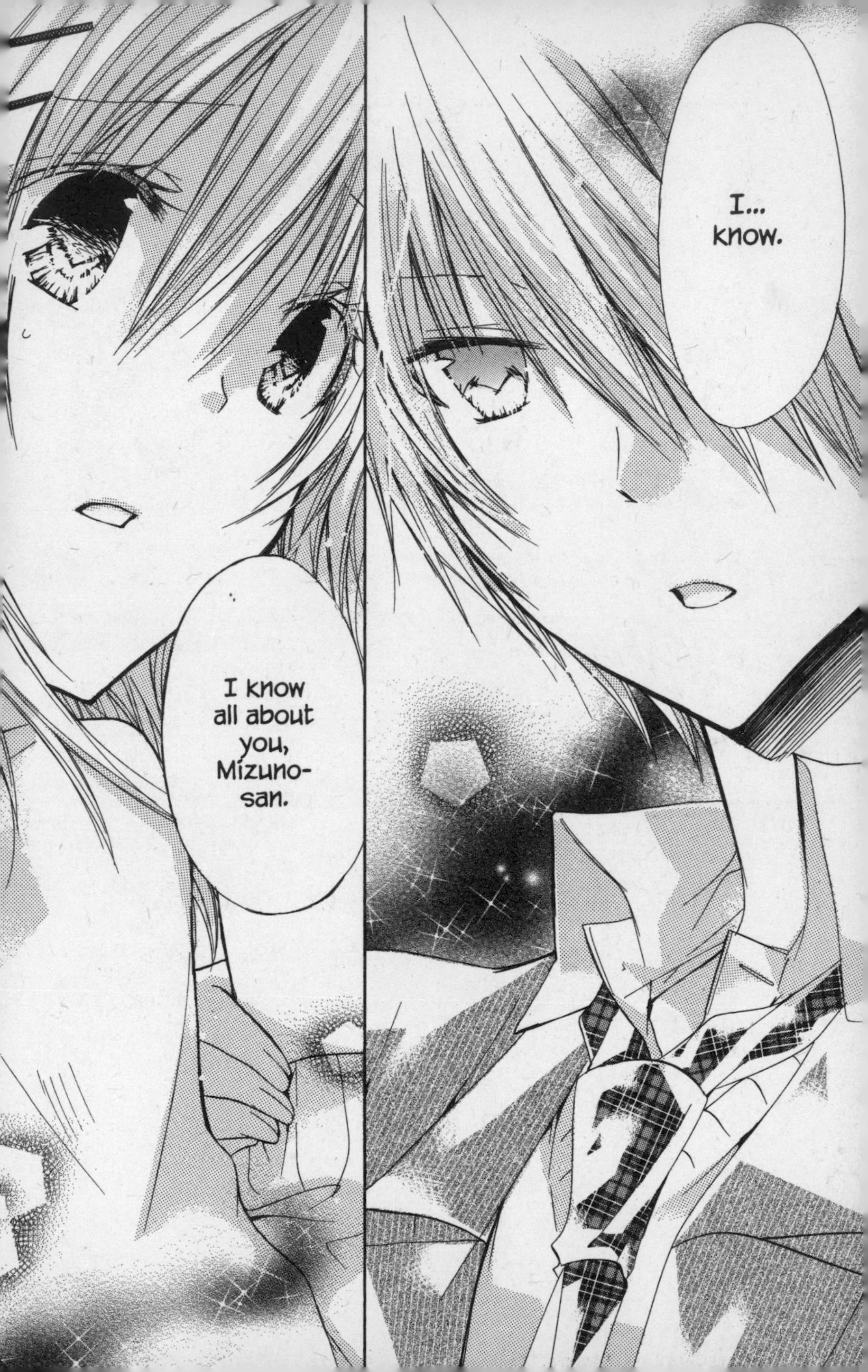
I... know.
I know all about you, Mizuno-san.

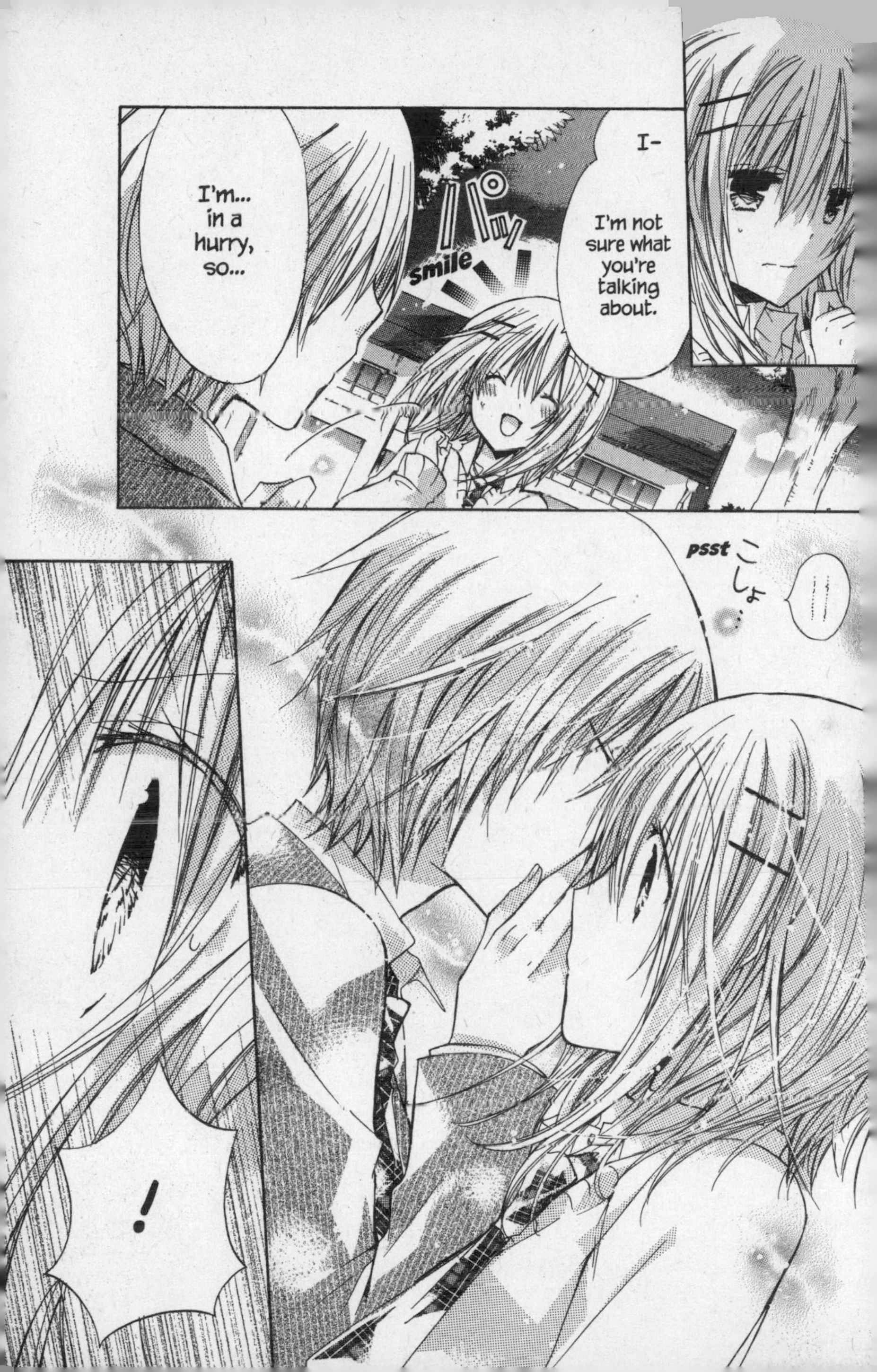
I-
I'm not sure what you're talking about.
パッ
smile
I'm... in a hurry, so...
psst
こしょ
...
!

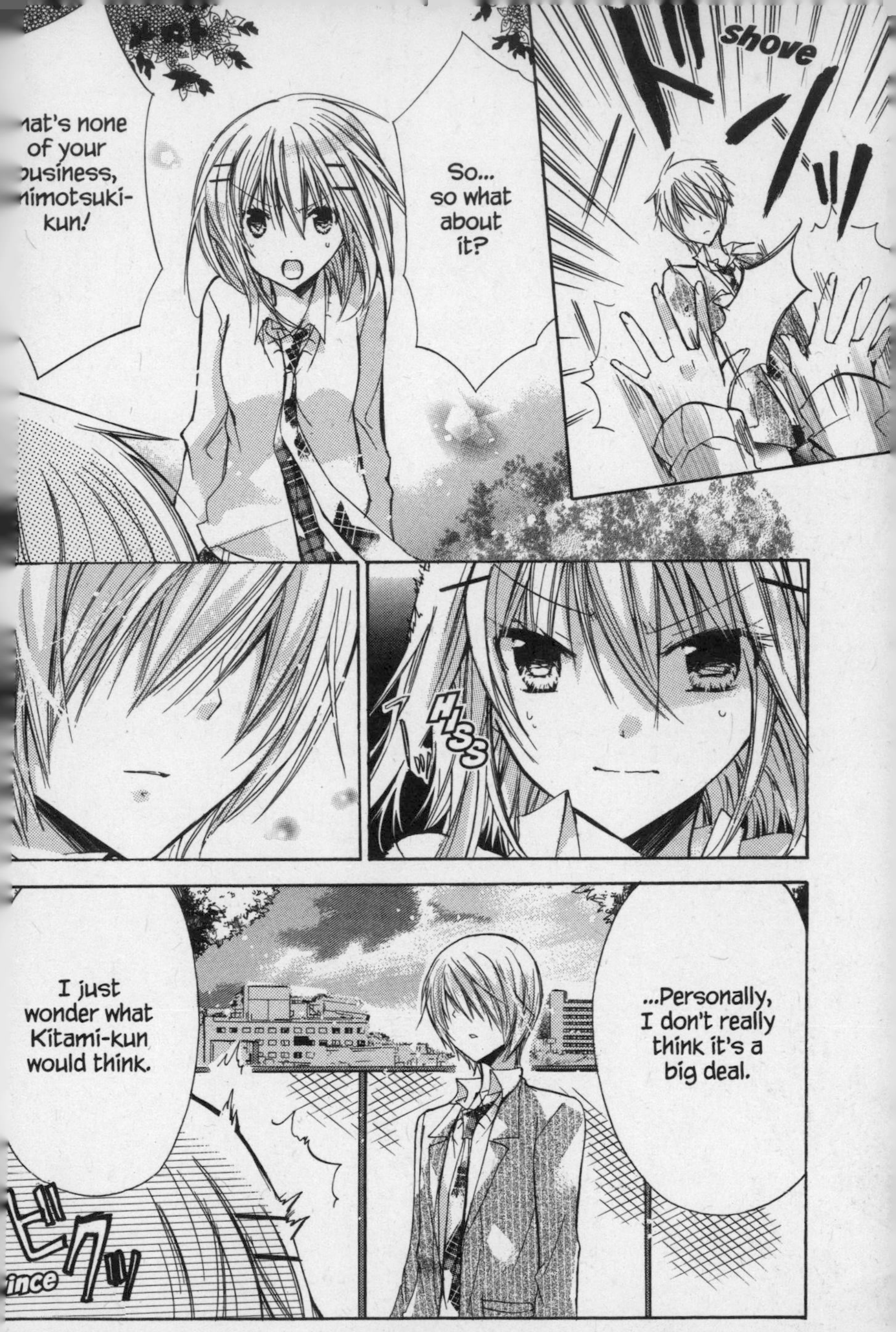
shove
So... so what about it?
at's none of your usiness, imotsuki-kun!
HISS
...Personally, I don't really think it's a big deal.
I just wonder what Kitami-kun would think.
ince

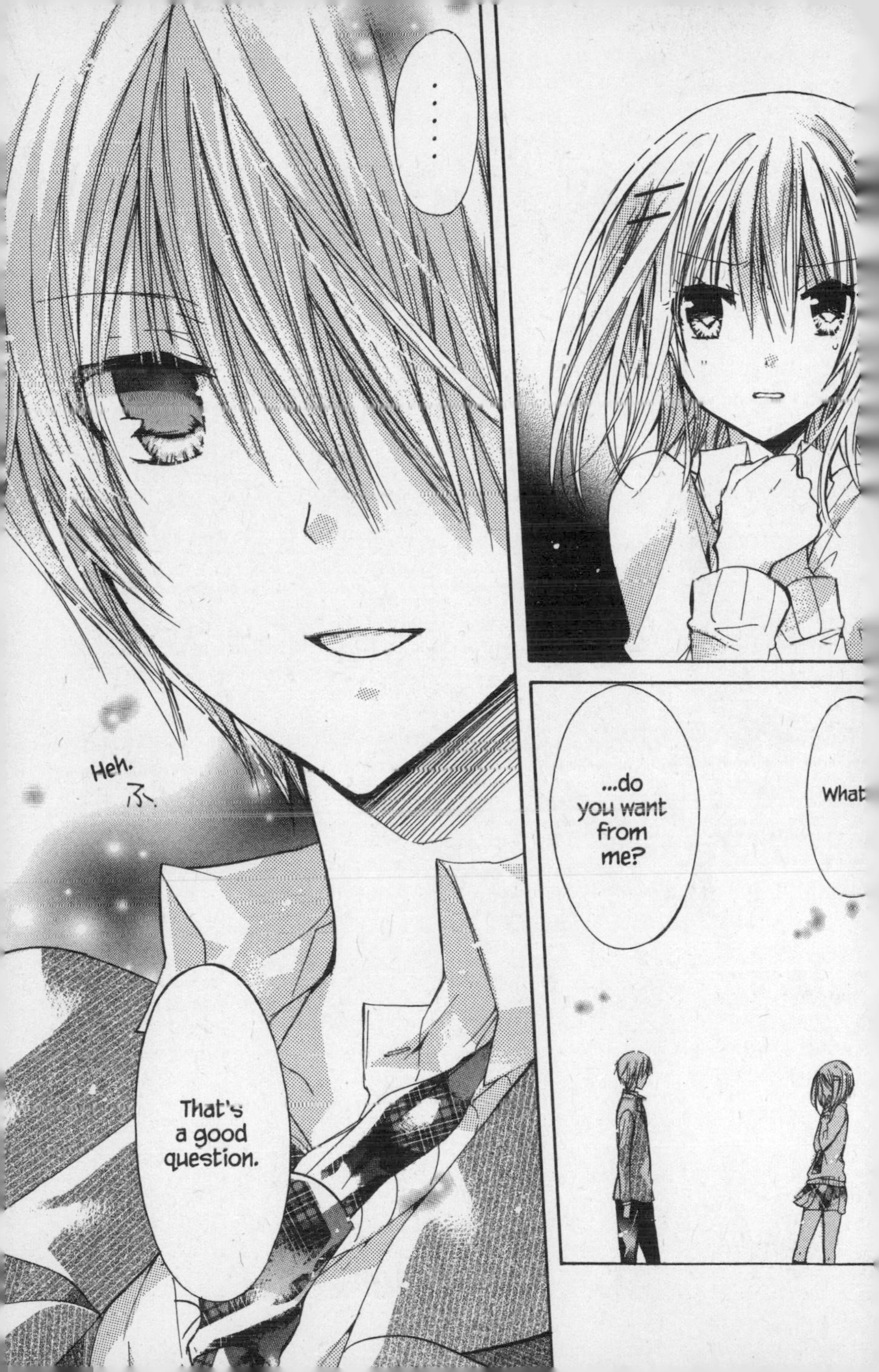
What
...do you want from me?
.....
Heh.
ふ.
That's a good question.

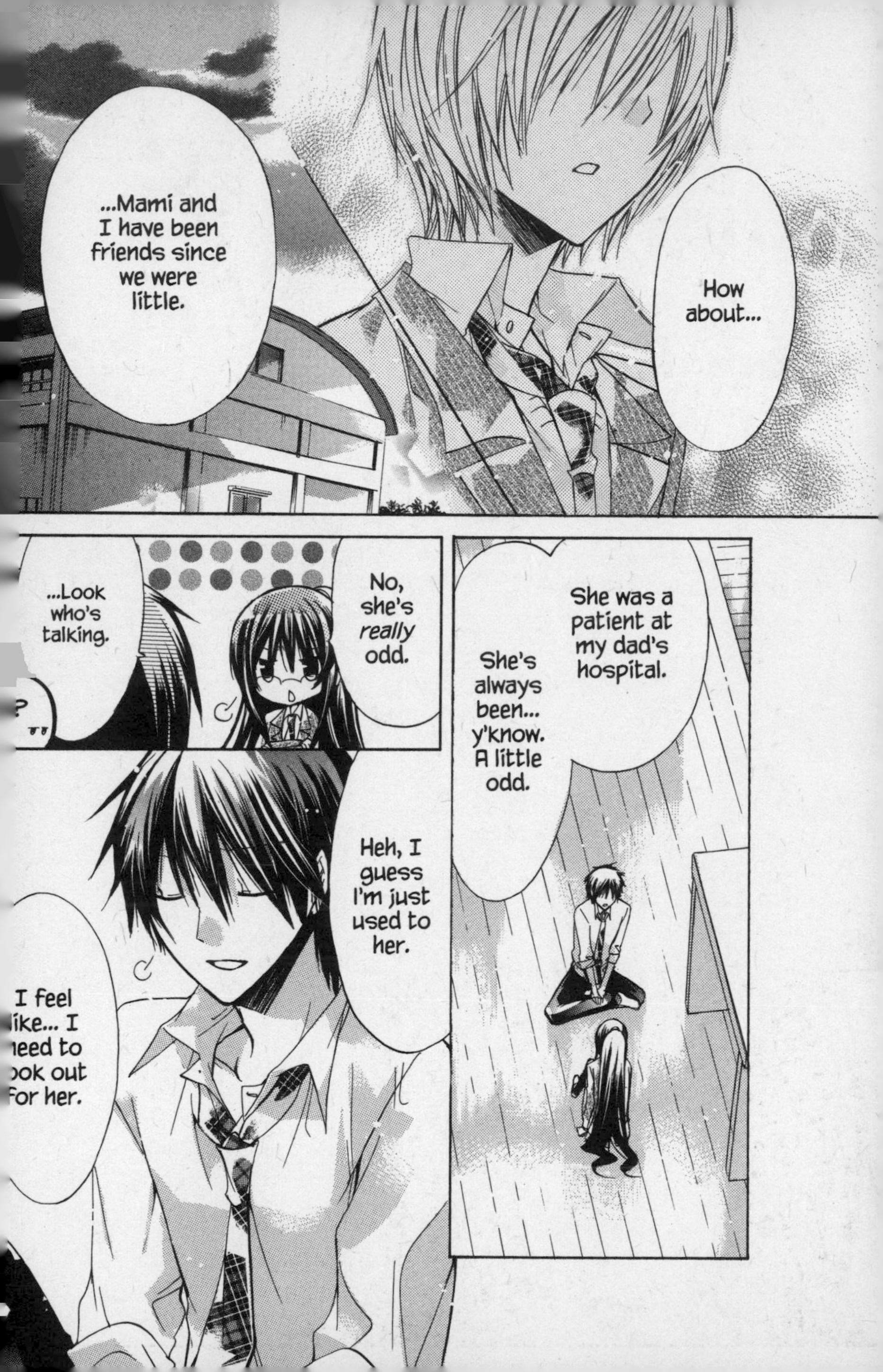
How about...
...Mami and I have been friends since we were little.
She was a patient at my dad's hospital.
She's always been... y'know. A little odd.
No, she's *really* odd.
...Look who's talking.
?
Heh, I guess I'm just used to her.
I feel ike... I eed to ook out for her.

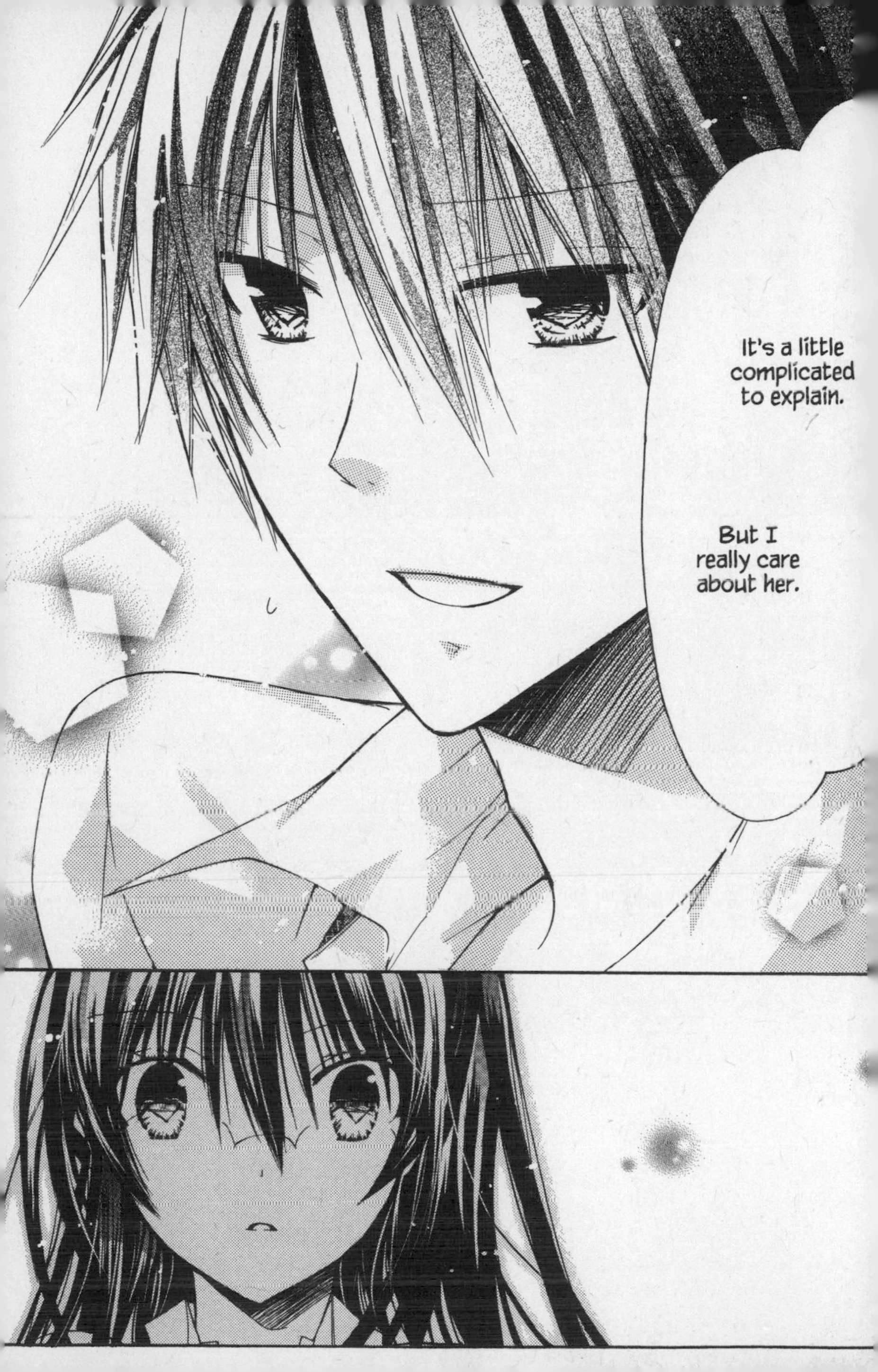
It's a little complicated to explain.
But I really care about her.

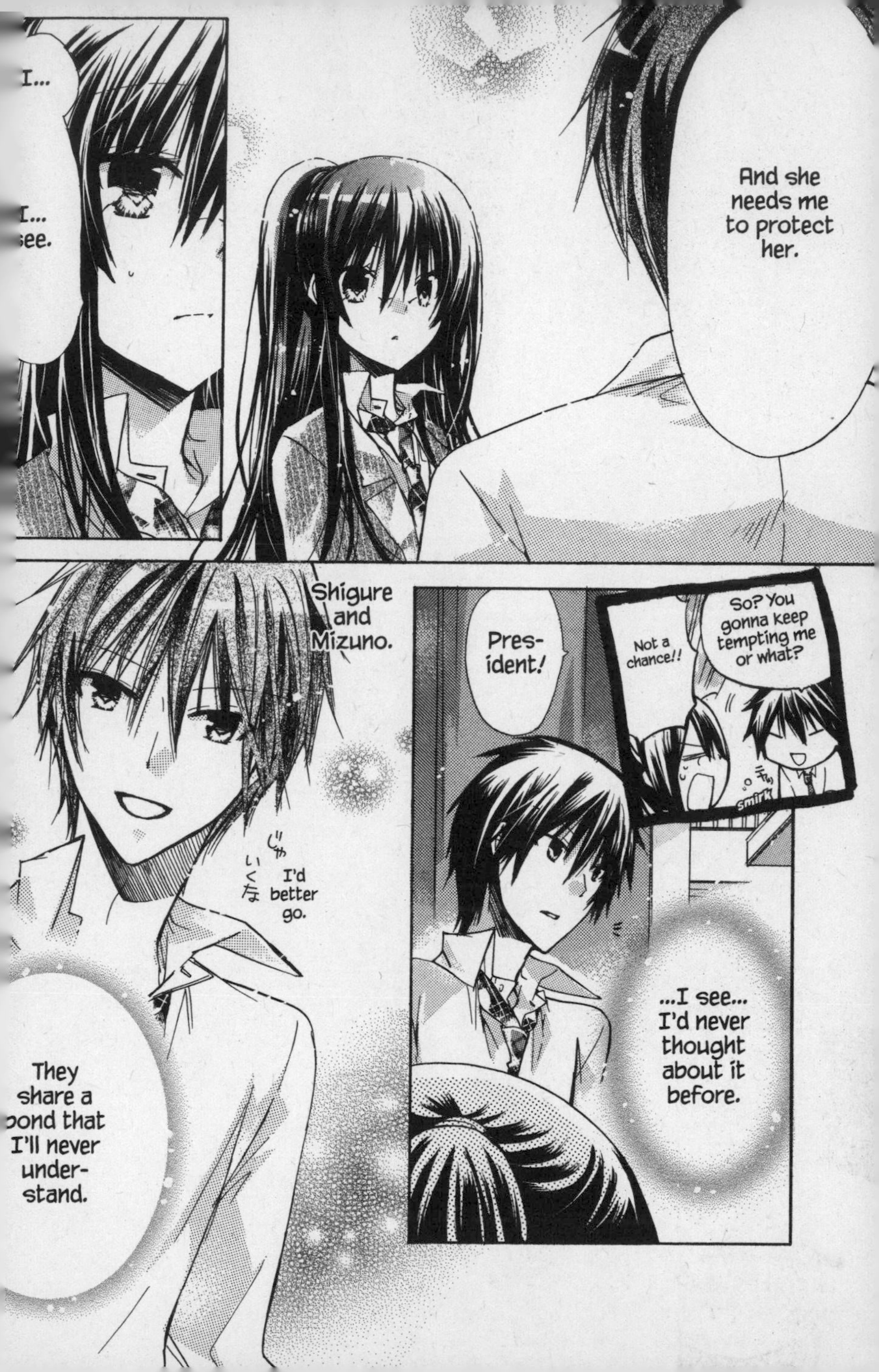
And she needs me to protect her.
I...
I... see.
So? You gonna keep tempting me or what?
Not a chance!!
smirk
Pres-ident!
...I see... I'd never thought about it before.
Shigure and Mizuno.
じゃいくな
I'd better go.
They share a bond that I'll never under-stand.

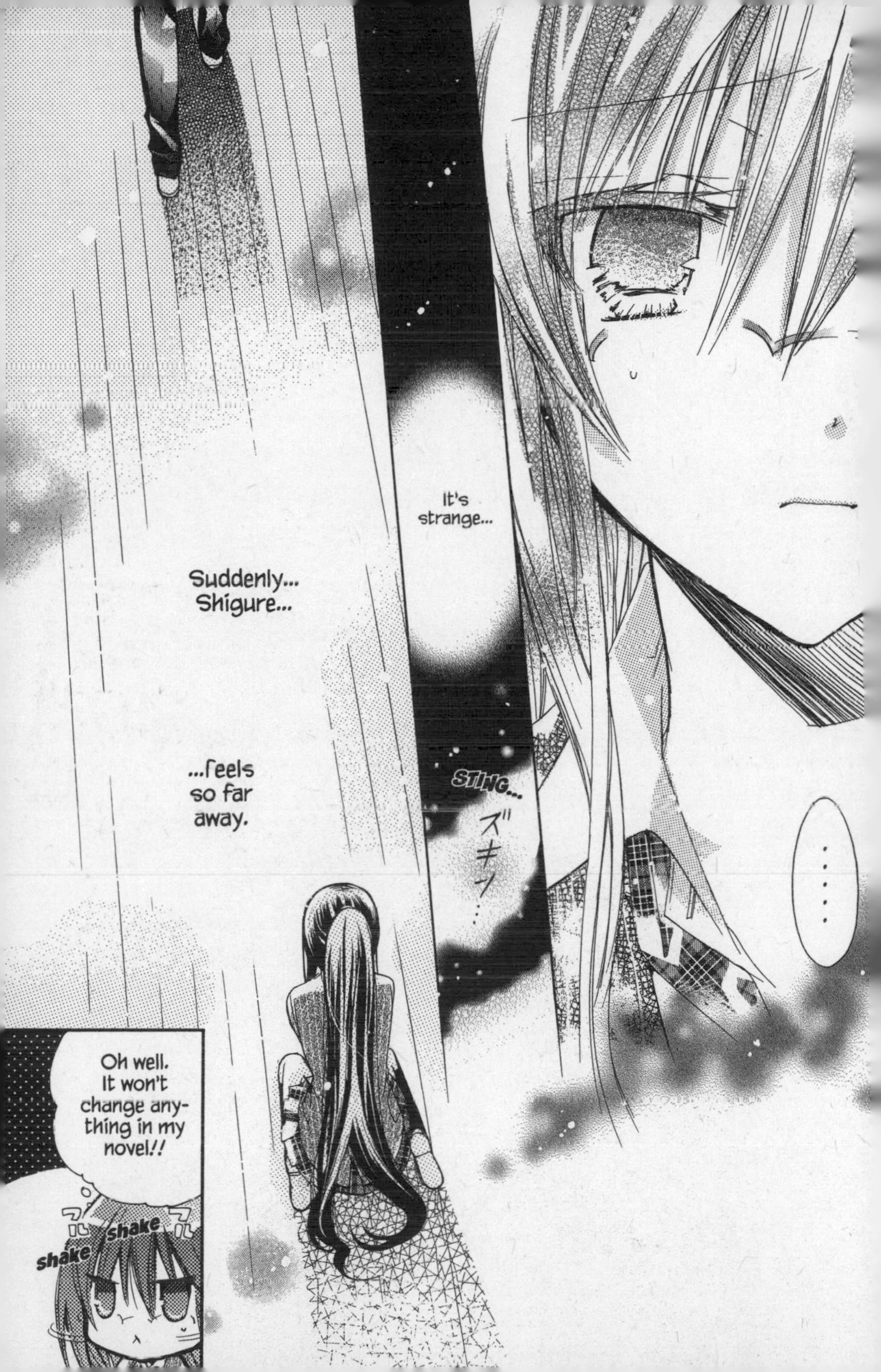
It's strange...
STING...
ズキッ...
......
Suddenly... Shigure...
...feels so far away.
Oh well. It won't change anything in my novel!!
shake
shake

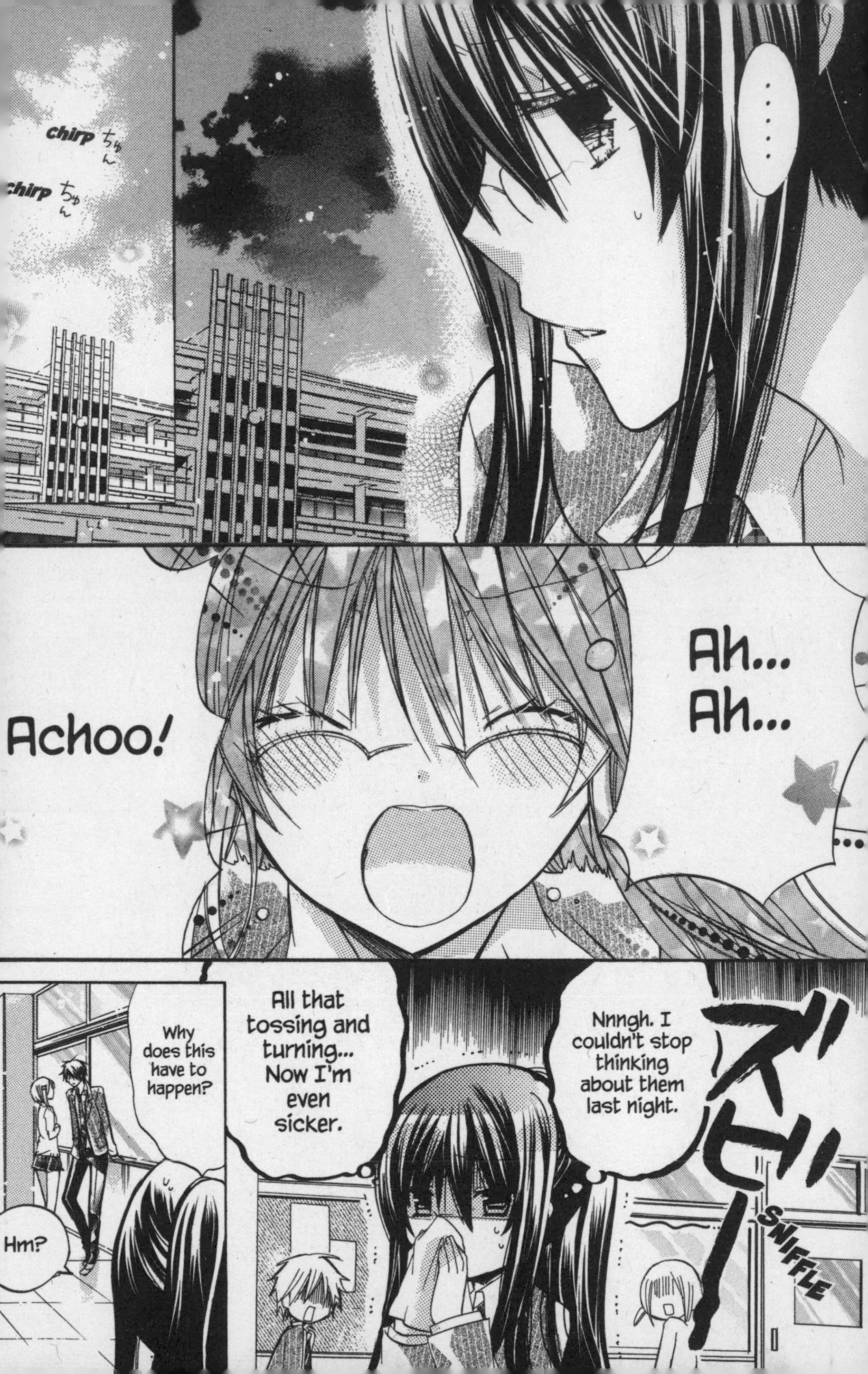
......
chirp ちゅん
chirp ちゅん
Ah... Ah...
...
Achoo!
ズビー
SNIFFLE
Nnngh. I couldn't stop thinking about them last night.
All that tossing and turning... Now I'm even sicker.
Why does this have to happen?
Hm?

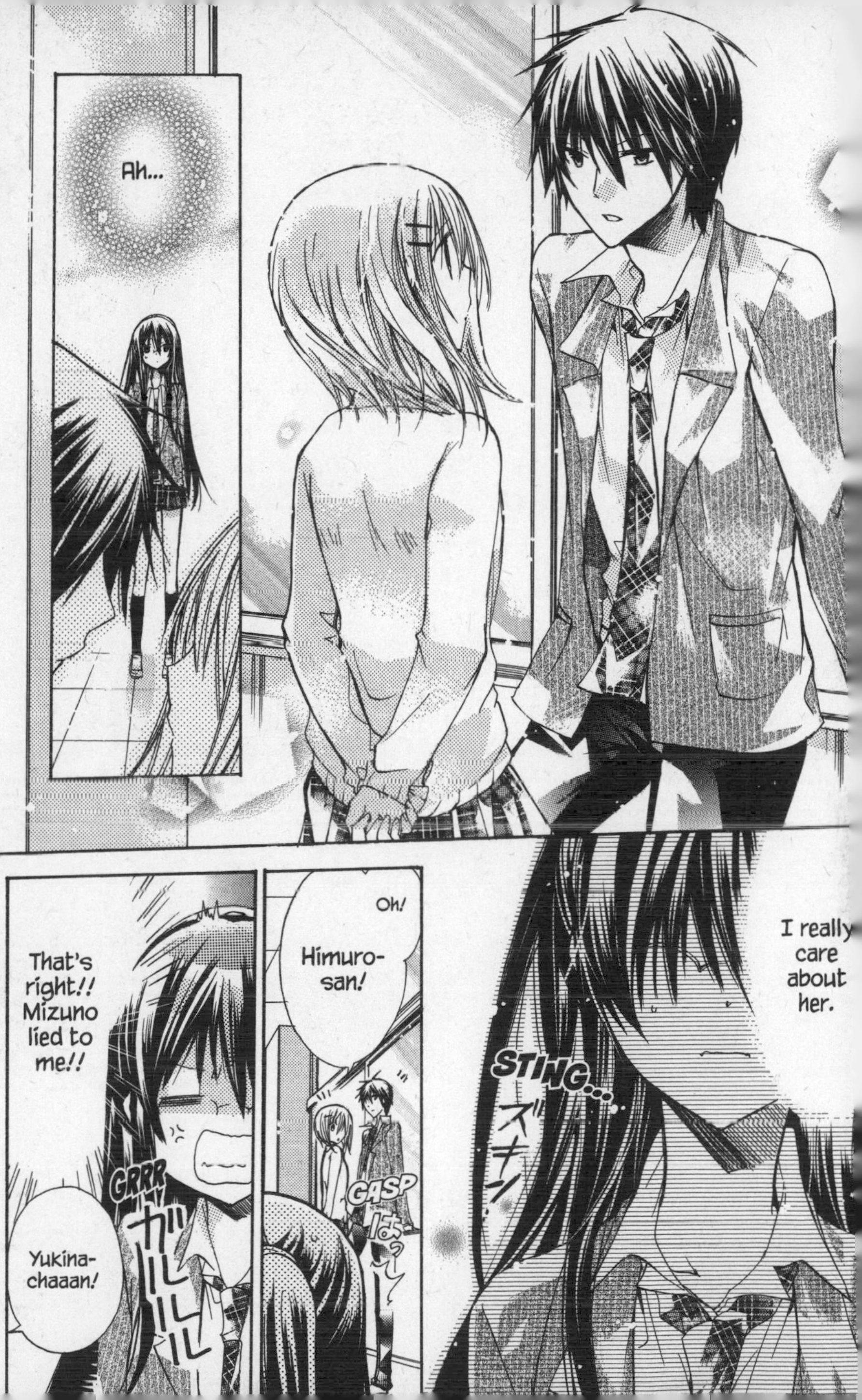
Ah...
I really care about her.
STING...
ズキン
Oh!
Himuro-san!
GASP
はっ
That's right!! Mizuno lied to me!!
GRRR
Yukina-chaaan!

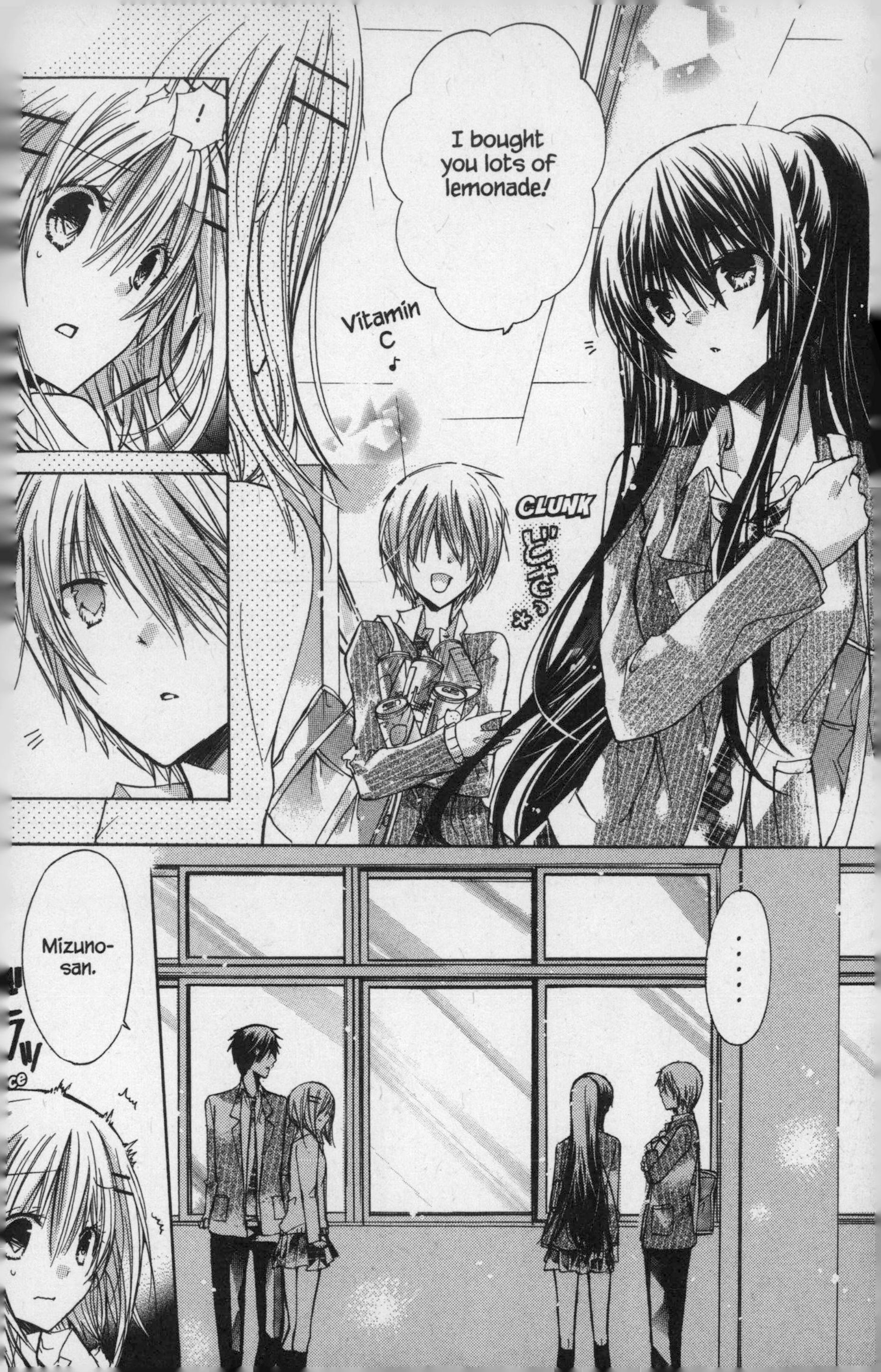
I bought you lots of lemonade!
Vitamin C ♪
CLUNK
!
......
Mizuno-san.

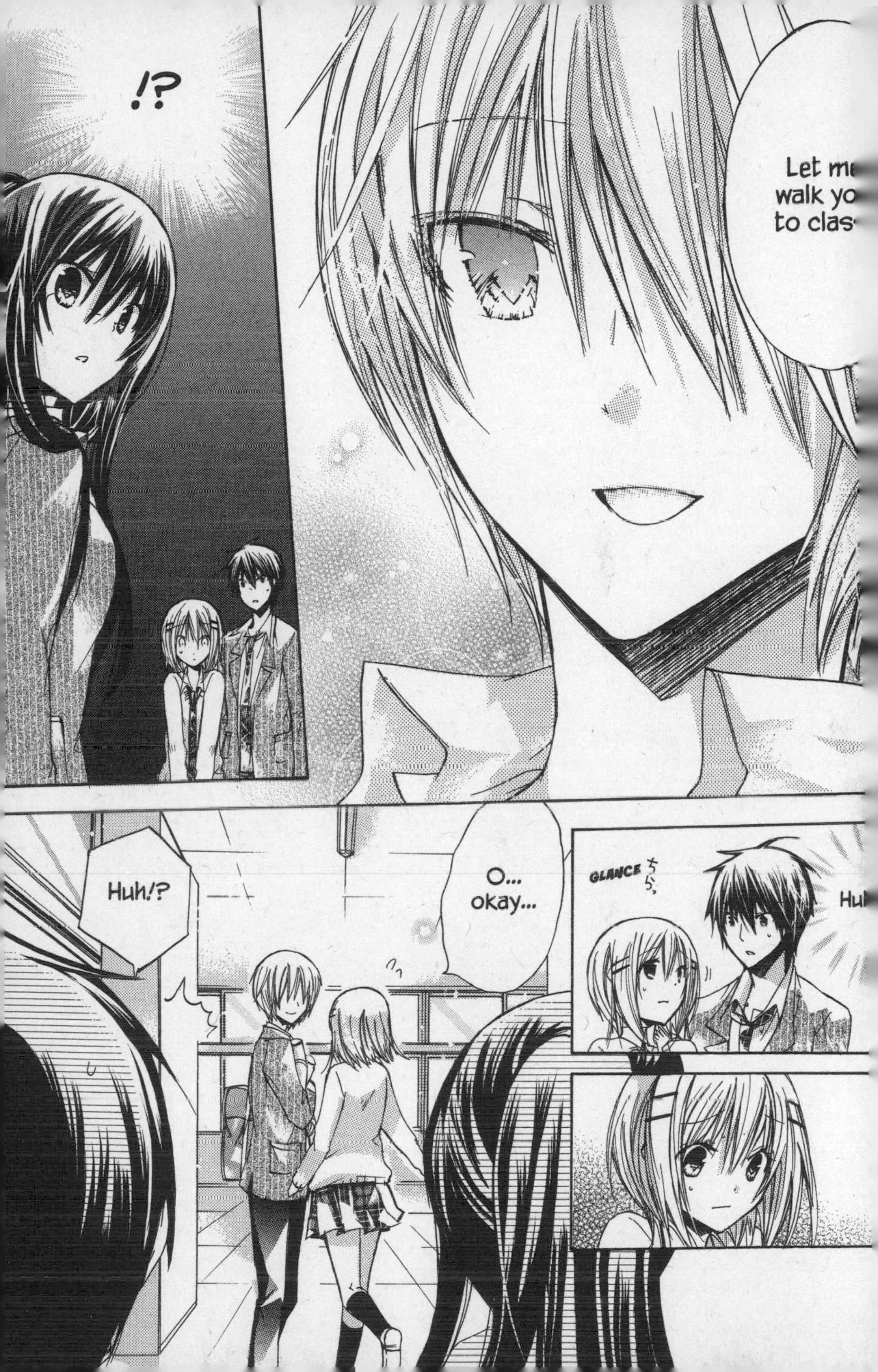
Let m
walk yo
to clas
!?
GLANCE ちら、
Hu
O... okay...
Huh!?

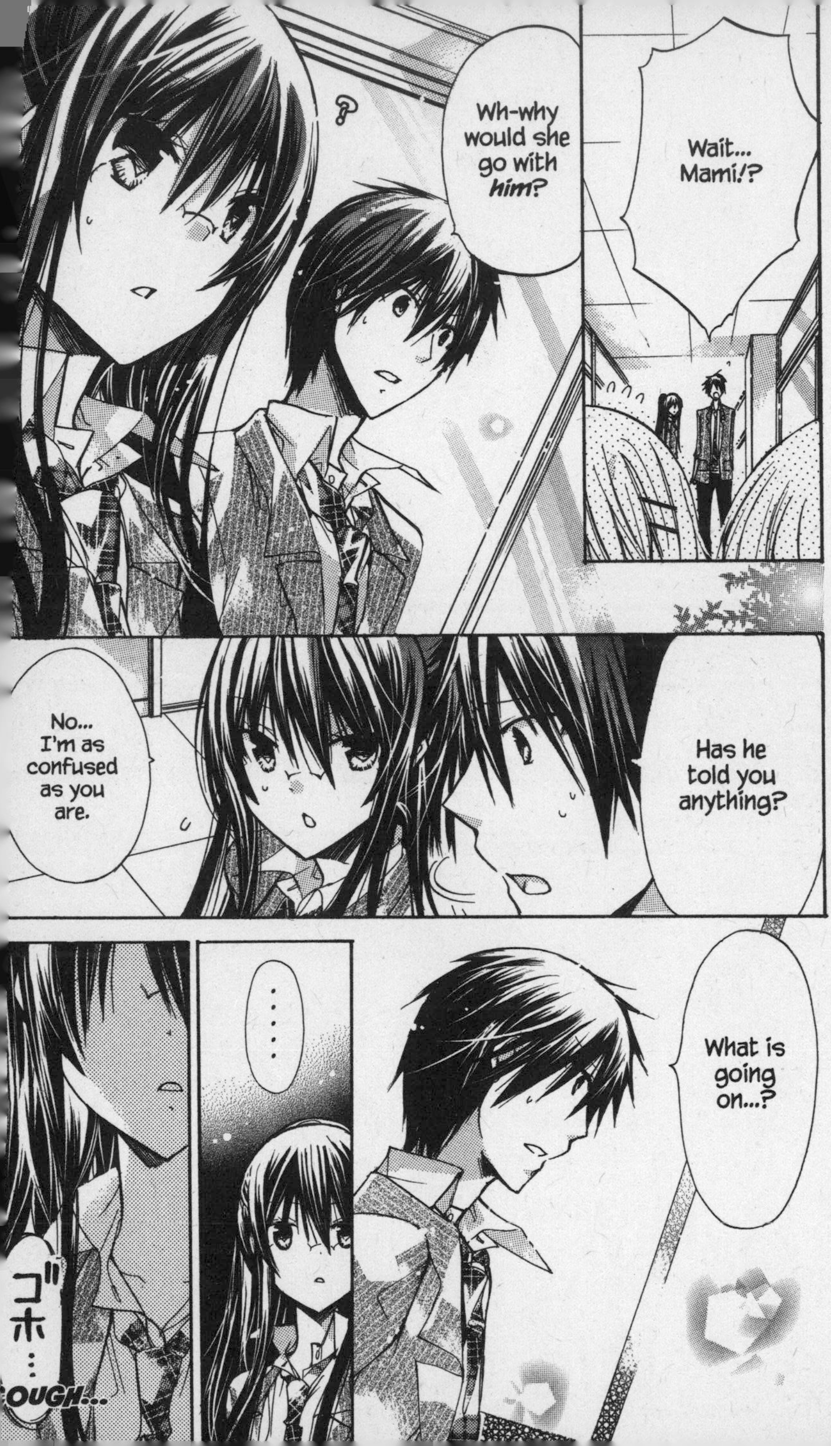
Wait... Mami!?
Wh-why would she go with *him*?
Has he told you anything?
No... I'm as confused as you are.
What is going on...?
......
ゴホ…
COUGH...

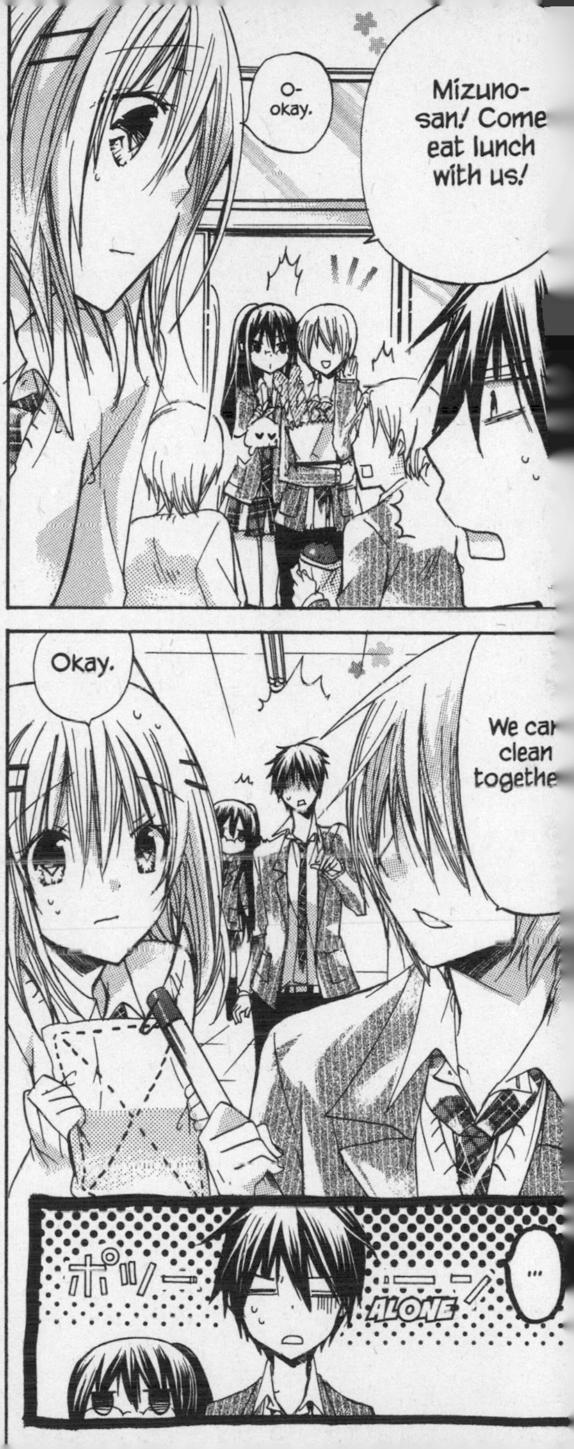
Mizuno-san! Come eat lunch with us!
O-okay.
We ca clean togethe
Okay.
...
ALONE

Last Time...

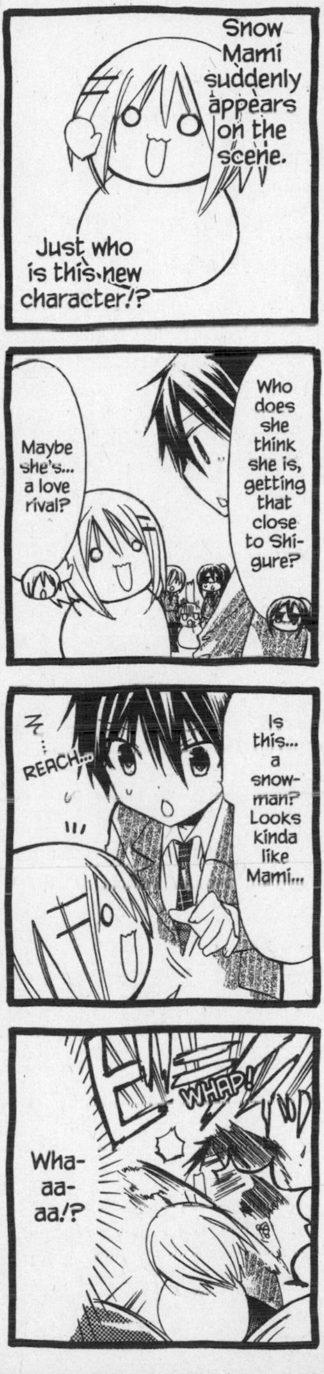
Snow Mami suddenly appears on the scene.
Just who is this new character!?
Who does she think she is, getting that close to Shigure?
Maybe she's... a love rival?
Is this... a snowman? Looks kinda like Mami...
REACH...
WHAP!
Wha-aa-aa!?

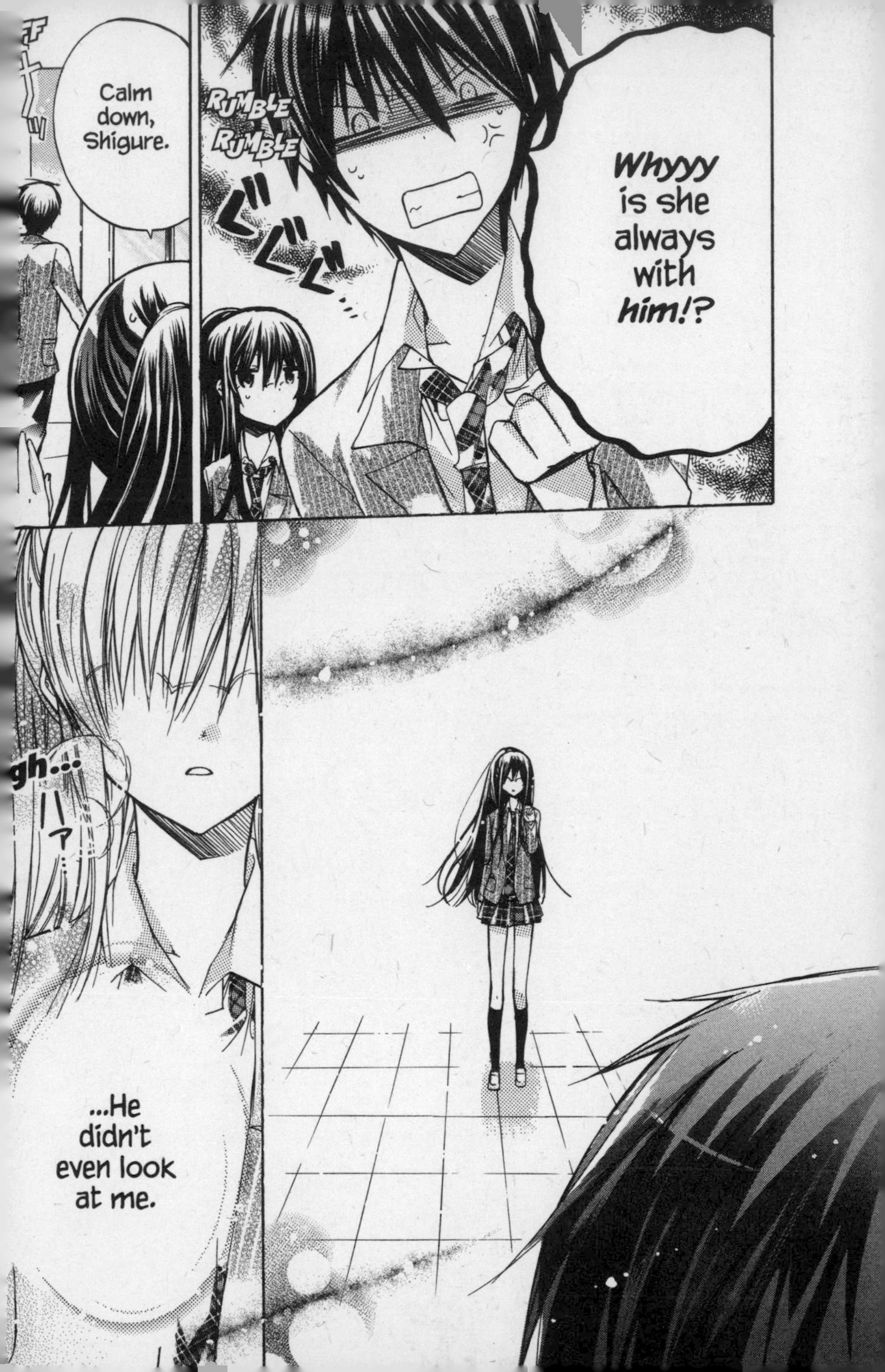
RUMBLE
RUMBLE
Whyyy is she always with *him!?*
Calm down, Shigure.
ハァ…
...He didn't even look at me.

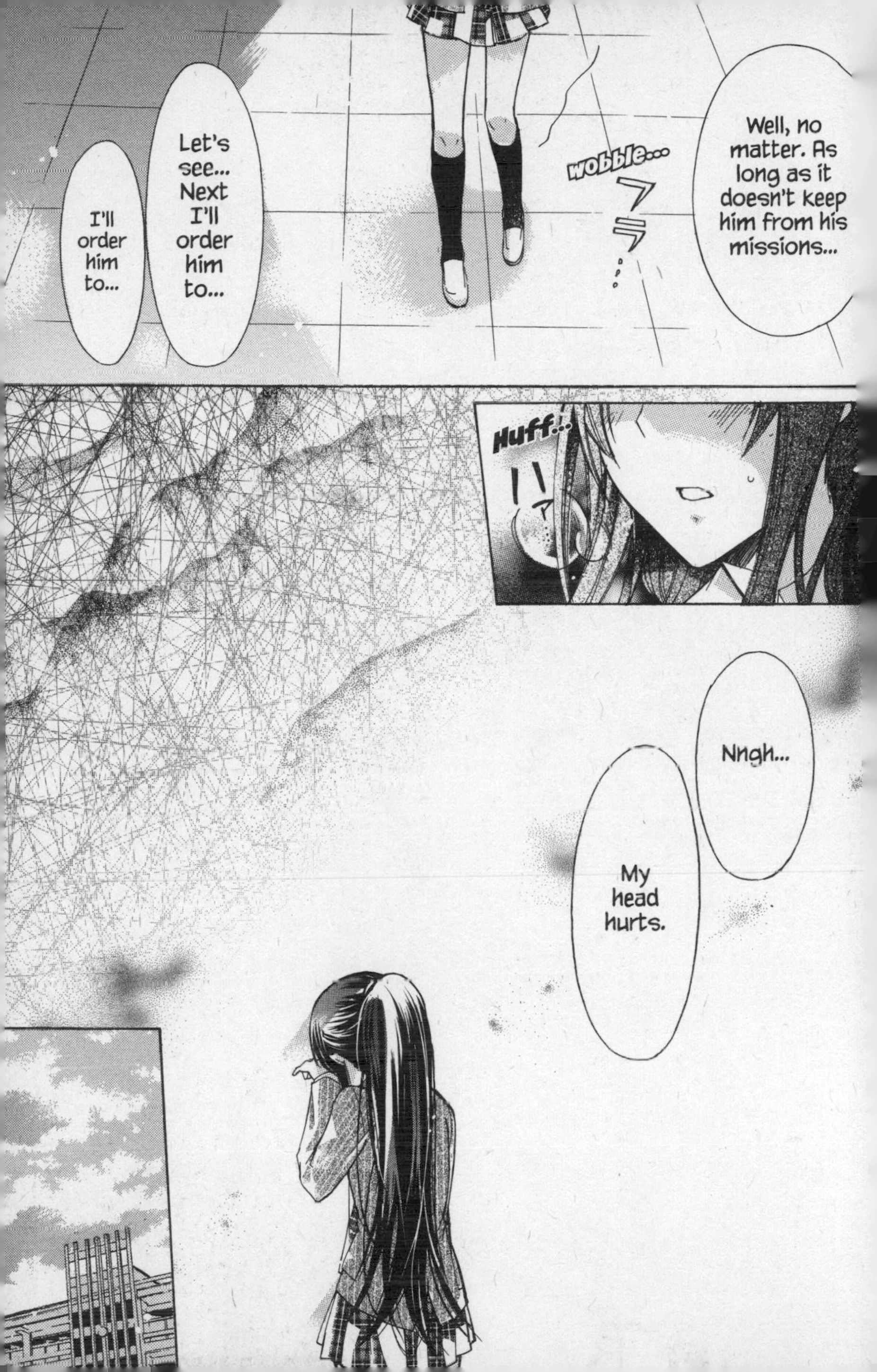
Well, no matter. As long as it doesn't keep him from his missions...
wobble...
Let's see... Next I'll order him to...
I'll order him to...
Huff...
Nngh...
My head hurts.

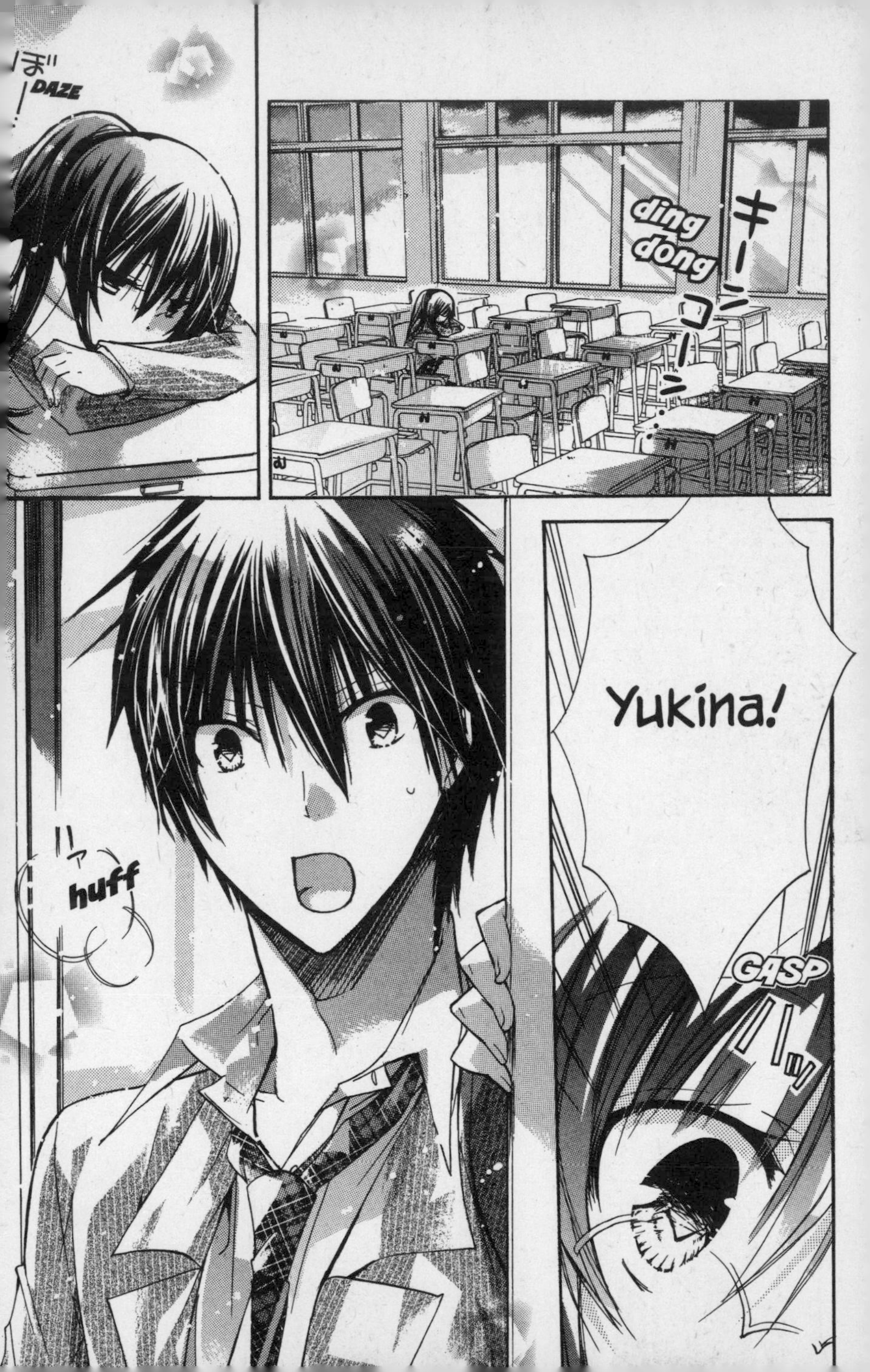
ding dong
DAZE
Yukina!
GASP
huff

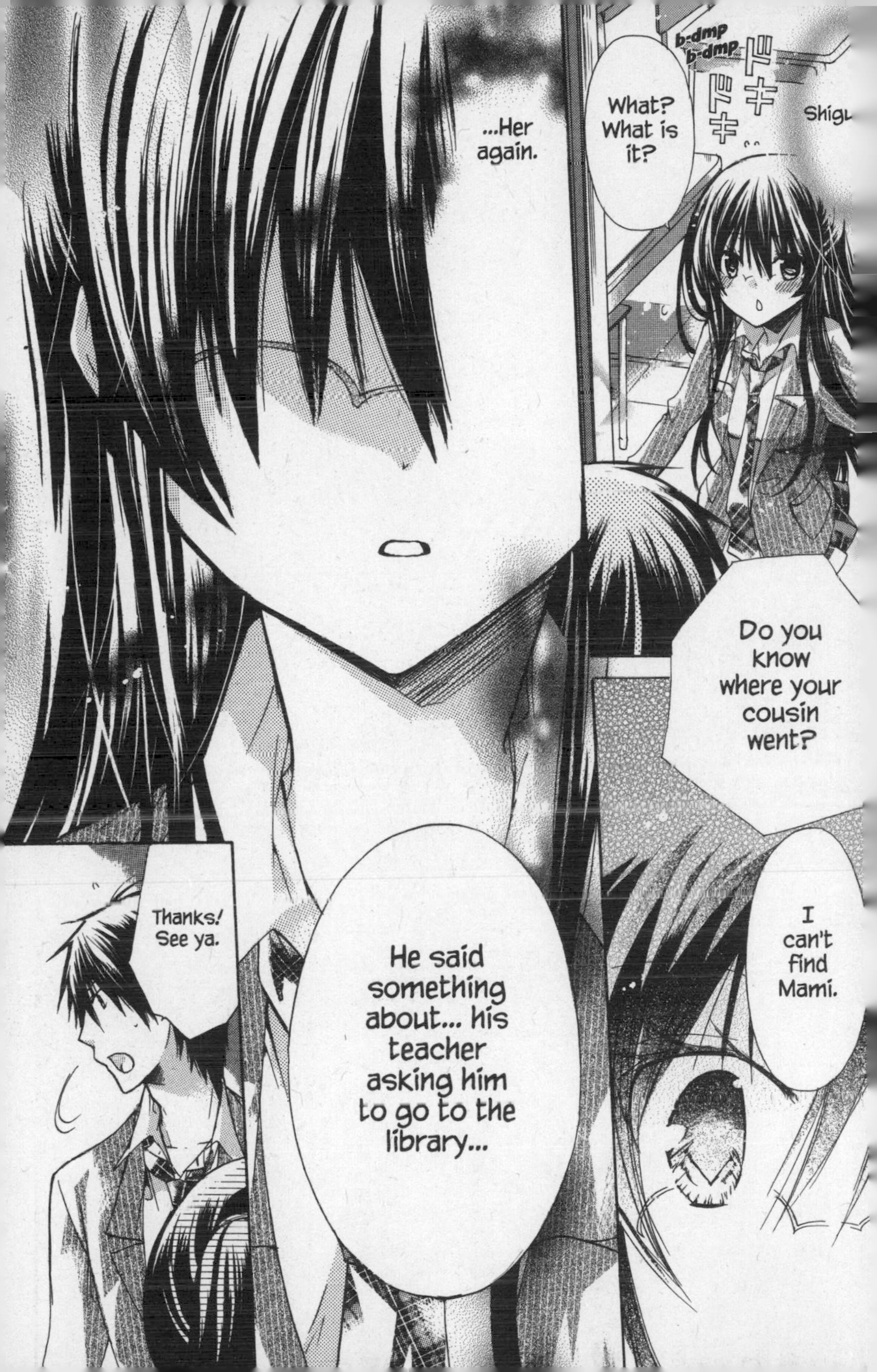
Shigu
b-dmp
b-dmp
ドキドキ
What? What is it?
Do you know where your cousin went?
I can't find Mami.
...Her again.
He said something about... his teacher asking him to go to the library...
Thanks! See ya.

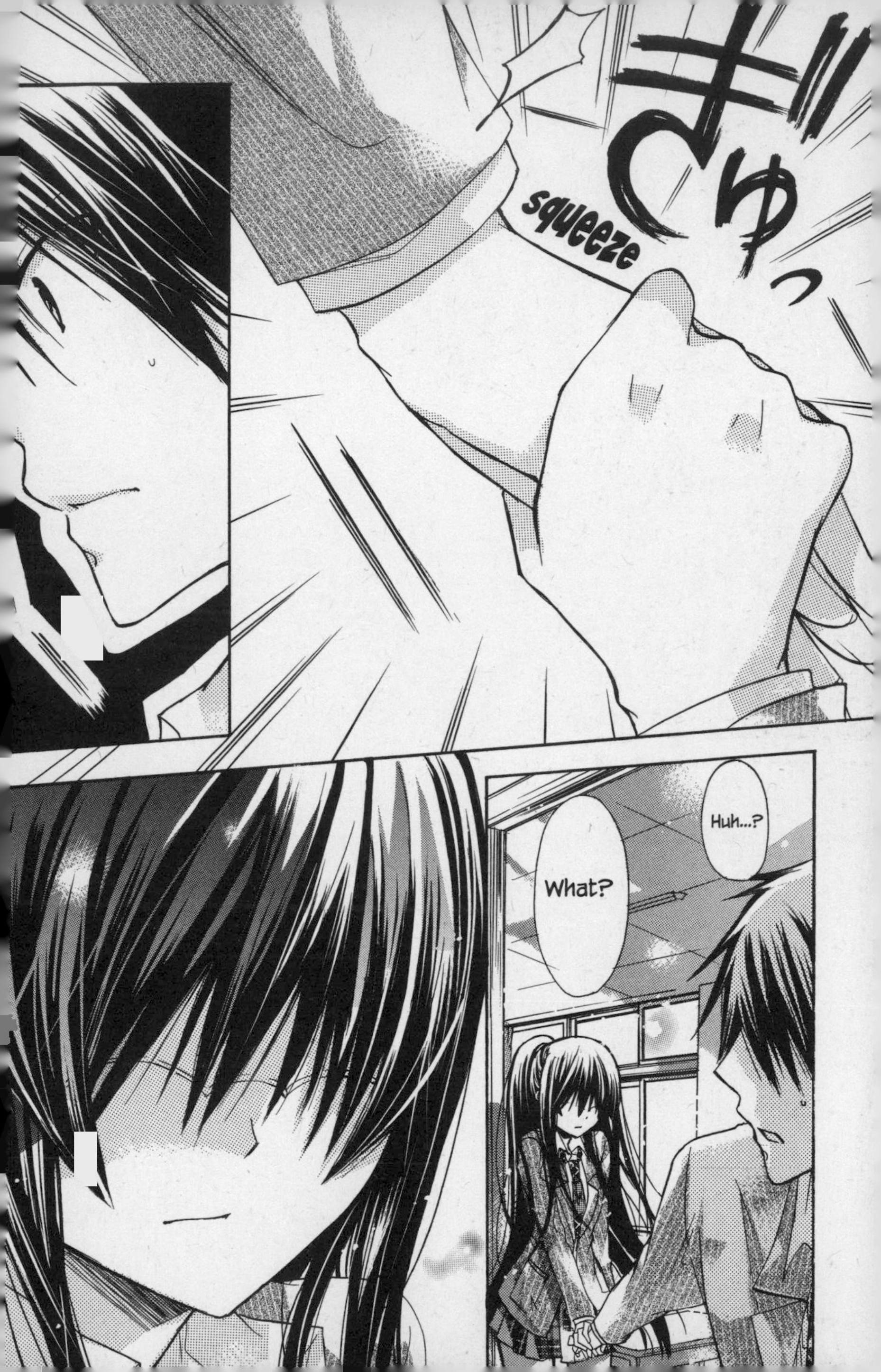
ぎゅっ
squeeze
Huh...?
What?

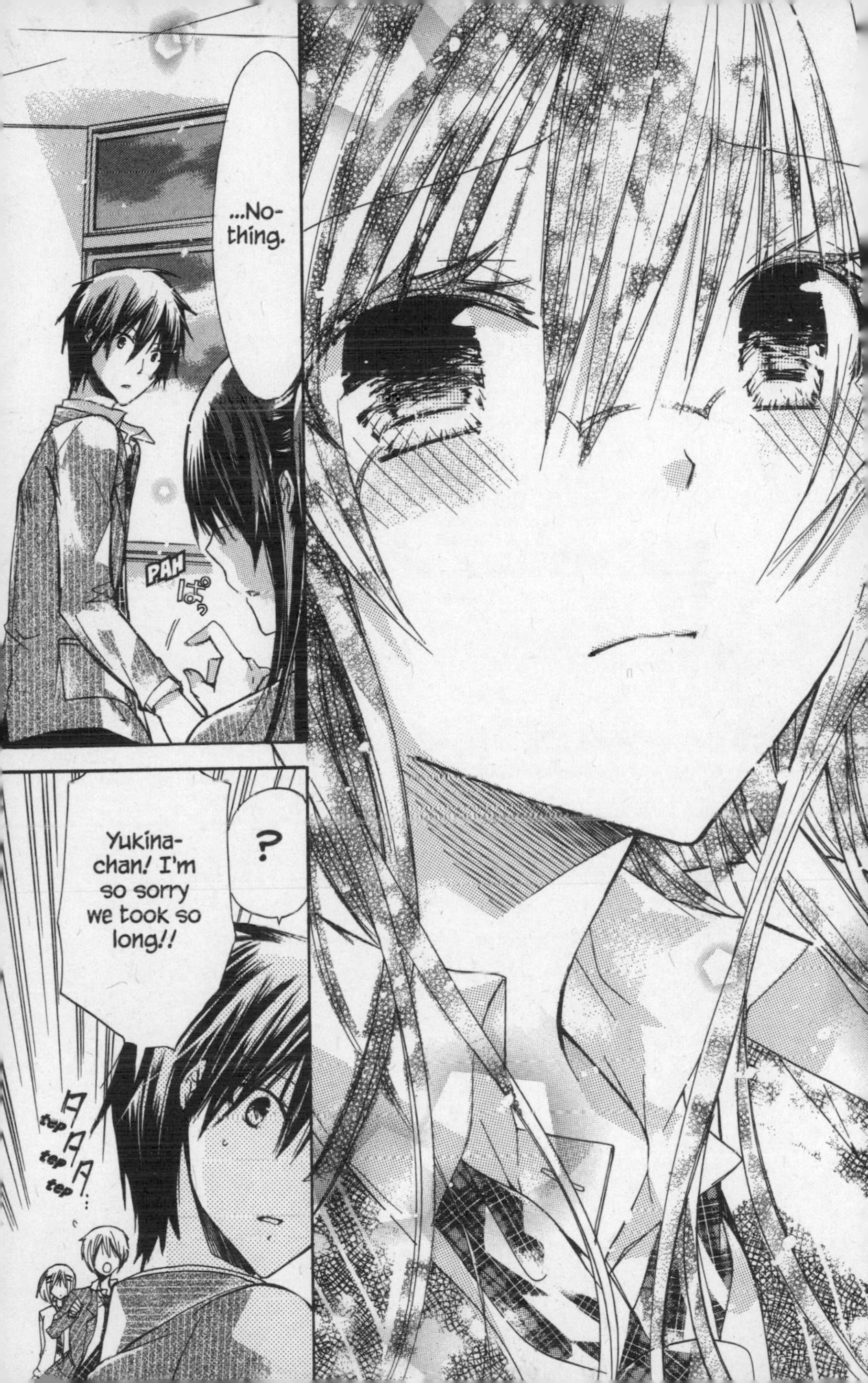
...No-thing.
PAH
ぱっ
?
Yukina-chan! I'm so sorry we took so long!!
tep tep tep

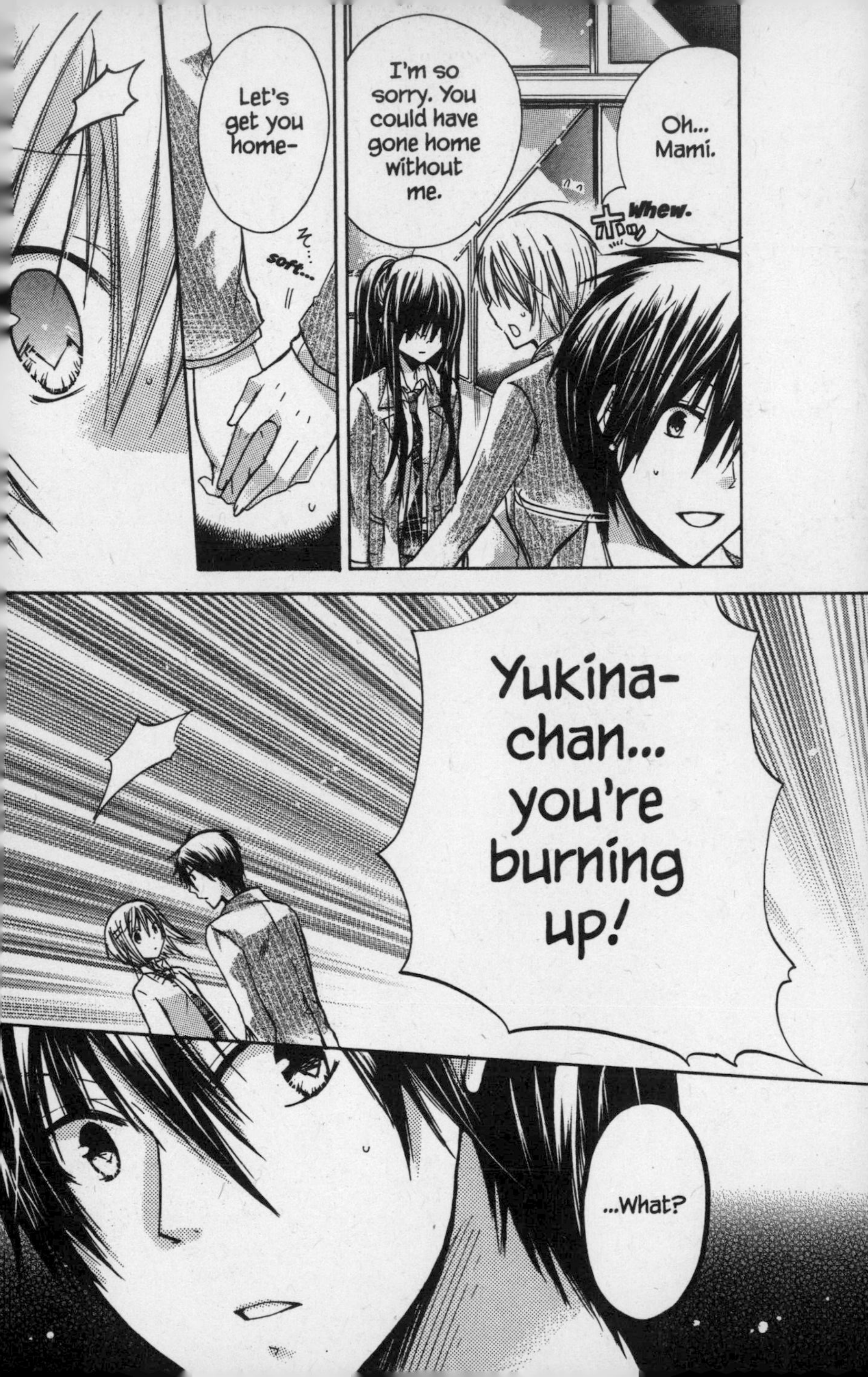
Oh... Mami.
Whew.
I'm so sorry. You could have gone home without me.
Let's get you home-
soft...
Yukina-chan... you're burning up!
...What?

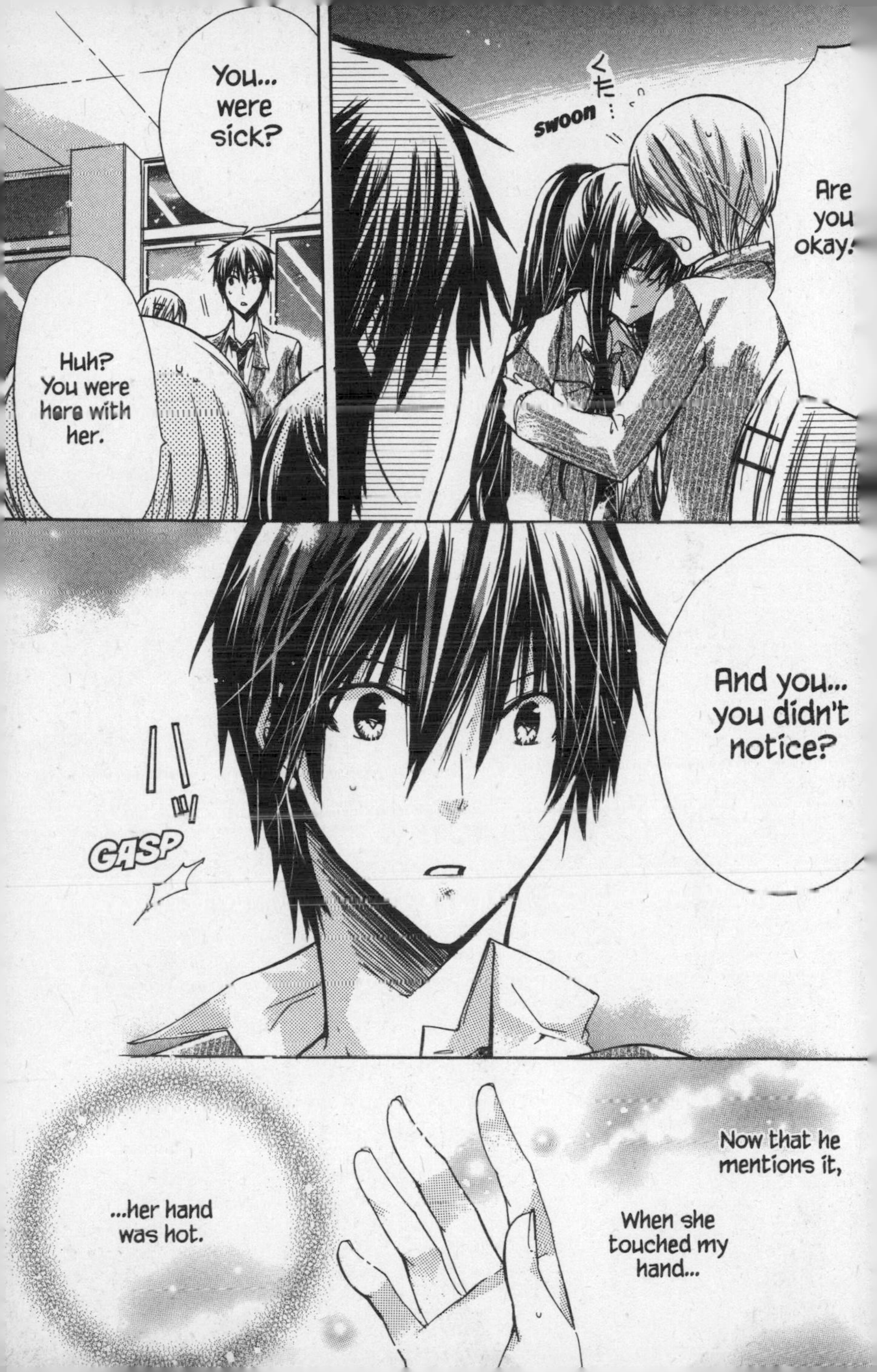
Are you okay!
くた…
swoon
You... were sick?
Huh? You were here with her.
And you... you didn't notice?
GASP
Now that he mentions it,
When she touched my hand...
...her hand was hot.

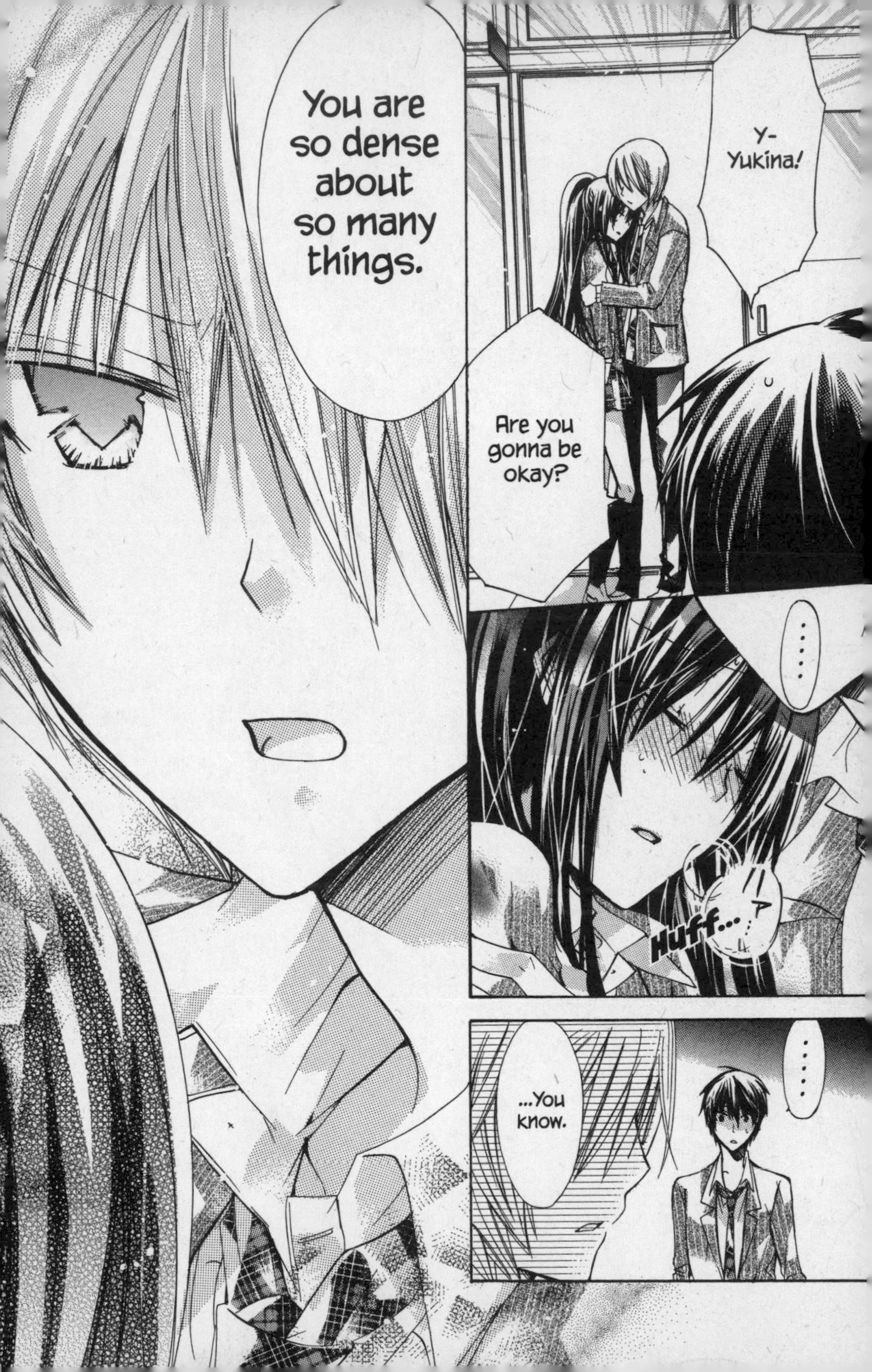
Y-Yukina!
Are you gonna be okay?
......
Huff...
......
...You know.
You are so dense about so many things.

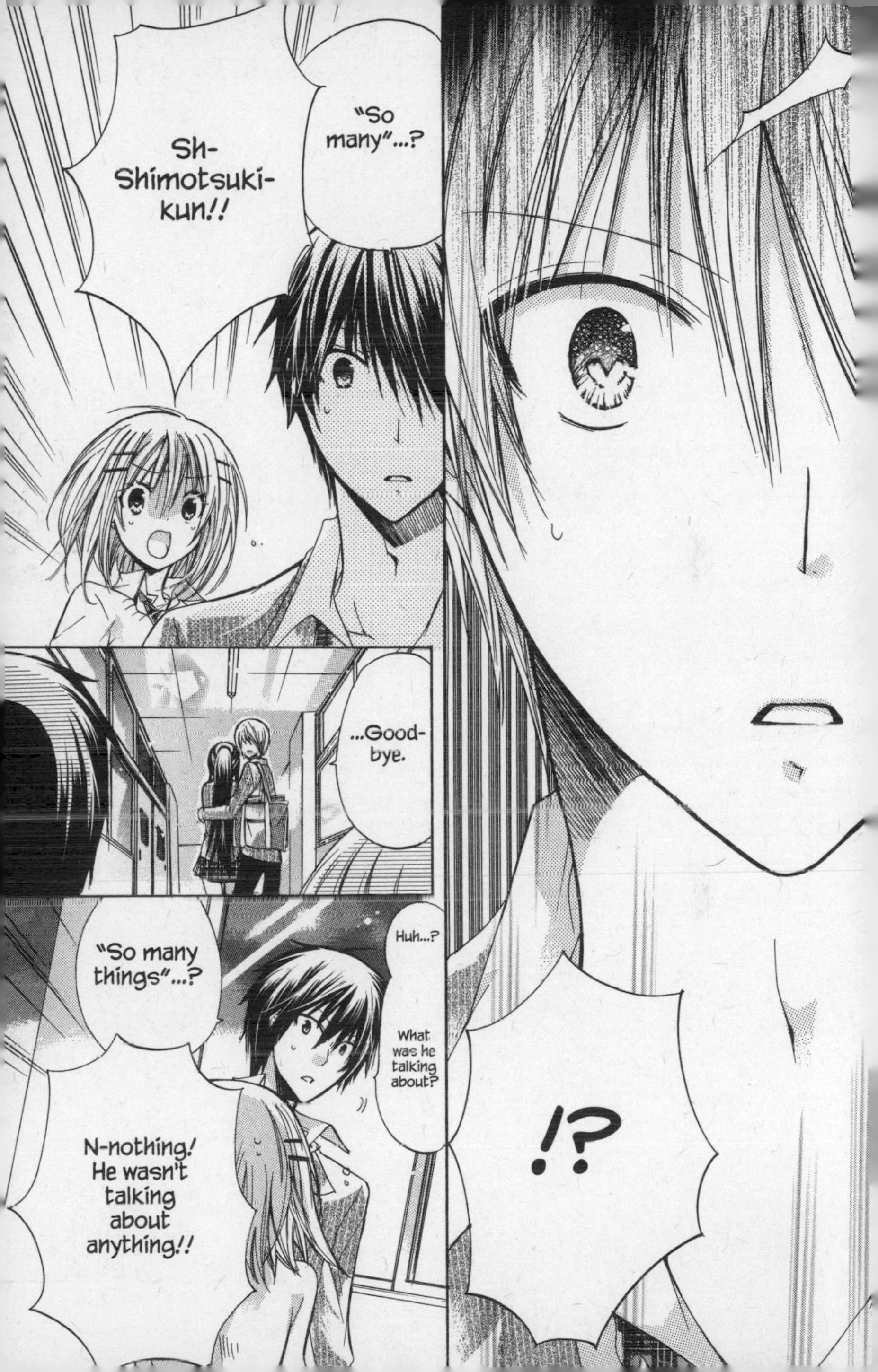
!?
"So many"...?
Sh-Shimotsuki-kun!!
...Good-bye.
Huh...?
"So many things"...?
What was he talking about?
N-nothing! He wasn't talking about anything!!

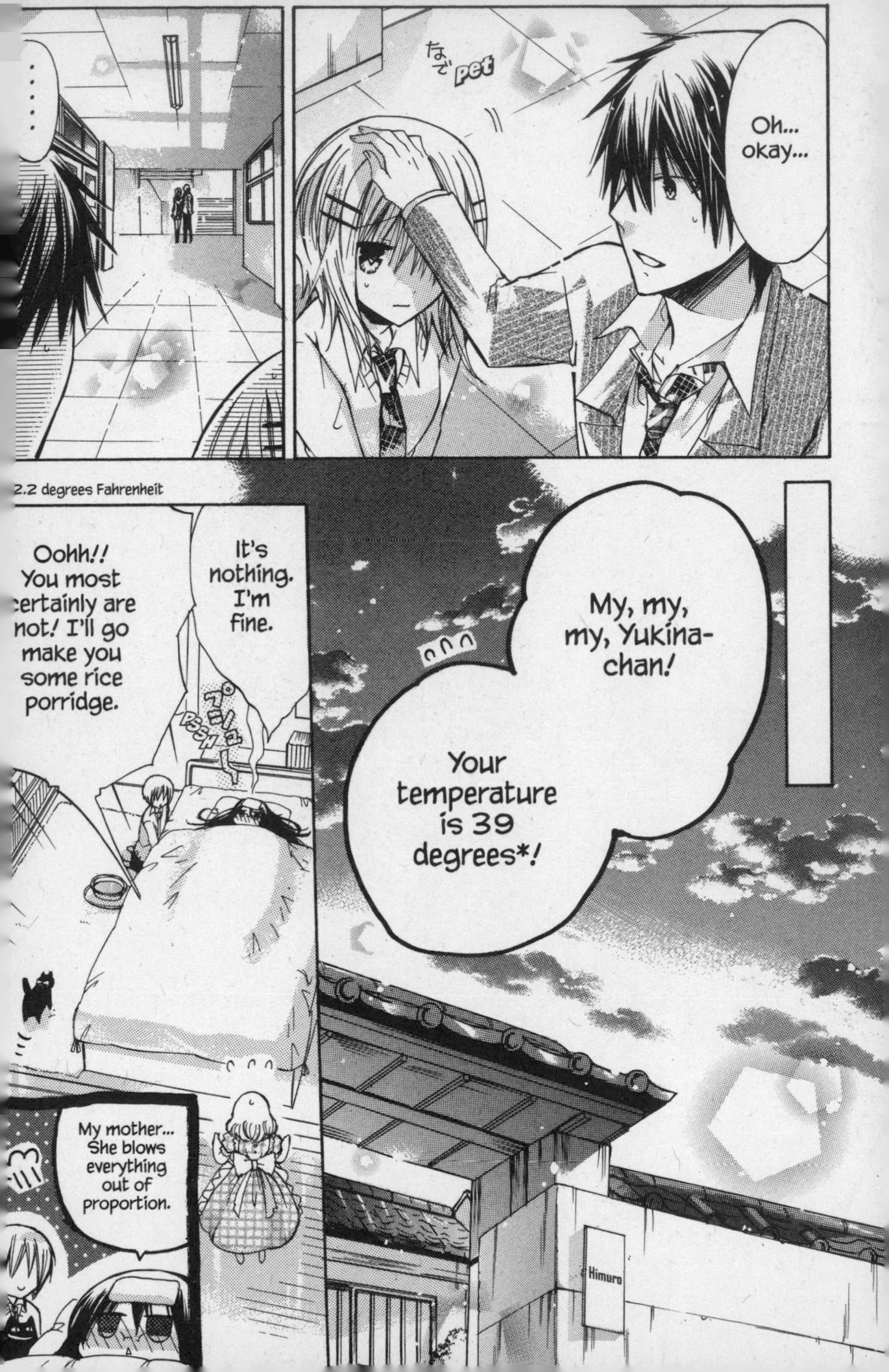
なで pet
Oh... okay...
......
My, my, my, Yukina-chan!
Your temperature is 39 degrees*!
Himuro
It's nothing. I'm fine.
Oohh!! You most certainly are not! I'll go make you some rice porridge.
PSSH
My mother... She blows everything out of proportion.

*2.2 degrees Fahrenheit

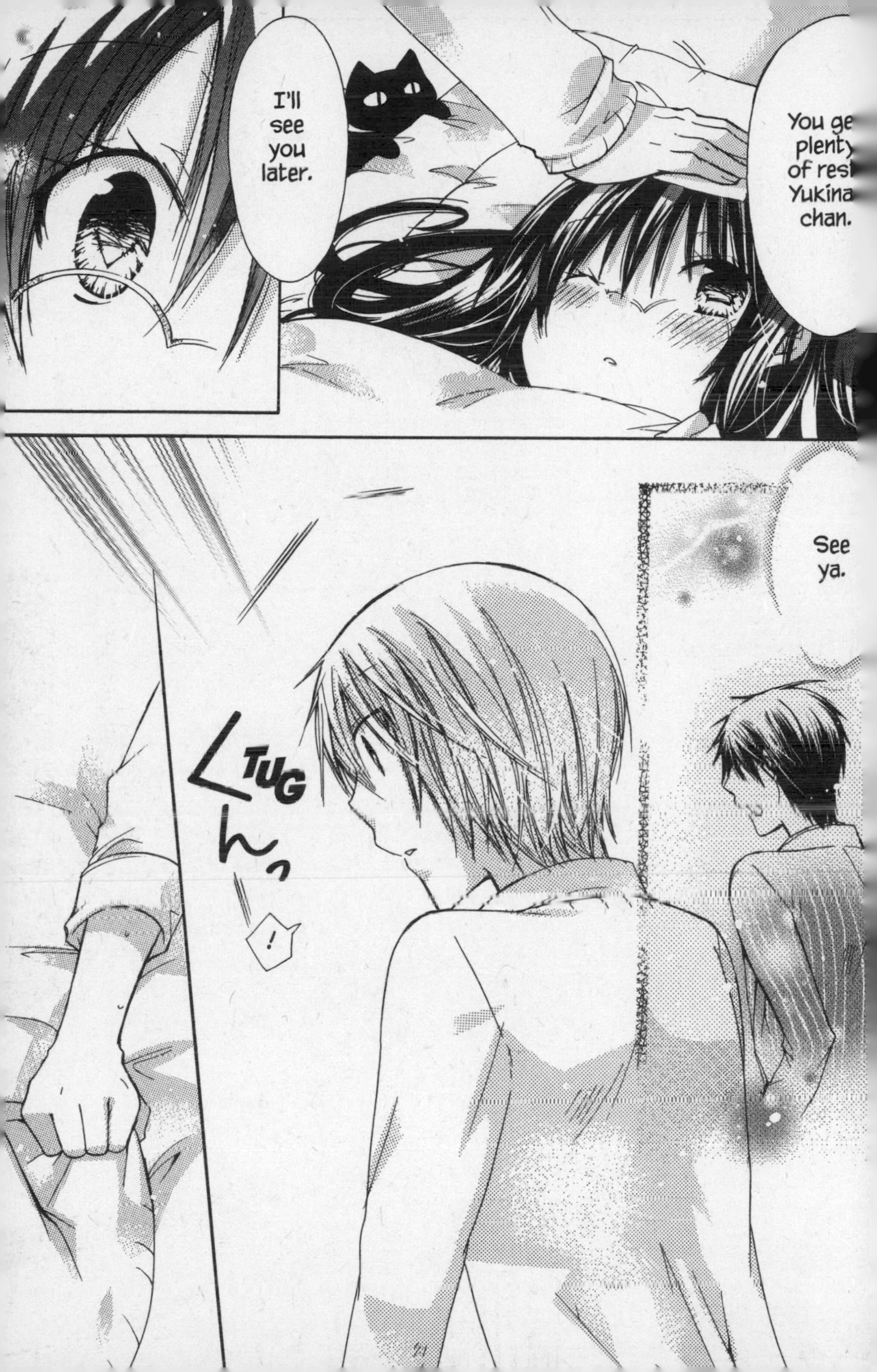
You ge plenty of res Yukina chan.
I'll see you later.
See ya.
TUG
!

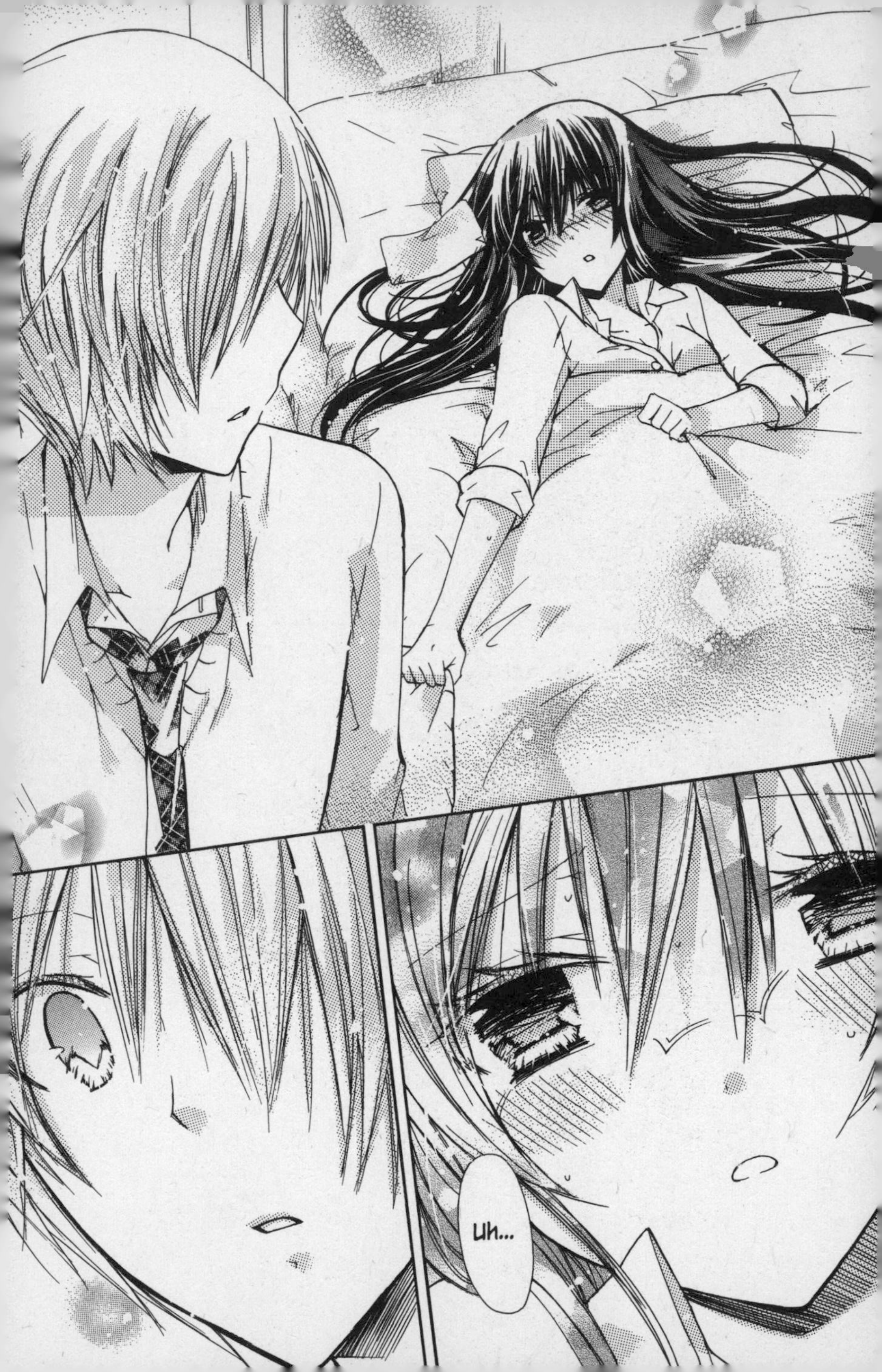
Uh...

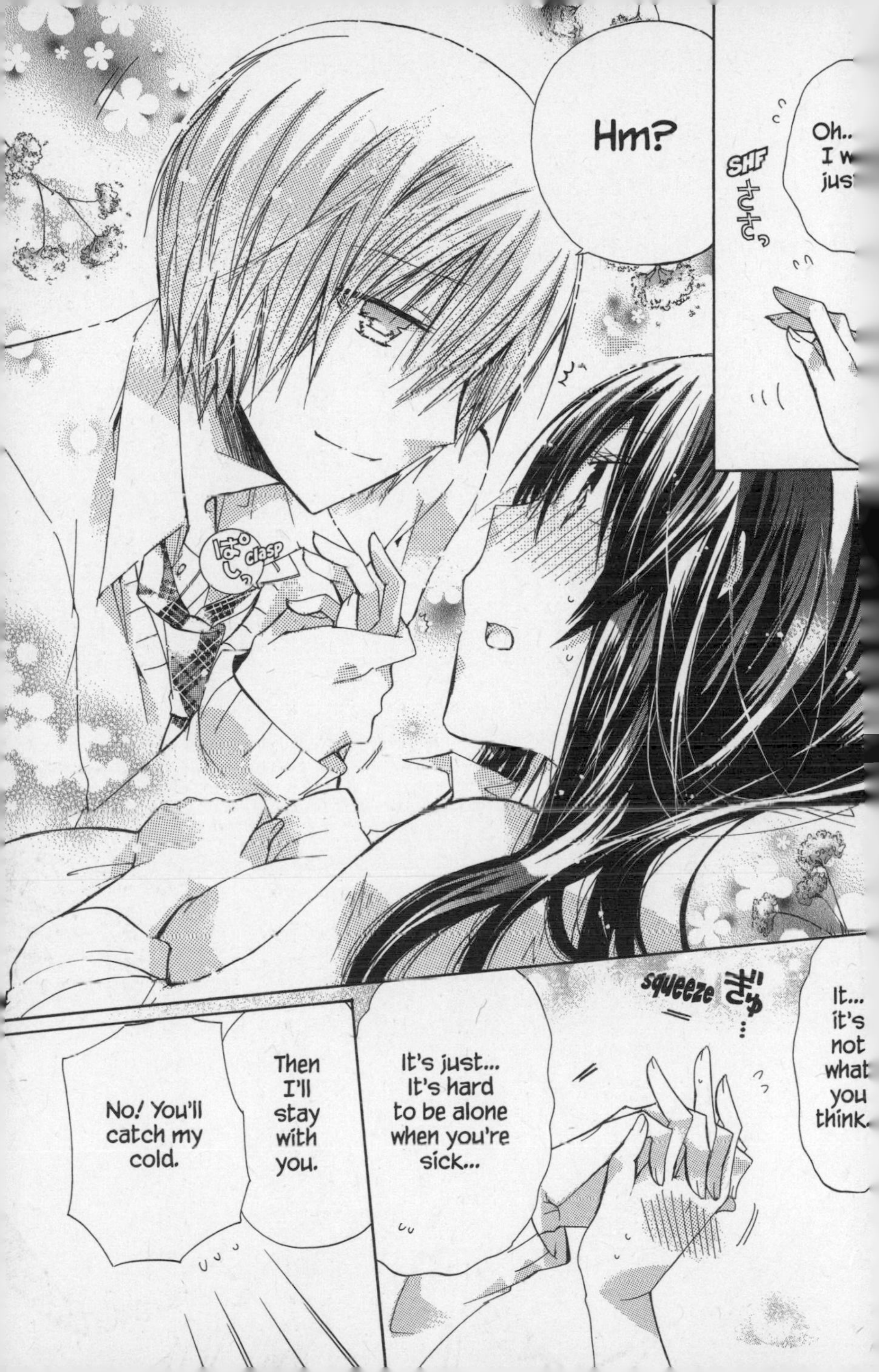
Oh..
I w
jus
SHF ささっ
Hm?
clasp はしっ
It... it's not what you think.
squeeze ぎゅ…
It's just... It's hard to be alone when you're sick...
Then I'll stay with you.
No! You'll catch my cold.

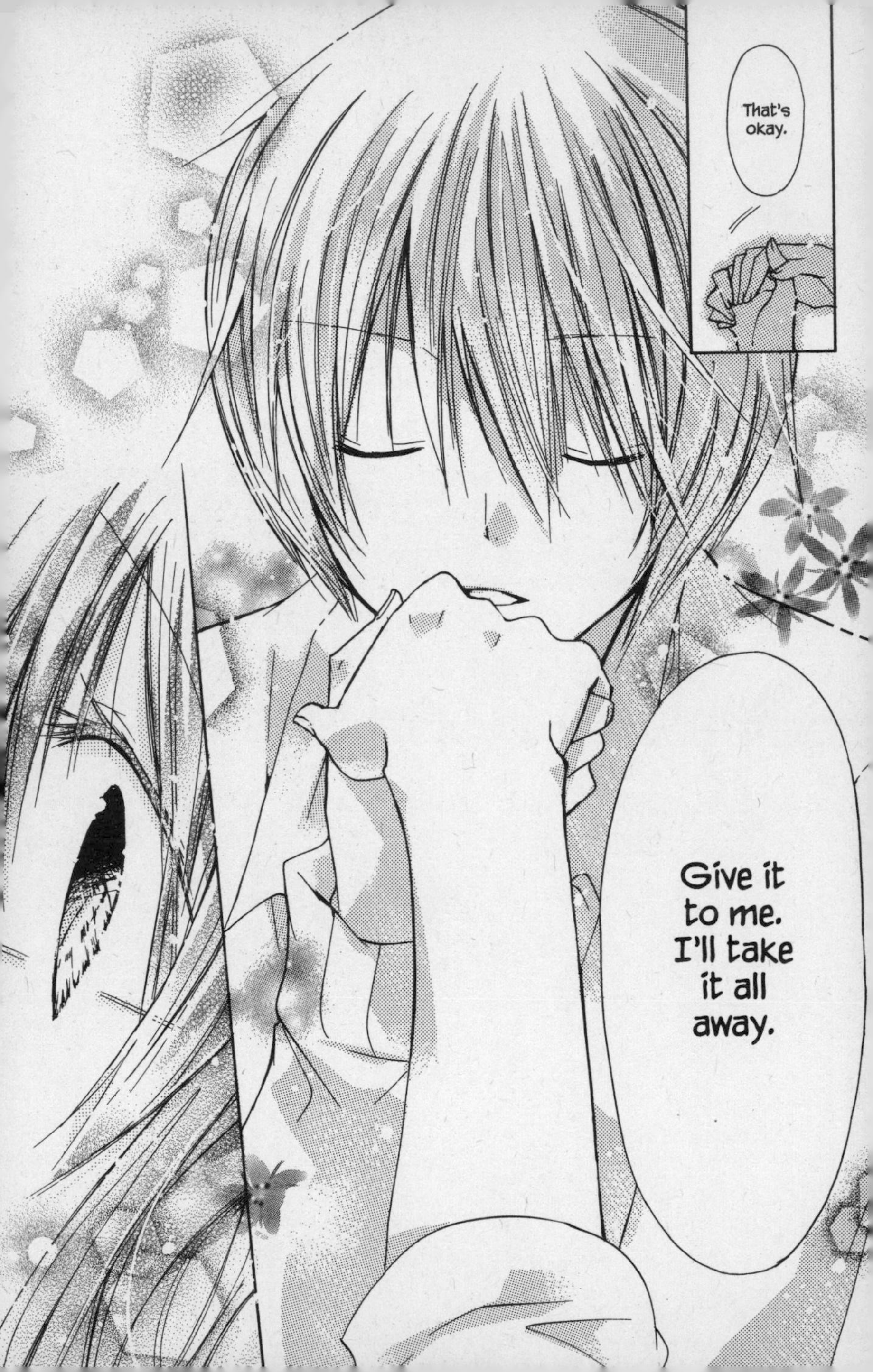
That's okay.
Give it to me. I'll take it all away.

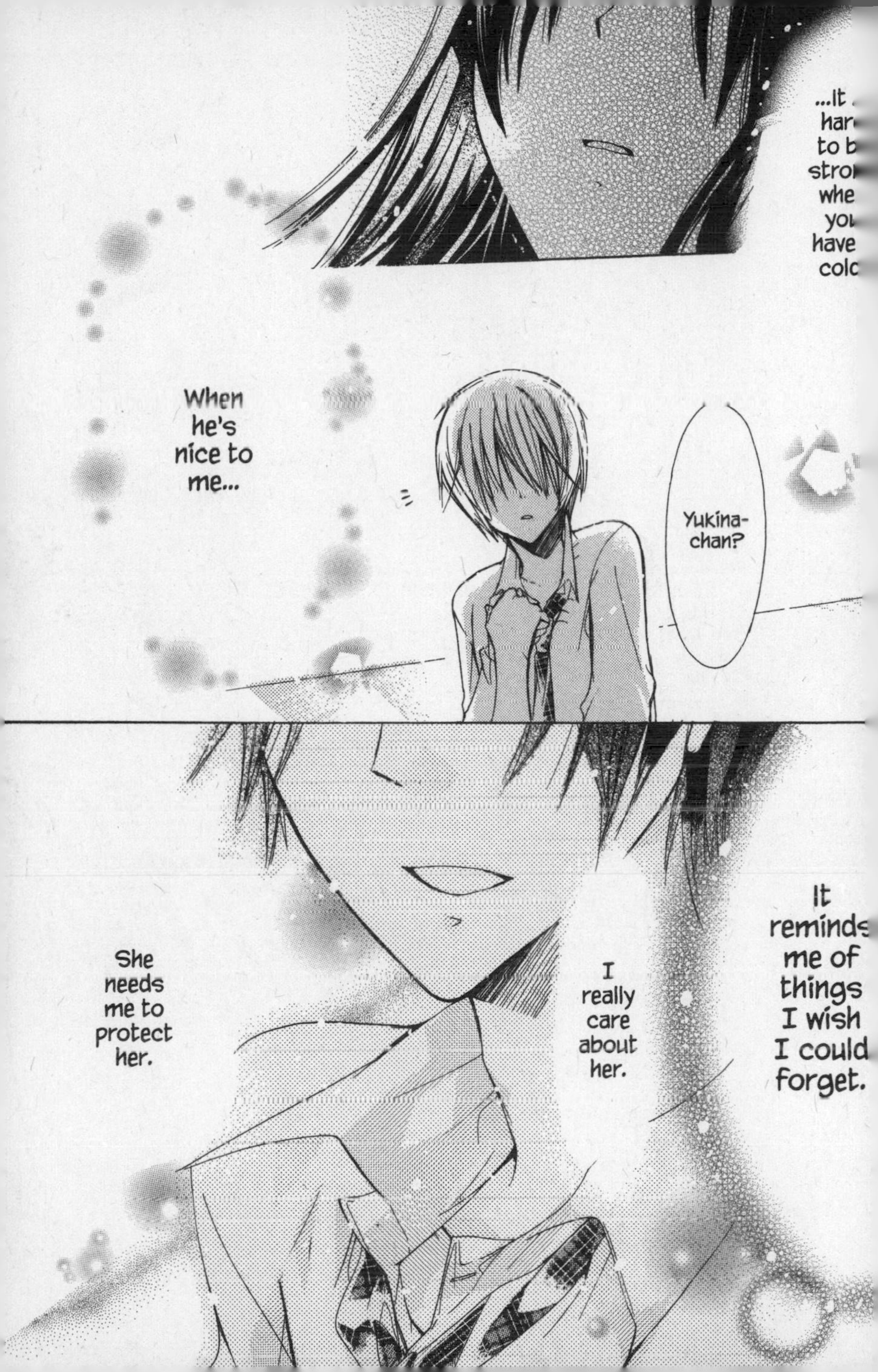
...It har to b stro whe you have colc
Yukina-chan?
When he's nice to me...
It reminds me of things I wish I could forget.
I really care about her.
She needs me to protect her.

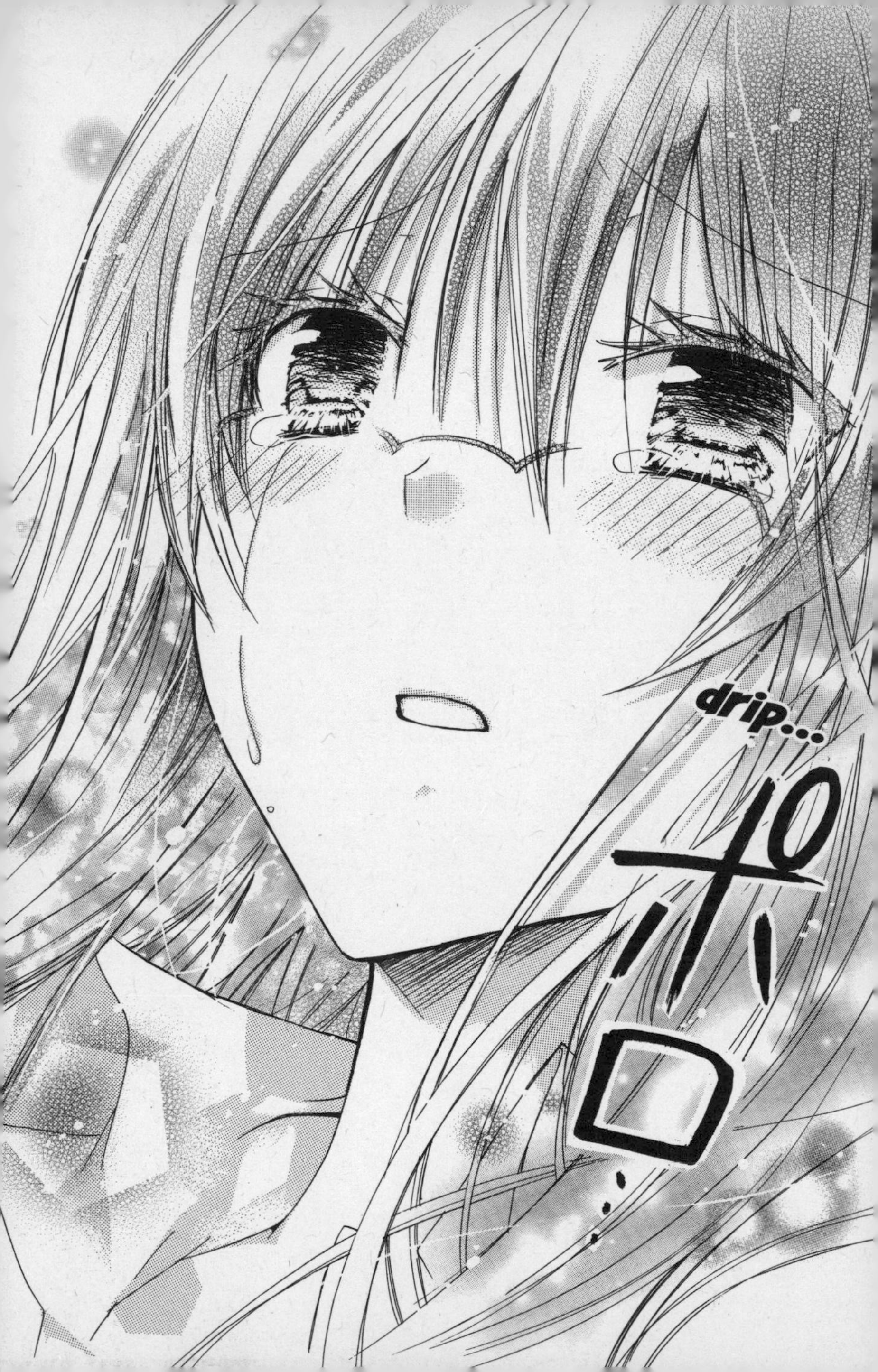
drip...
ポロ

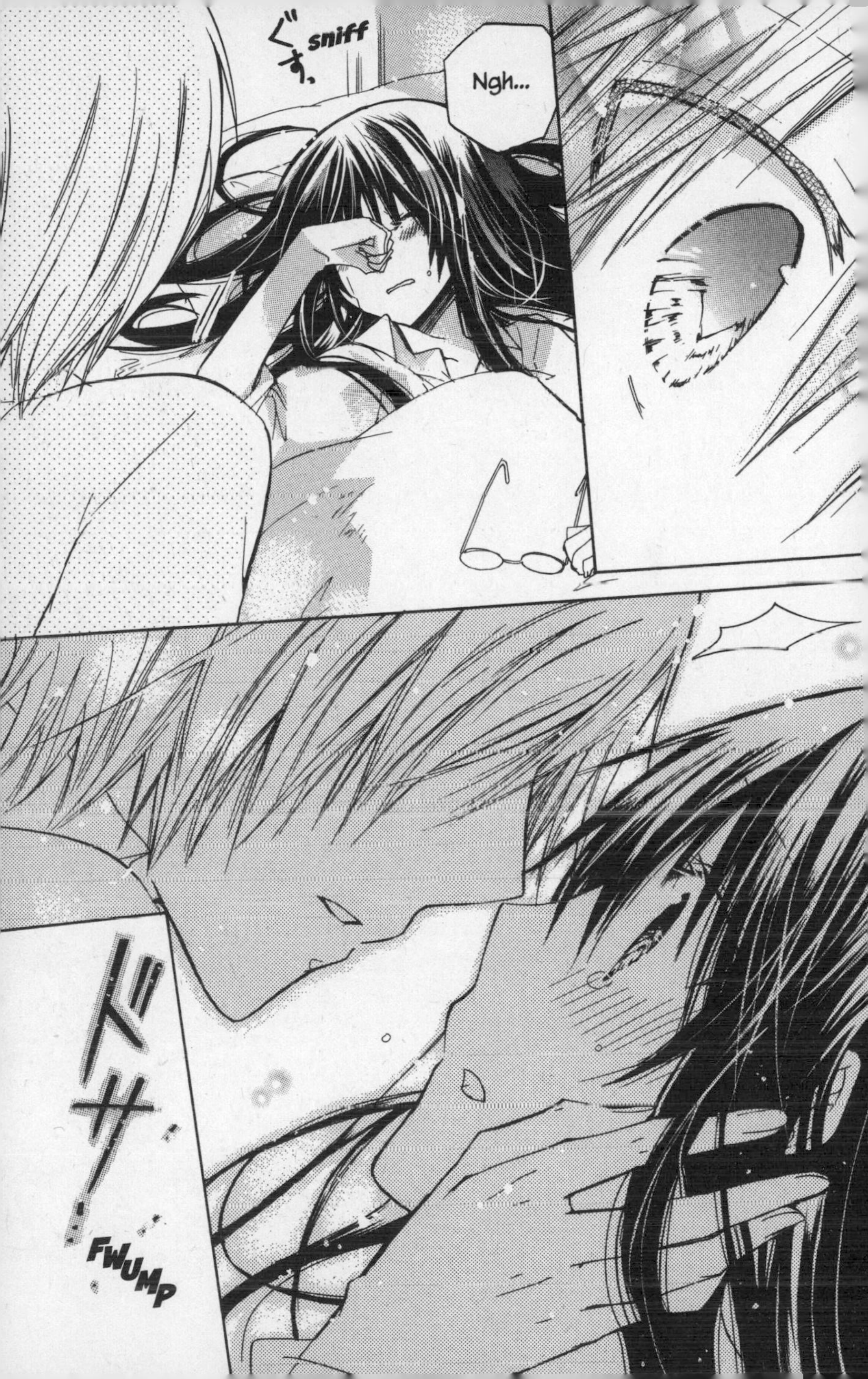
ぐすっ
sniff
Ngh...
ドサー
FWUMP

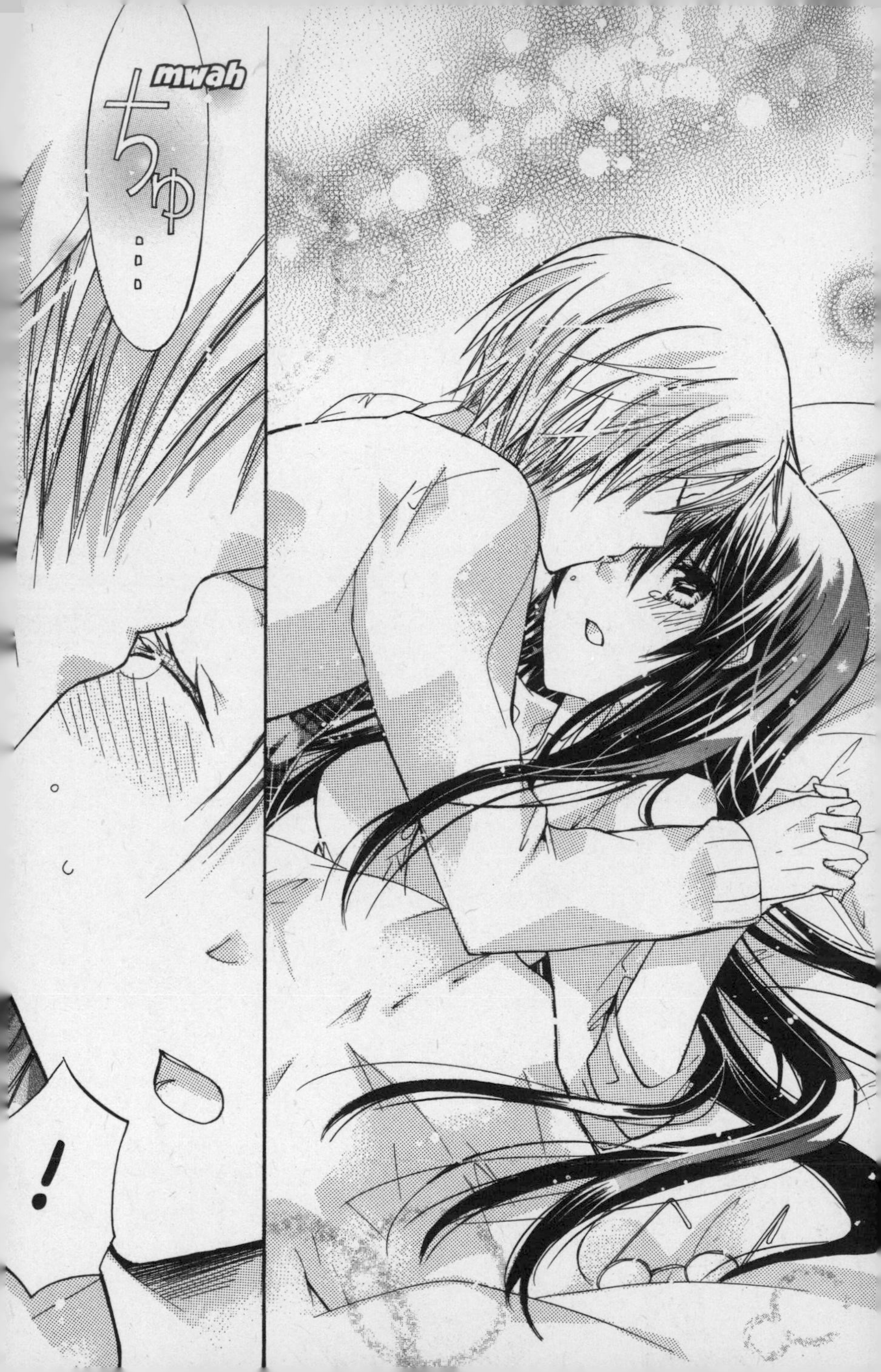
mwah
ちゅ…
!

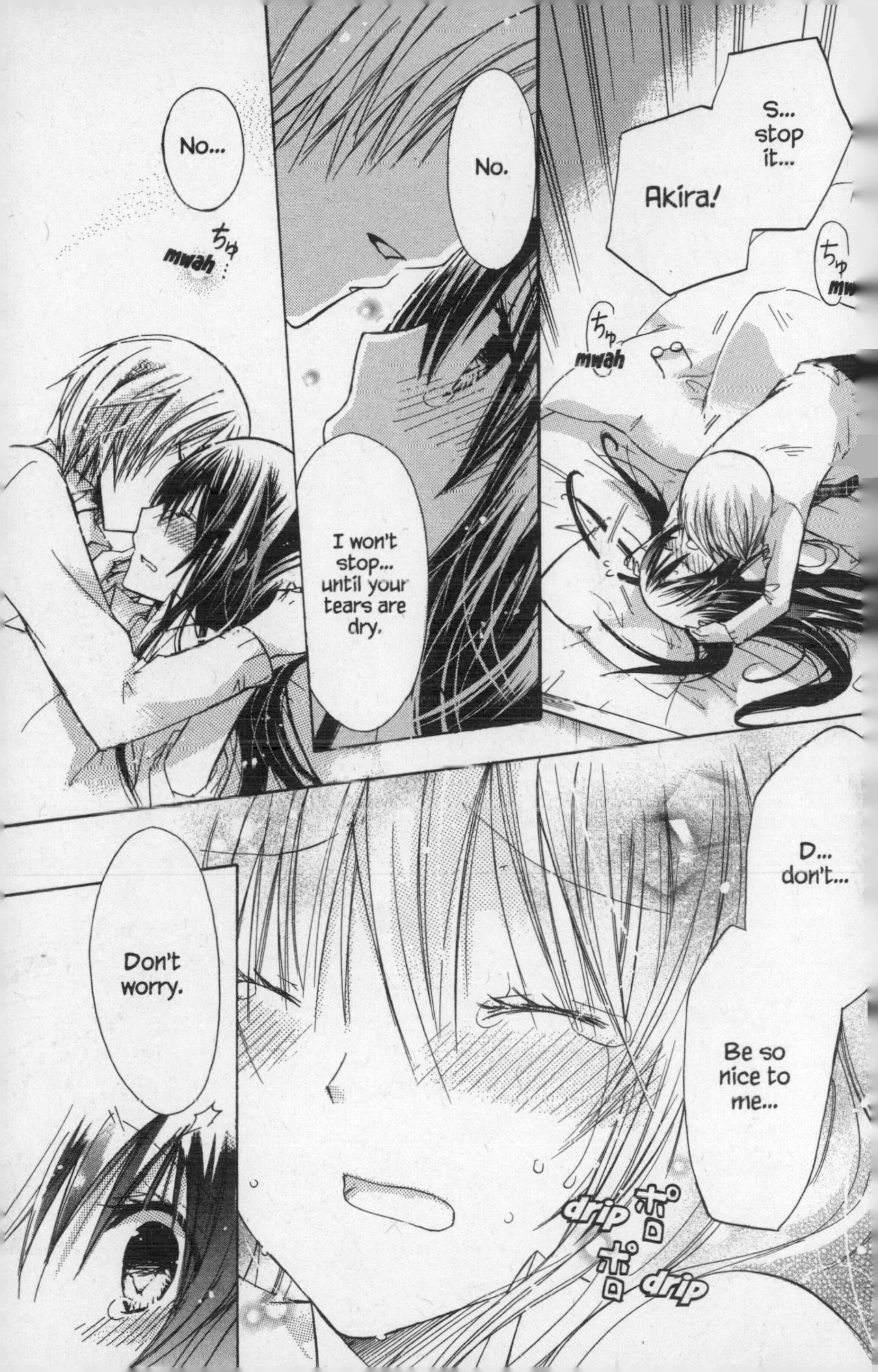
S... stop it...
Akira!
ちゅ
ちゅ
mwah
No.
I won't stop... until your tears are dry.
No...
ちゅ
mwah
D... don't...
Be so nice to me...
ポロ
drip
ポロ
drip
Don't worry.

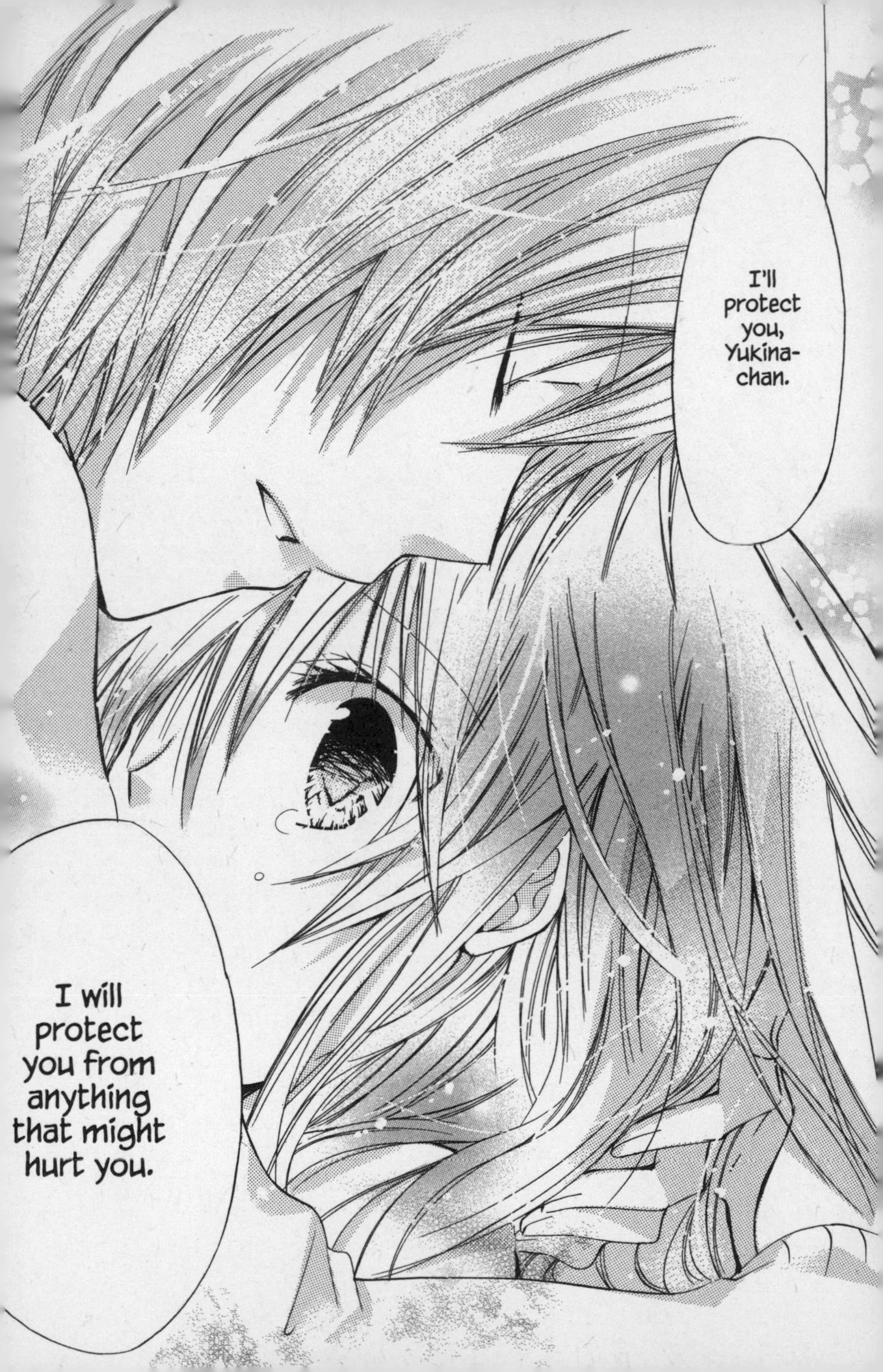
I'll protect you, Yukina-chan.
I will protect you from anything that might hurt you.

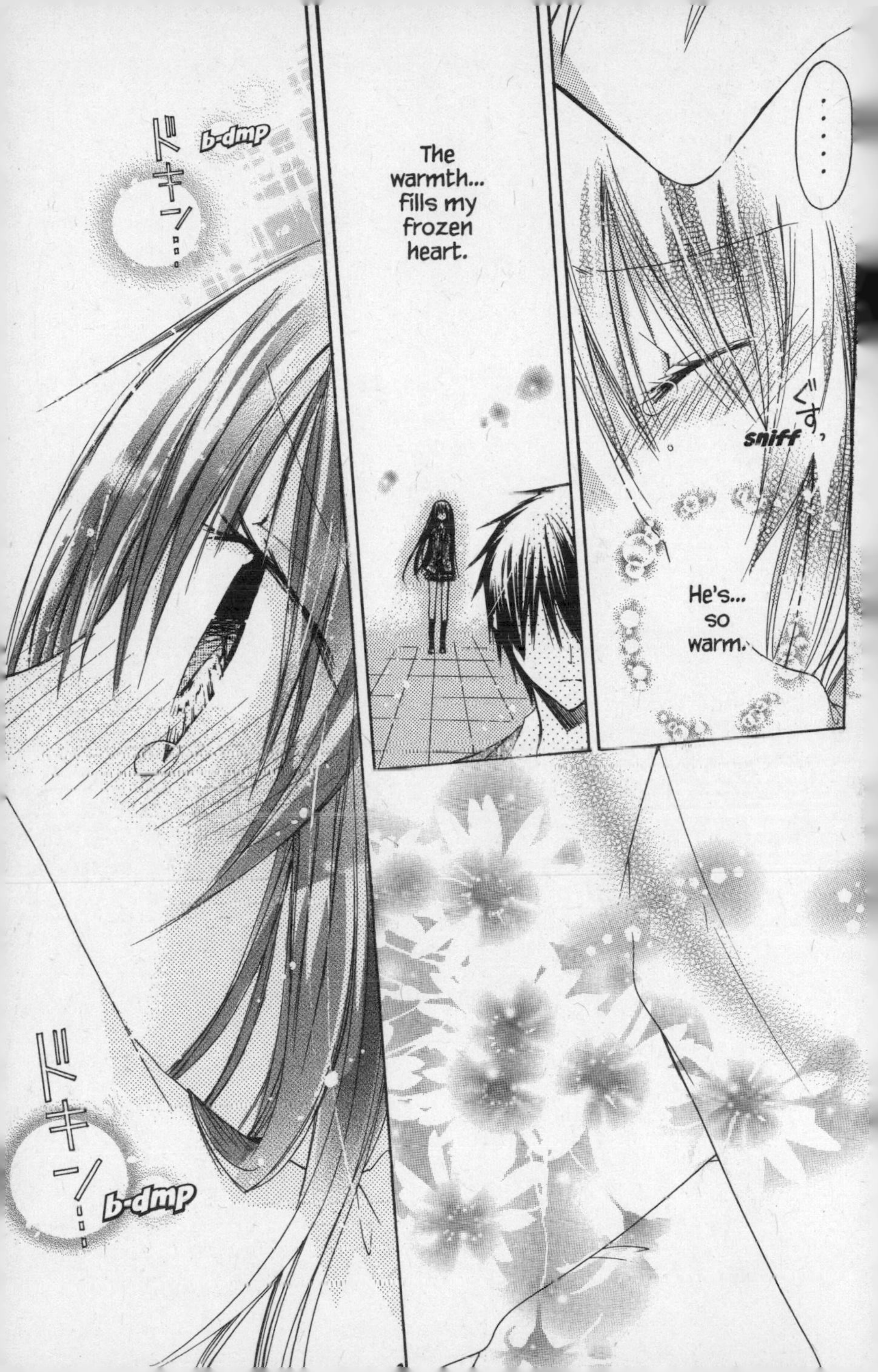
.....
ぐす、
sniff
He's... so warm.
The warmth... fills my frozen heart.
ドキン…
b-dmp
ドキーン…
b-dmp

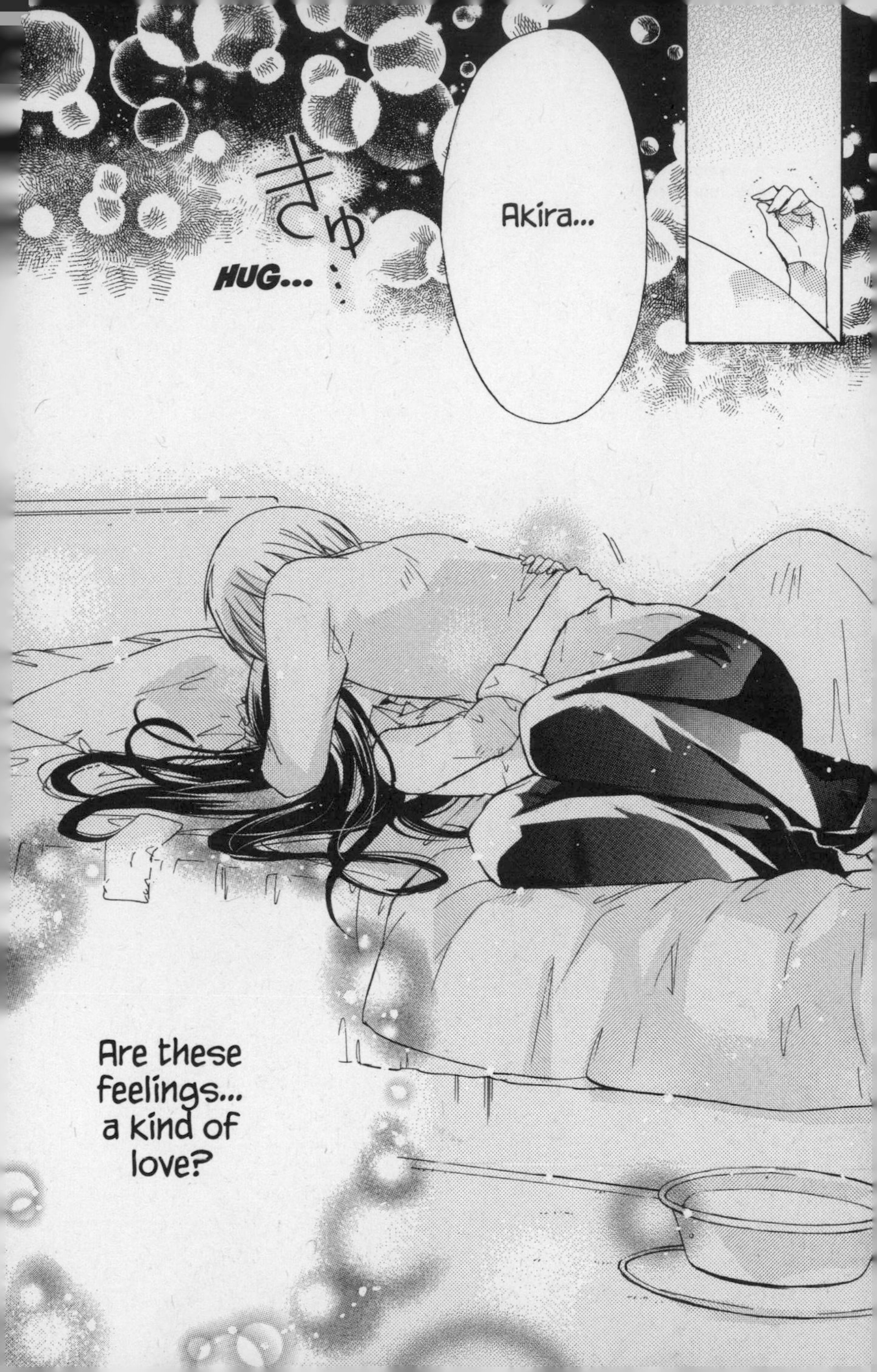
Akira...
きゅ…
HUG...
Are these feelings... a kind of love?

Missions of Love

**It is time for love.
Secret cell phone novelist vs. the most popular boy in school.
A mission of love for absolute servitude.**

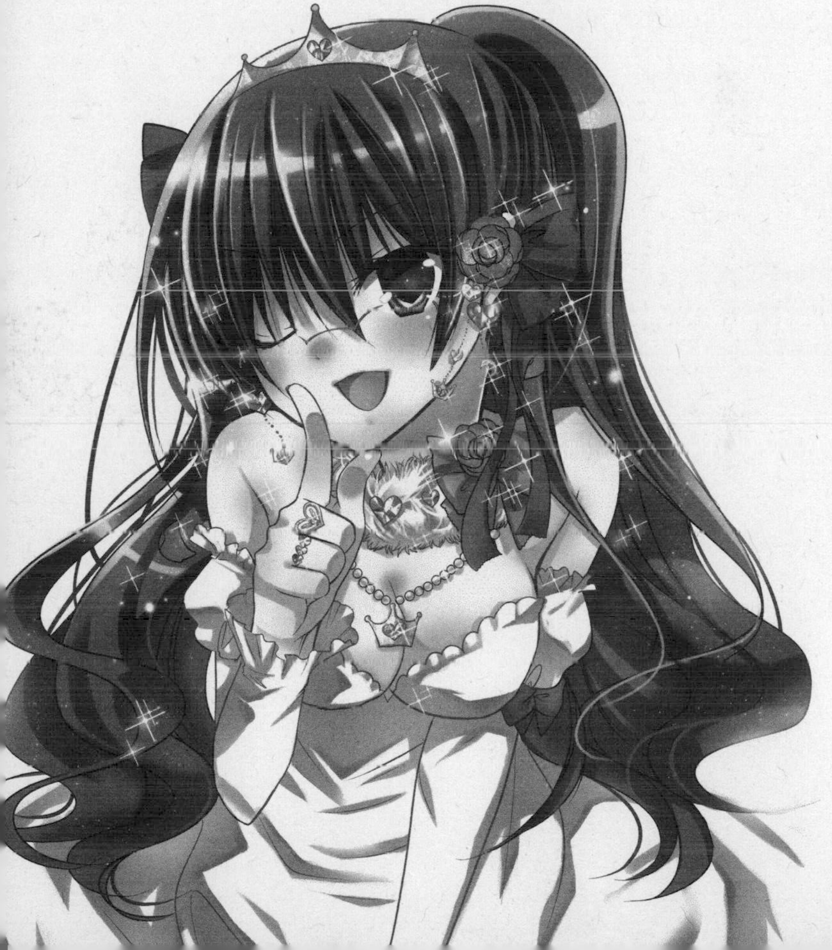

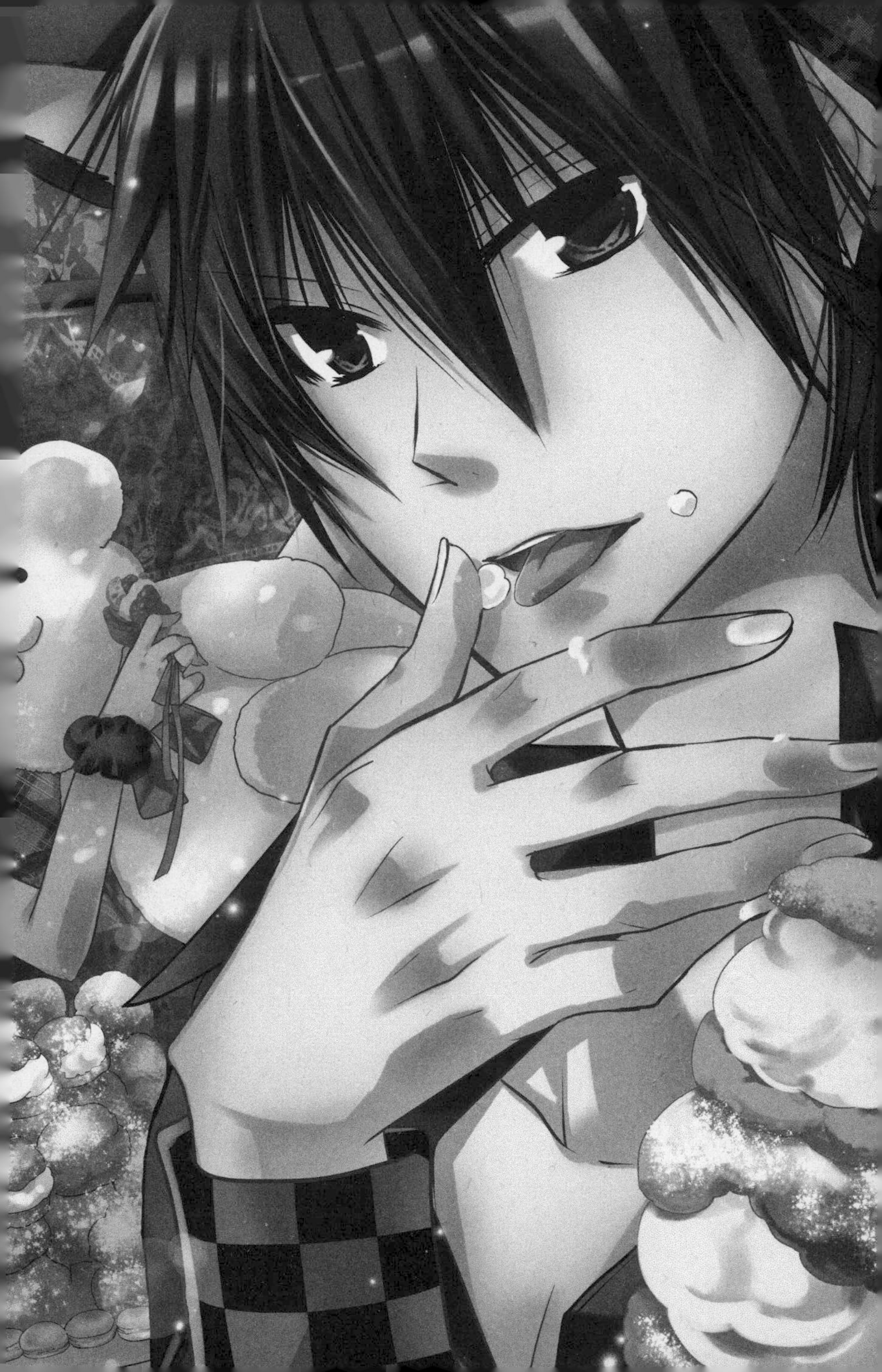

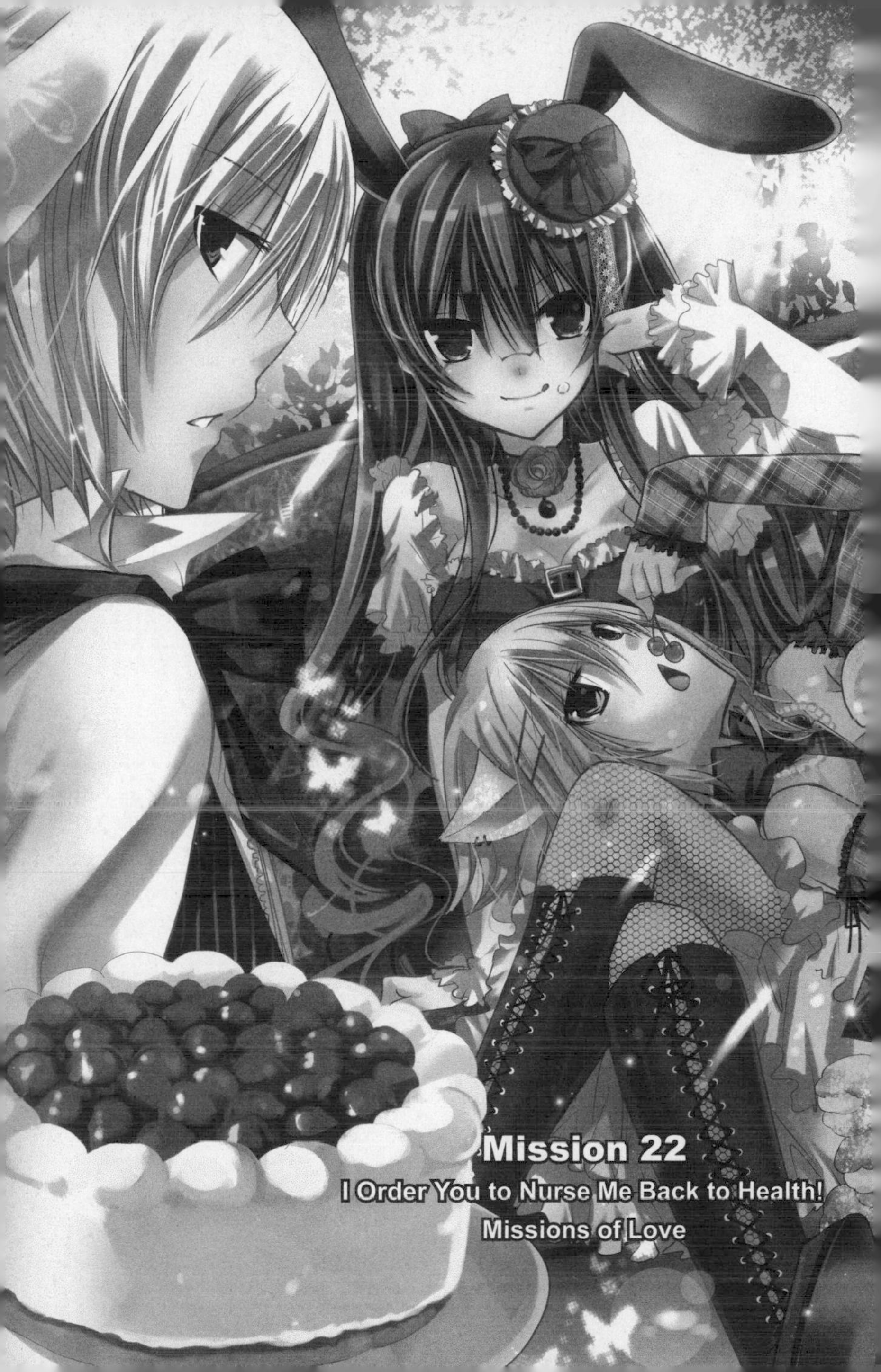
Mission 22
I Order You to Nurse Me Back to Health!
Missions of Love

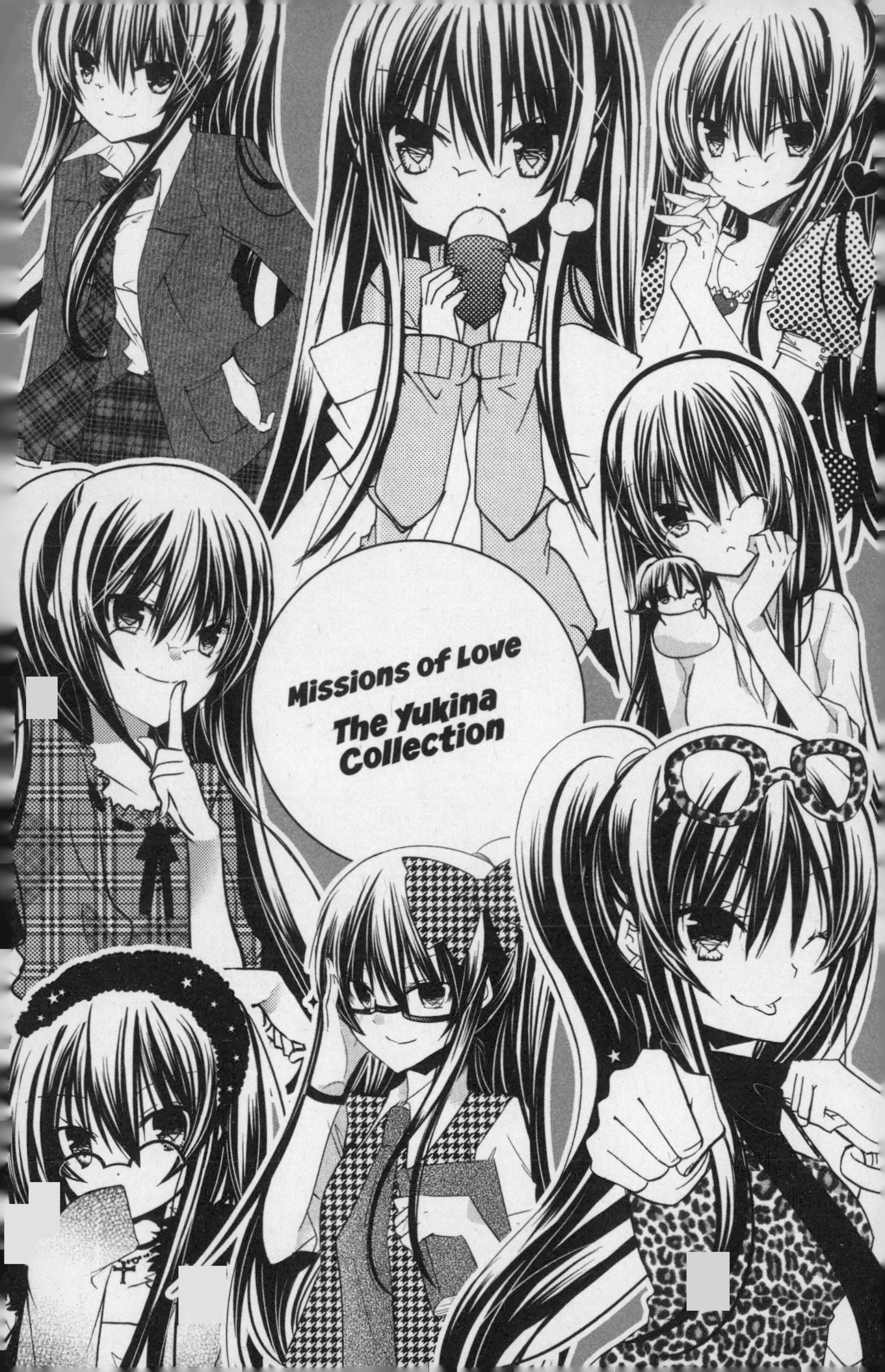
Missions of Love
The Yukina Collection

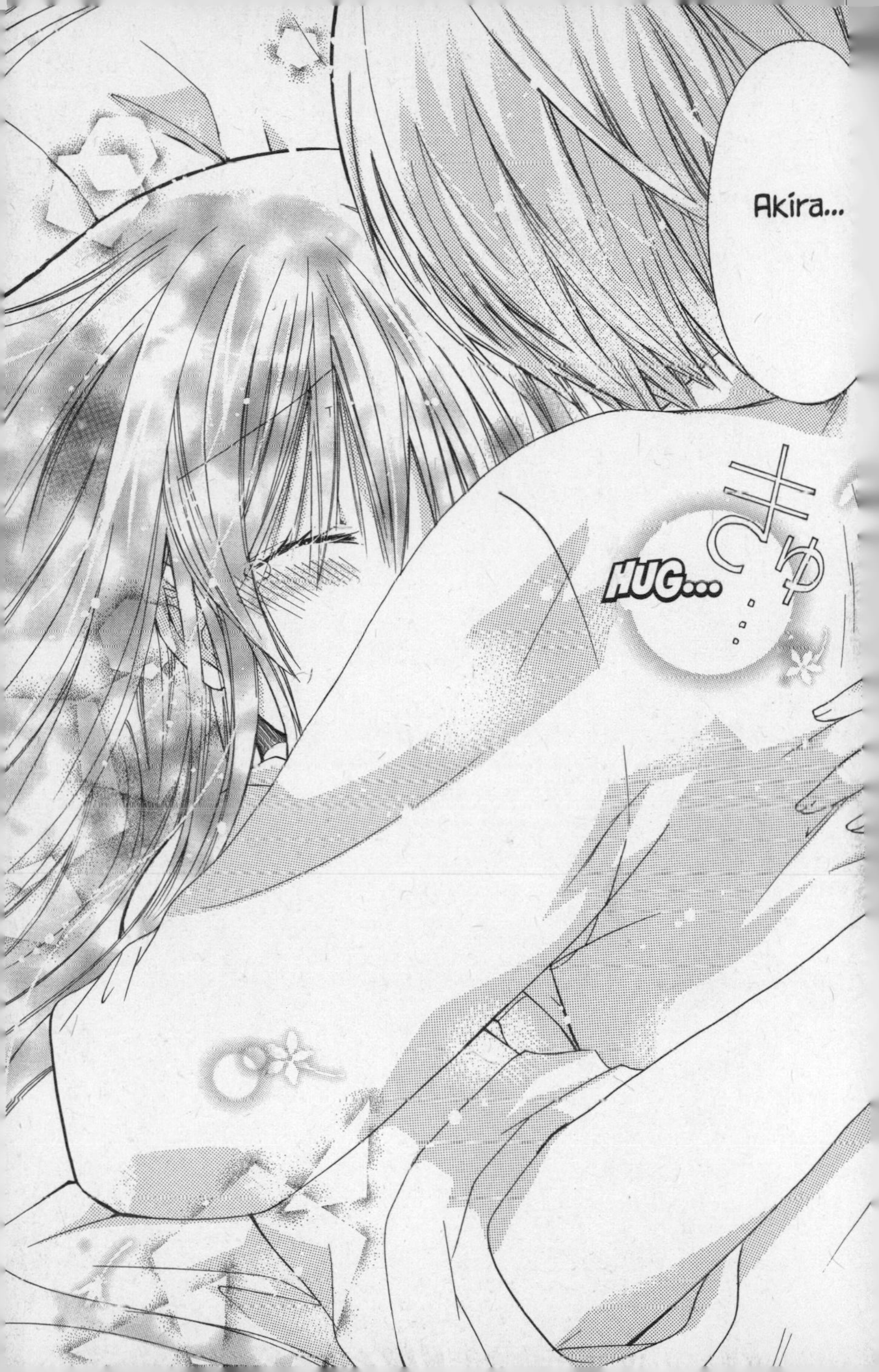
Akira...
HUG...

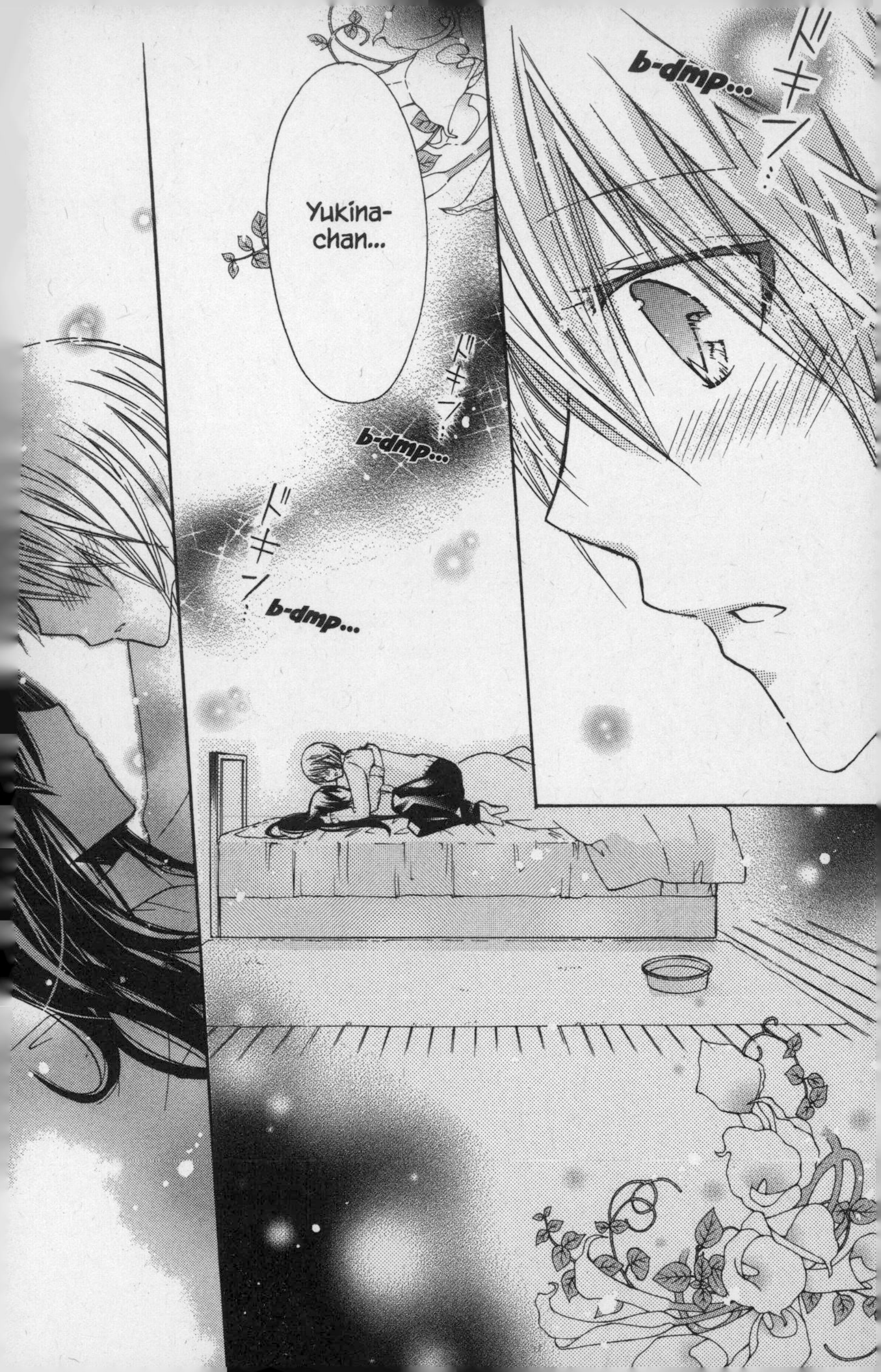
b-dmp...
Yukina-chan...
b-dmp...
b-dmp...

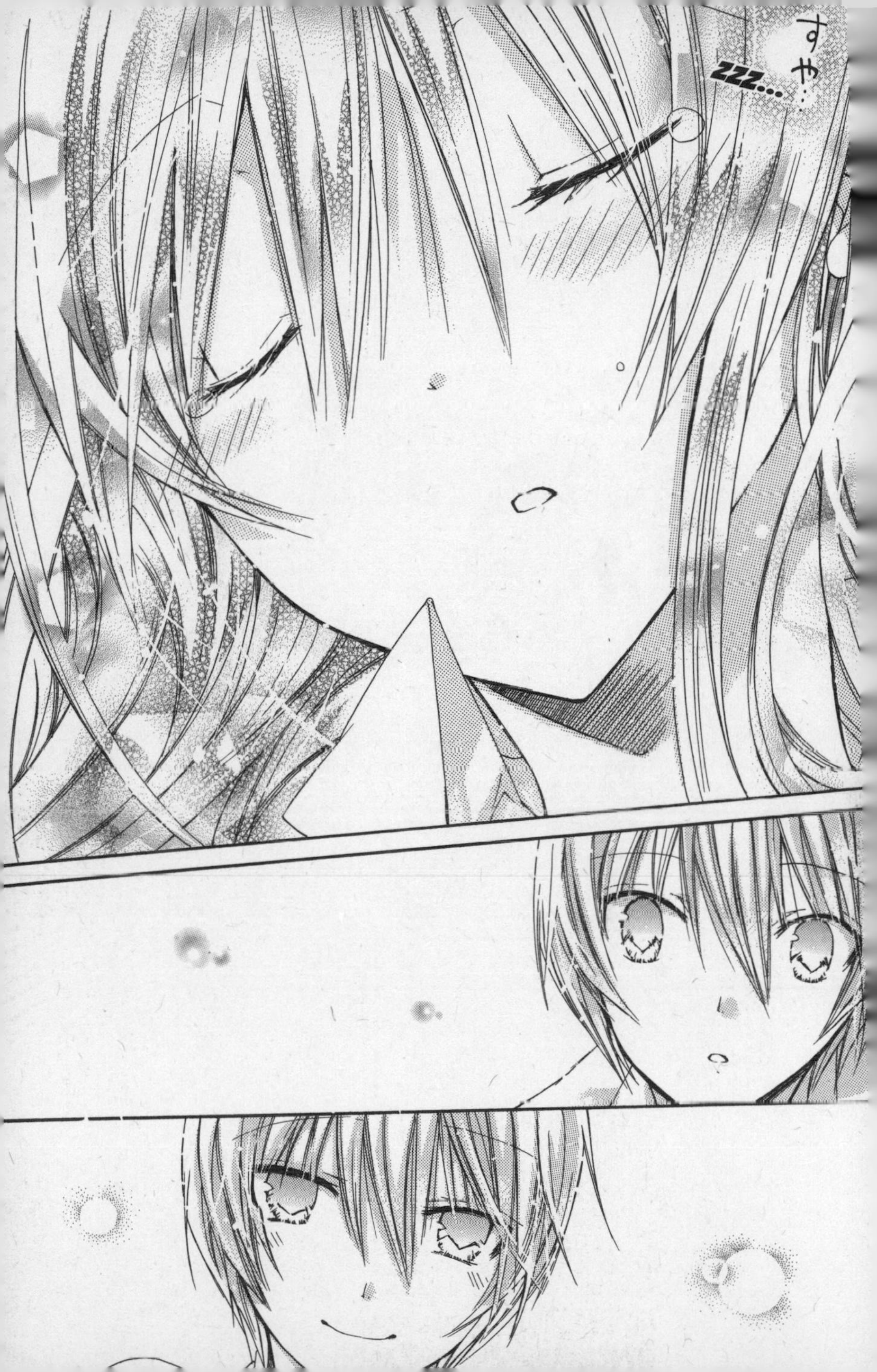
すやっ
zzz...

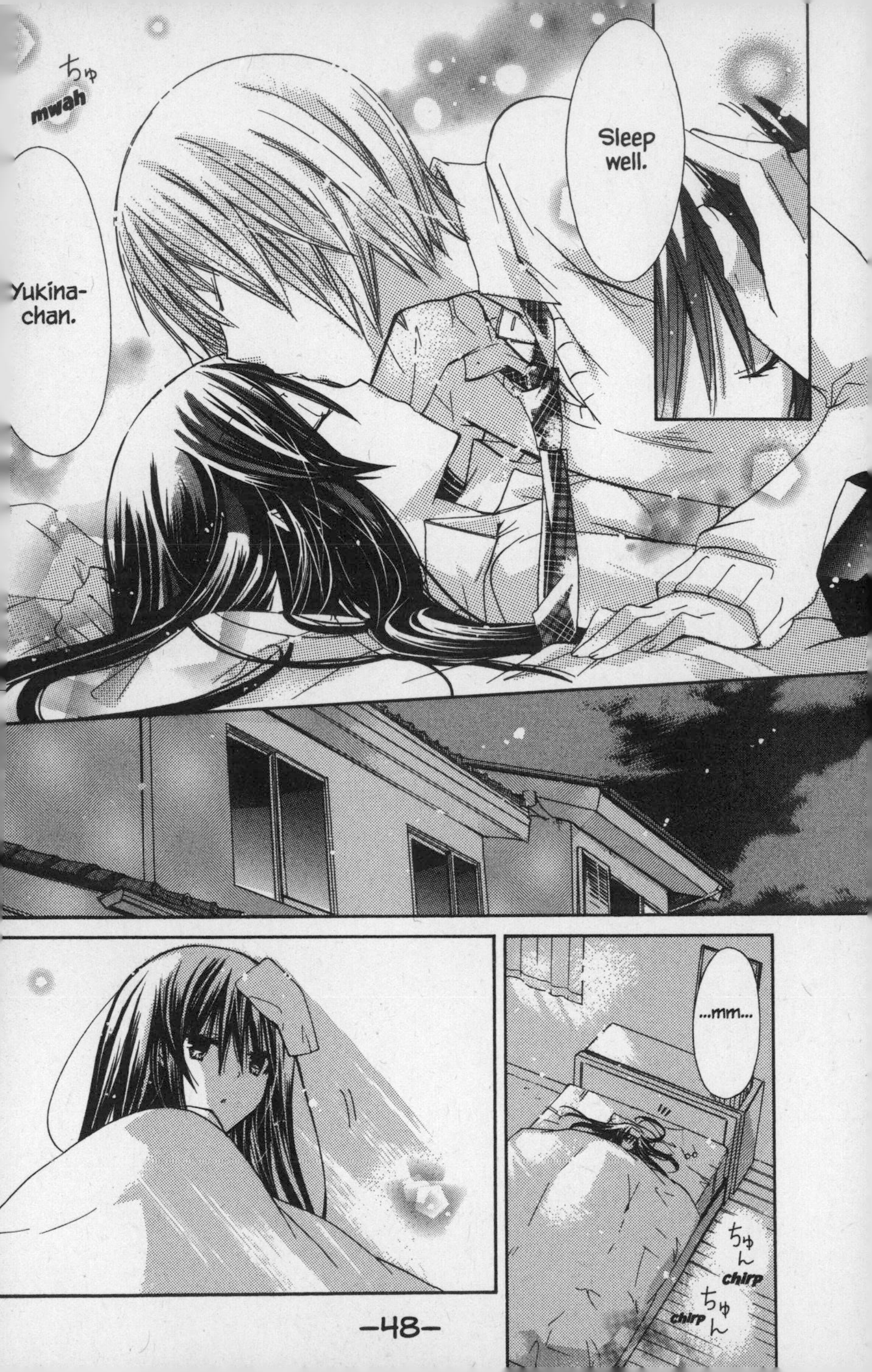
Sleep well.
ちゅ
mwah
Yukina-chan.
...mm...
ちゅん
chirp
ちゅん
chirp

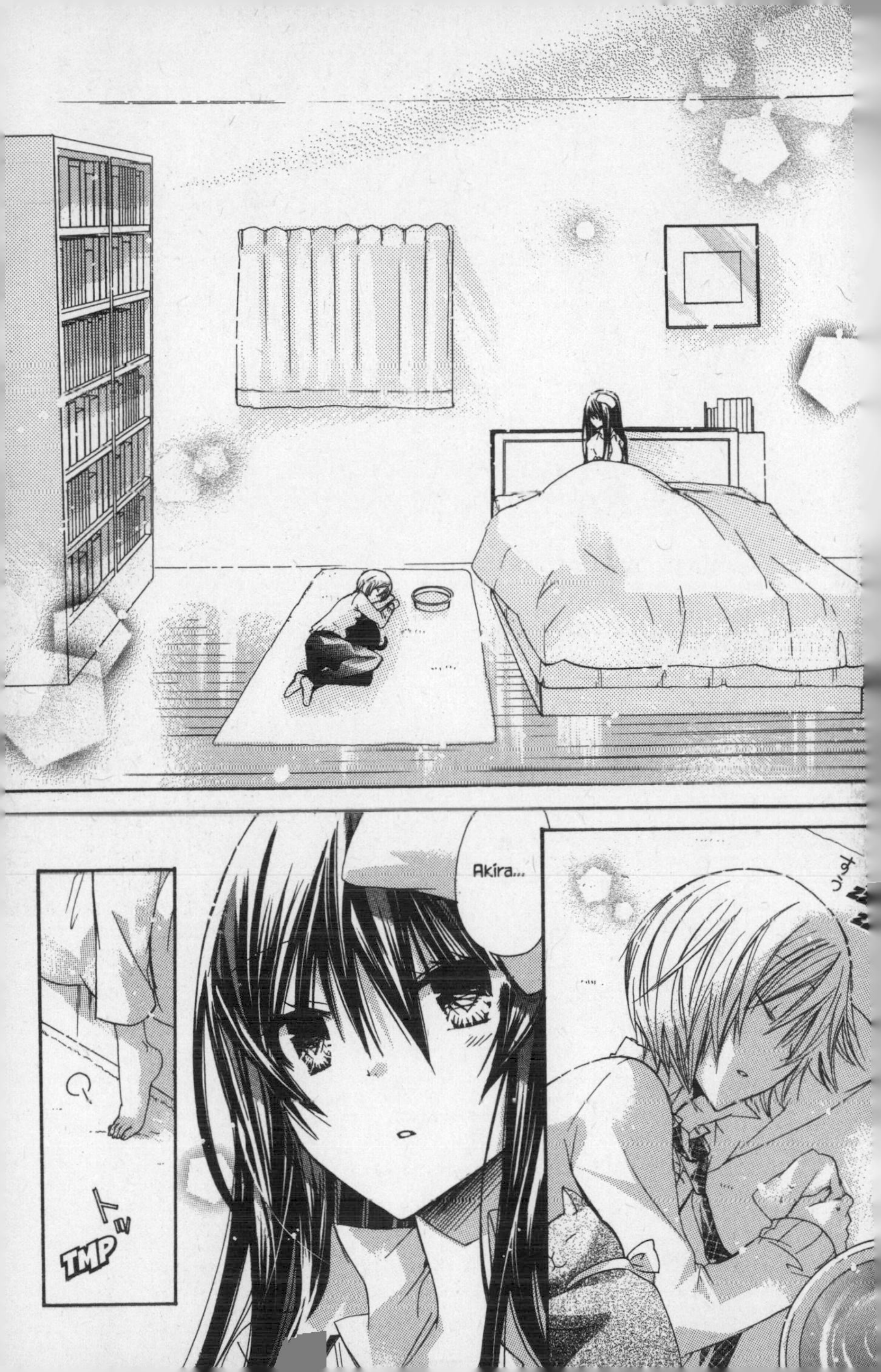
Akira...
TMP

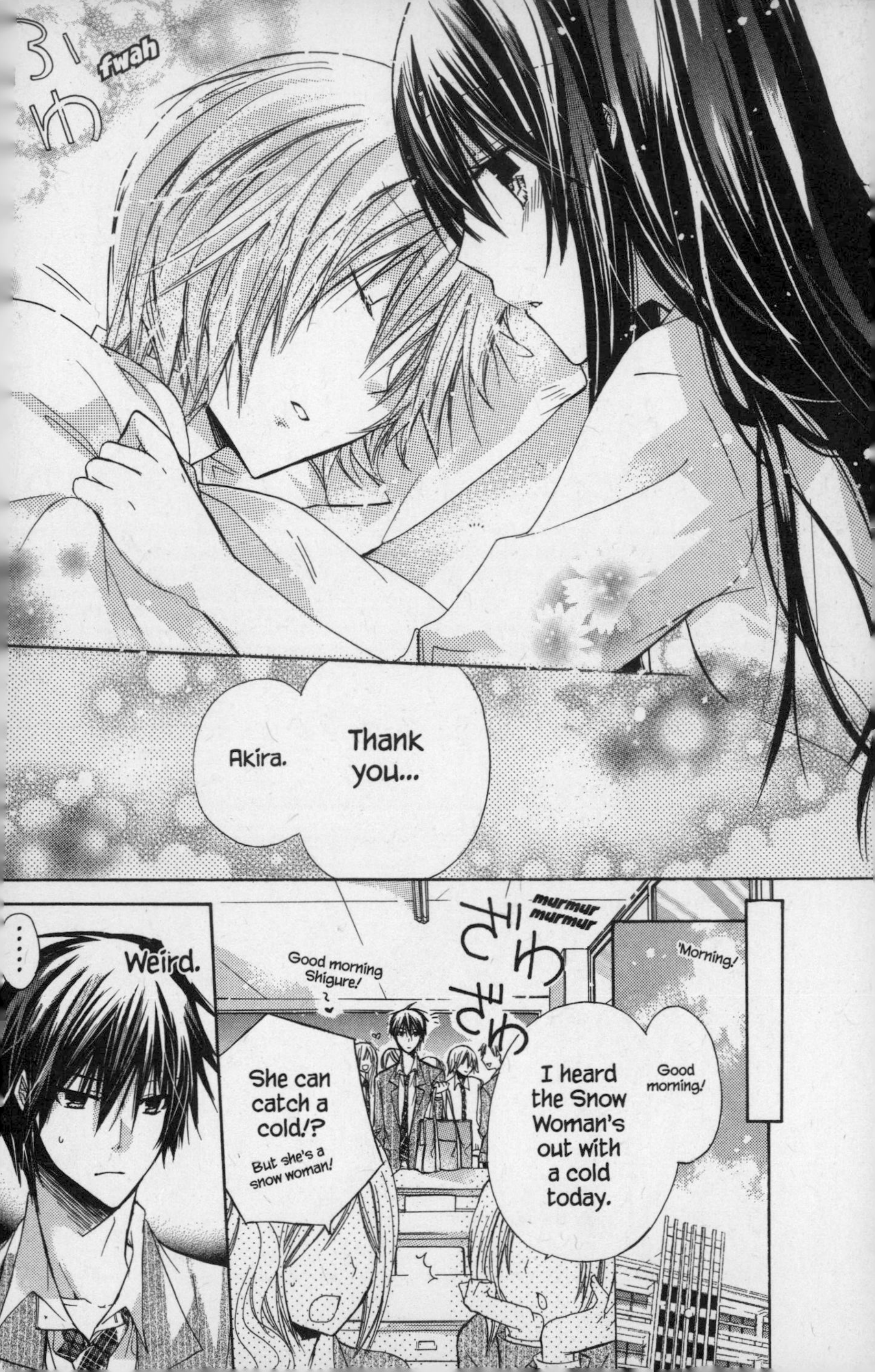
fwah
Thank you...
Akira.
murmur murmur
'Morning!
Good morning!
I heard the Snow Woman's out with a cold today.
She can catch a cold!?
But she's a snow woman!
Good morning Shigure!
......
Weird.

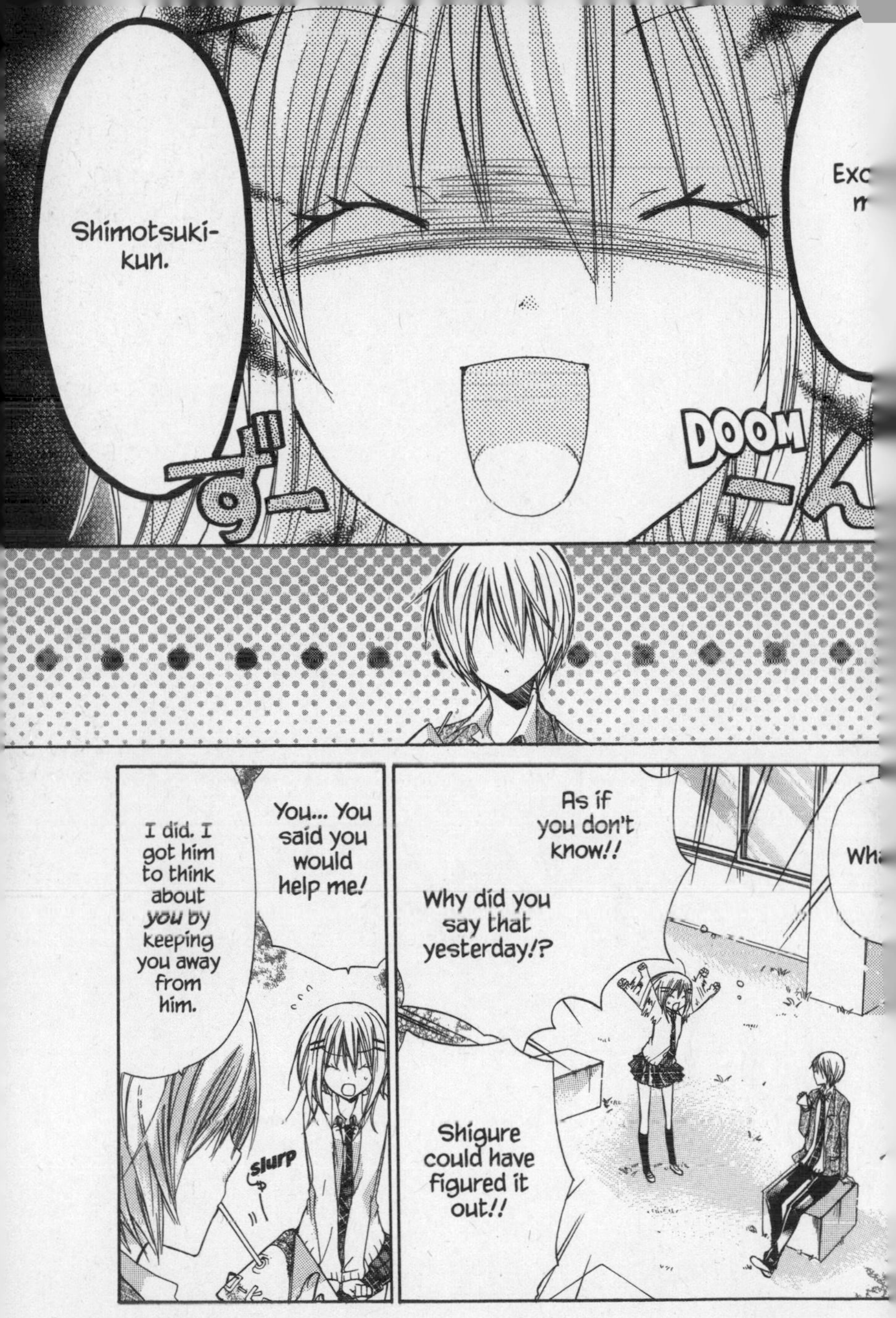

Exc
m
Shimotsuki-kun.
DOOM
....
Wh
As if you don't know!!
Why did you say that yesterday!?
Shigure could have figured it out!!
You... You said you would help me!
I did. I got him to think about *you* by keeping you away from him.
slurp

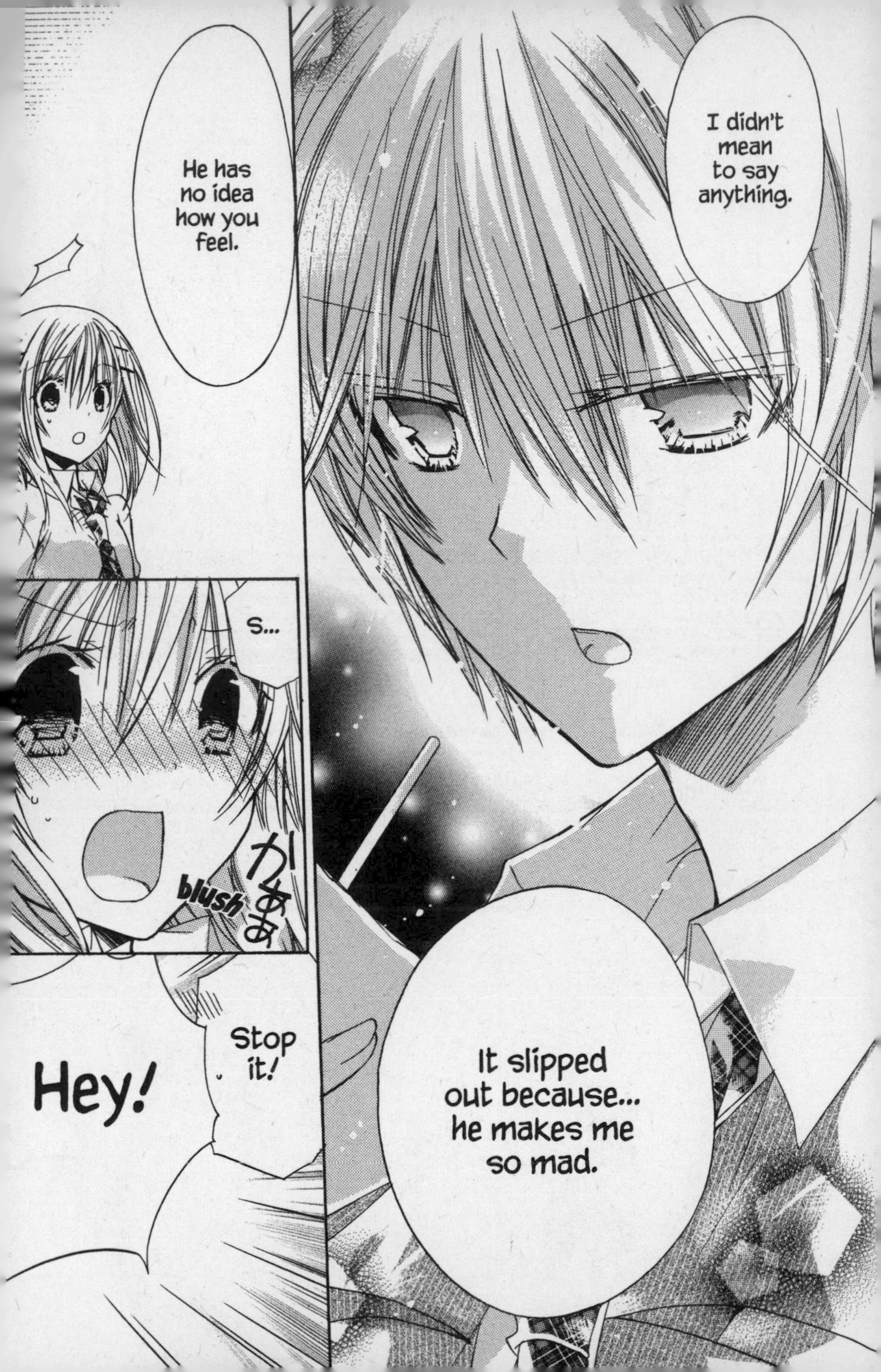
I didn't mean to say anything.
It slipped out because... he makes me so mad.
He has no idea how you feel.
S...
blush
Stop it!
Hey!

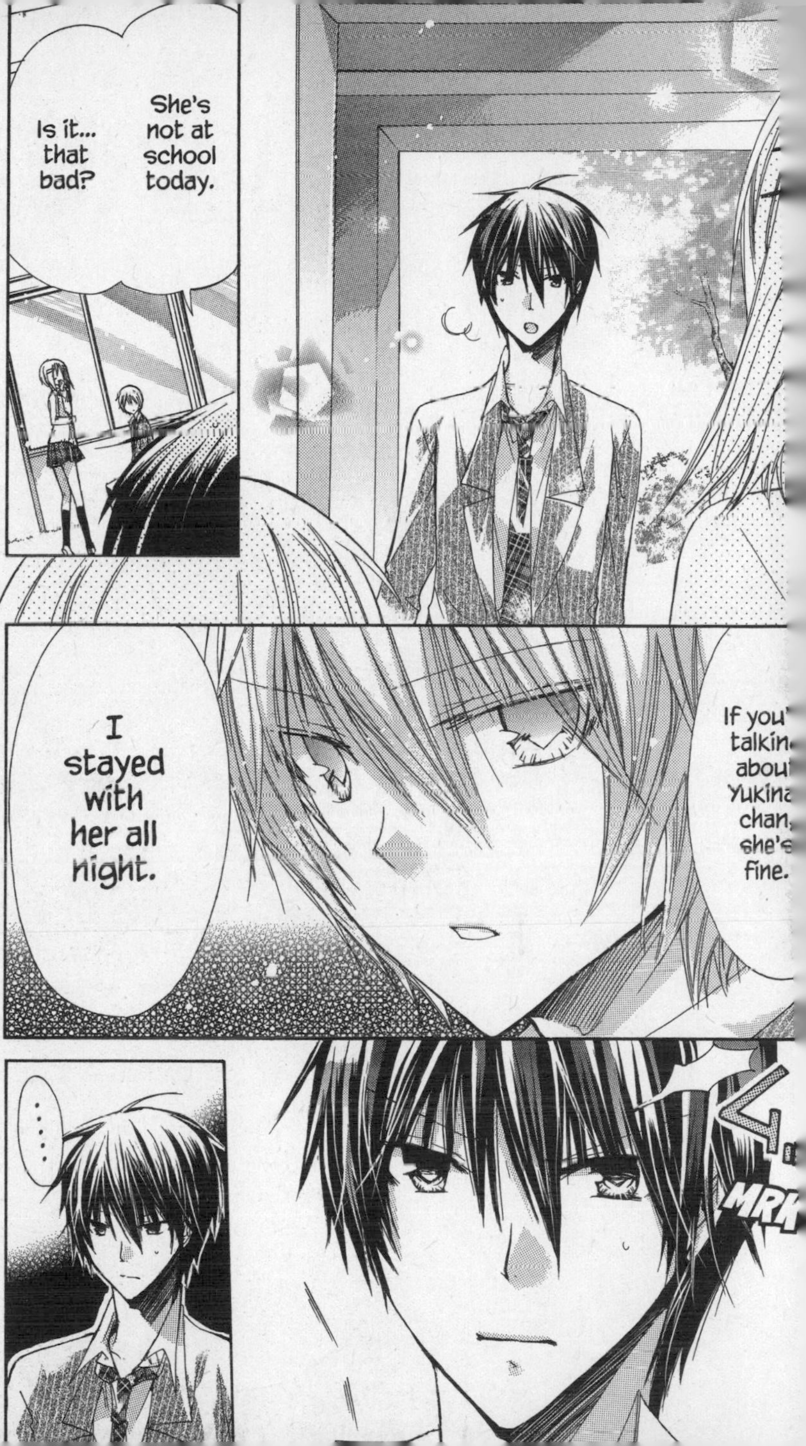
She's not at school today.
Is it... that bad?
If you' talkin abou Yukina chan, she's fine.
I stayed with her all night.
MRK
.....

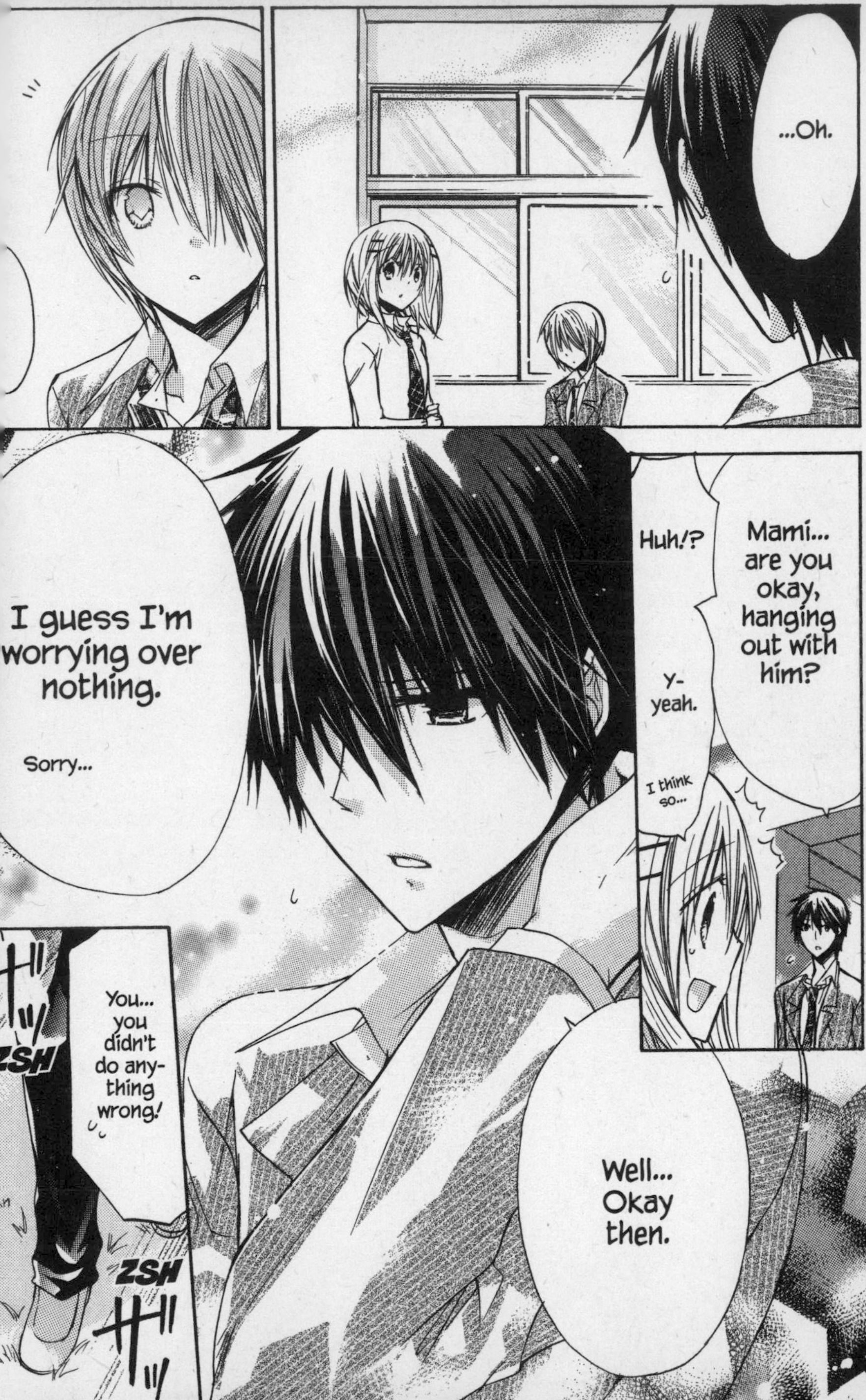
...Oh.
Mami... are you okay, hanging out with him?
Huh!?
Y-yeah.
I think so...
Well... Okay then.
I guess I'm worrying over nothing.
Sorry...
ZSH
You... you didn't do any-thing wrong!
ZSH

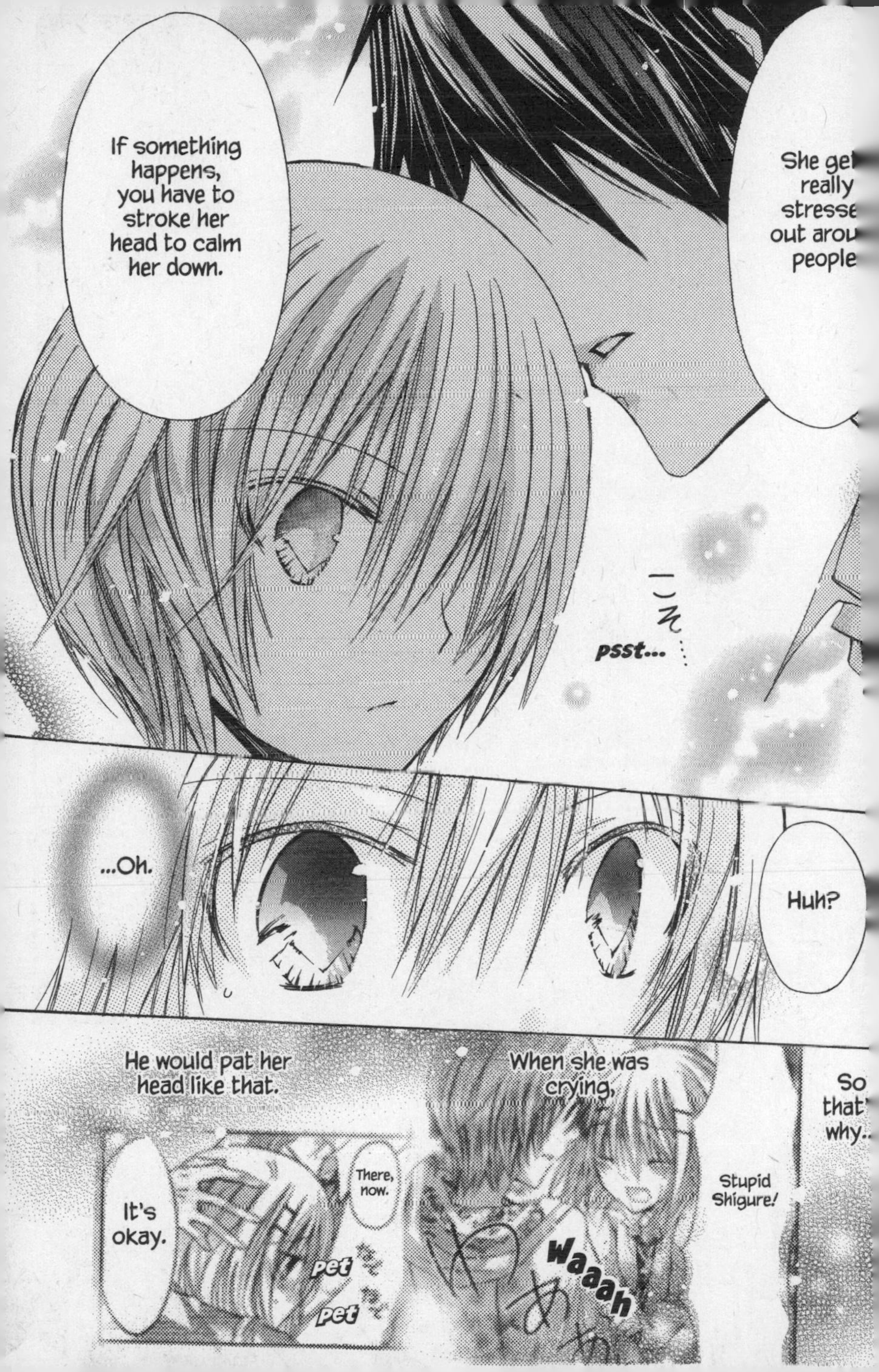
She get
really
stresse
out arou
people
psst...
If something happens, you have to stroke her head to calm her down.
Huh?
...Oh.
So
that
why..
When she was crying,
Stupid Shigure!
Waaah
He would pat her head like that.
There, now.
pet
pet
It's okay.

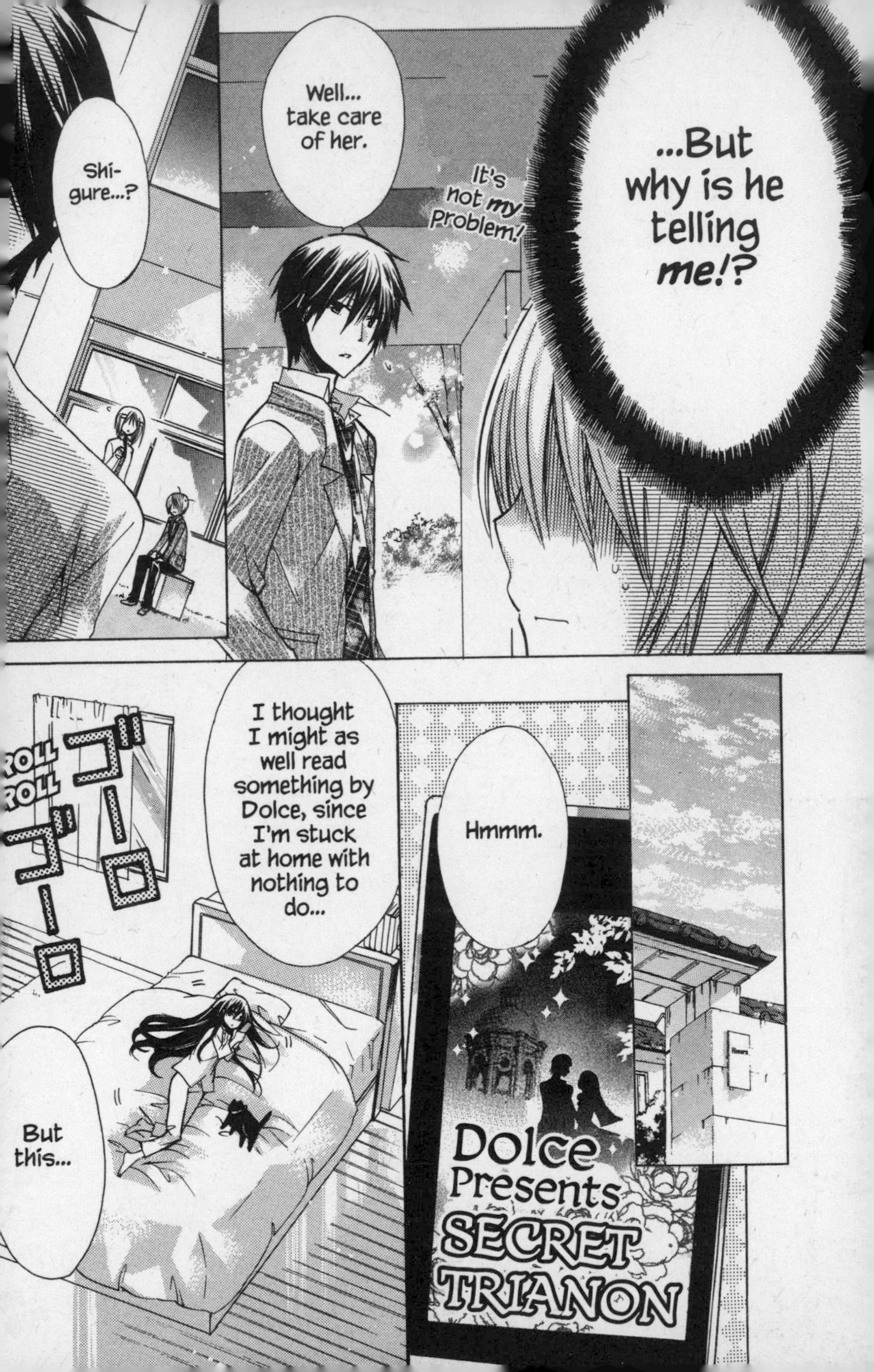
Shi-gure...?
Well... take care of her.
It's not my problem!
...But why is he telling me!?
ROLL ROLL
I thought I might as well read something by Dolce, since I'm stuck at home with nothing to do...
But this...
Hmmm.
Dolce Presents SECRET TRIANON

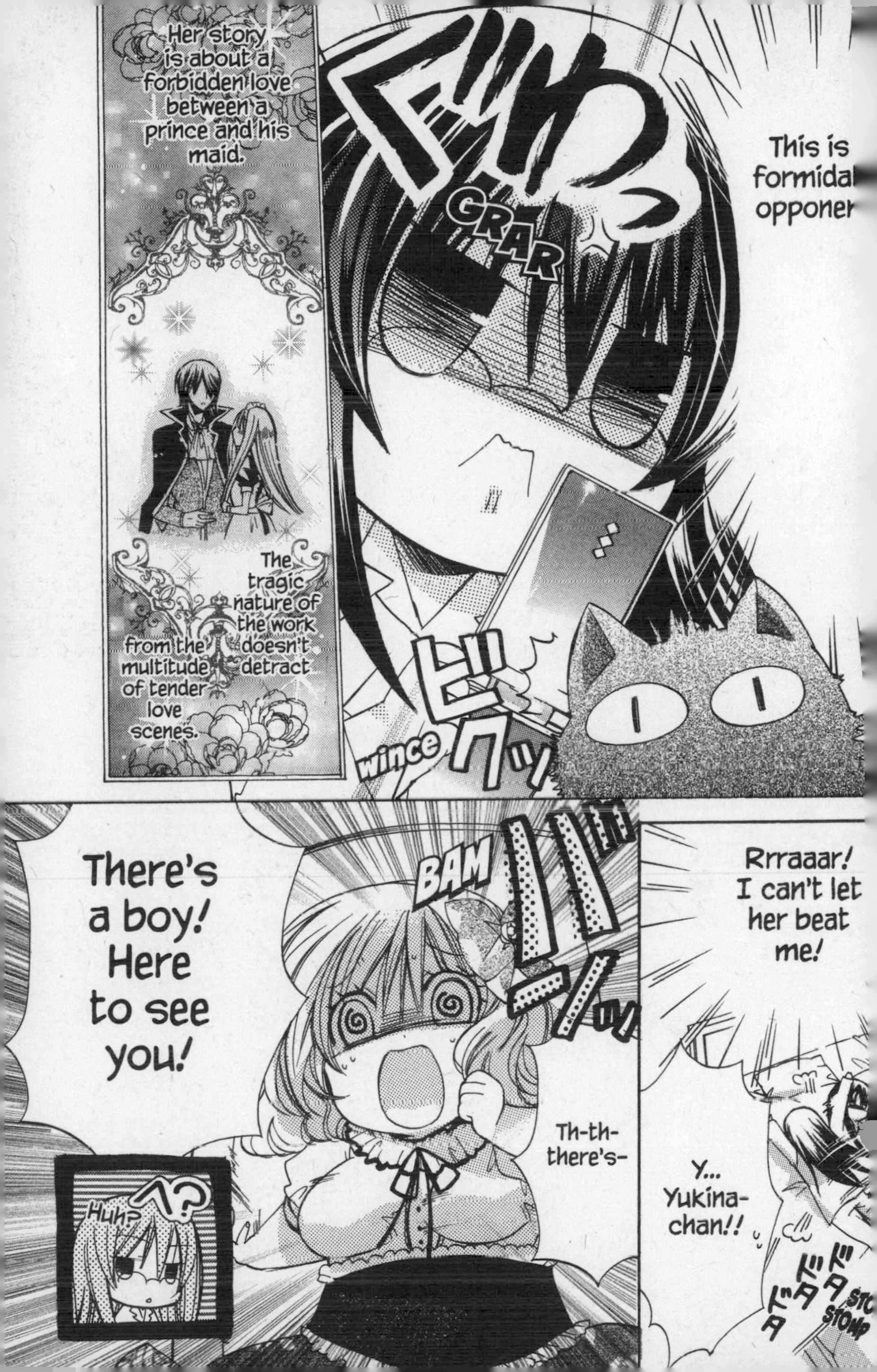
This is formidab opponen
GRAR
wince
Her story is about a forbidden love between a prince and his maid.
The tragic nature of the work doesn't detract from the multitude of tender love scenes.
Rrraaar! I can't let her beat me!
Y... Yukina-chan!!
STOMP
BAM
Th-th-there's-
There's a boy! Here to see you!
Huh?

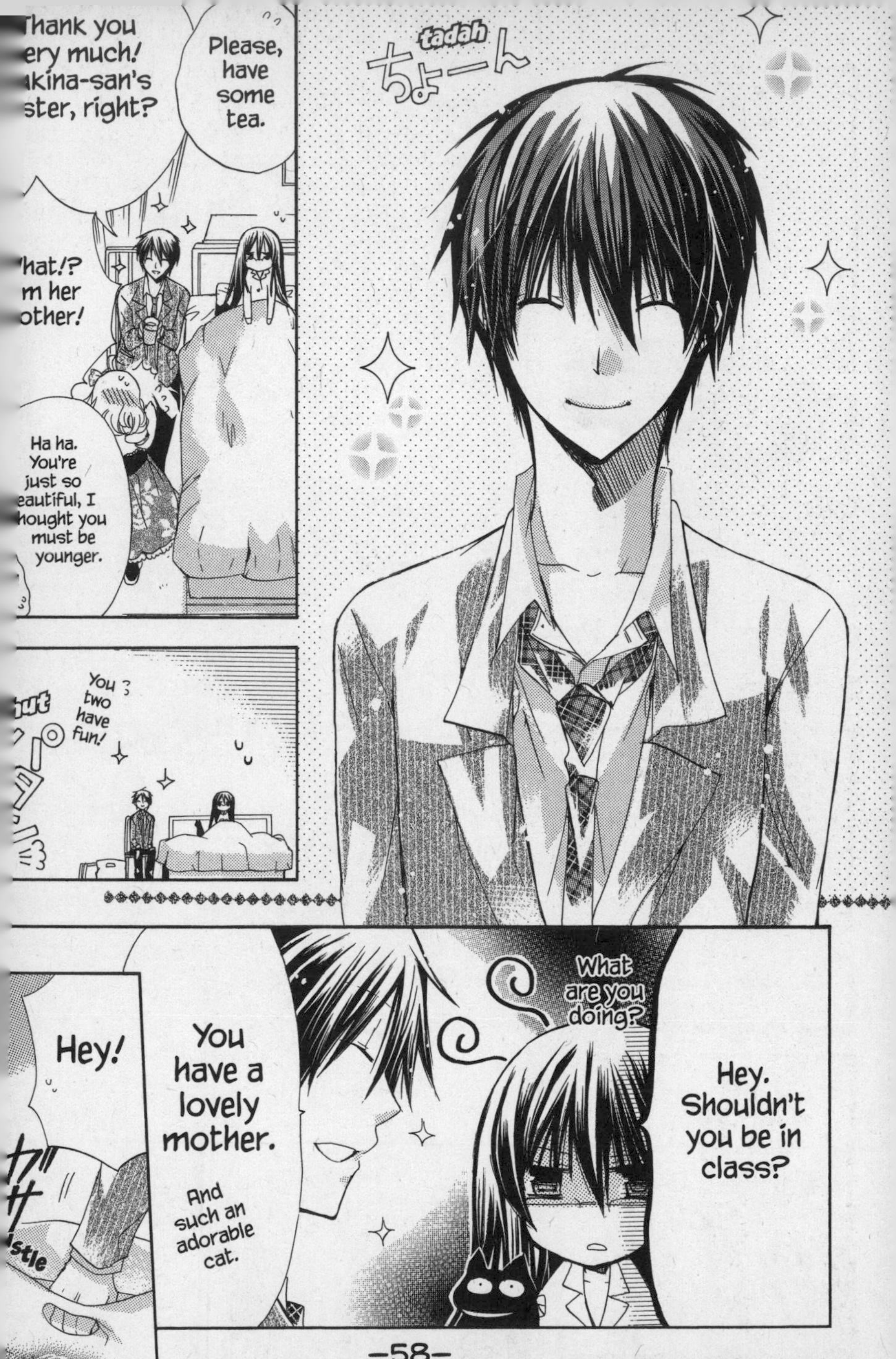
tadah
ちょーん
Please, have some tea.
Thank you ery much! kina-san's ster, right?
hat!? m her other!
Ha ha. You're just so eautiful, I hought you must be younger.
You two have fun!
What are you doing?
Hey. Shouldn't you be in class?
You have a lovely mother.
And such an adorable cat.
Hey!

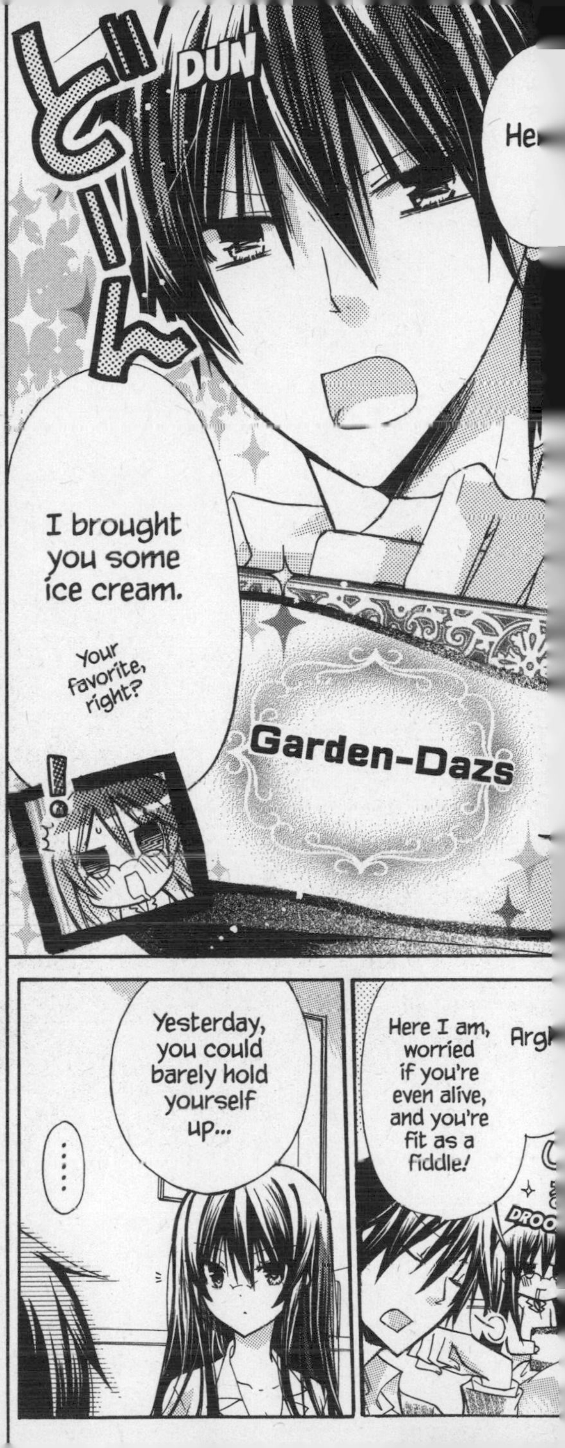
DUN
He
I brought you some ice cream.
Your favorite, right?
Garden-Dazs
!
Arg
Here I am, worried if you're even alive, and you're fit as a fiddle!
DROO
Yesterday, you could barely hold yourself up...
......

Snow Mami 1

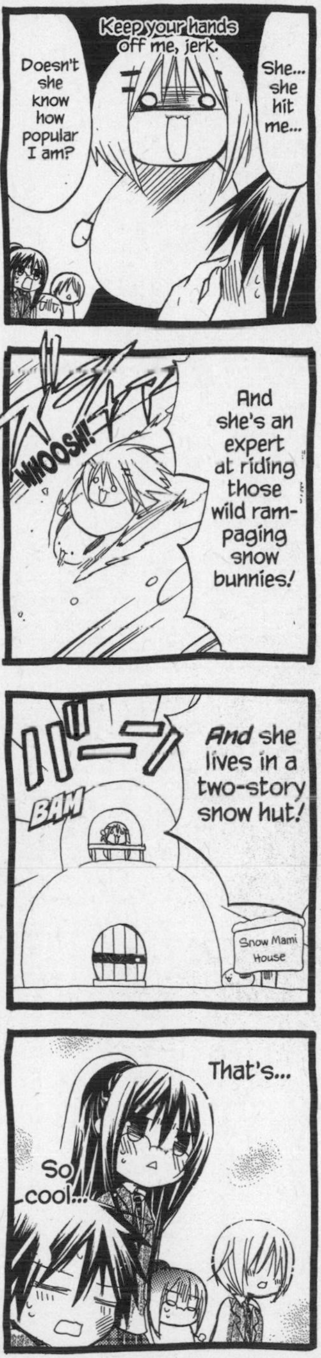
She... she hit me...
Keep your hands off me, jerk.
Doesn't she know how popular I am?
And she's an expert at riding those wild ram-paging snow bunnies!
WHOOSH!
And she lives in a two-story snow hut!
BAM
Snow Mami House
That's...
So cool...

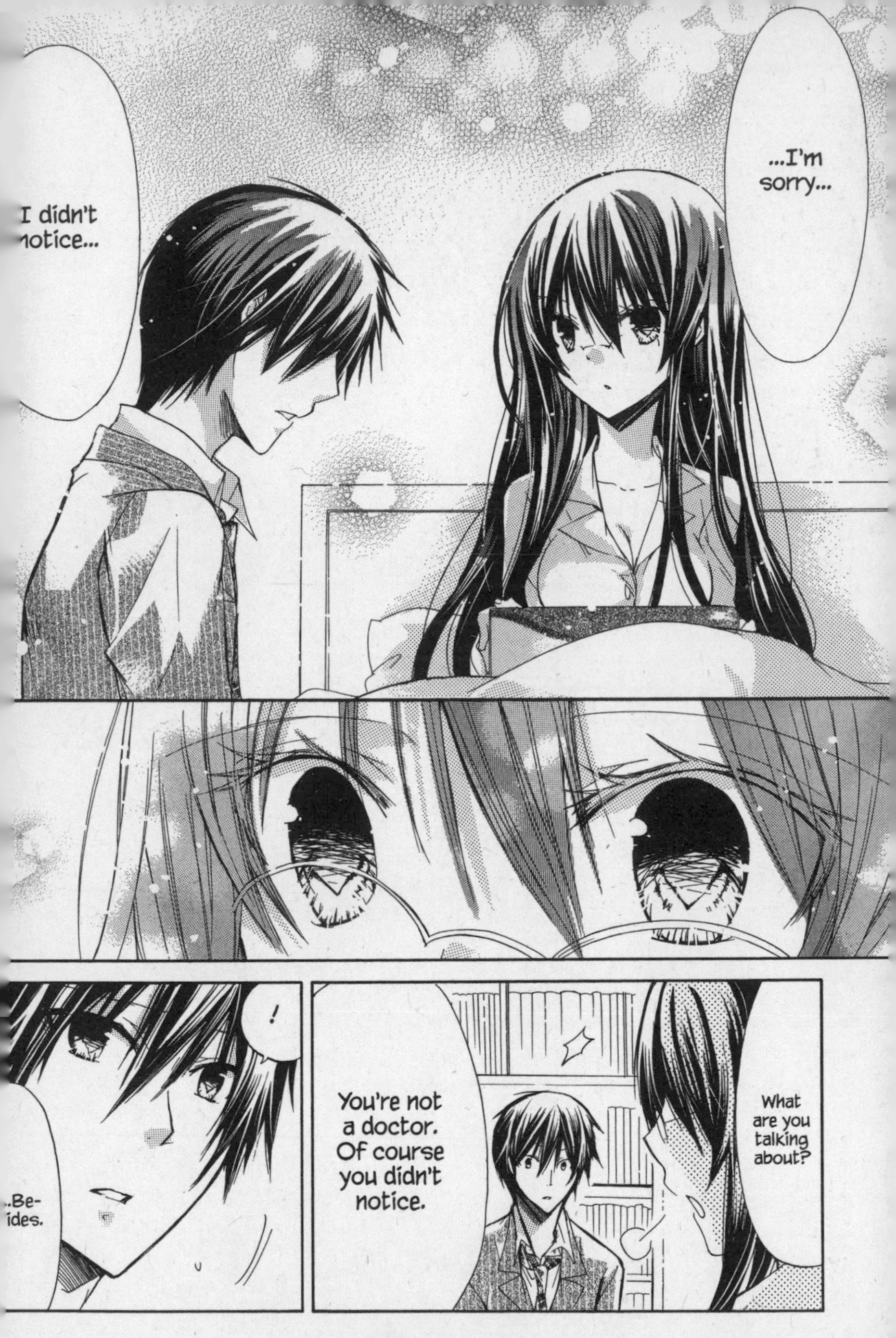
...I'm sorry...
I didn't notice...
What are you talking about?
You're not a doctor. Of course you didn't notice.
!
..Be- ides.

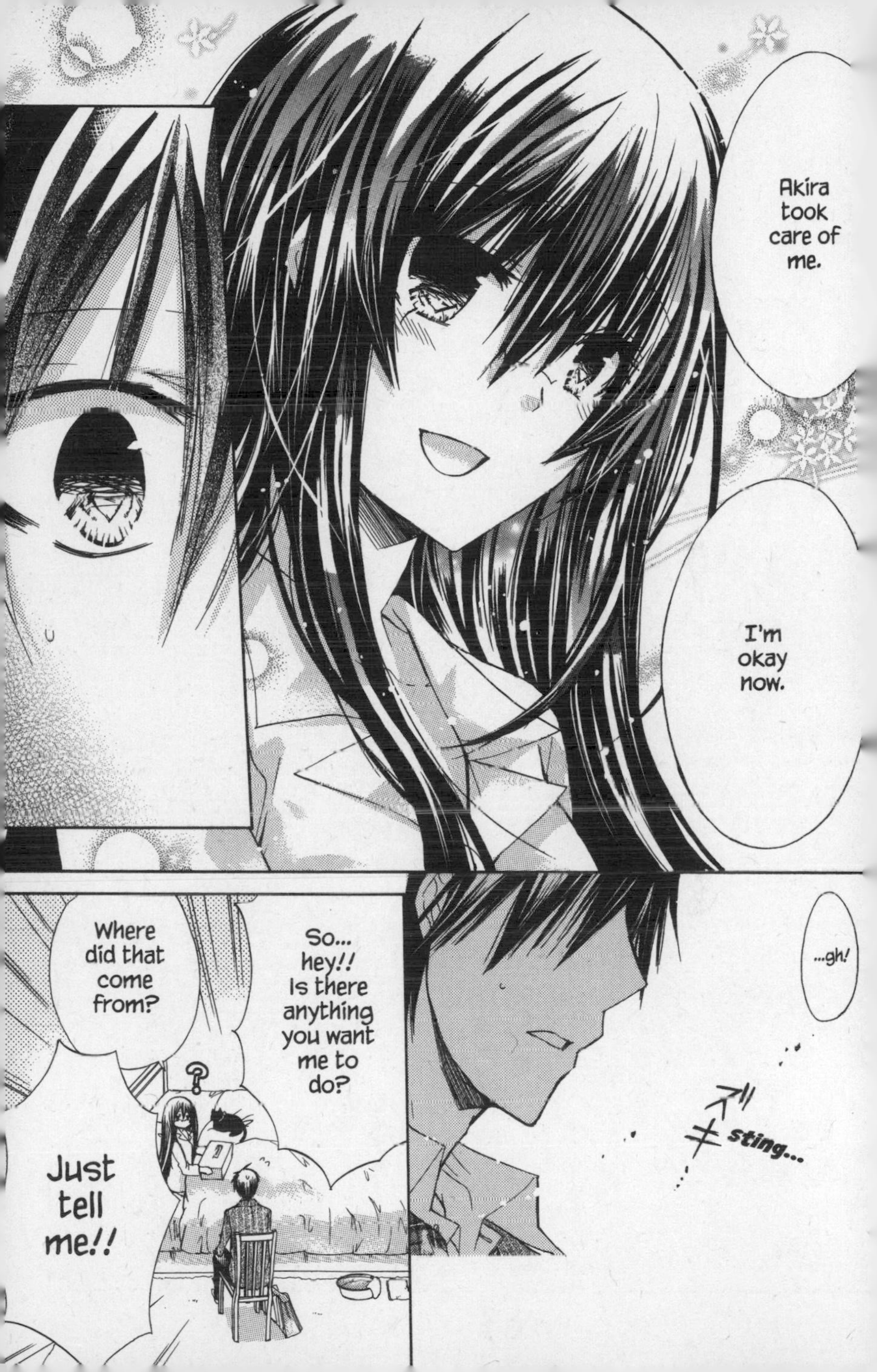
Akira took care of me.
I'm okay now.
...gh!
ズキ
sting...
So... hey!! Is there anything you want me to do?
Where did that come from?
Just tell me!!

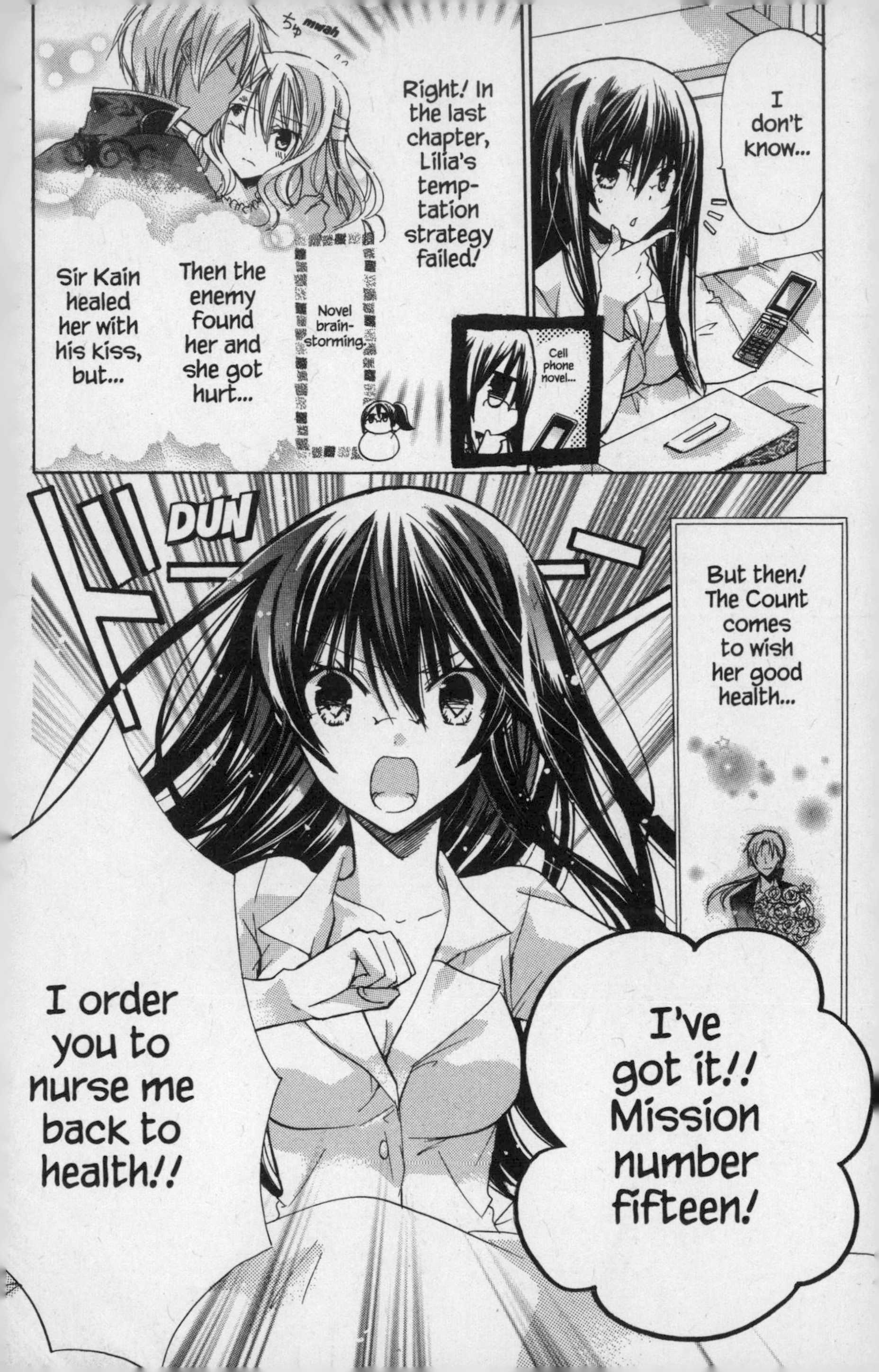
I don't know...
Cell phone novel...
Right! In the last chapter, Lilia's temptation strategy failed!
ちゅ mwah
Novel brain-storming.
Then the enemy found her and she got hurt...
Sir Kain healed her with his kiss, but...
But then! The Count comes to wish her good health...
DUN
I've got it!! Mission number fifteen!
I order you to nurse me back to health!!

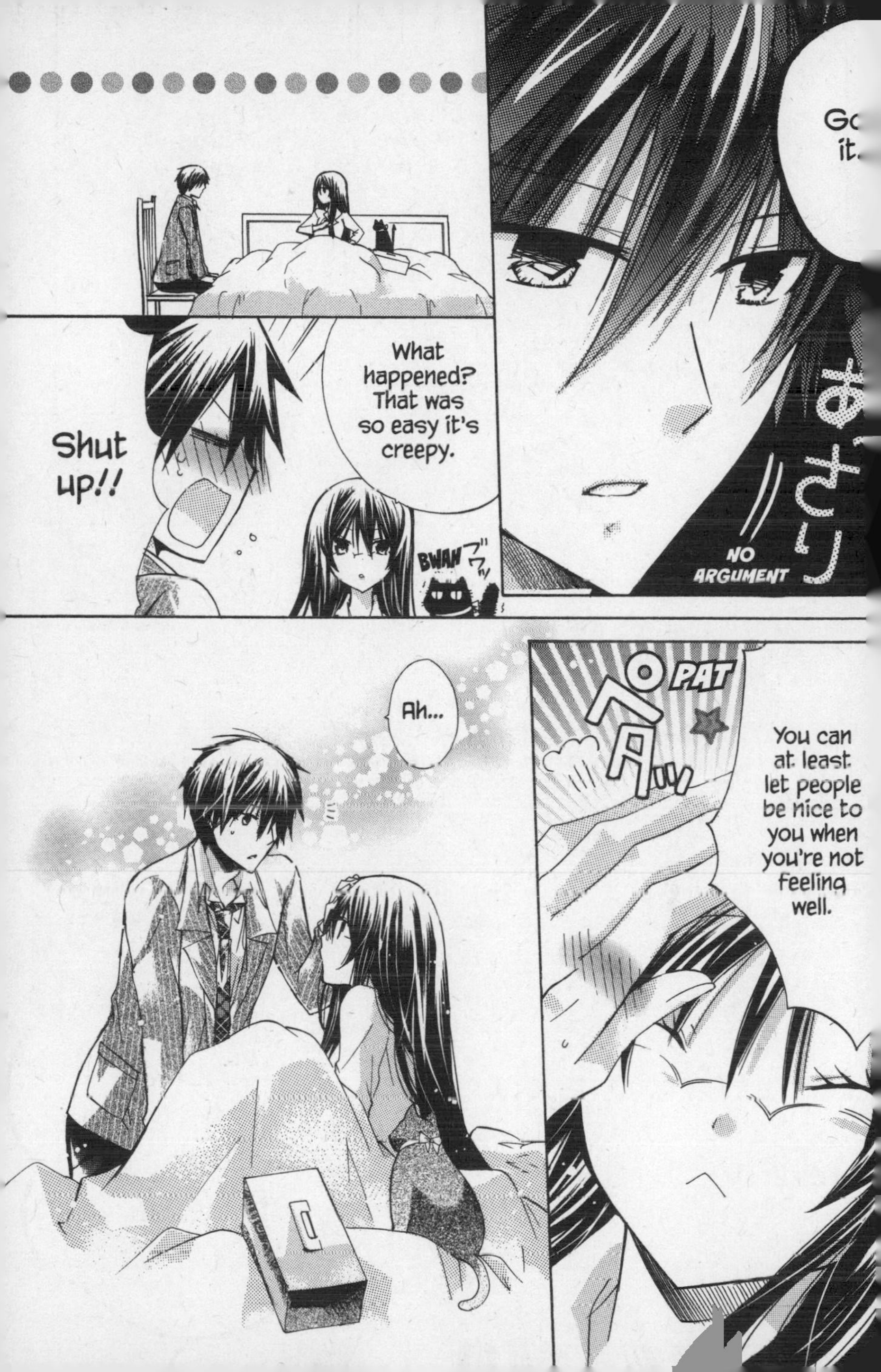
Go
it.
NO ARGUMENT
What happened? That was so easy it's creepy.
BWAH
Shut up!!
PAT
You can at least let people be nice to you when you're not feeling well.
Ah...

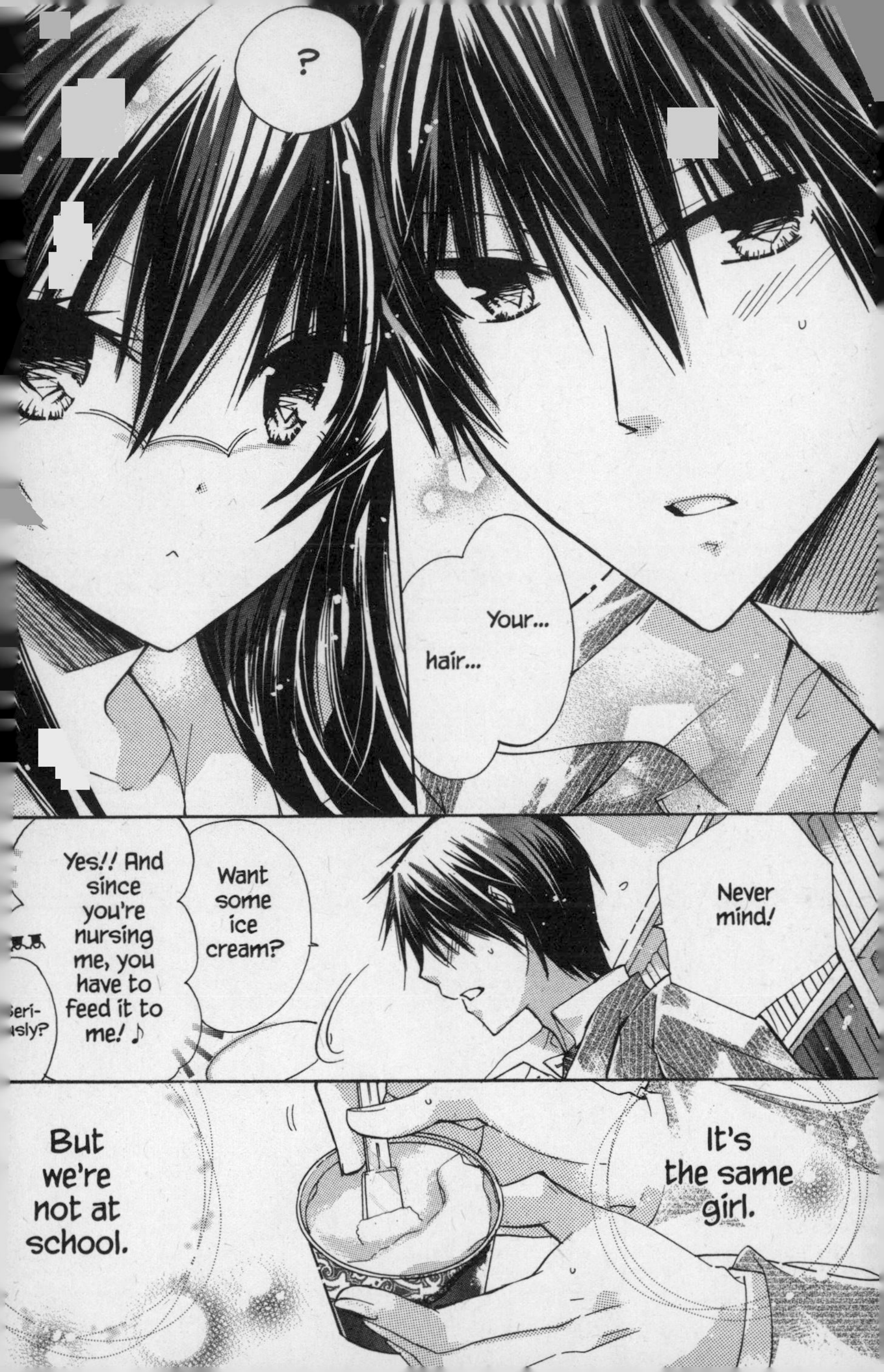
?
Your... hair...
Never mind!
Want some ice cream?
Yes!! And since you're nursing me, you have to feed it to me! ♪
Seri- usly?
It's the same girl.
But we're not at school.

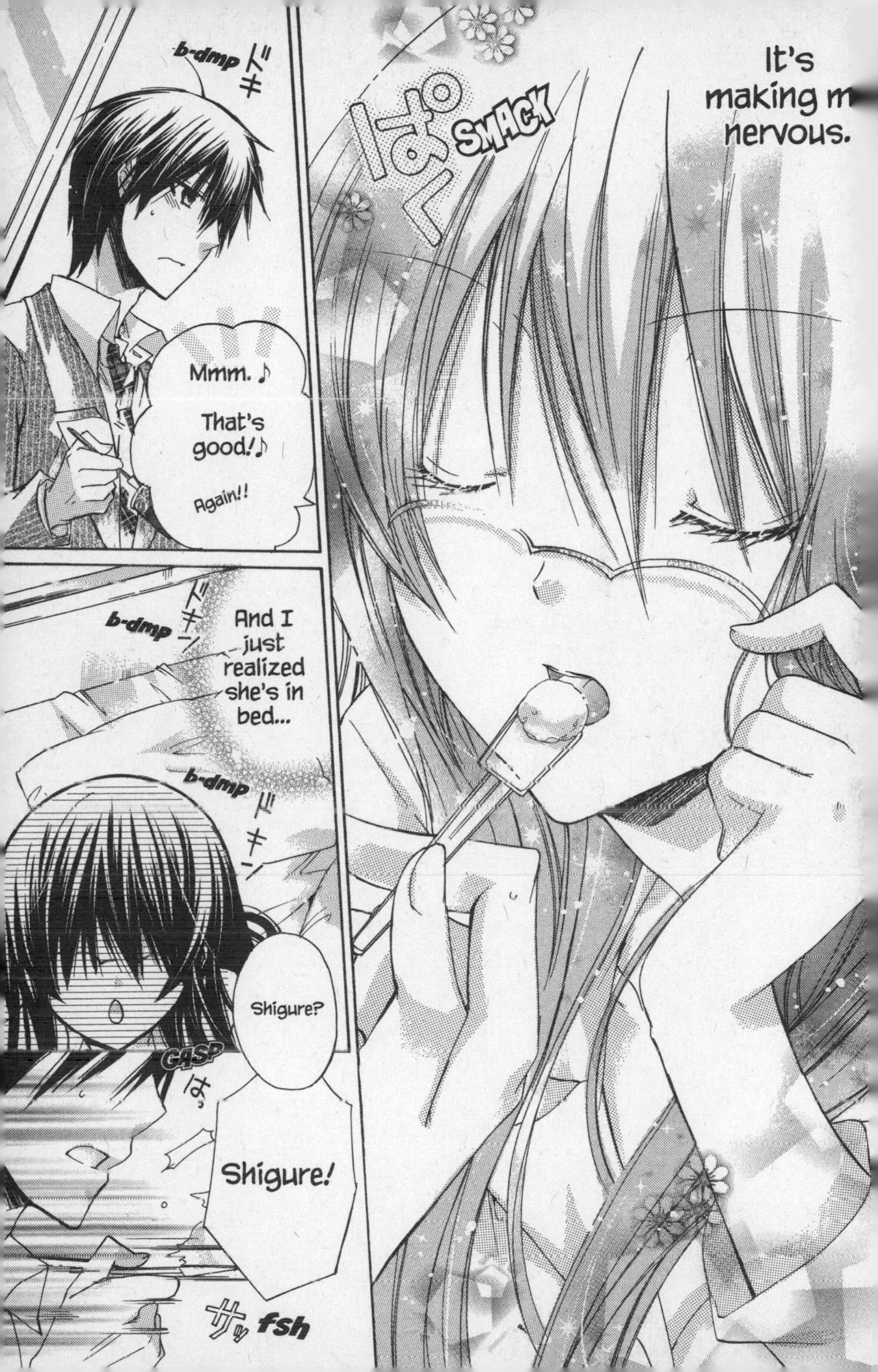
It's making m nervous.
ぱく
SMACK
ドキ
b-dmp
Mmm. ♪
That's good!♪
Again!!
ドキン
b-dmp
And I just realized she's in bed...
ドキン
b-dmp
Shigure?
は
GASP
Shigure!
サッ
fsh

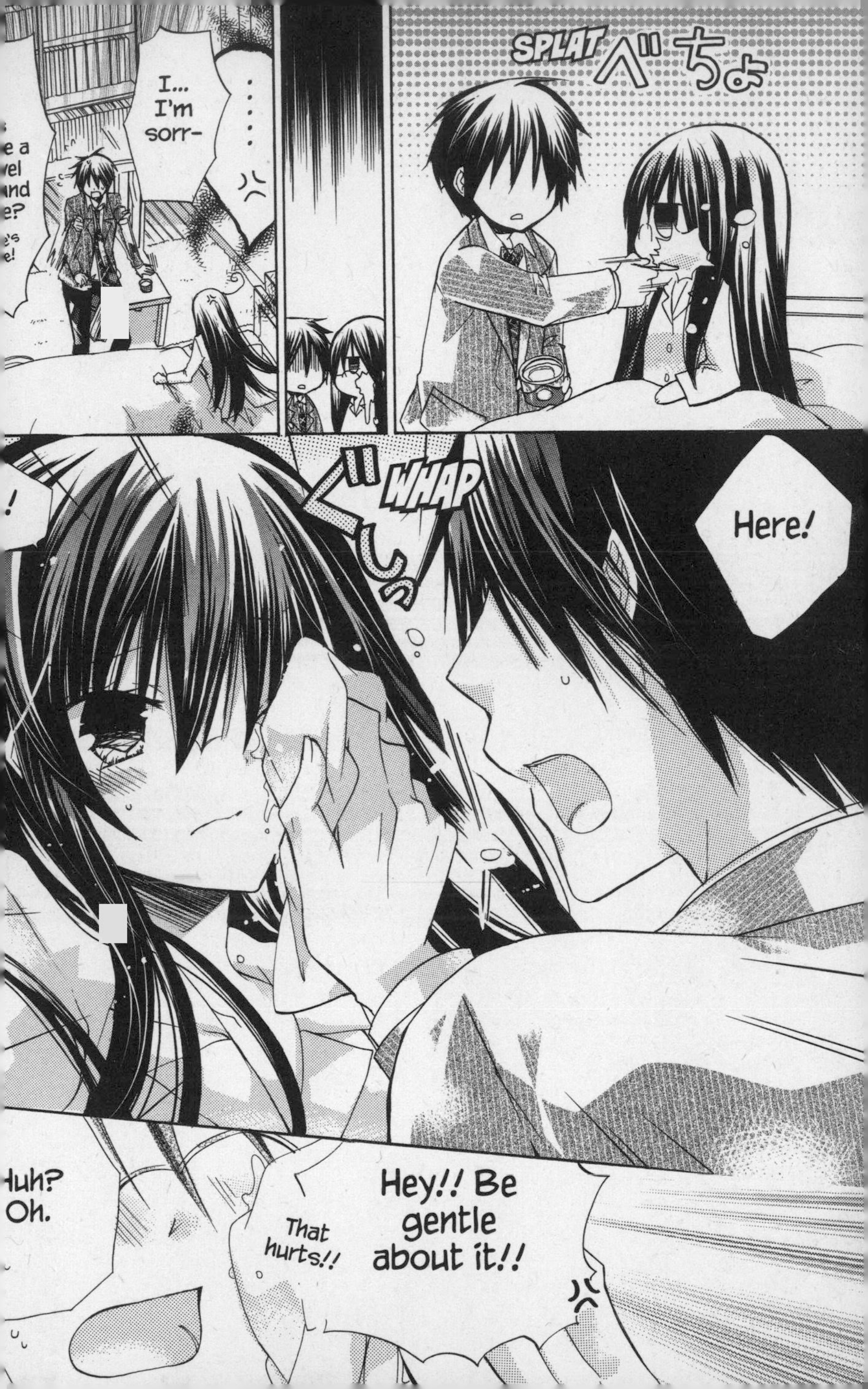
SPLAT べちょ
I... I'm sorr-
......
Here!
WHAP
Hey!! Be gentle about it!!
That hurts!!
Huh? Oh.

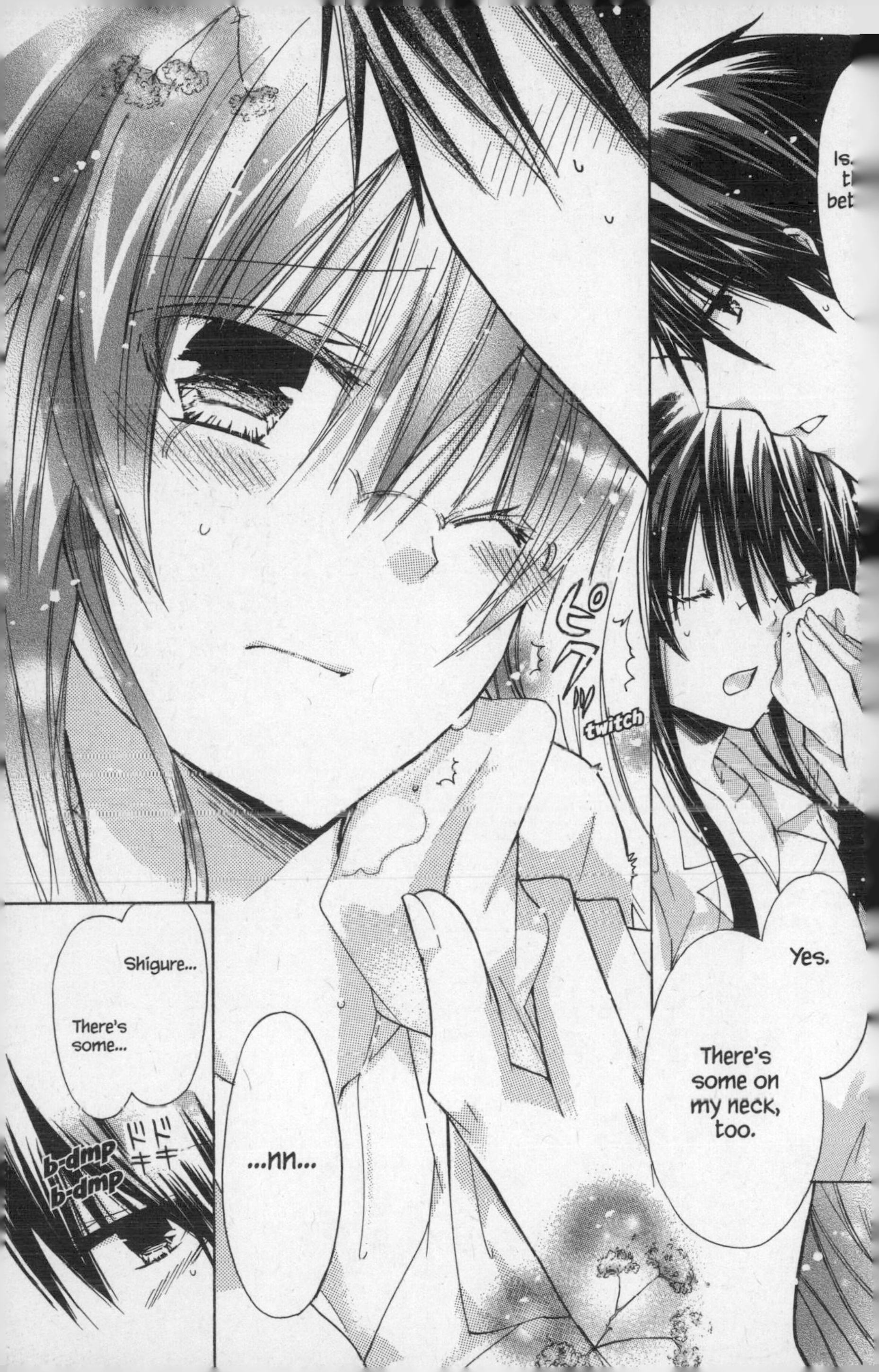
Yes.
There's some on my neck, too.
ピクッ
twitch
...nn...
Shigure...
There's some...
ドキドキ
b-dmp b-dmp

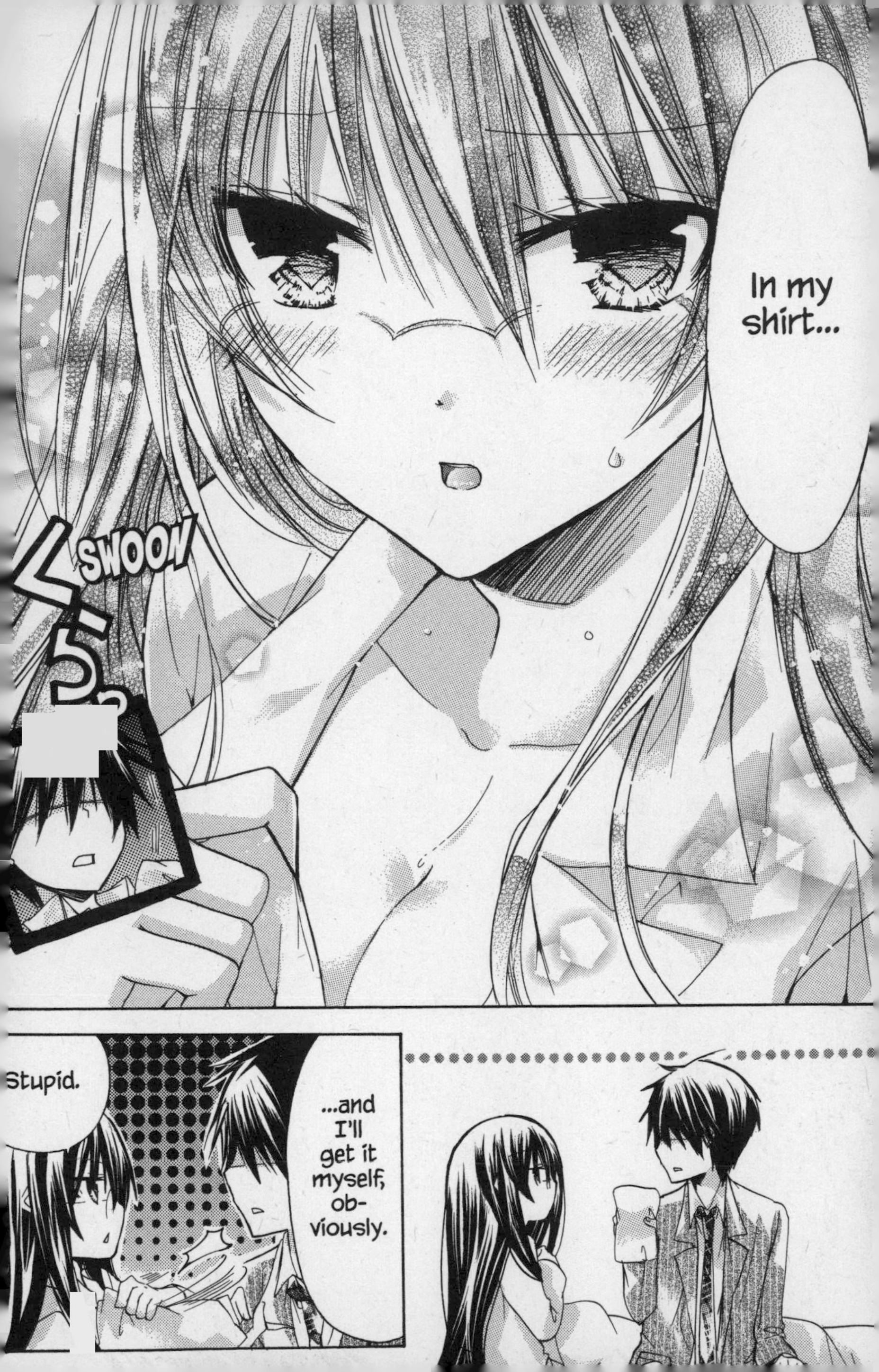
In my shirt...
SWOON
...and I'll get it myself, ob-viously.
Stupid.

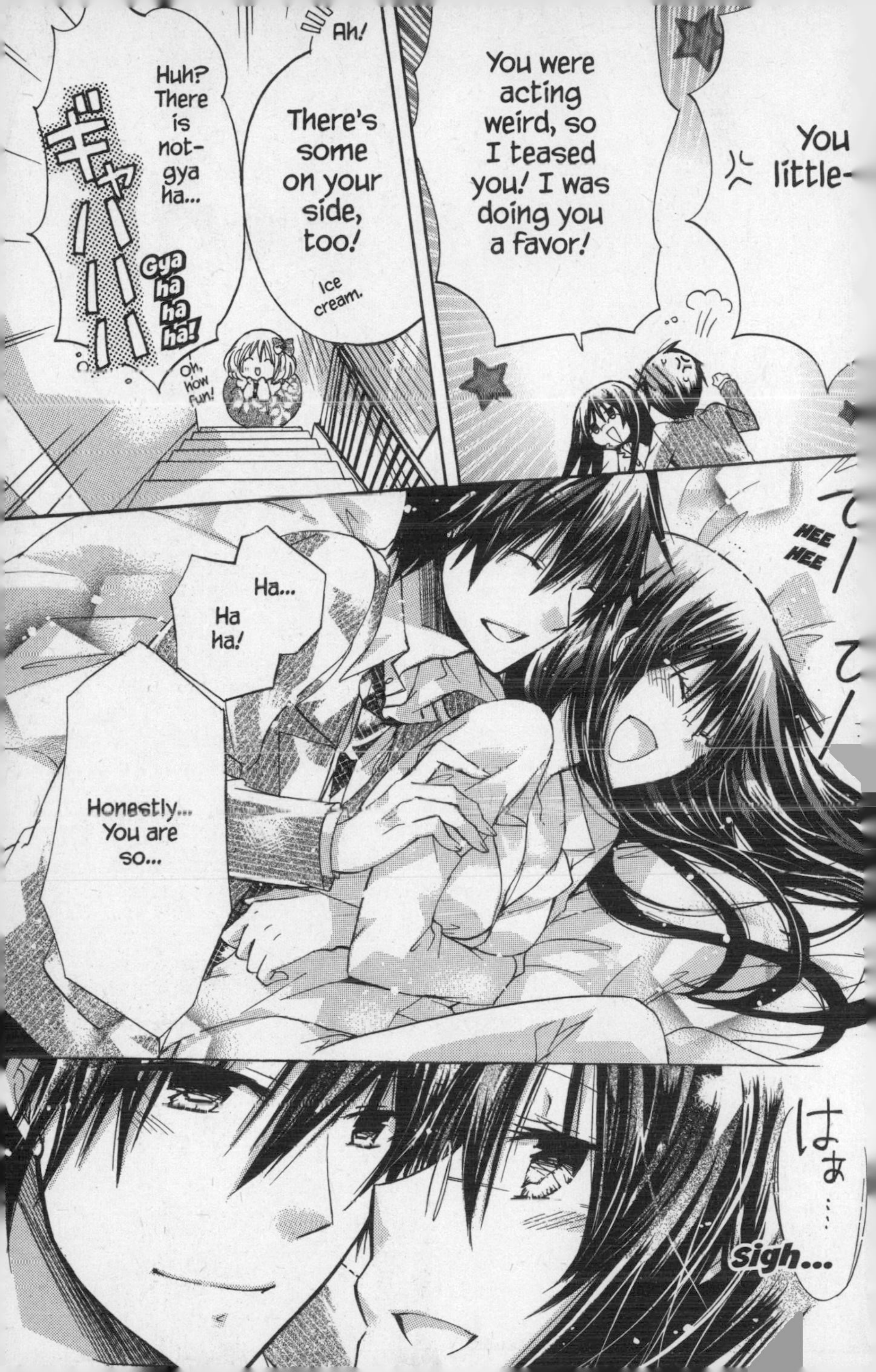
You little-
You were acting weird, so I teased you! I was doing you a favor!
Ah!
There's some on your side, too!
Ice cream.
Huh? There is not-gya ha...
Gya ha ha ha!
Oh, how fun!
HEE HEE
Ha... Ha ha!
Honestly... You are so...
Sigh...

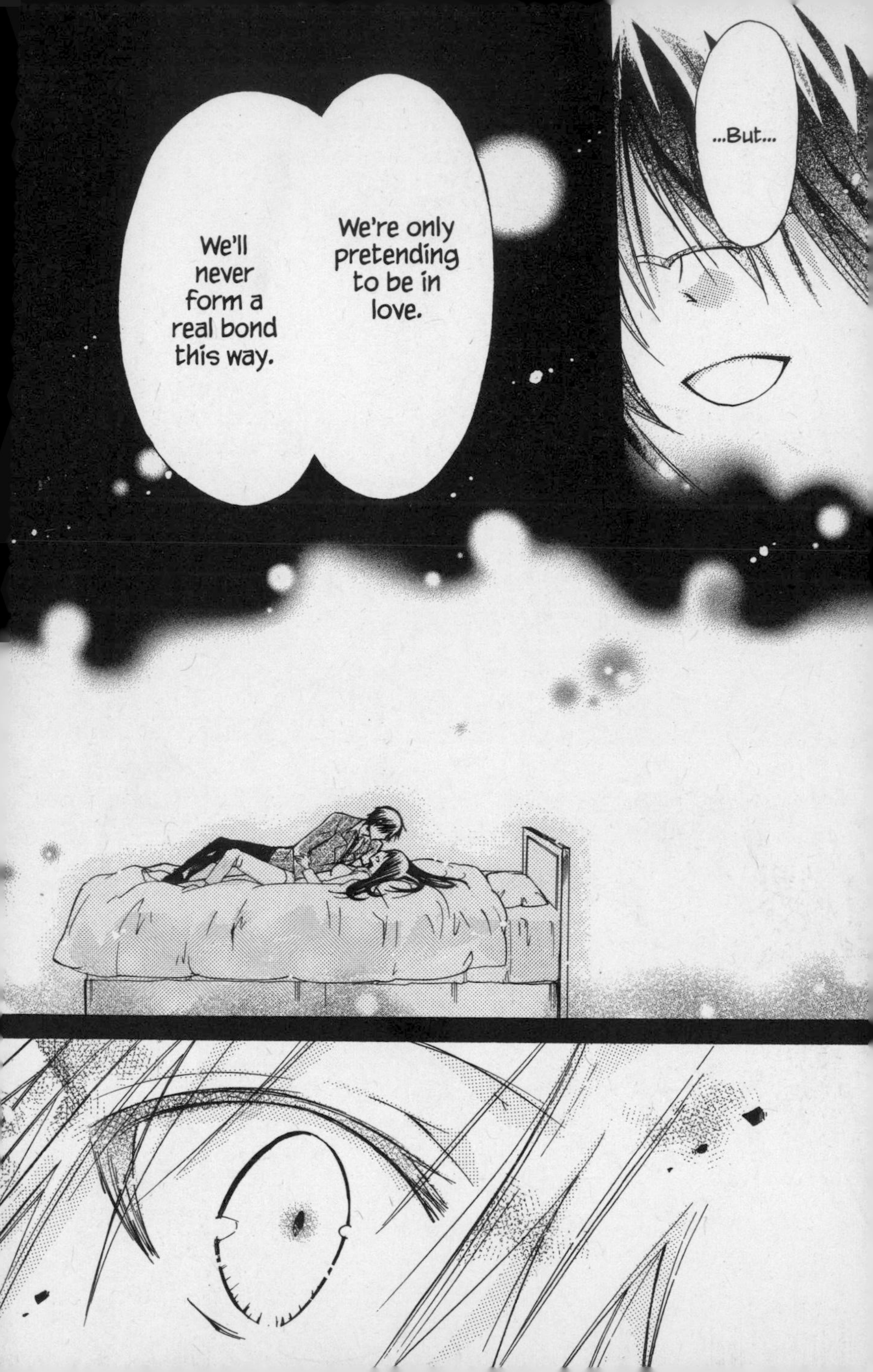
...But...
We're only pretending to be in love.
We'll never form a real bond this way.

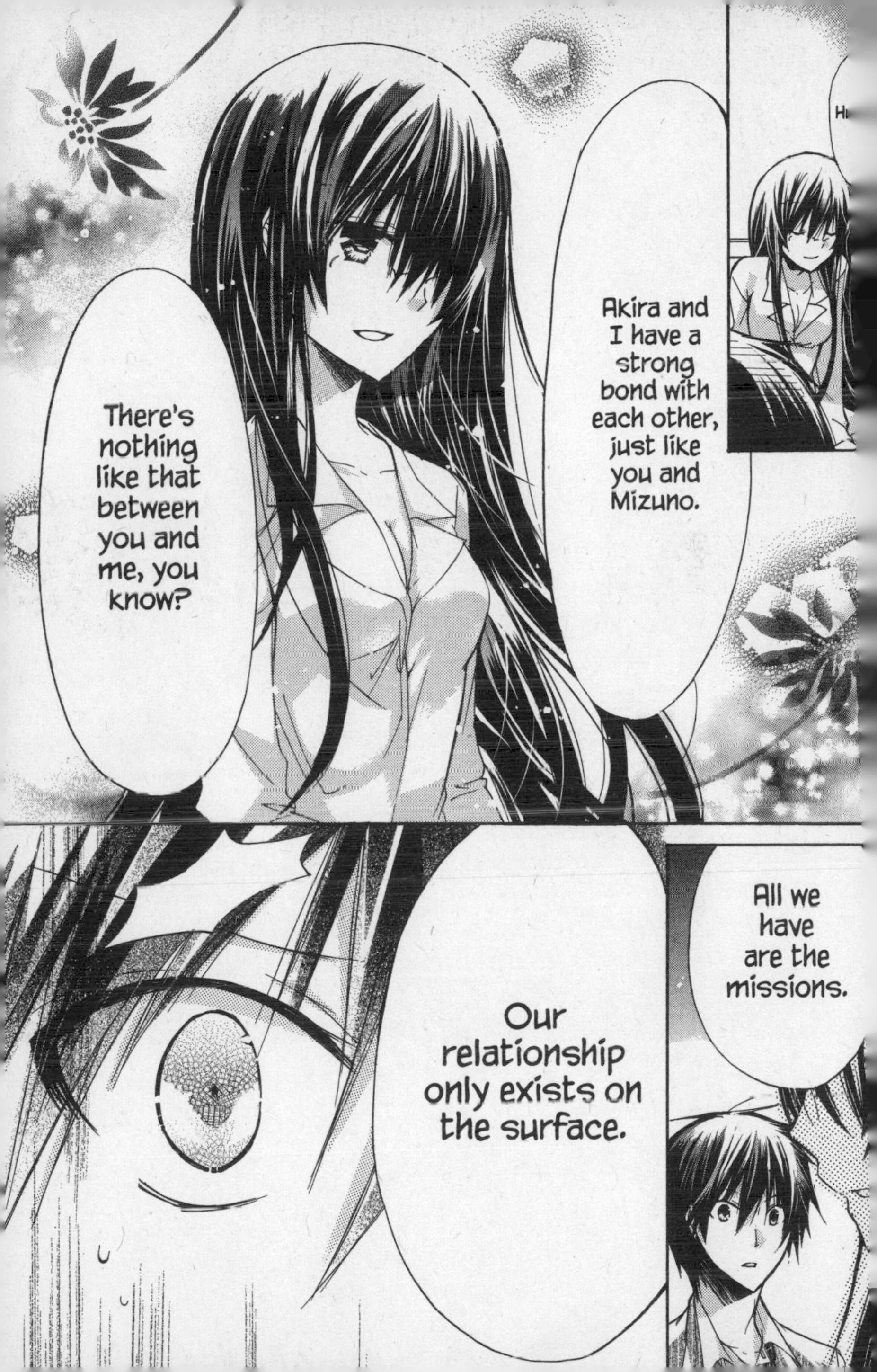
Akira and I have a strong bond with each other, just like you and Mizuno.
There's nothing like that between you and me, you know?
All we have are the missions.
Our relationship only exists on the surface.

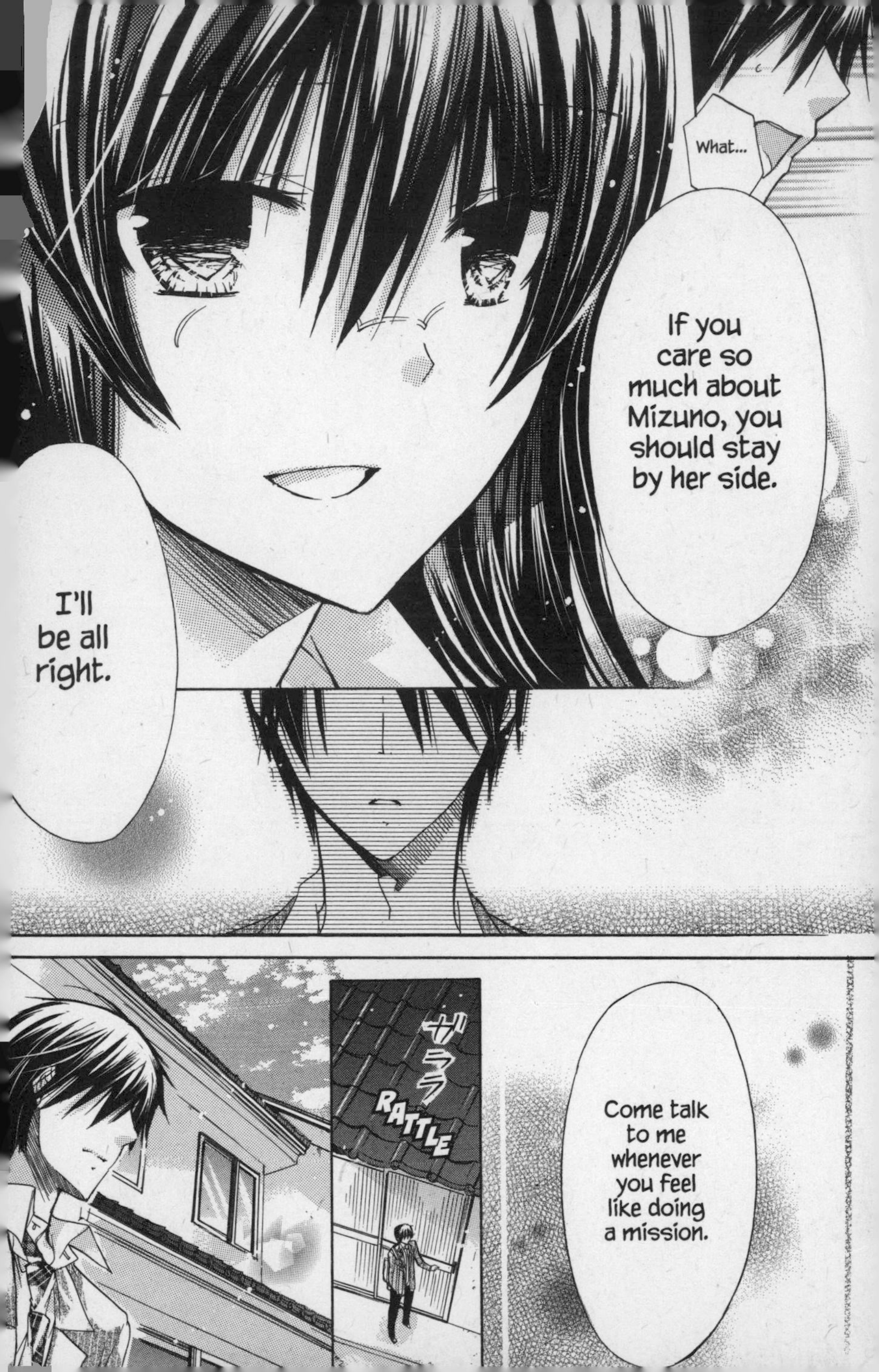
What...
If you care so much about Mizuno, you should stay by her side.
I'll be all right.
Come talk to me whenever you feel like doing a mission.
RATTLE

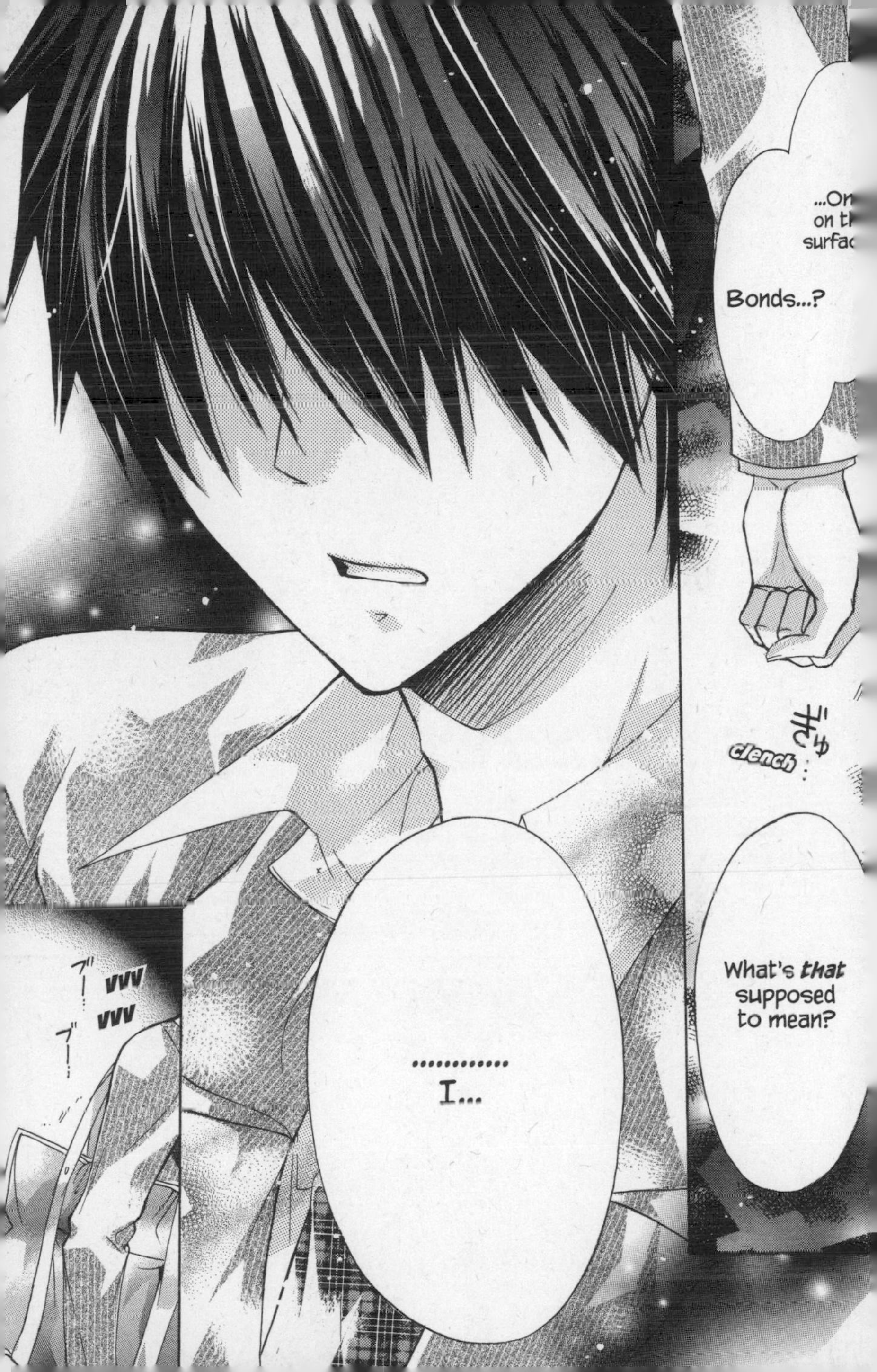
...On
on th
surfac
Bonds...?
ぎゅ
clench
What's *that* supposed to mean?
....
I...
ブー VVV
ブー VVV

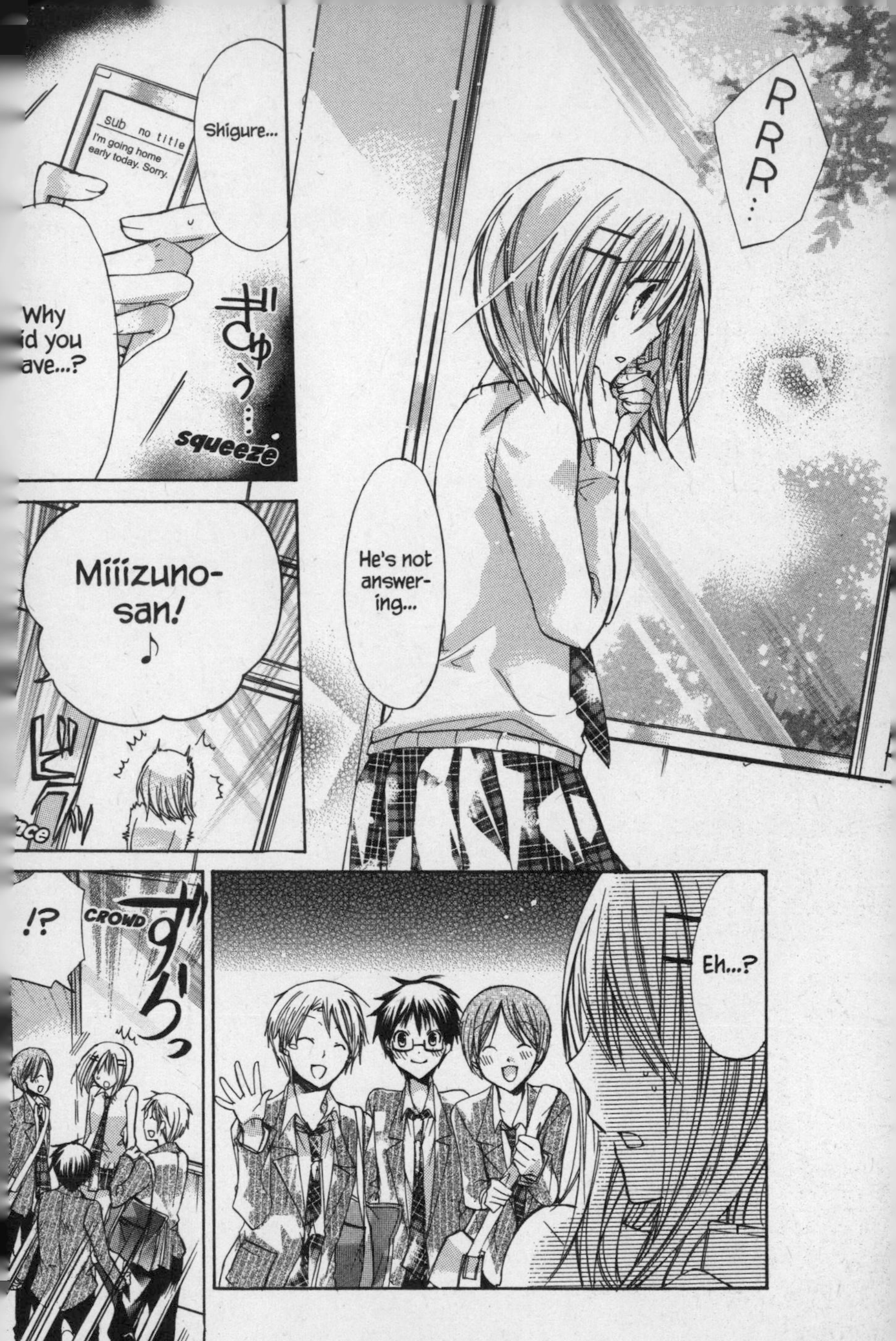
RRR...
He's not answering...
sub no title
I'm going home early today. Sorry.
Shigure...
squeeze
Why
id you
ave...?
Miiizuno-san! ♪
Eh...?
!?
CROWD

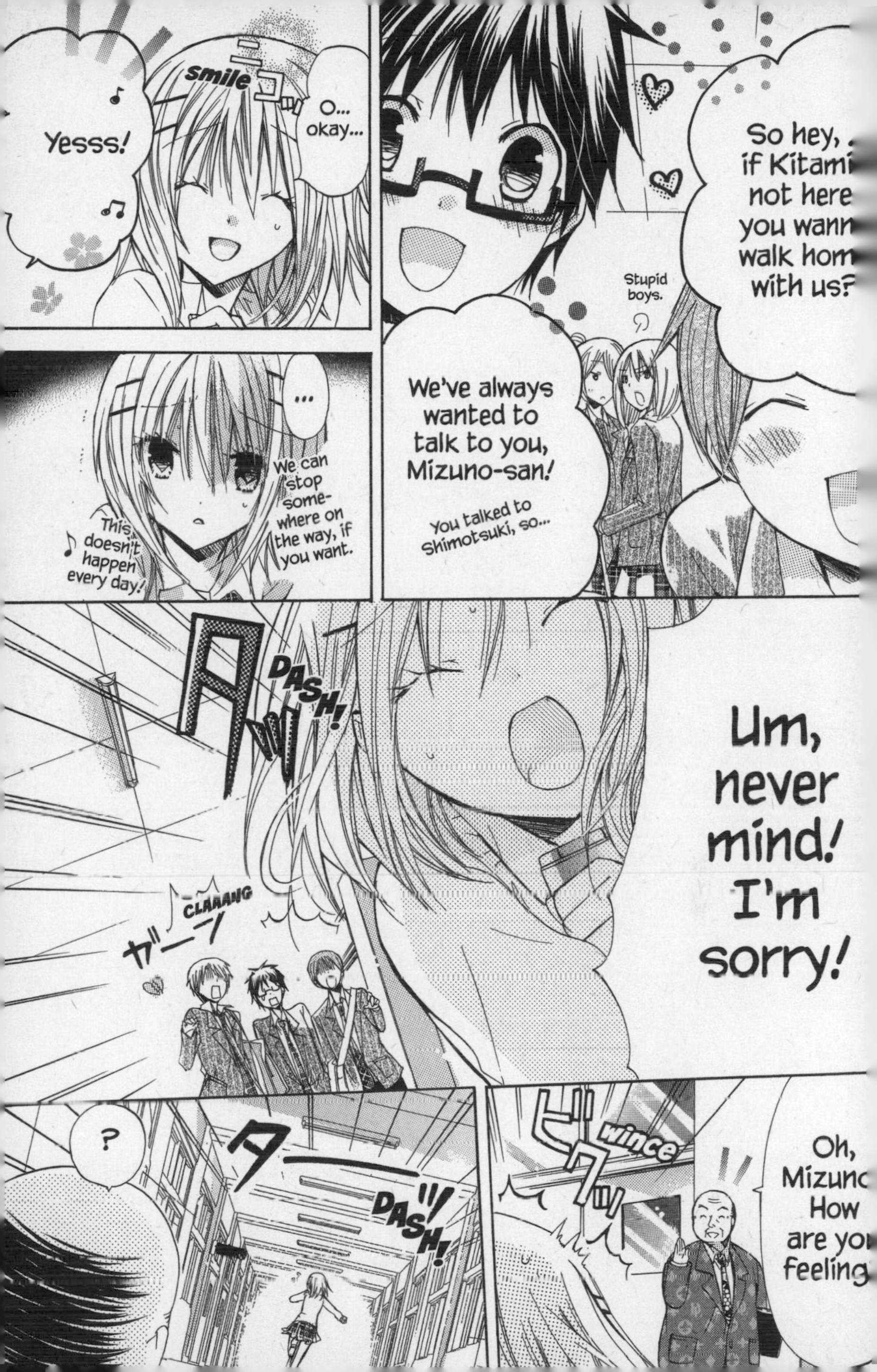

So hey, if Kitami not here you wann walk hom with us?
Stupid boys.
O... okay...
smile
Yesss!
We've always wanted to talk to you, Mizuno-san!
You talked to Shimotsuki, so...
...
We can stop some-where on the way, if you want.
This doesn't happen every day!
Um, never mind! I'm sorry!
DASH!
CLAAANG
Oh, Mizuno How are yo feeling
wince
?
DASH!

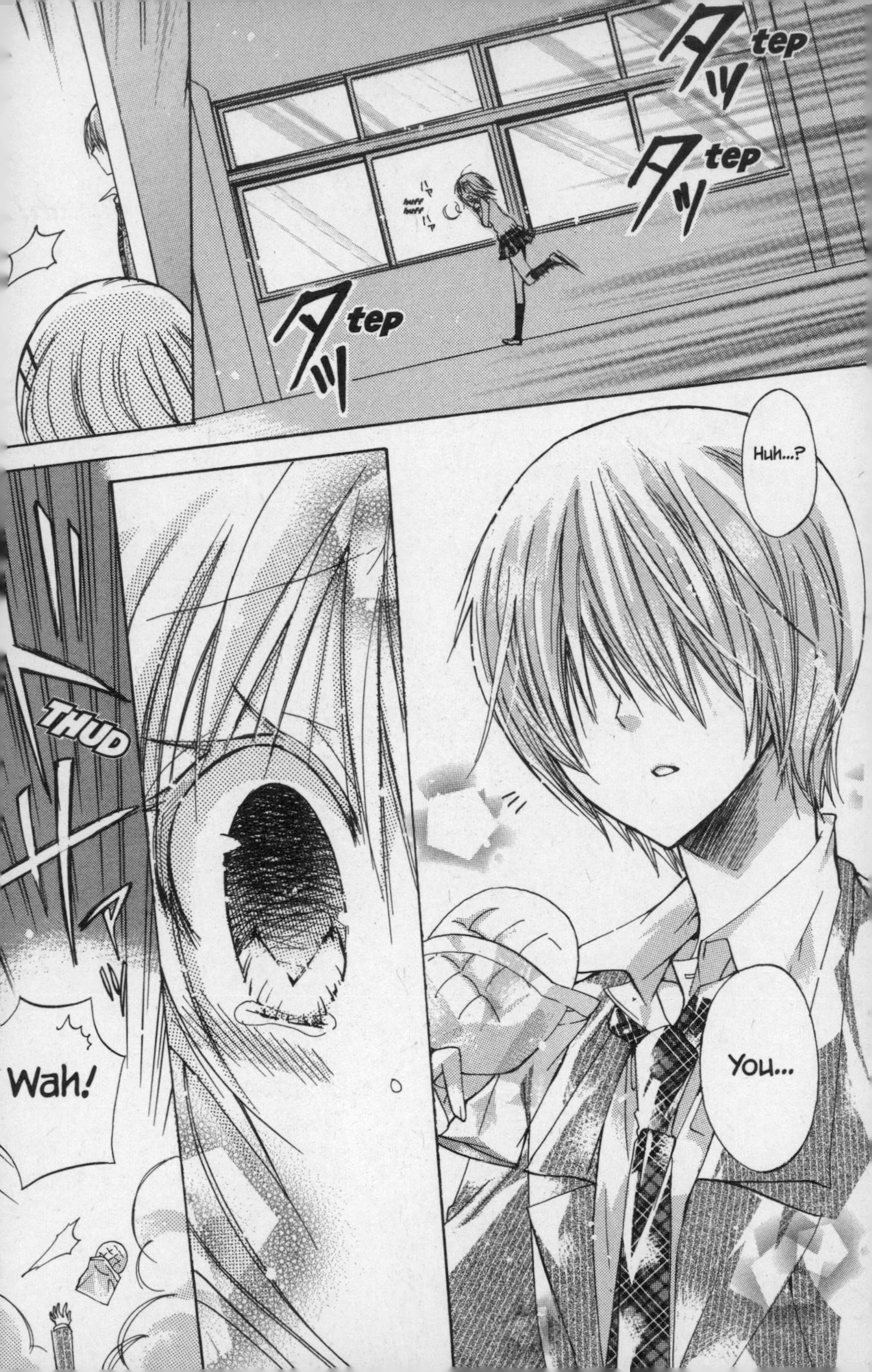
タッ tep
タッ tep
huff huff
タッ tep
Huh...?
You...
THUD
Wah!

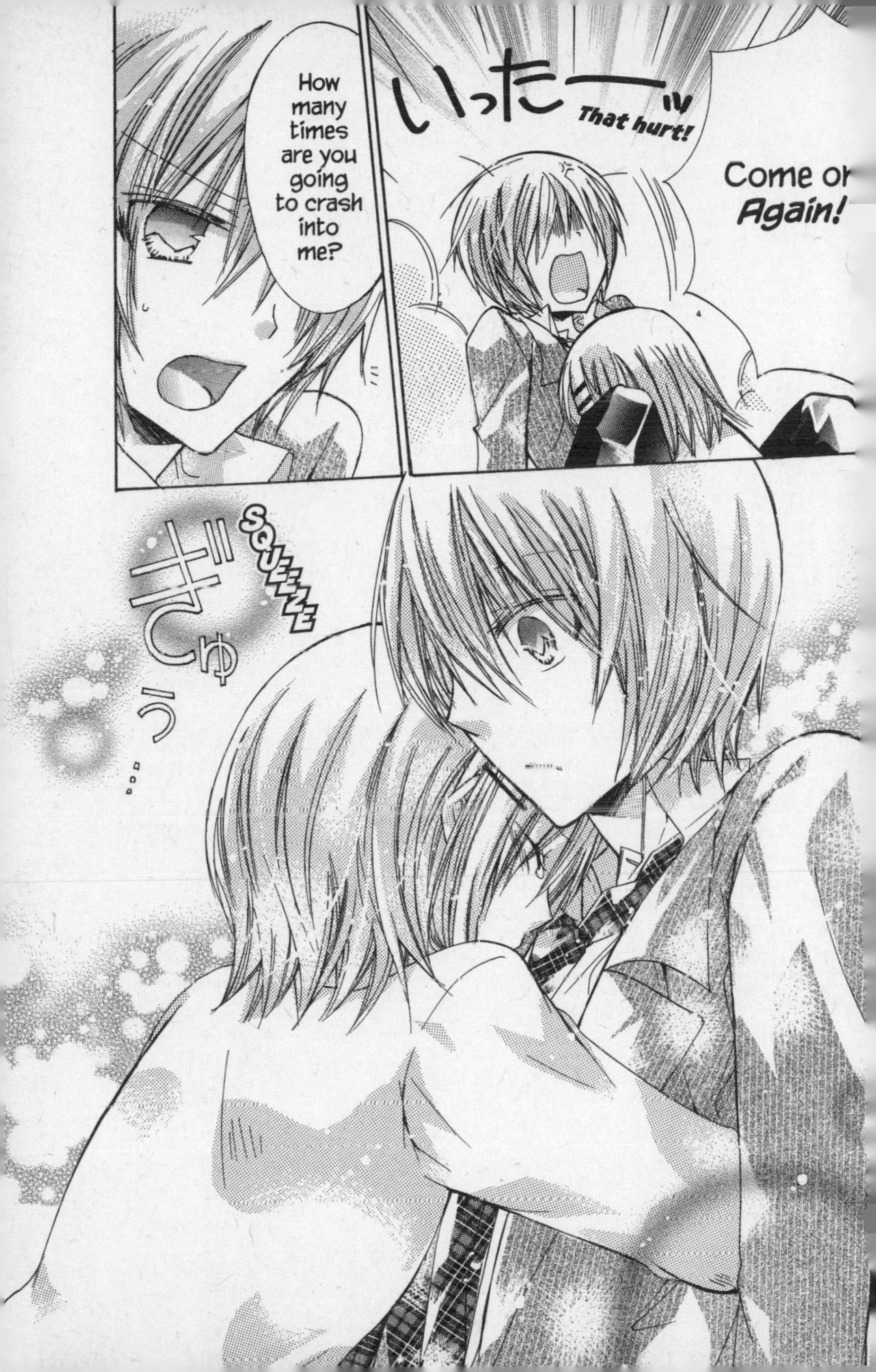
いったーーッ
That hurt!
Come on
Again!
How many times are you going to crash into me?
ぎゅう…
SQUEEZE

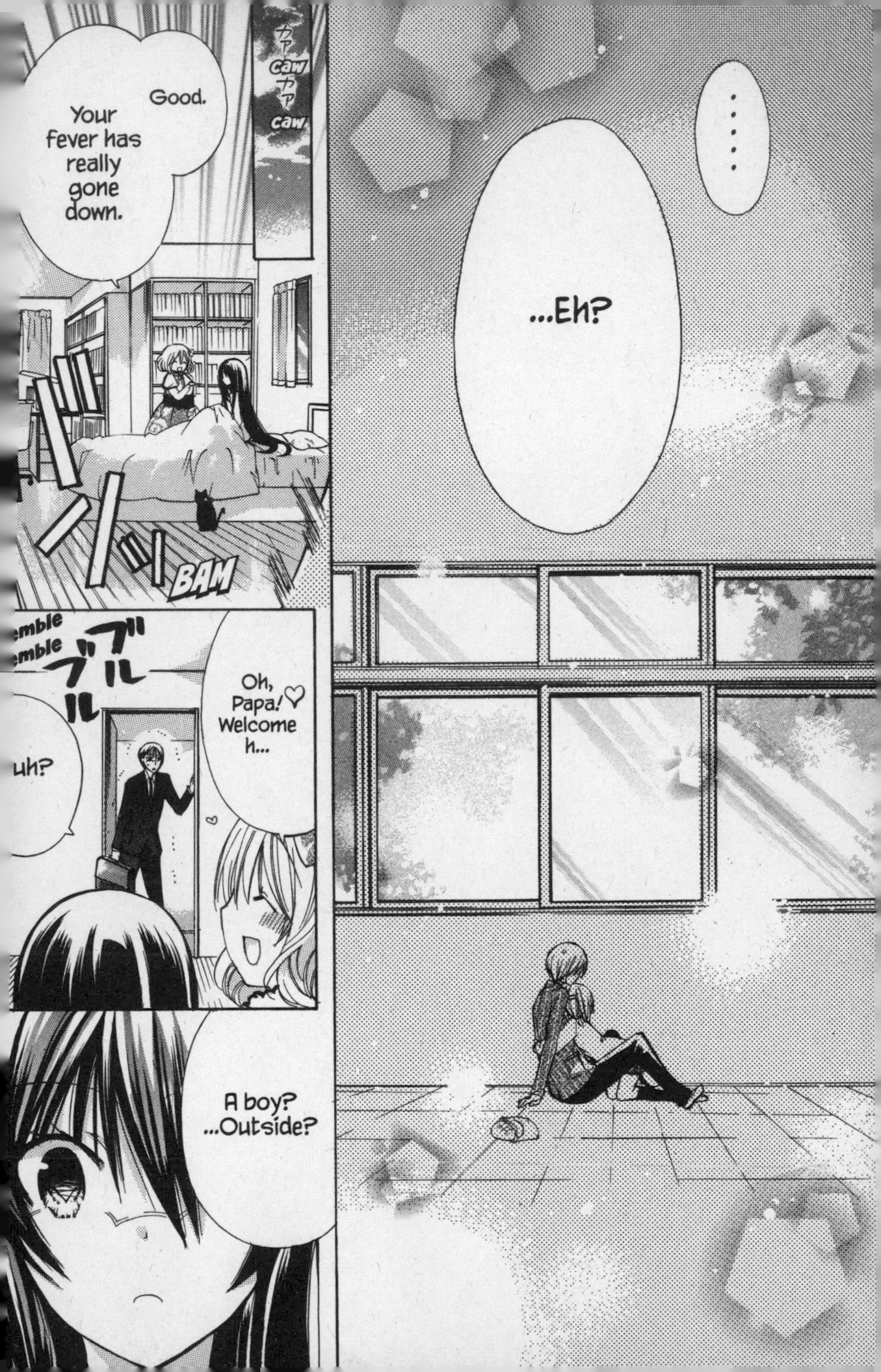

.....
...Eh?
カア caw カア caw
Good. Your fever has really gone down.
BAM
Oh, Papa!♡ Welcome h...
emble emble ブルブル
uh?
A boy? ...Outside?

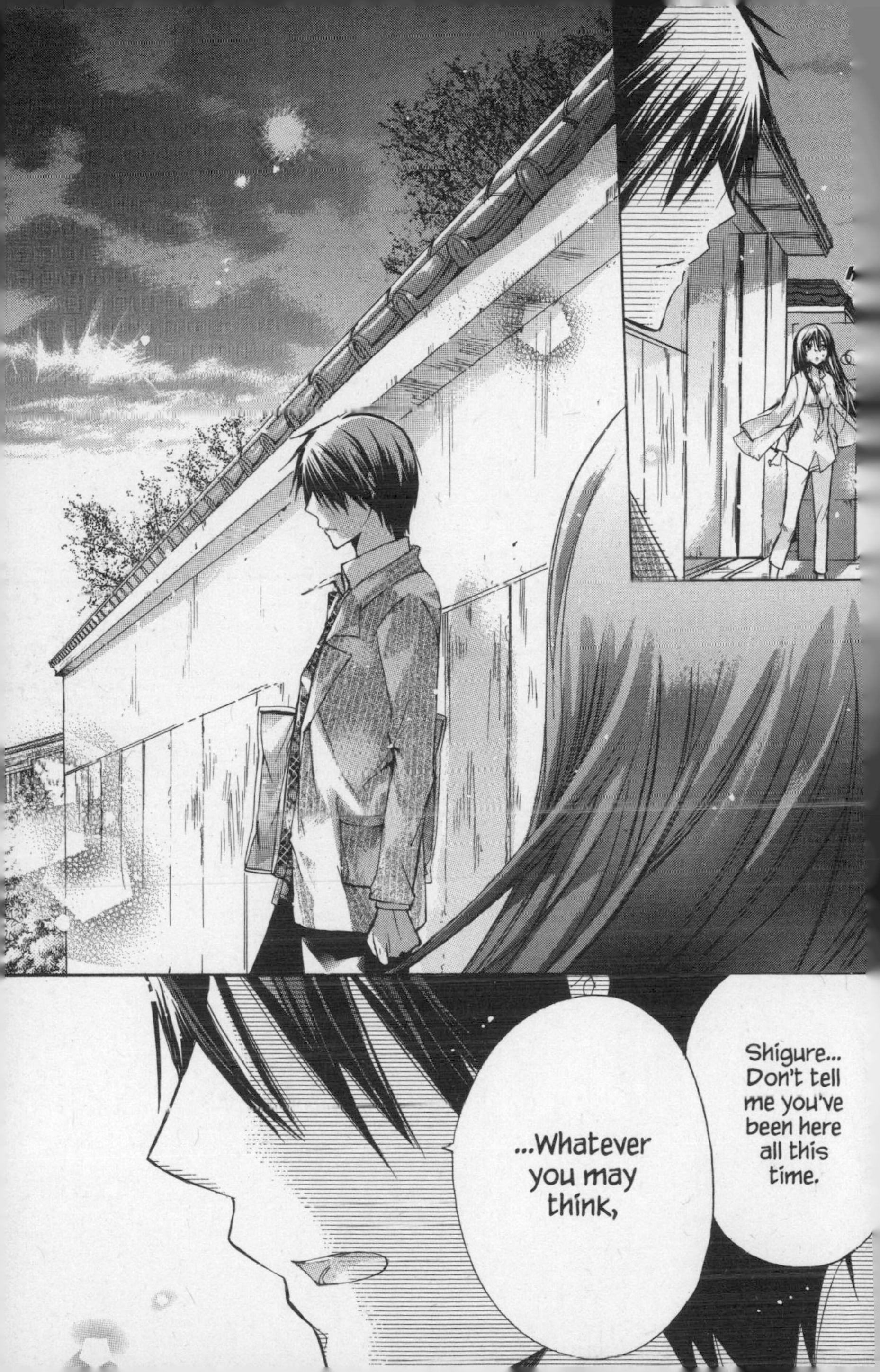
Shigure... Don't tell me you've been here all this time.
...Whatever you may think,

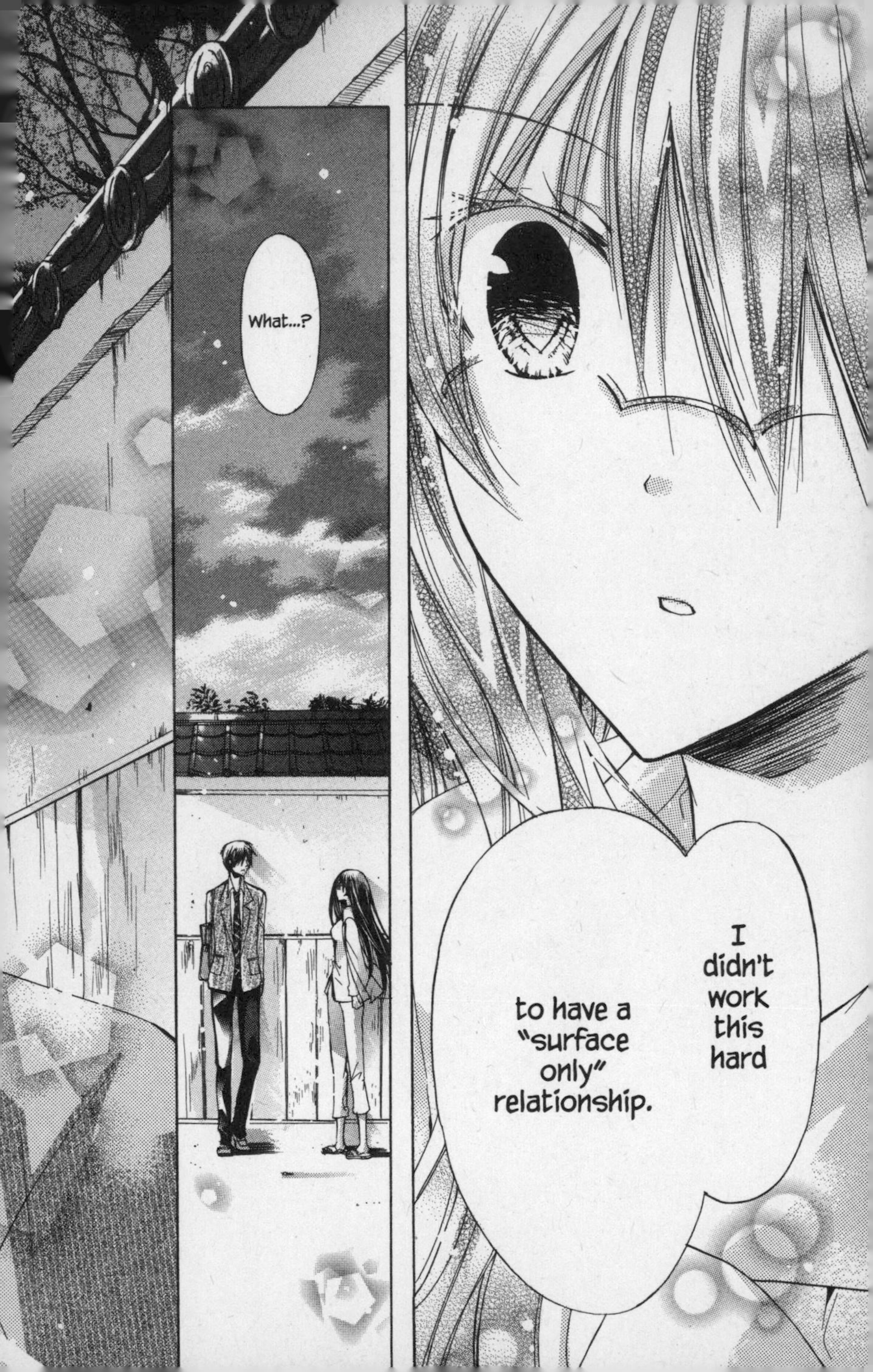
I didn't work this hard to have a "surface only" relationship.
What...?

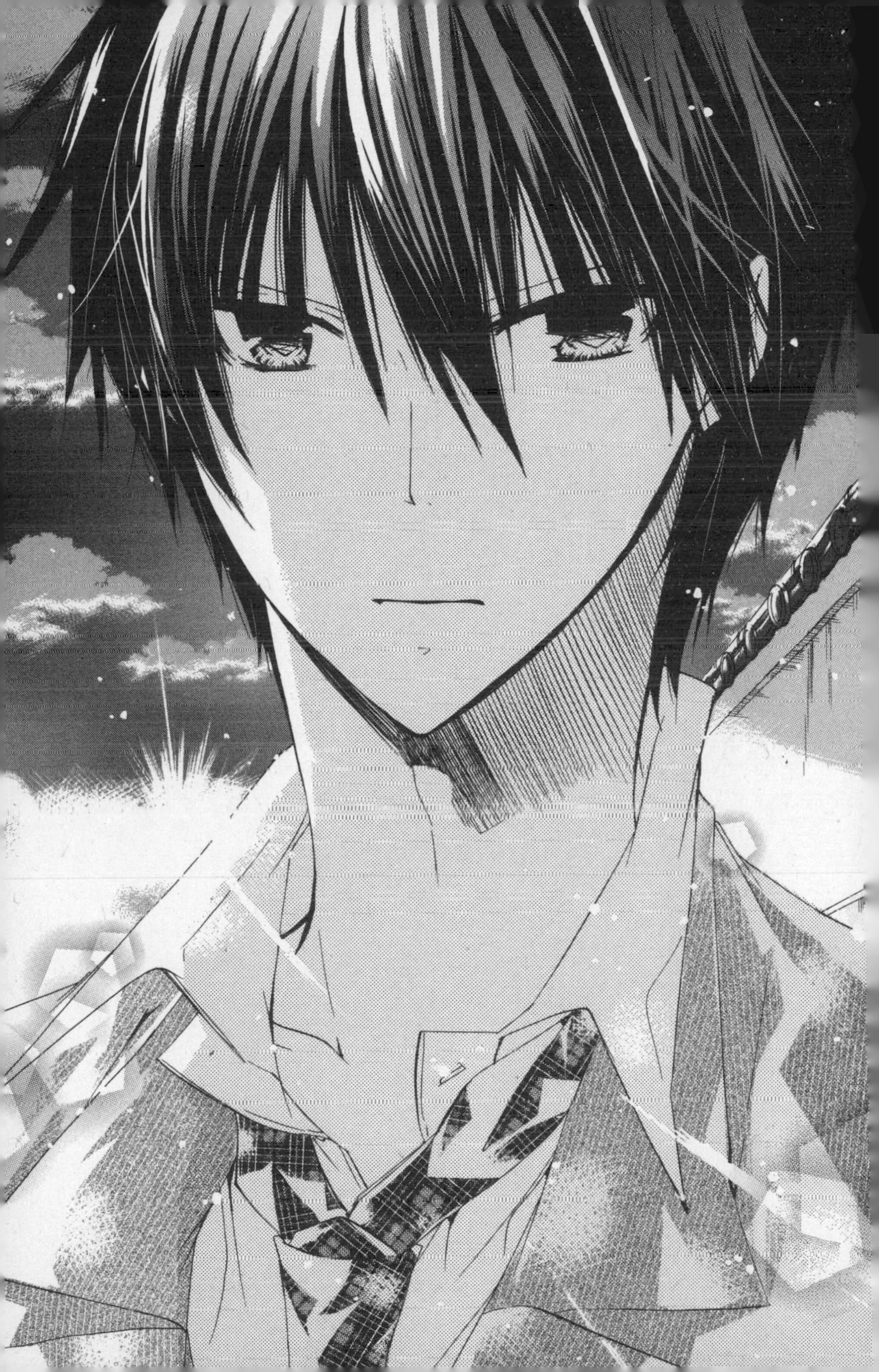

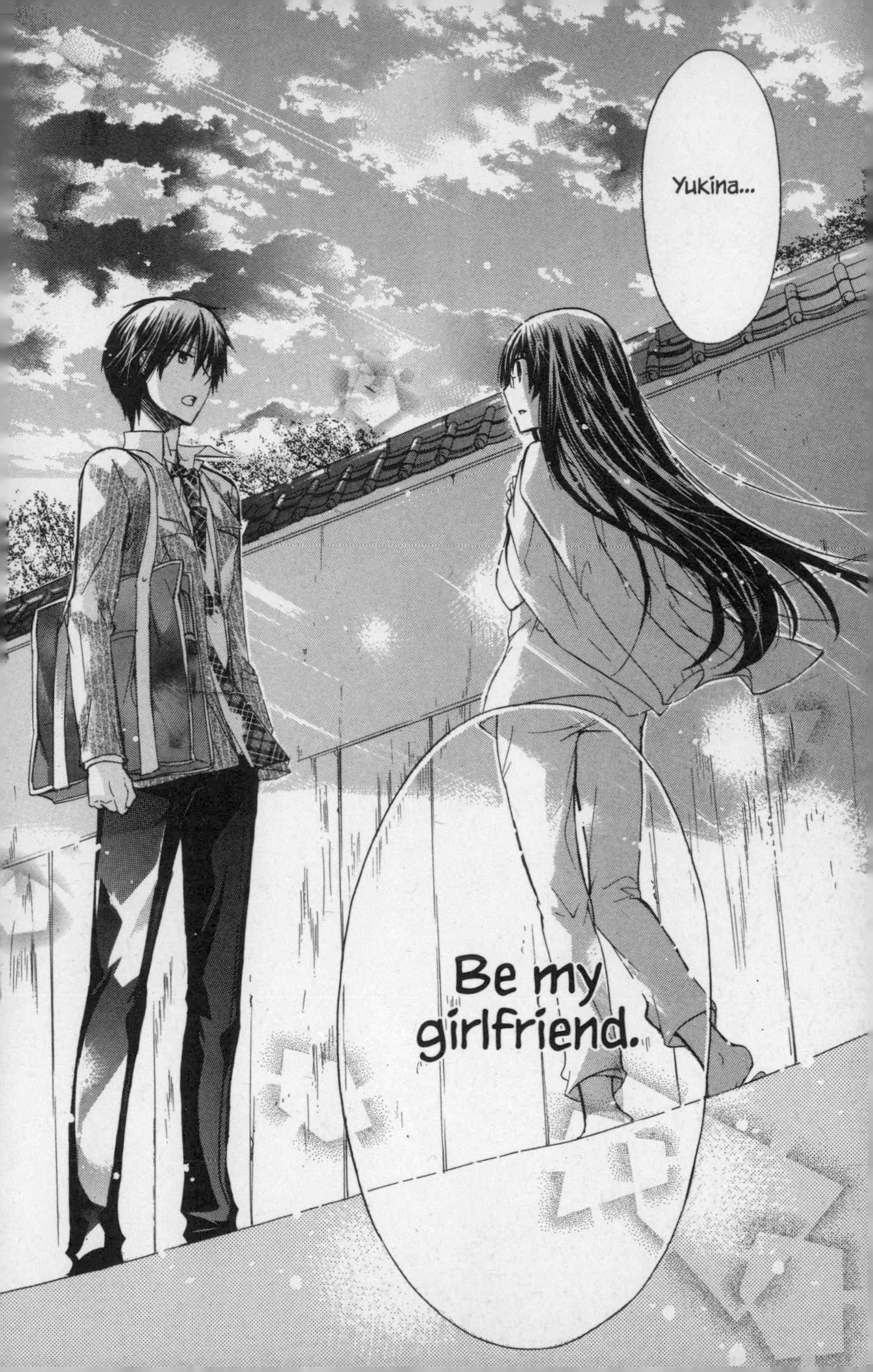
Yukina...
Be my girlfriend.

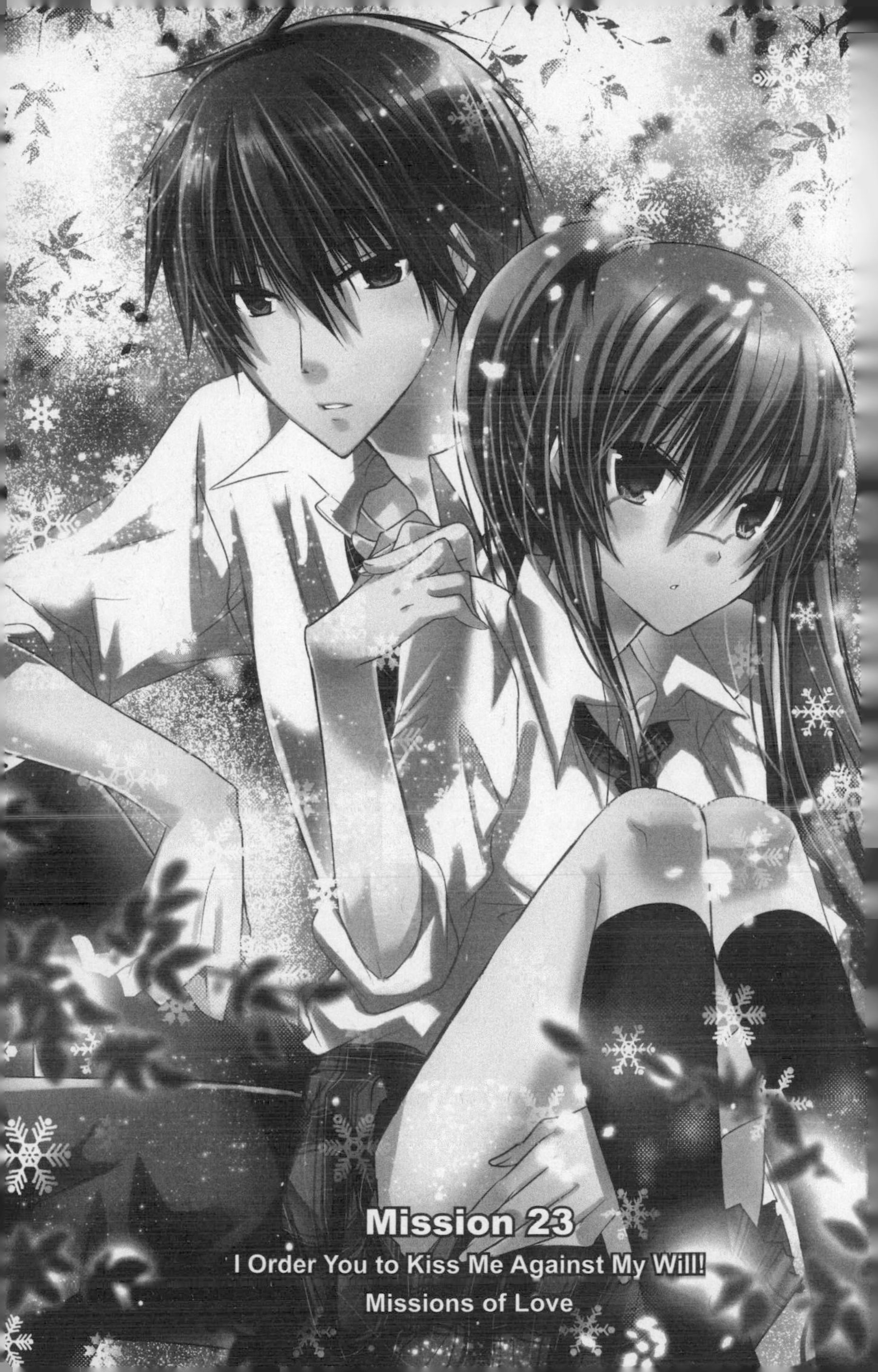
Mission 23
I Order You to Kiss Me Against My Will!
Missions of Love

Missions of Love

It is time for love.
Secret cell phone novelist vs. the most popular boy in school.
A mission of love for absolute servitude.

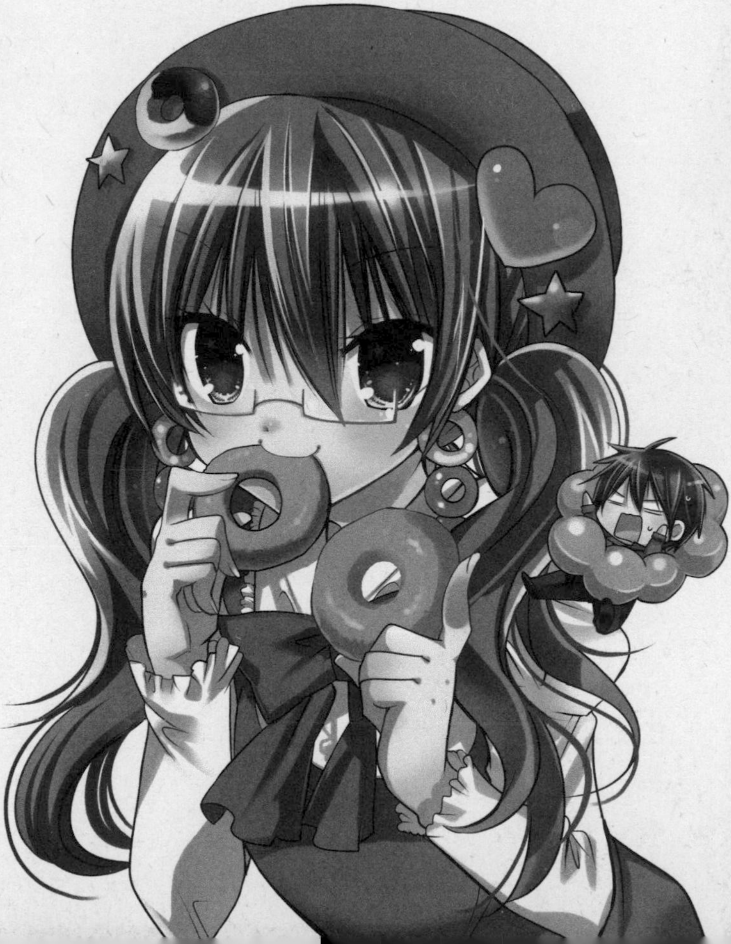

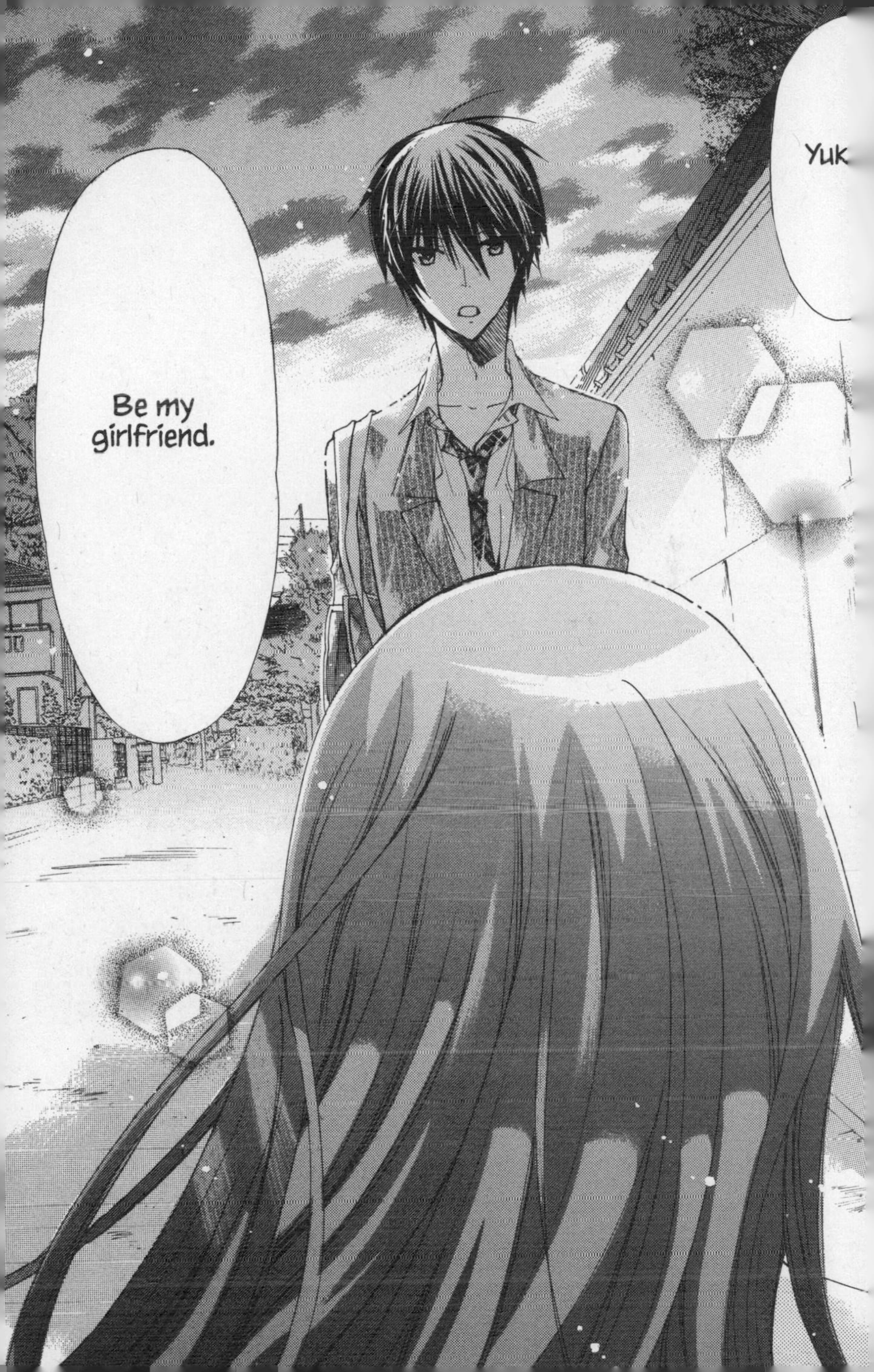
Yuk
Be my girlfriend.

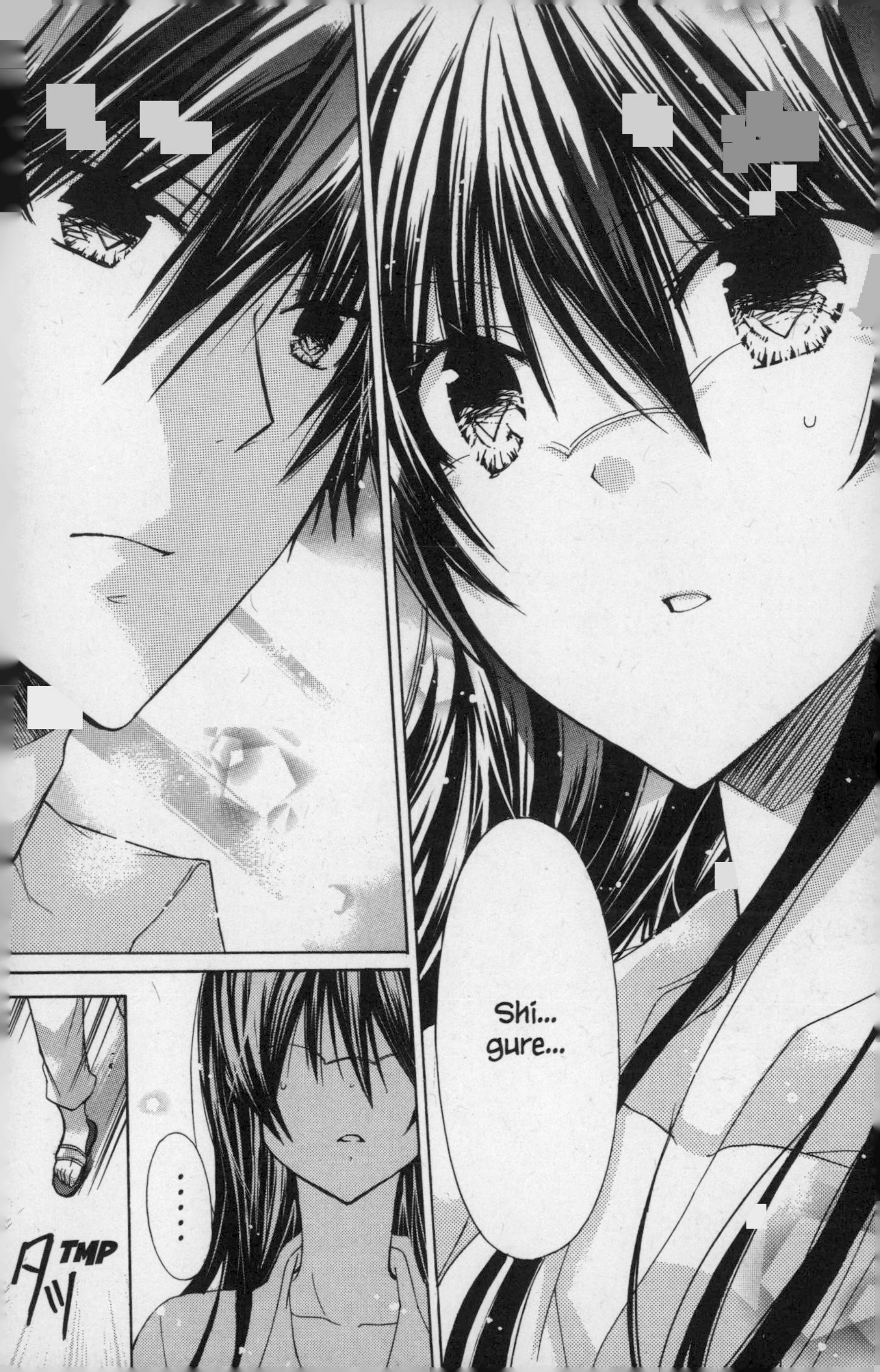
Shi... gure...
.....
TMP

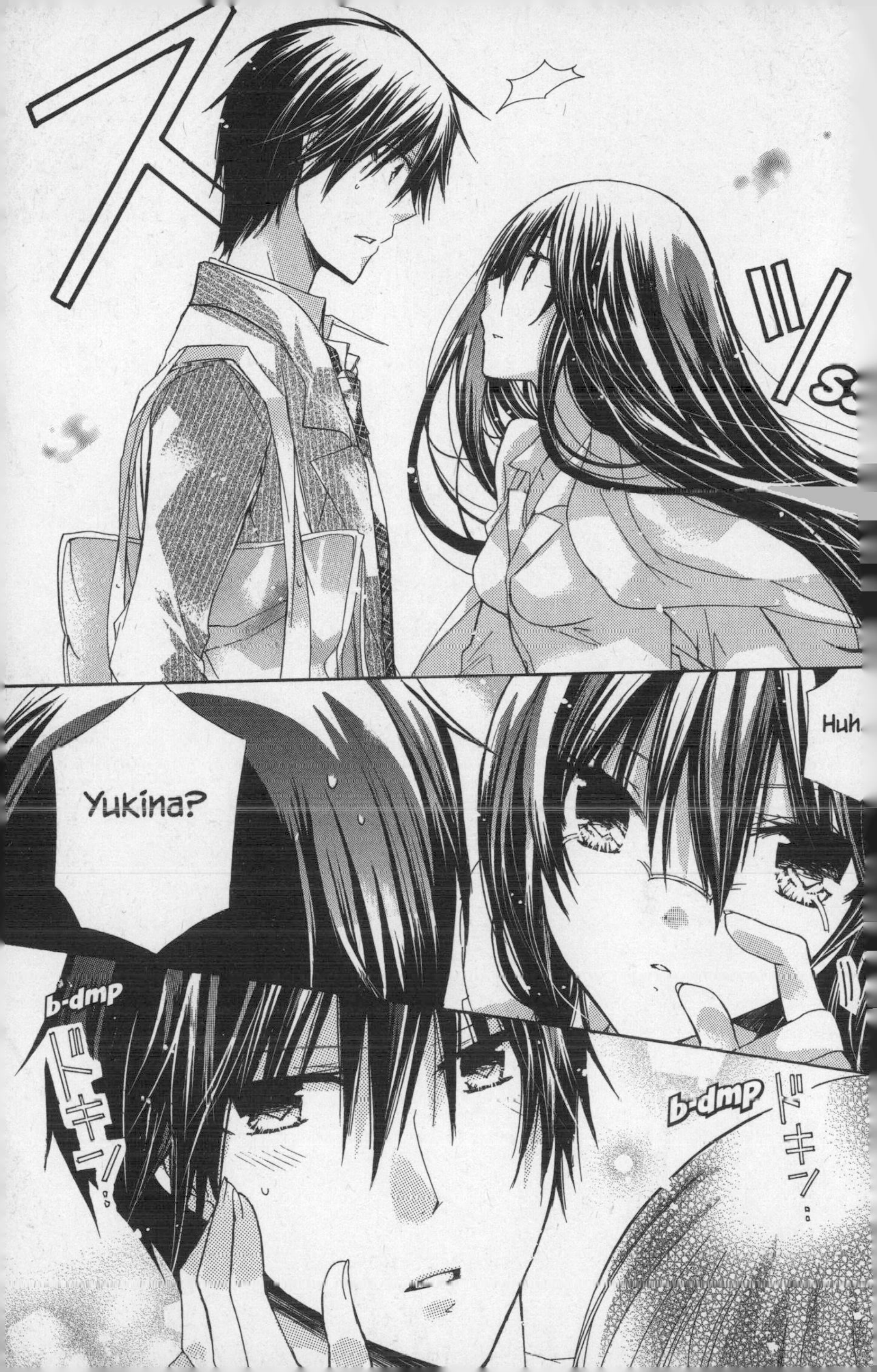

スッ
Huh
Yukina?
b-dmp
ドキン
b-dmp
ドキン

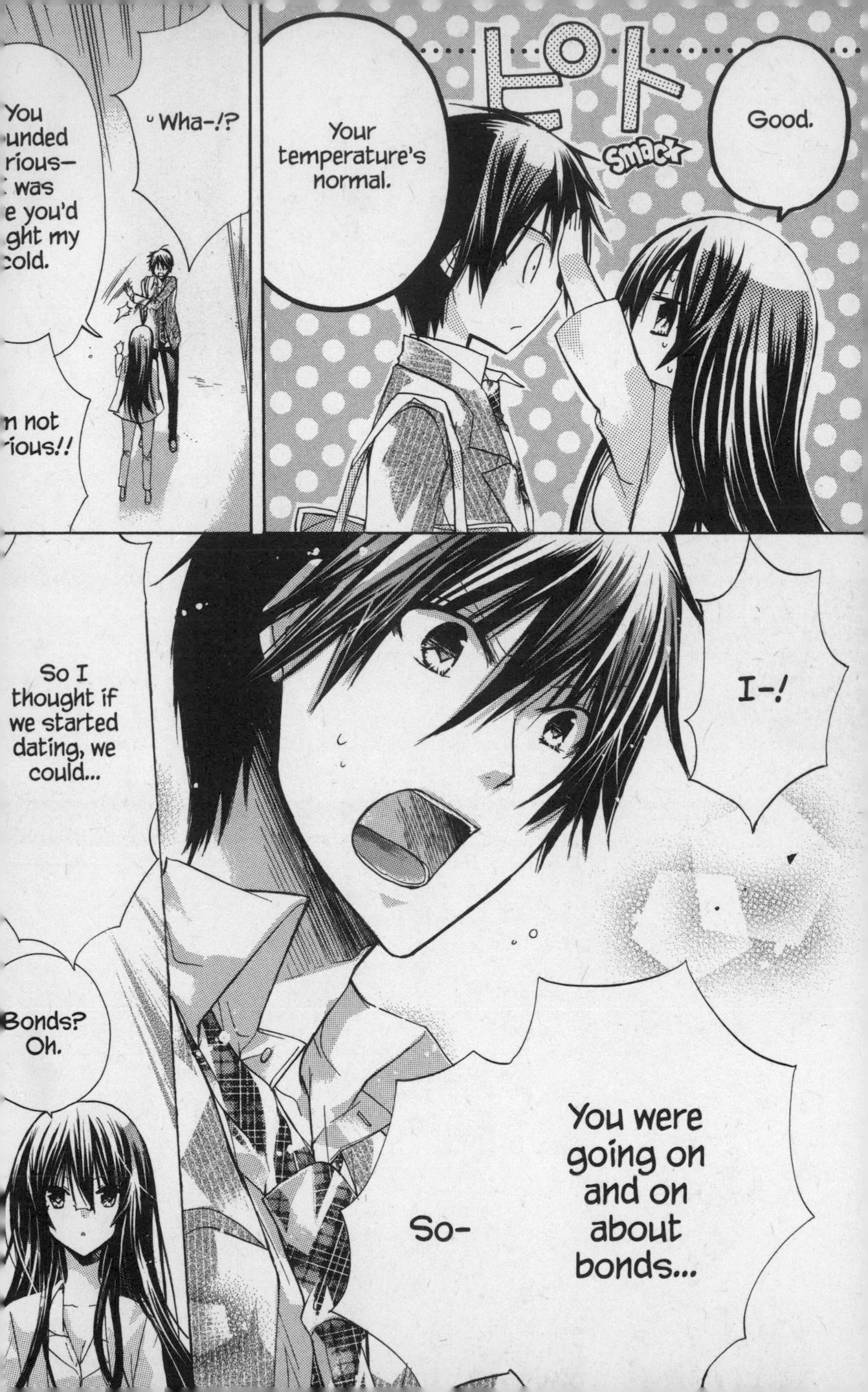
Good.
SMACK
Your temperature's normal.
Wha-!?
You
unded
rious—
was
e you'd
ght my
cold.
n not
rious!!
I-!
You were going on and on about bonds...
So-
So I thought if we started dating, we could...
Bonds? Oh.

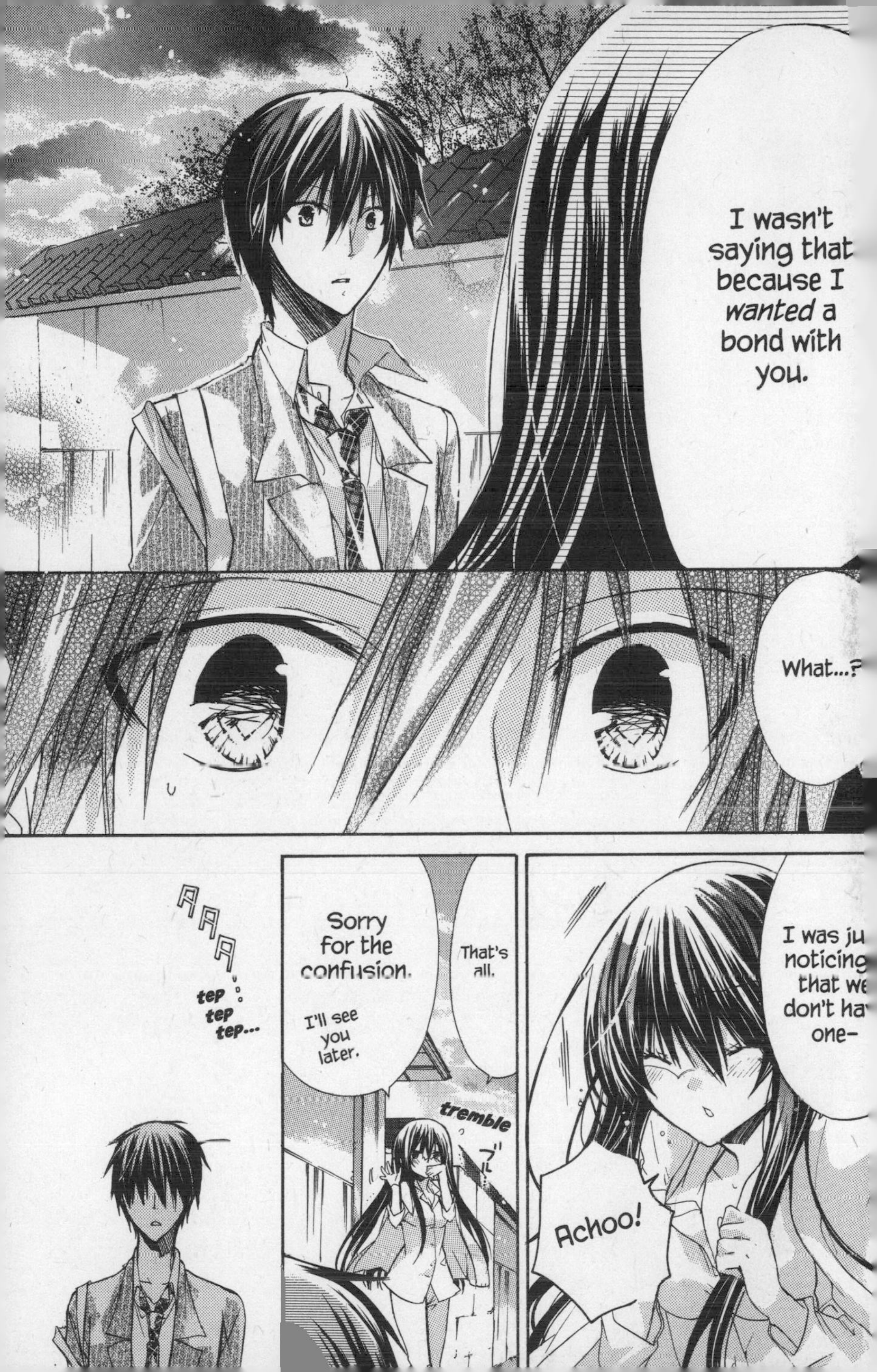

I wasn't saying that because I *wanted* a bond with you.
What...?
I was ju noticing that we don't ha one-
Achoo!
That's all.
Sorry for the confusion.
I'll see you later.
tremble
AAA
tep tep tep...

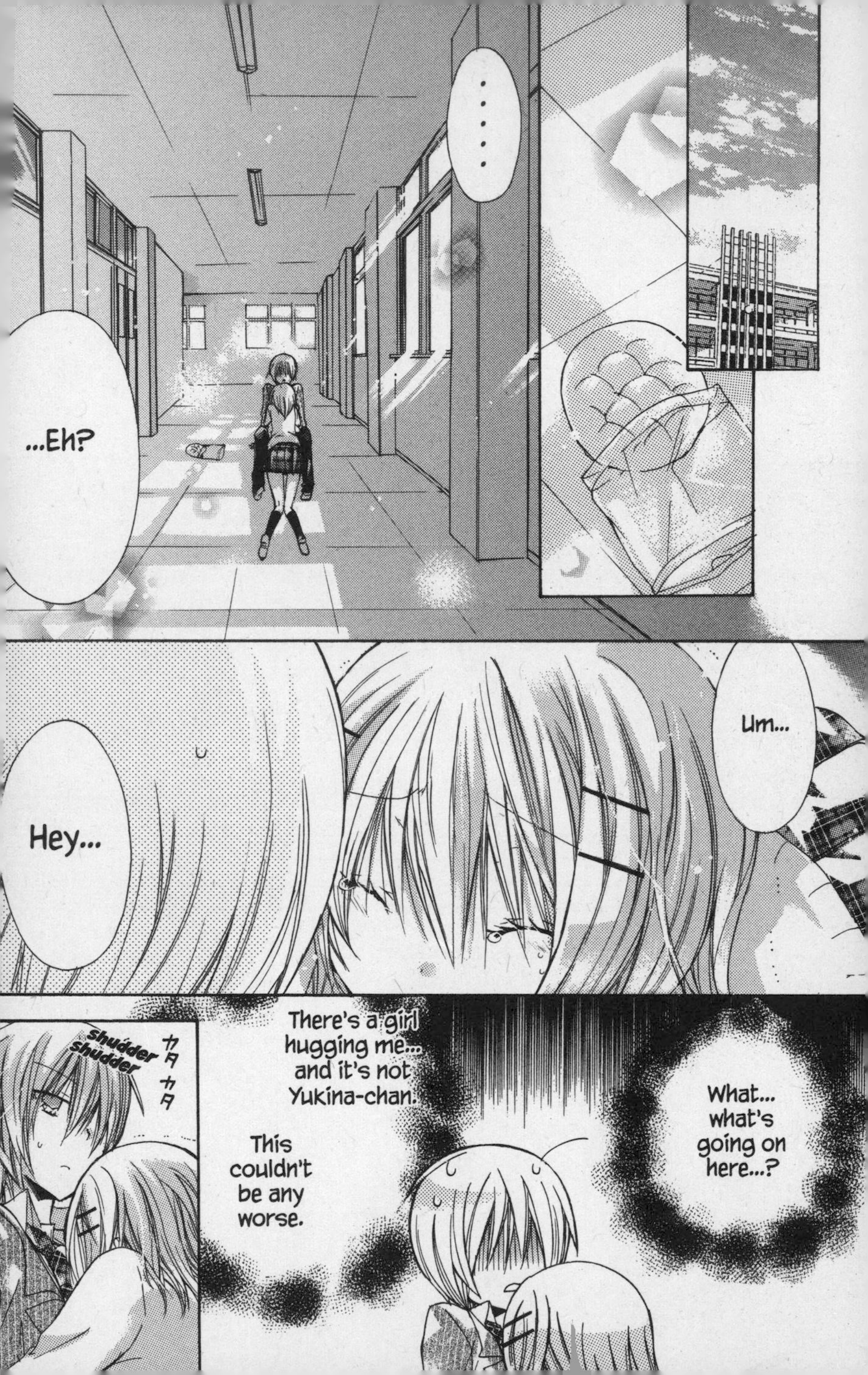
.....
...Eh?
Um...
Hey...
What... what's going on here...?
There's a girl hugging me... and it's not Yukina-chan.
This couldn't be any worse.
Shudder shudder
カタ カタ

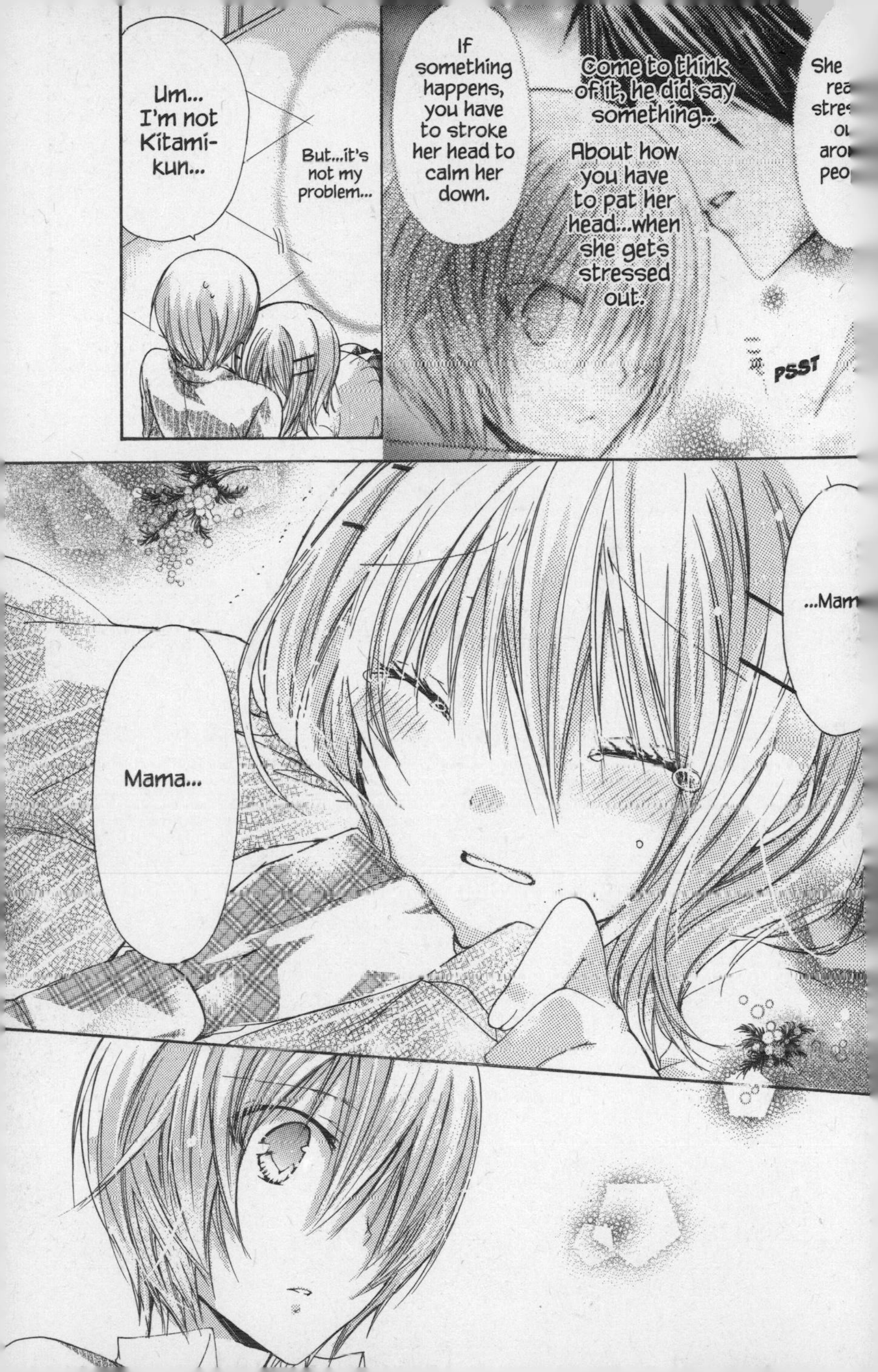
She rea stres ou aro peo
PSST
Come to think of it, he did say something...
About how you have to pat her head...when she gets stressed out.
If something happens, you have to stroke her head to calm her down.
Um... I'm not Kitami-kun...
But...it's not my problem...
...Mam
Mama...

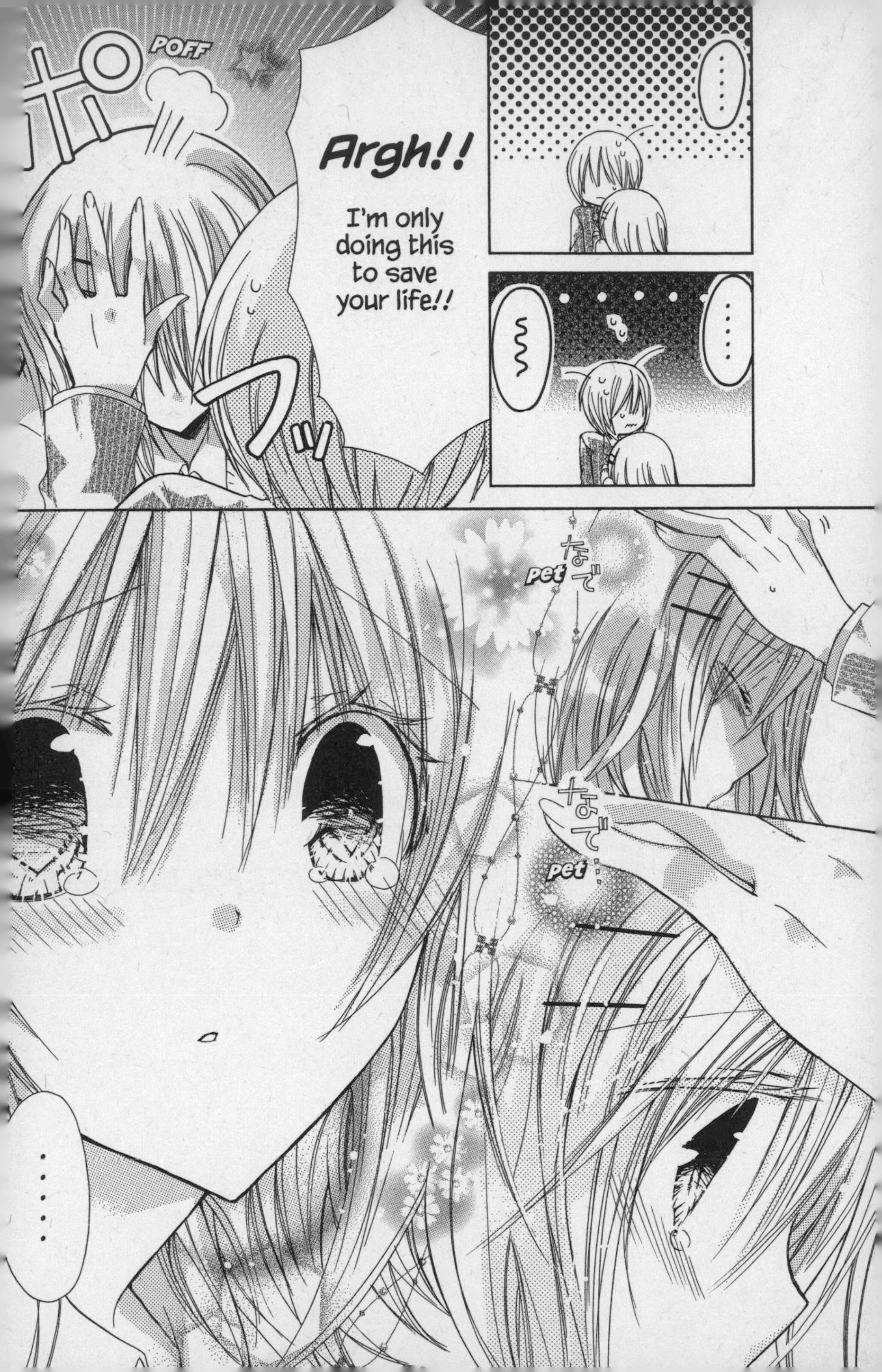
......
......
ポ
POFF
Argh!!
I'm only doing this to save your life!!
なで
pet
なで
pet
......

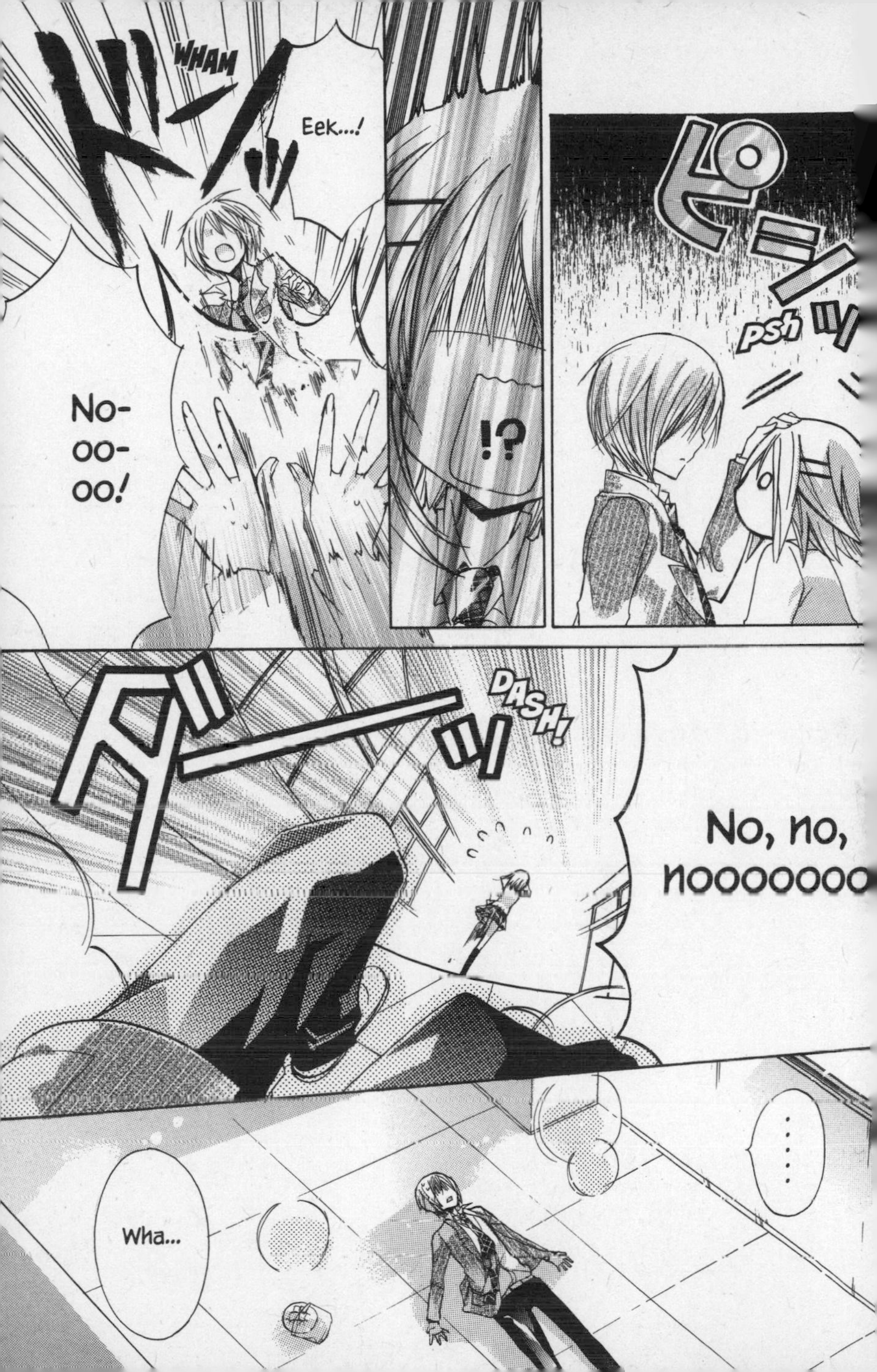
psh
!?
WHAM
Eek...!
No-oo-oo!
DASH!
No, no, noooooo
......
Wha...

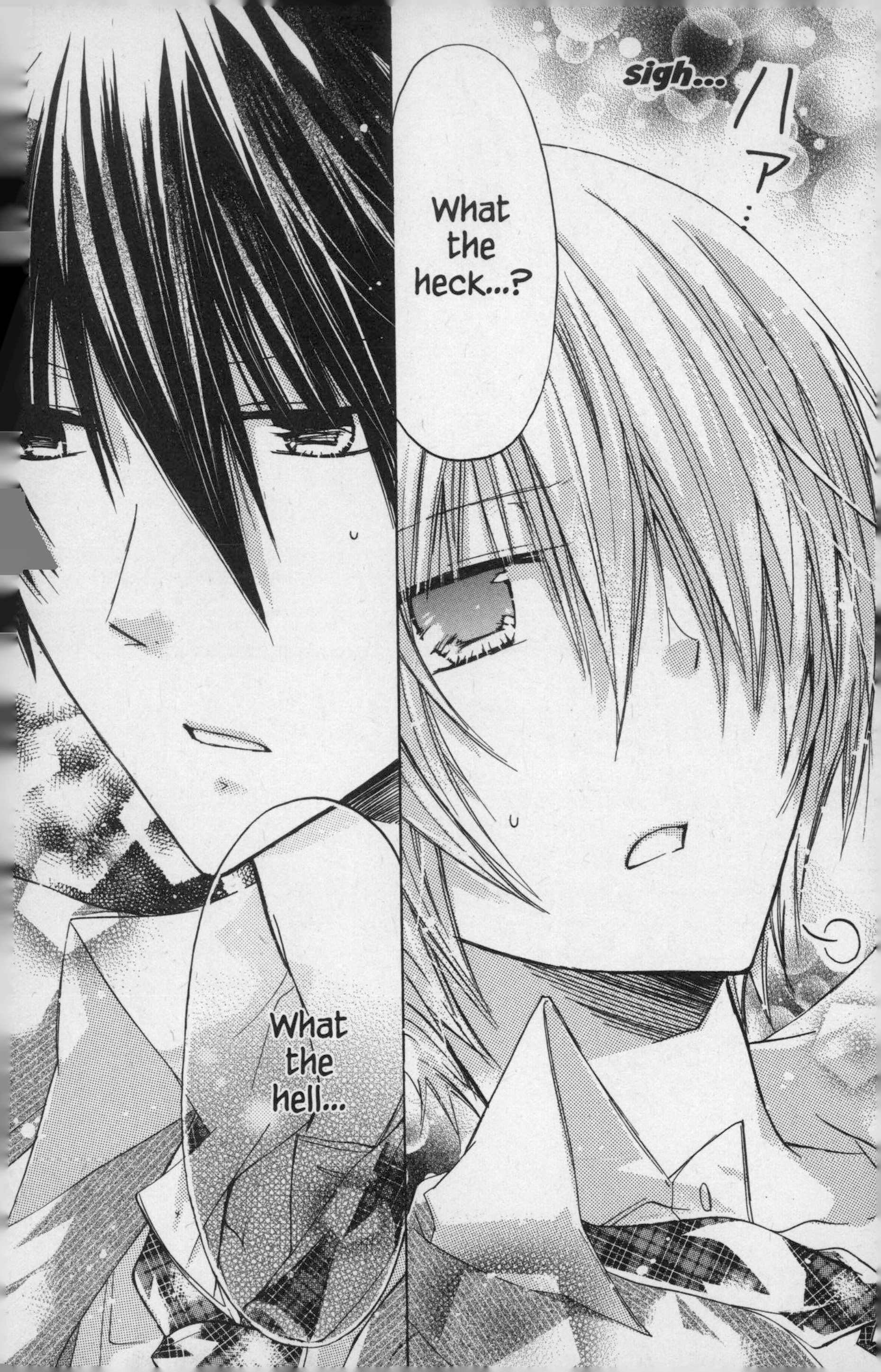
sigh...
ハア…
What the heck...?
What the hell...

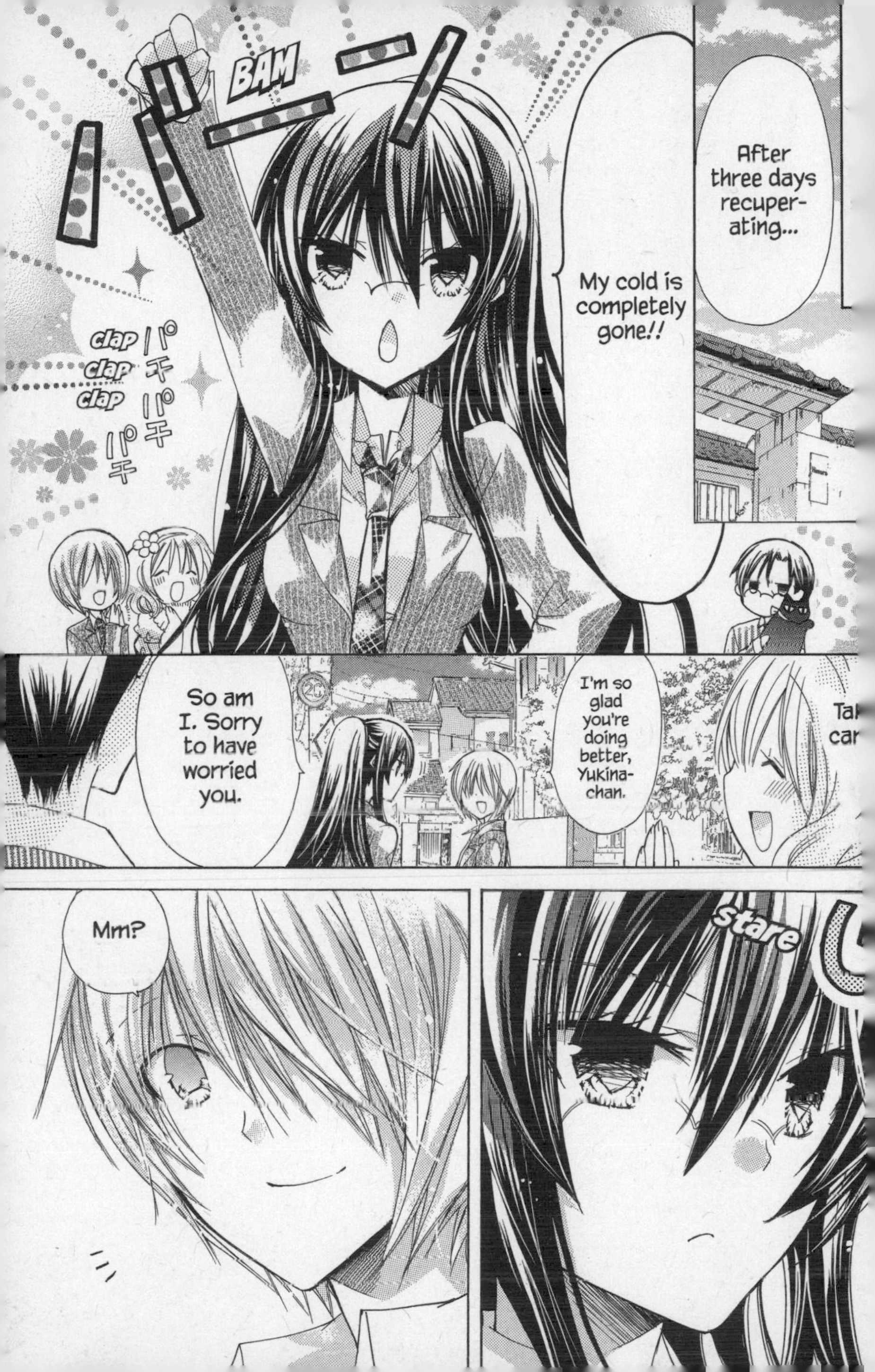
After three days recuperating...
My cold is completely gone!!
BAM
clap clap clap
パチパチパチ
I'm so glad you're doing better, Yukina-chan.
So am I. Sorry to have worried you.
stare
Mm?

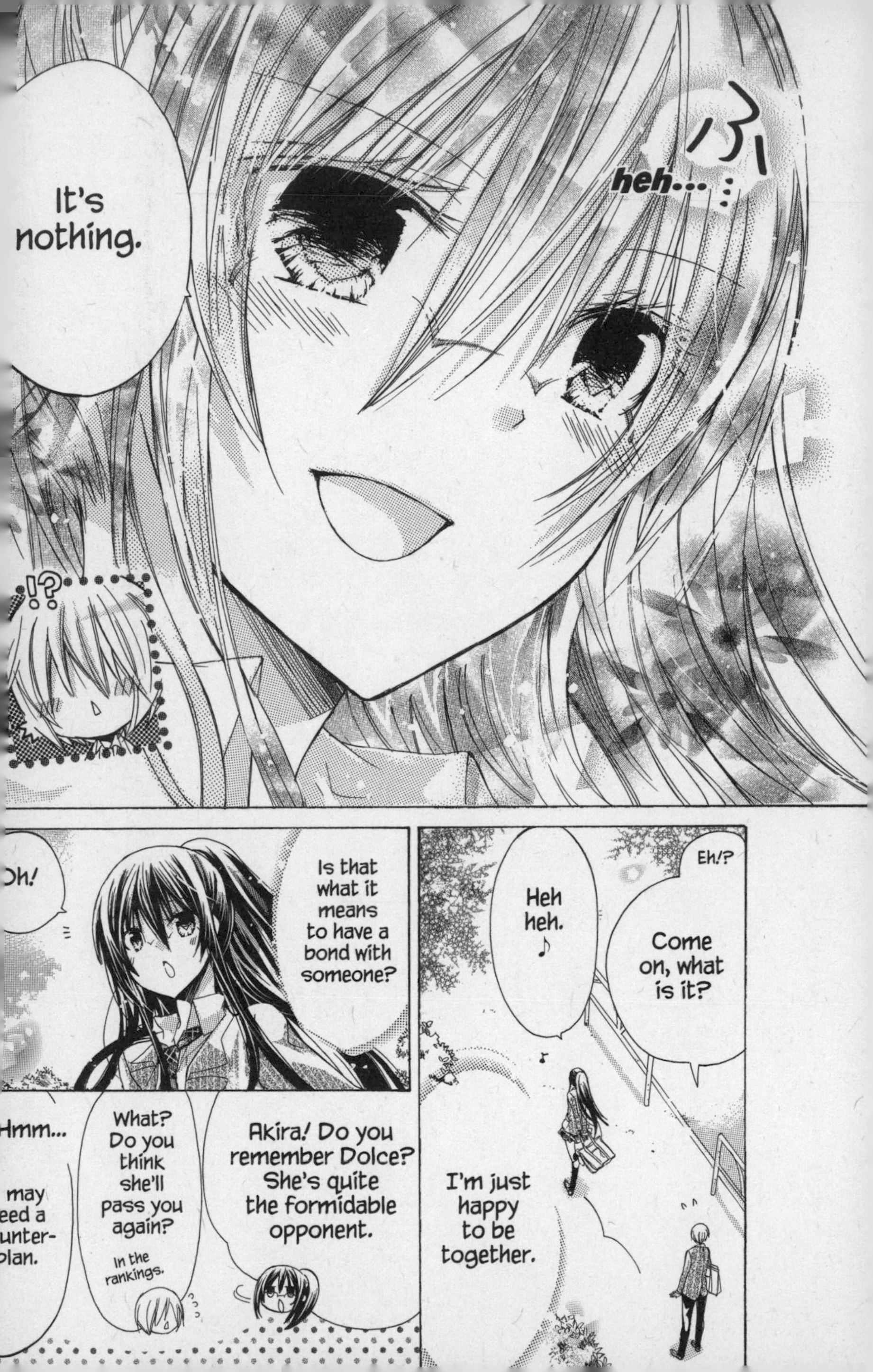
ふ
heh...
It's nothing.
!?
Eh!?
Come on, what is it?
Heh heh. ♪
I'm just happy to be together.
Is that what it means to have a bond with someone?
Oh!
Akira! Do you remember Dolce? She's quite the formidable opponent.
What? Do you think she'll pass you again?
In the rankings.
Hmm...
may eed a unter-plan.

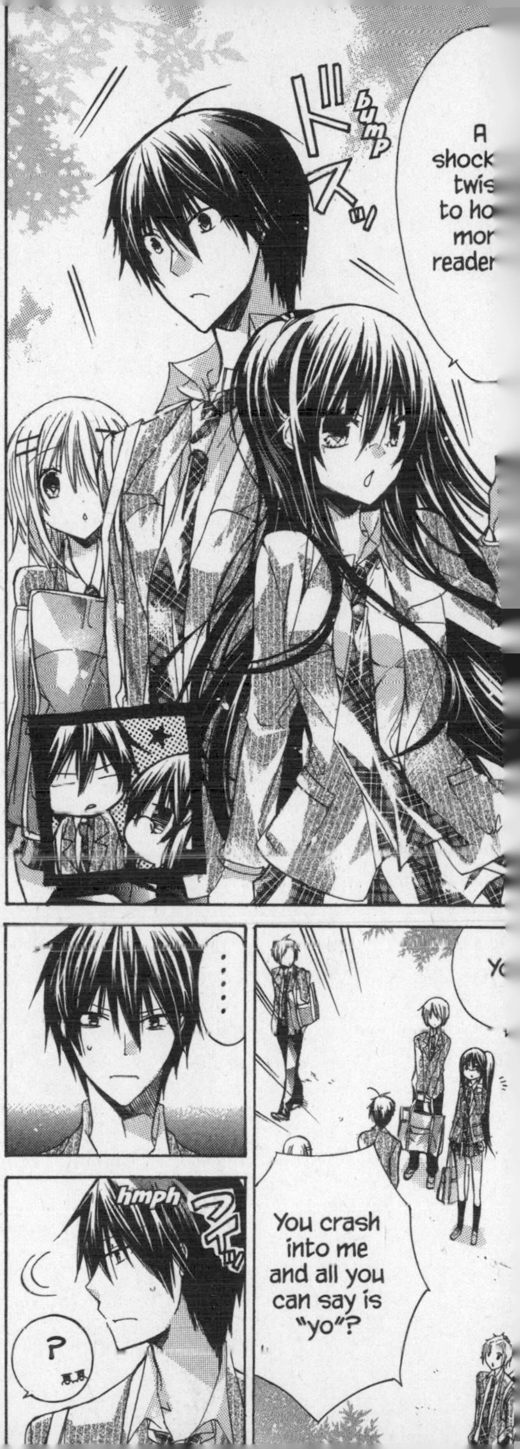
bump
A shock twis to ho mor reader
Yo
You crash into me and all you can say is "yo"?
.....
hmph
?

Snow Mami 2

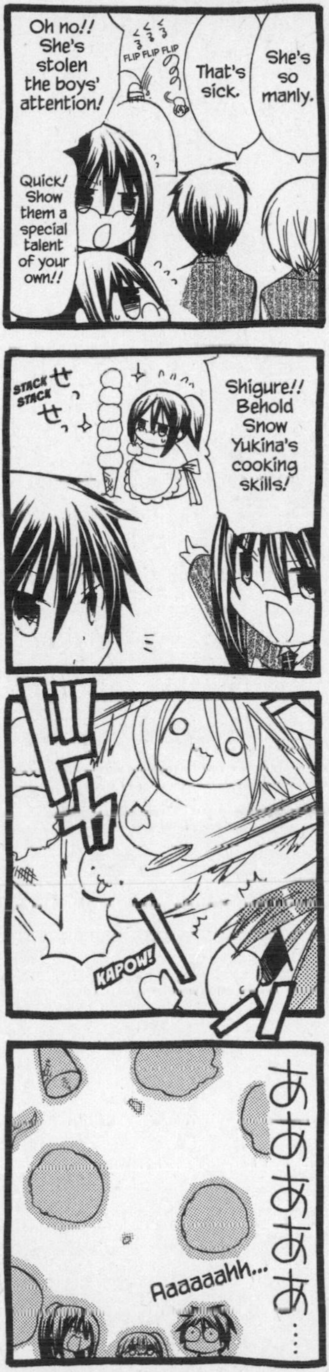
She's so manly.
That's sick.
FLIP FLIP FLIP
Oh no!! She's stolen the boys' attention!
Quick! Show them a special talent of your own!!
Shigure!! Behold Snow Yukina's cooking skills!
STACK STACK
KAPOW!
あああああ…
Aaaaaahh...

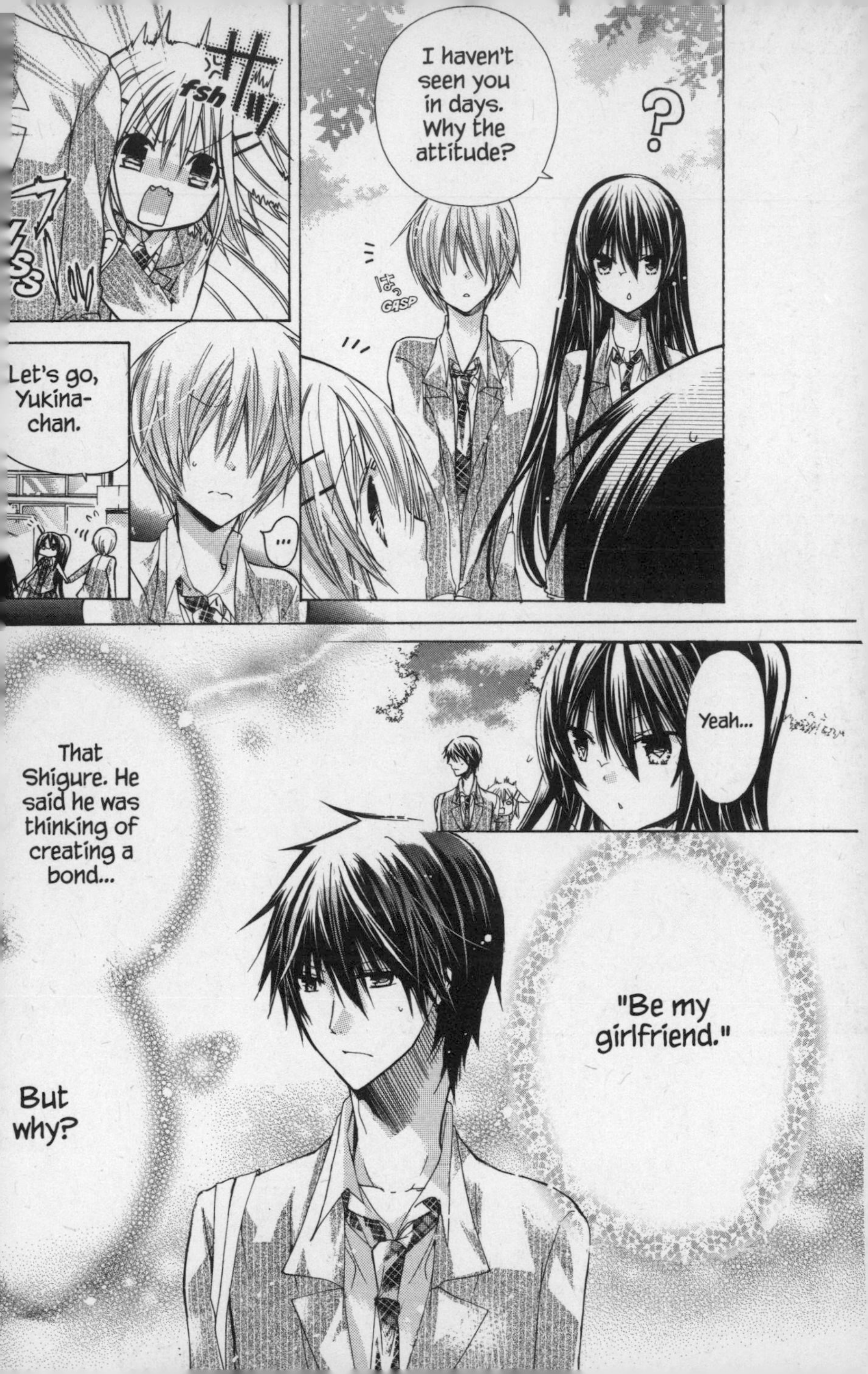
I haven't seen you in days. Why the attitude?
?
GASP
fsh
Let's go, Yukina-chan.
...
Yeah...
That Shigure. He said he was thinking of creating a bond...
"Be my girlfriend."
But why?

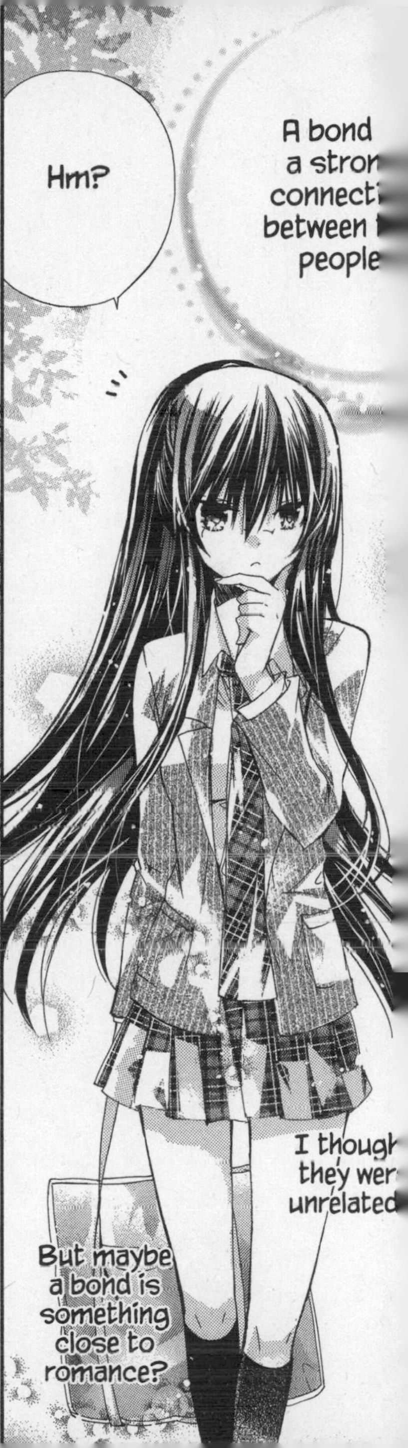
A bond
a stron
connecti
between
people
Hm?
I though
they wer
unrelated
But maybe a bond is something close to romance?
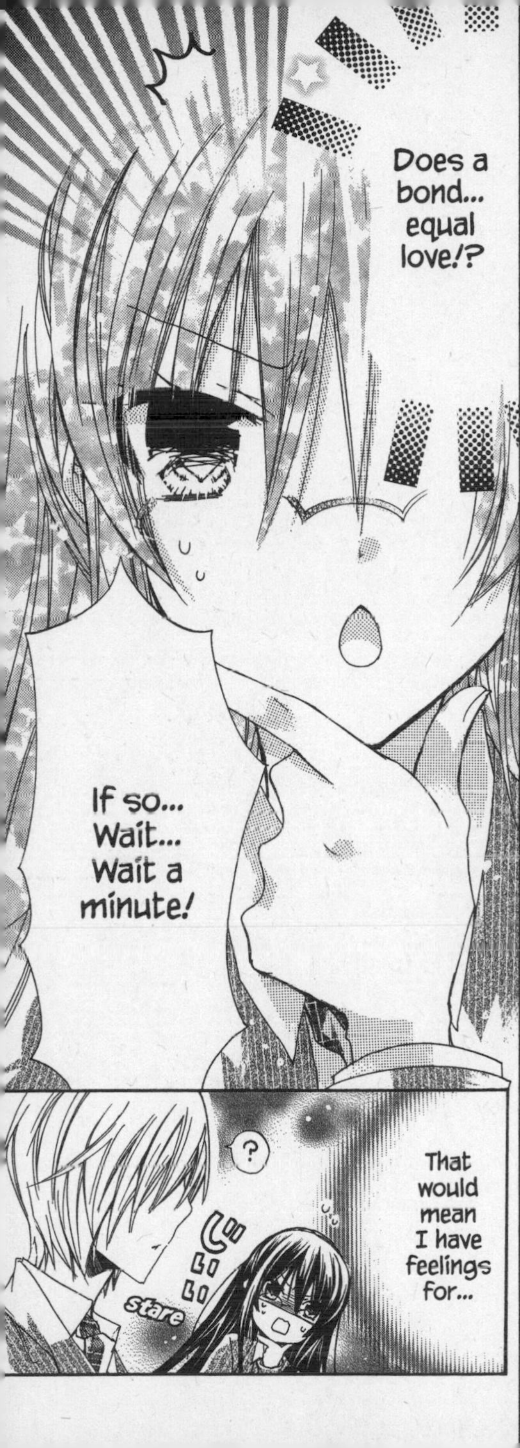
Does a bond... equal love!?
If so... Wait... Wait a minute!
That would mean I have feelings for...
?
stare

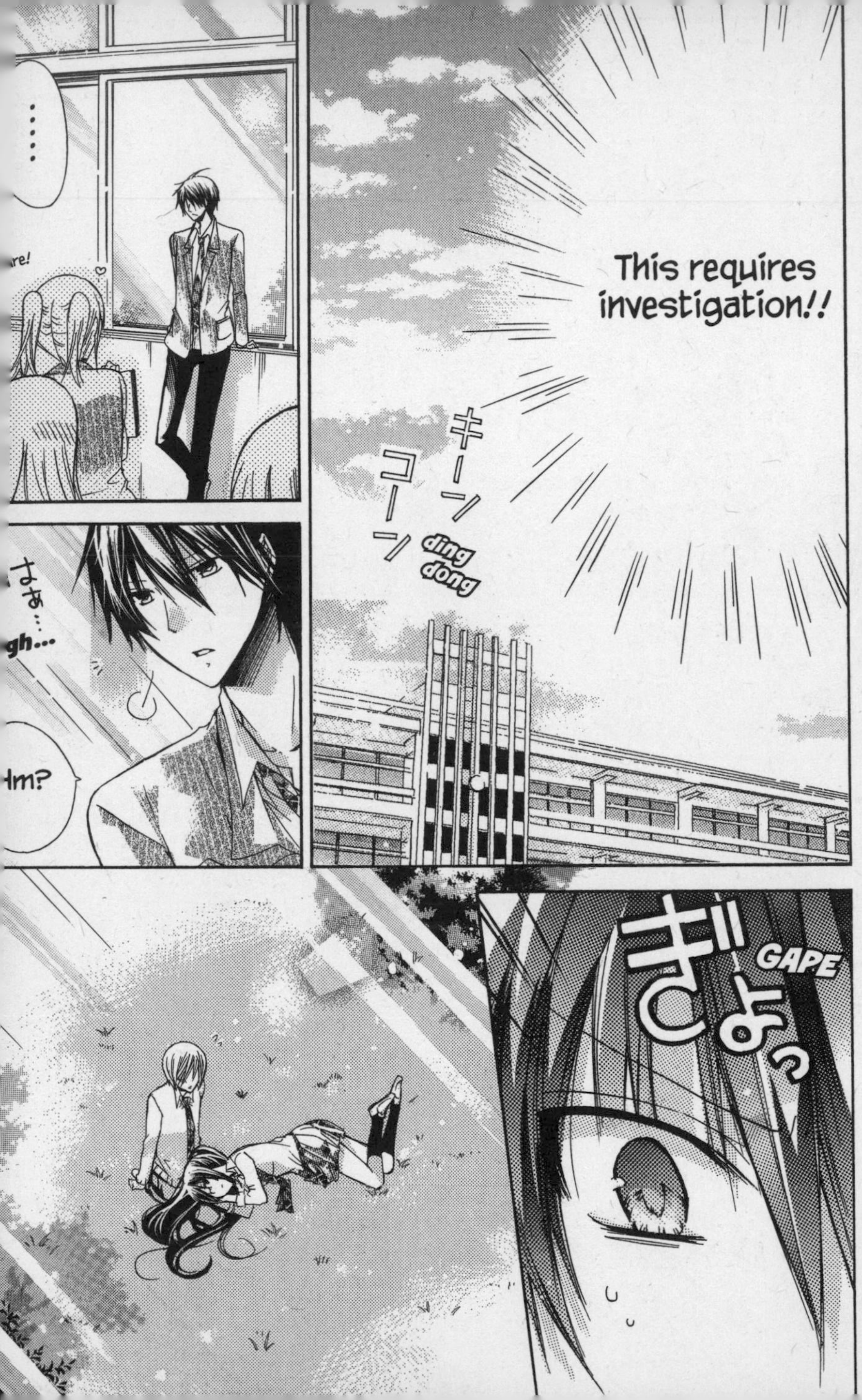
This requires investigation!!
キーンコーン
ding dong
......
re!
はぁ…
gh...
Hm?
ぎょっ
GAPE

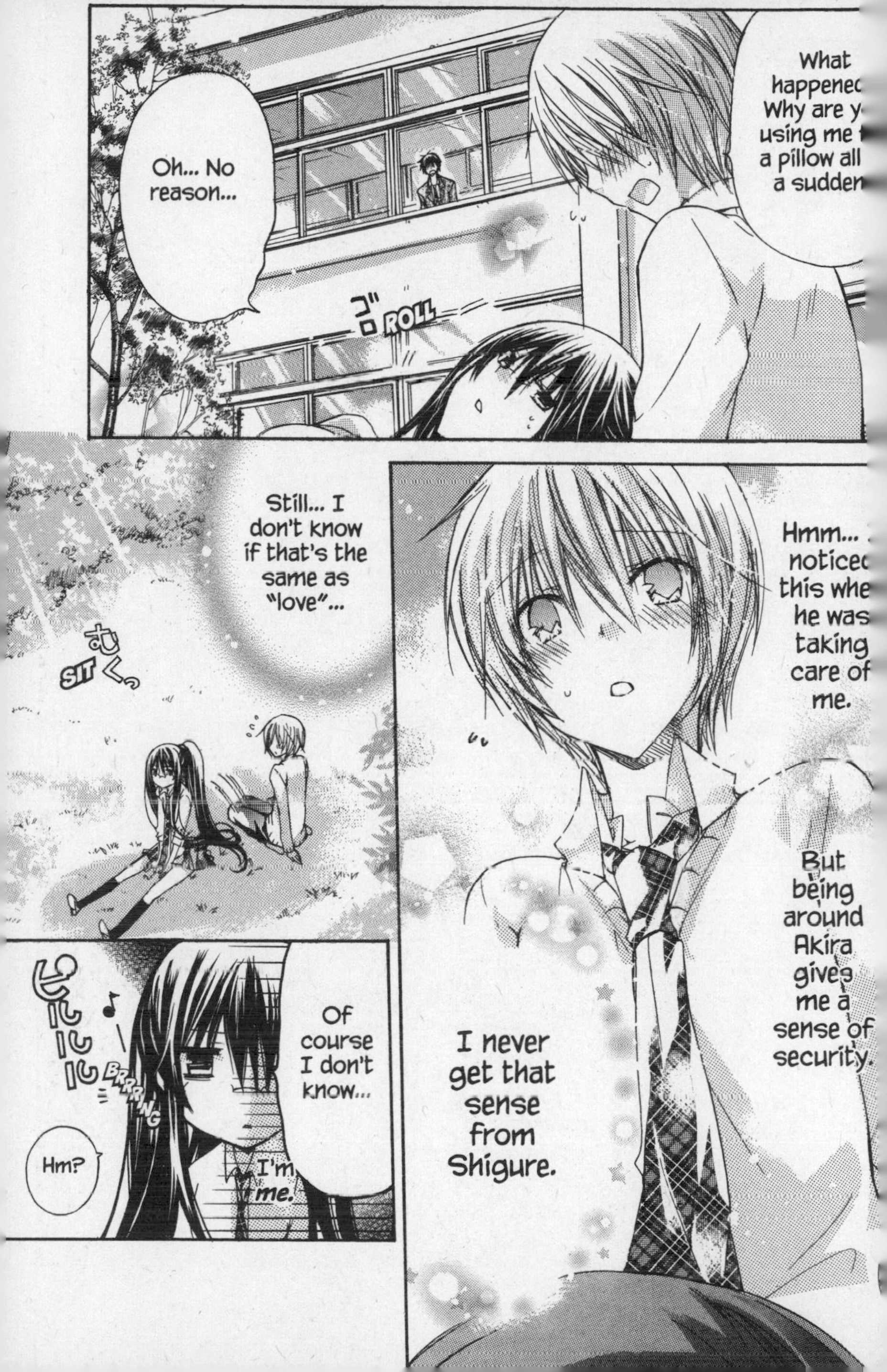
What happenec Why are y using me f a pillow all a sudden
Oh... No reason...
ゴロ ROLL
Hmm... noticec this whe he was taking care of me.
But being around Akira gives me a sense of security.
I never get that sense from Shigure.
Still... I don't know if that's the same as "love"...
むくっ SIT
Of course I don't know...
I'm me.
BRRRING
Hm?

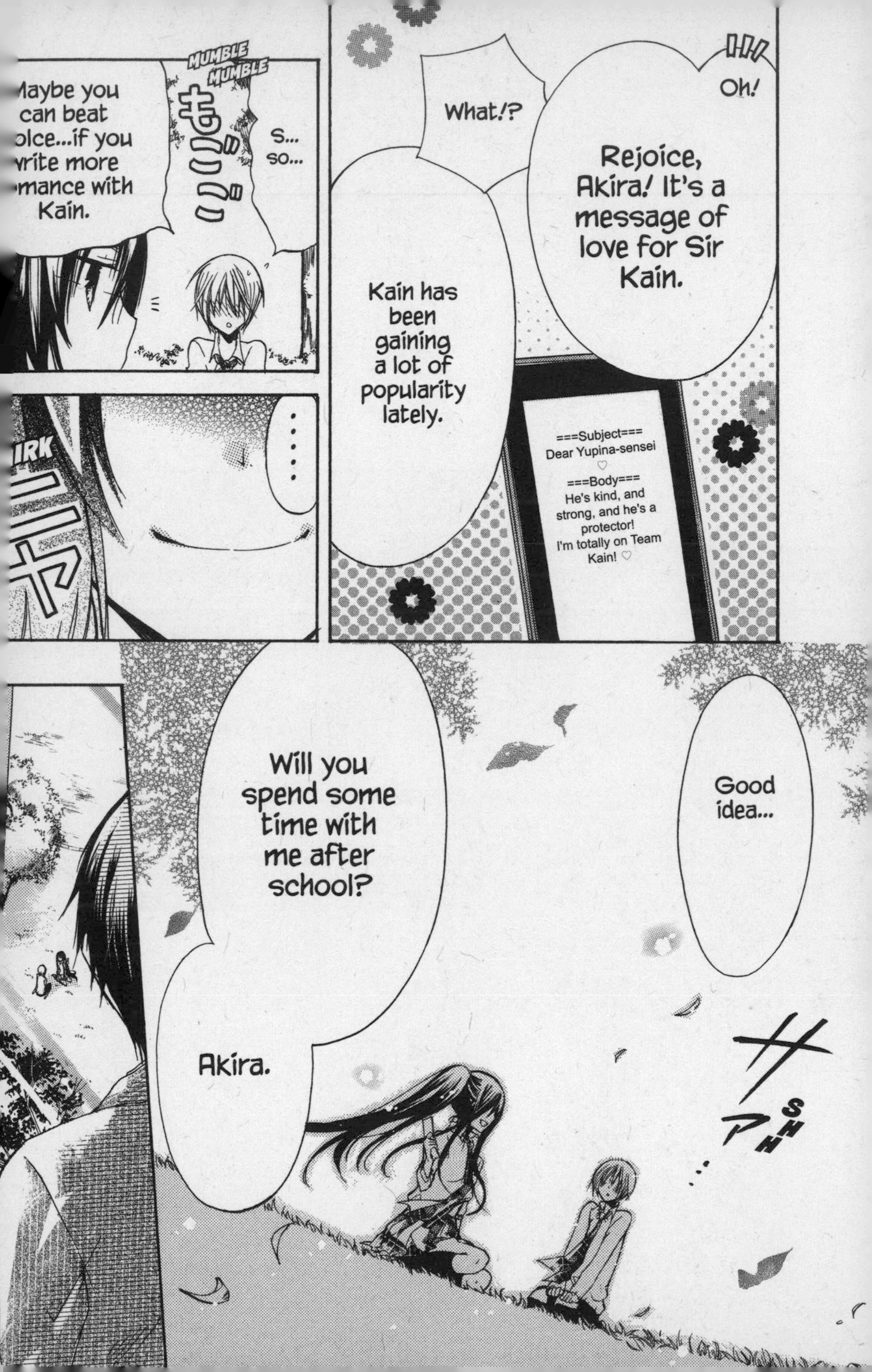
!!!
Oh!
Rejoice, Akira! It's a message of love for Sir Kain.
What!?
Kain has been gaining a lot of popularity lately.
===Subject=== Dear Yupina-sensei ♡ ===Body=== He's kind, and strong, and he's a protector! I'm totally on Team Kain! ♡
MUMBLE MUMBLE
S... so...
aybe you can beat olce...if you rite more mance with Kain.
......
IRK
Good idea...
Will you spend some time with me after school?
Akira.
SHH

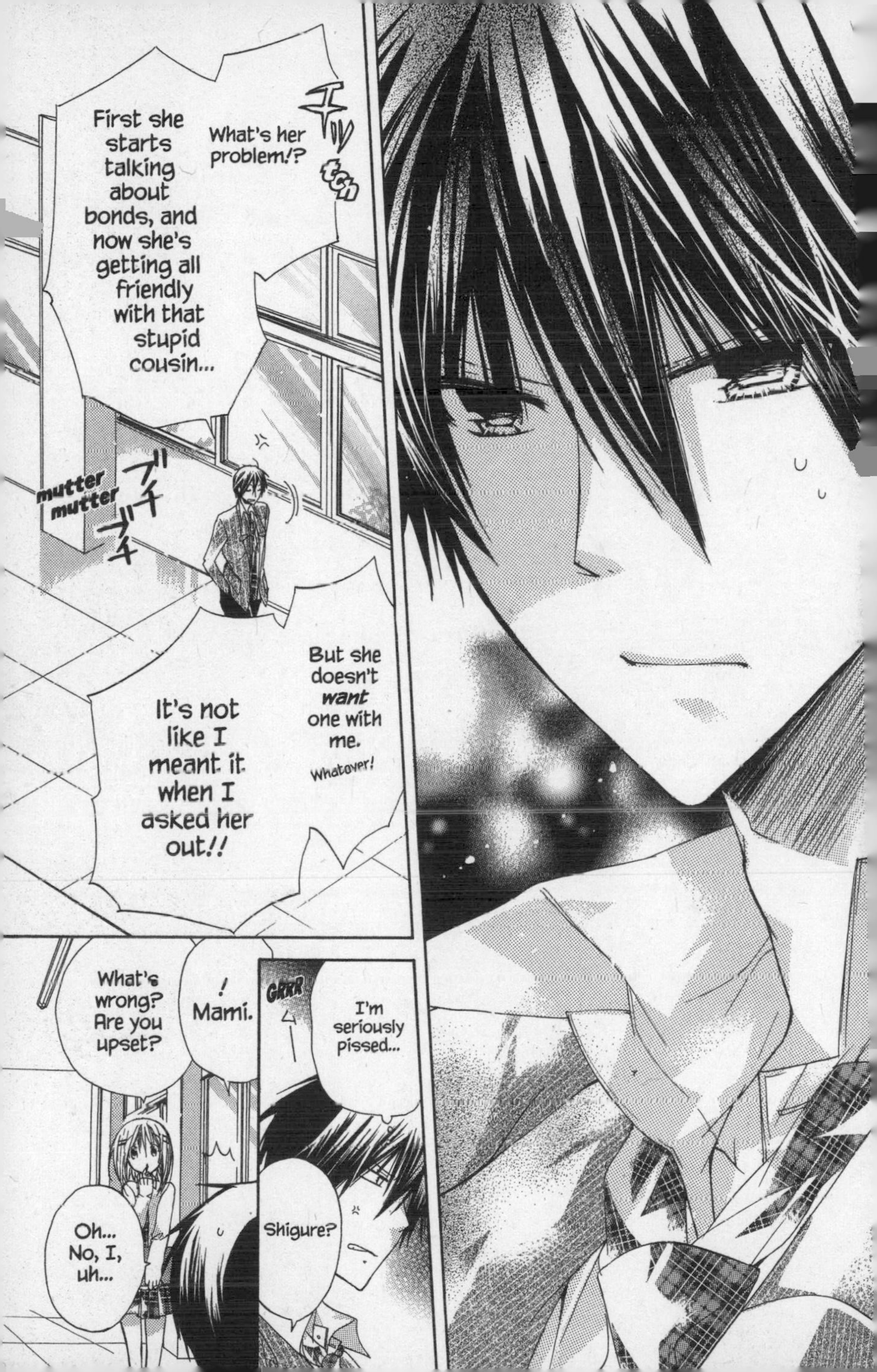
tch
What's her problem!?
First she starts talking about bonds, and now she's getting all friendly with that stupid cousin...
mutter mutter
But she doesn't *want* one with me.
Whatever!
It's not like I meant it when I asked her out!!
GRRR
I'm seriously pissed...
Shigure?
! Mami.
What's wrong? Are you upset?
Oh... No, I, uh...

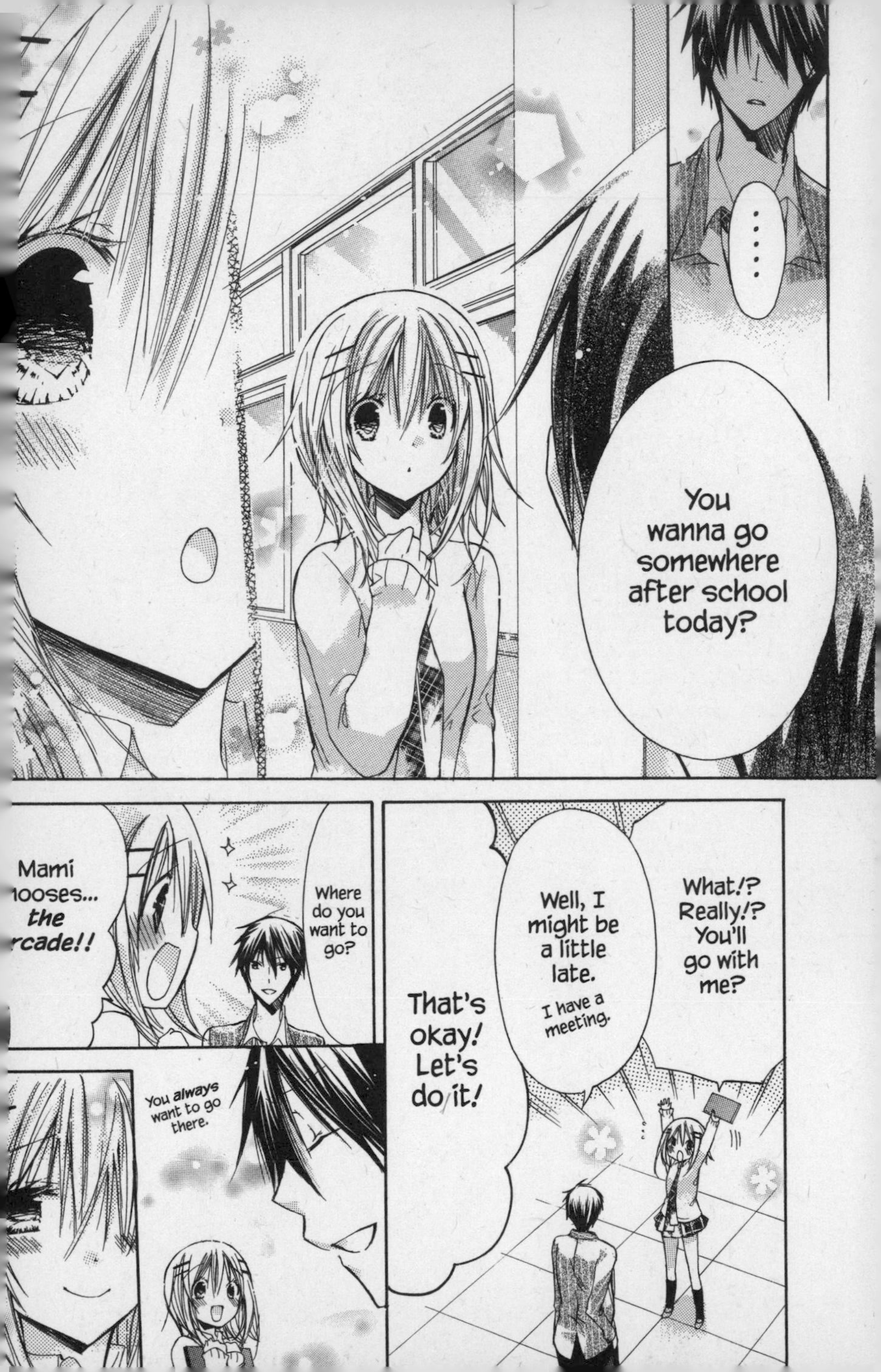
......
You wanna go somewhere after school today?
What!? Really!? You'll go with me?
Well, I might be a little late.
I have a meeting.
That's okay! Let's do it!
Where do you want to go?
Mami hooses... *the* rcade!!
You *always* want to go there.

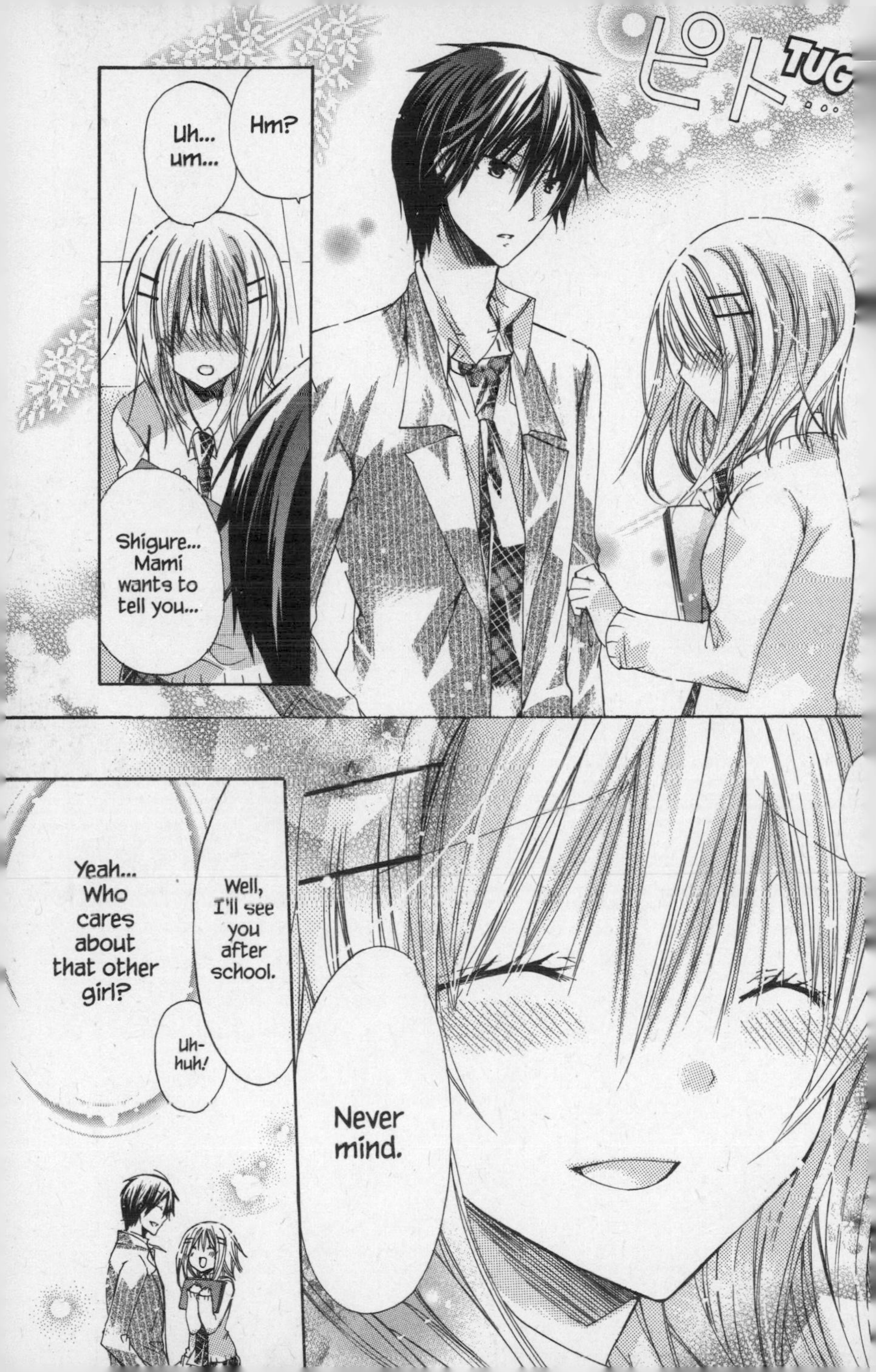
ピト
TUG...
Hm?
Uh... um...
Shigure... Mami wants to tell you...
Never mind.
Well, I'll see you after school.
Yeah... Who cares about that other girl?
Uh-huh!

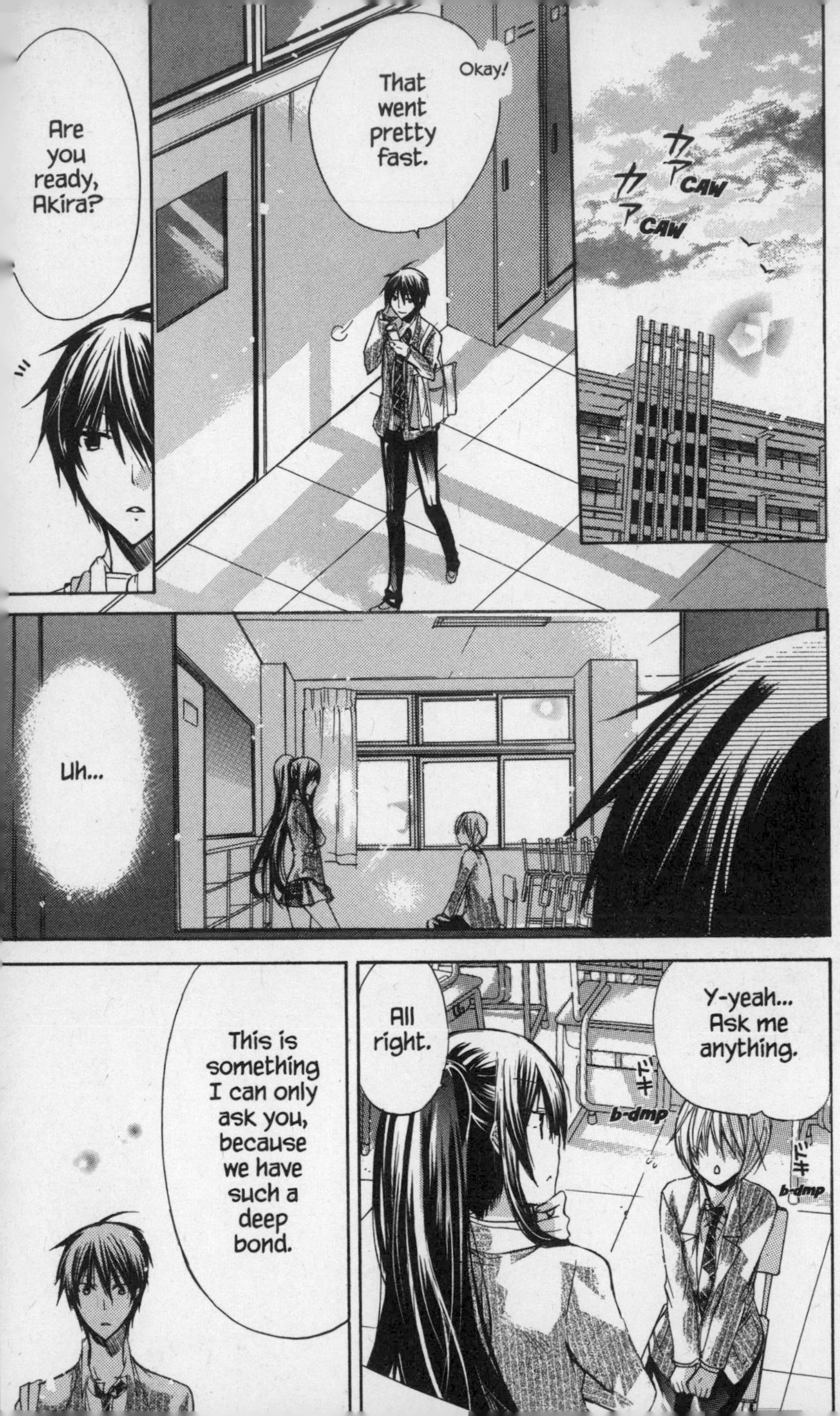
カァ CAW
カァ CAW
Okay!
That went pretty fast.
Are you ready, Akira?
Uh...
Y-yeah... Ask me anything.
ドキ b-dmp
ドキ b-dmp
All right.
This is something I can only ask you, because we have such a deep bond.

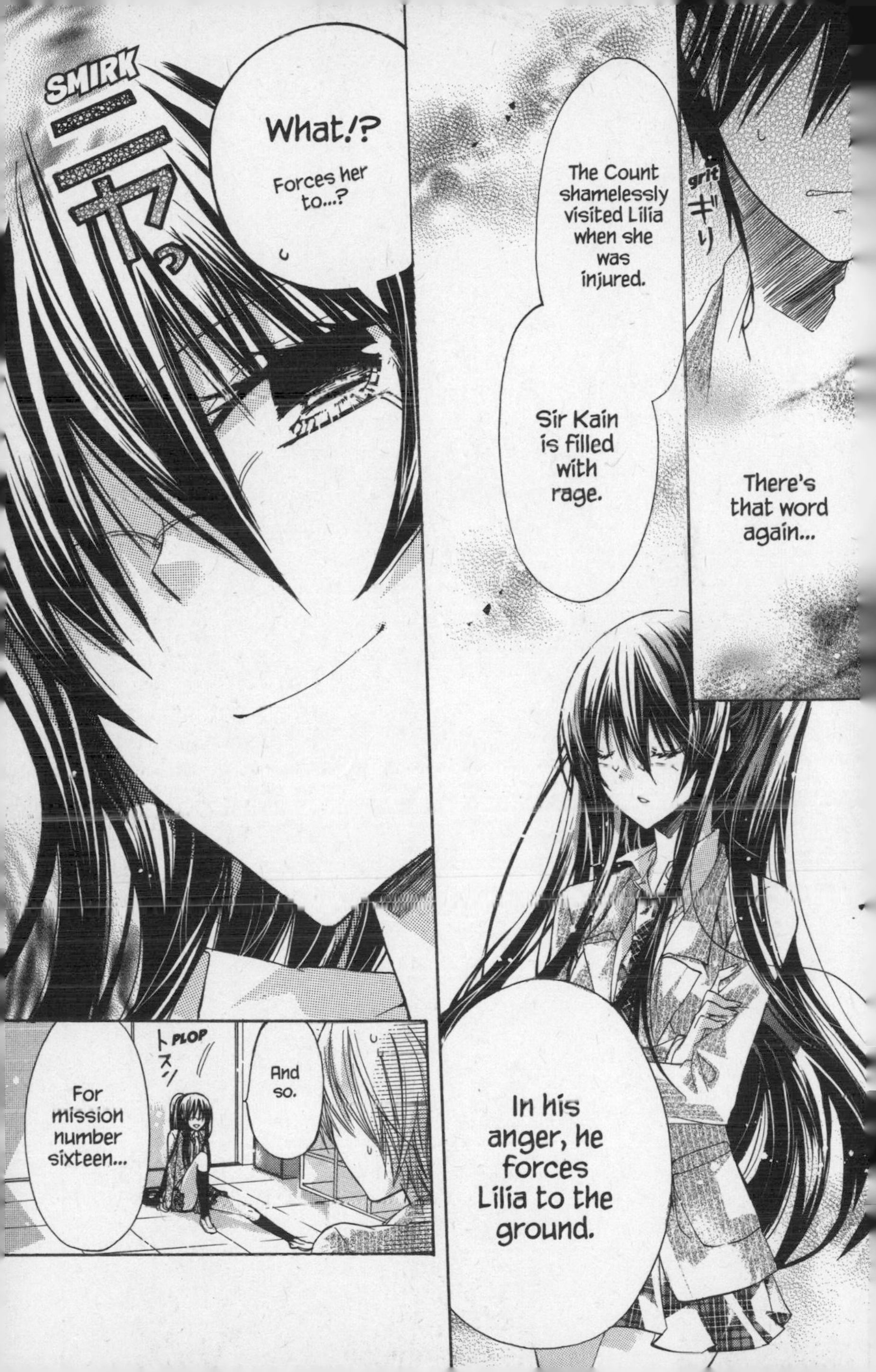
grit
ギリ
There's that word again...
The Count shamelessly visited Lilia when she was injured.
Sir Kain is filled with rage.
In his anger, he forces Lilia to the ground.
SMIRK
ニヤッ
What!? Forces her to...?
And so.
PLOP
トスッ
For mission number sixteen...

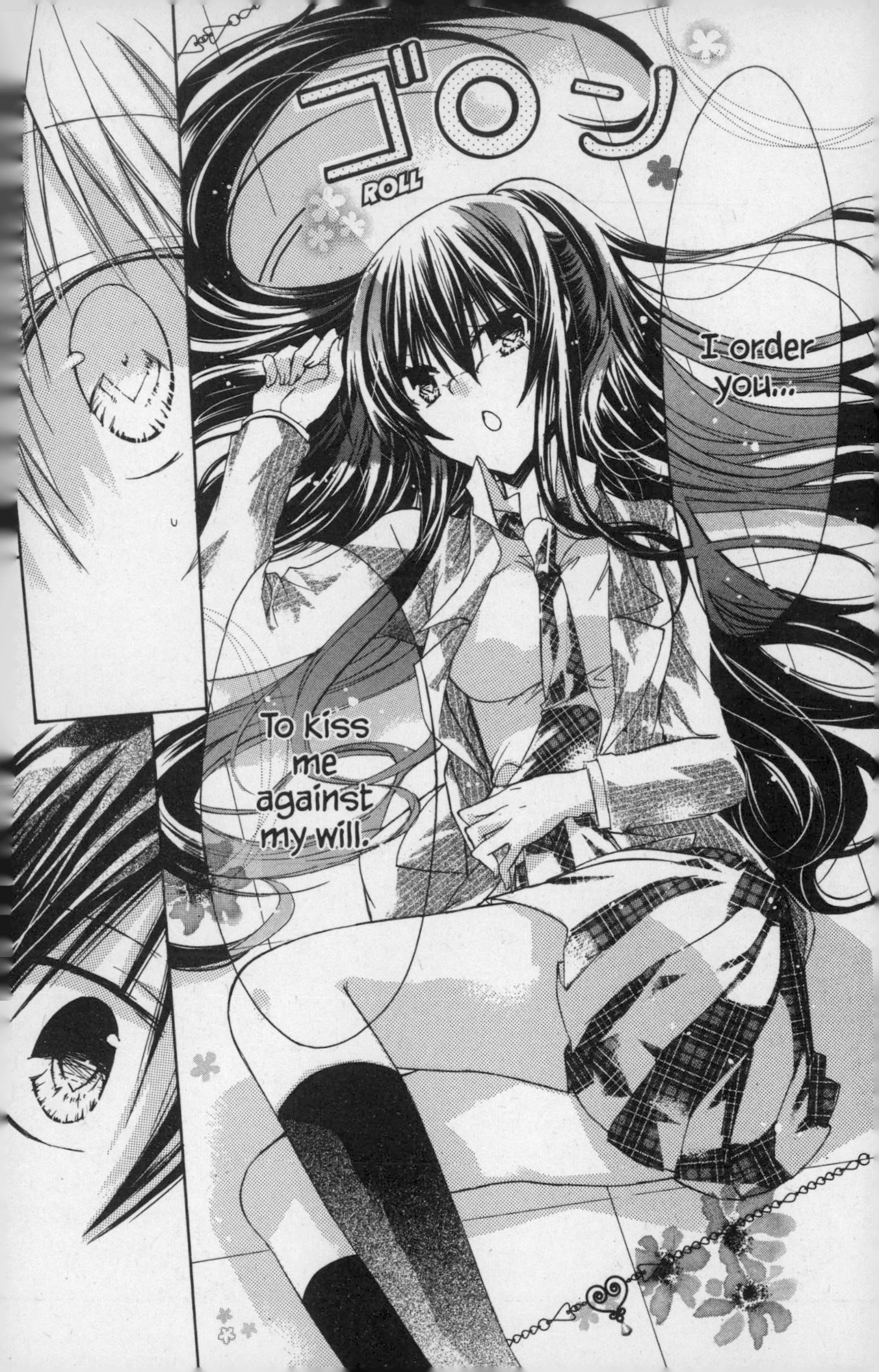
ゴローン
ROLL
I order you...
To kiss me against my will.

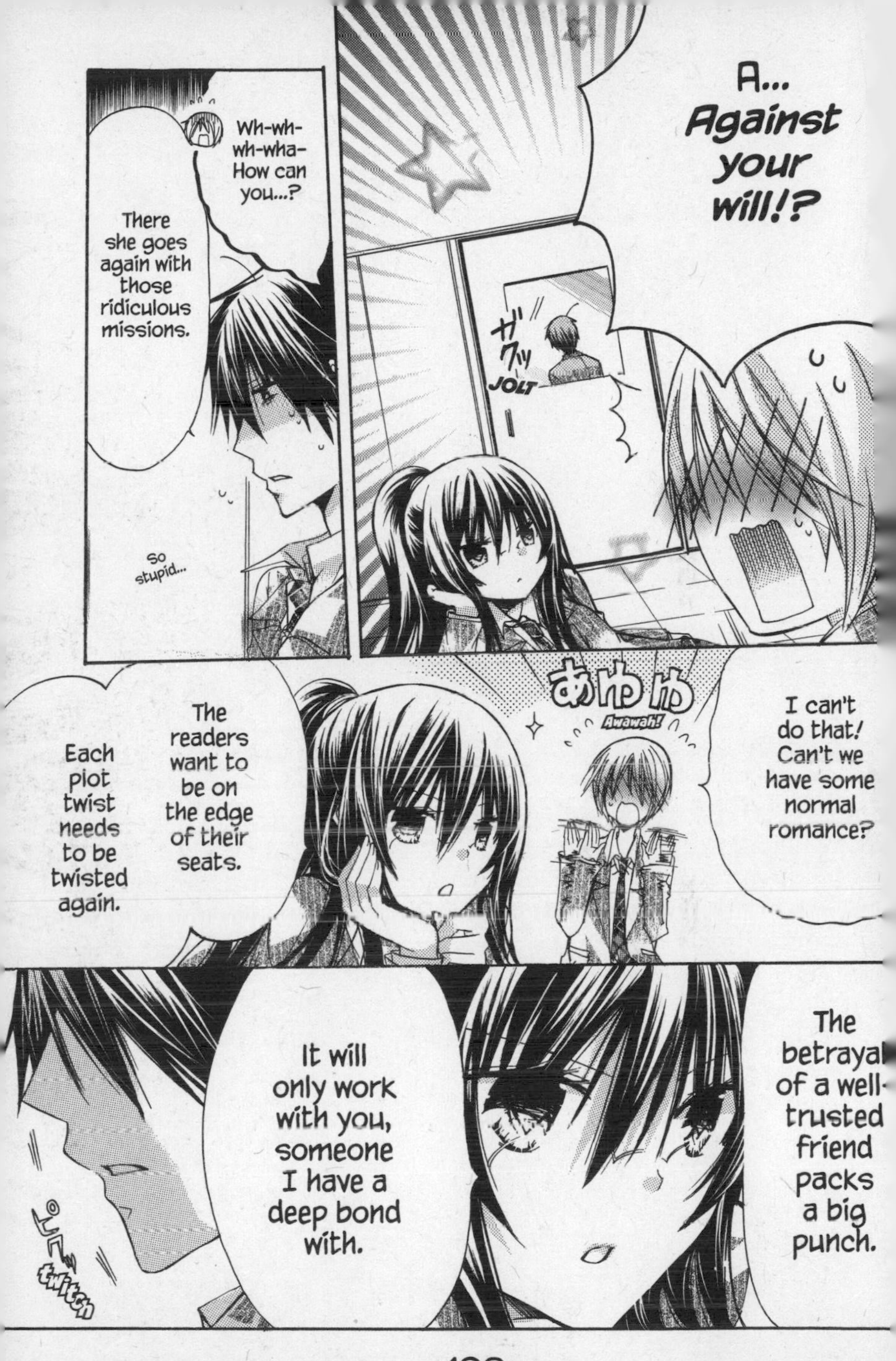
A... Against your will!?
ガクッ
JOLT
Wh-wh-wh-wha- How can you...?
There she goes again with those ridiculous missions.
So stupid...
I can't do that! Can't we have some normal romance?
あゆゆ
Awawah!
The readers want to be on the edge of their seats.
Each plot twist needs to be twisted again.
The betrayal of a well-trusted friend packs a big punch.
It will only work with you, someone I have a deep bond with.
ぴくっ
twitch

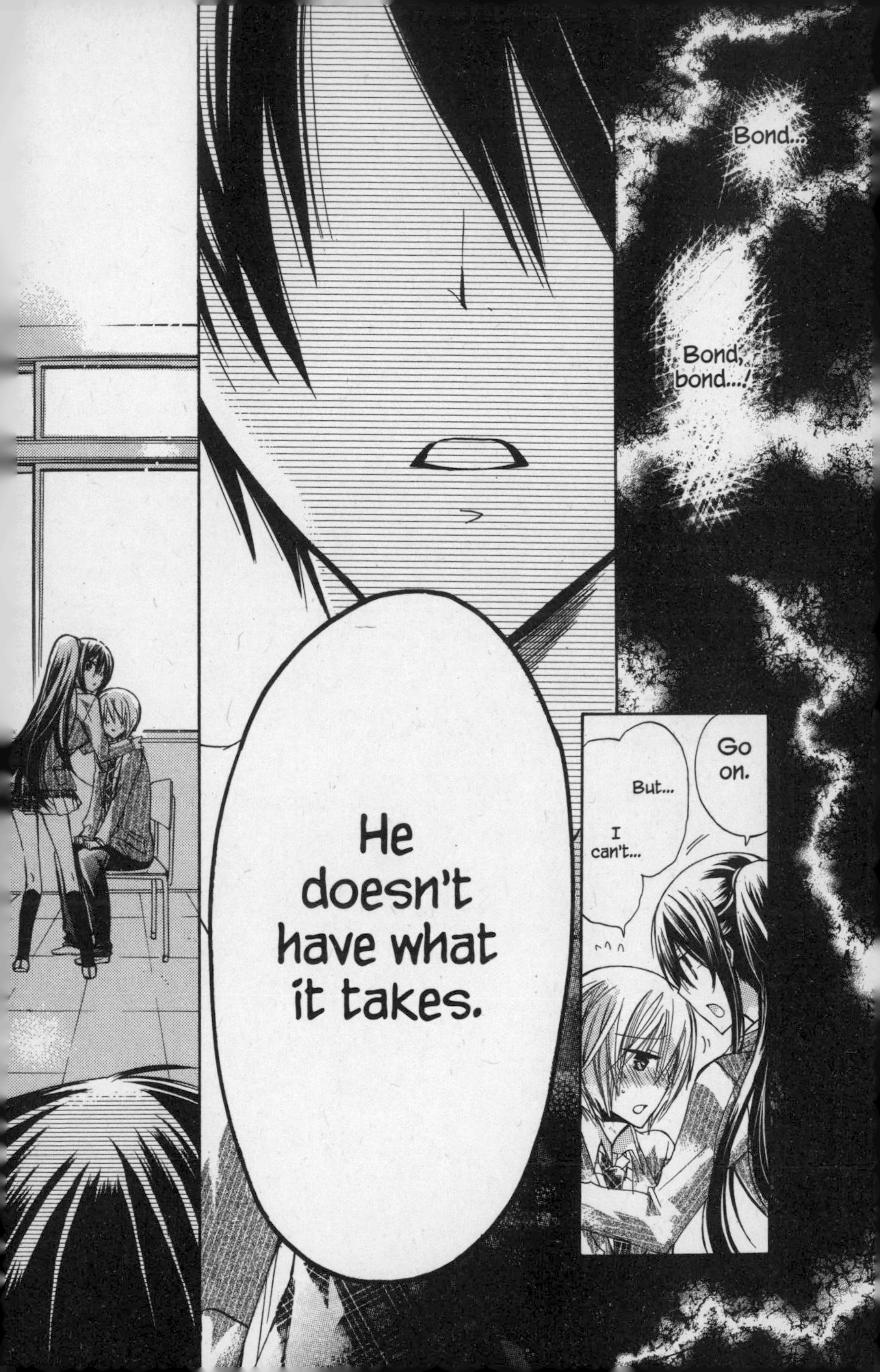
Bond...
Bond, bond...!
Go on.
But...
I can't...
He doesn't have what it takes.

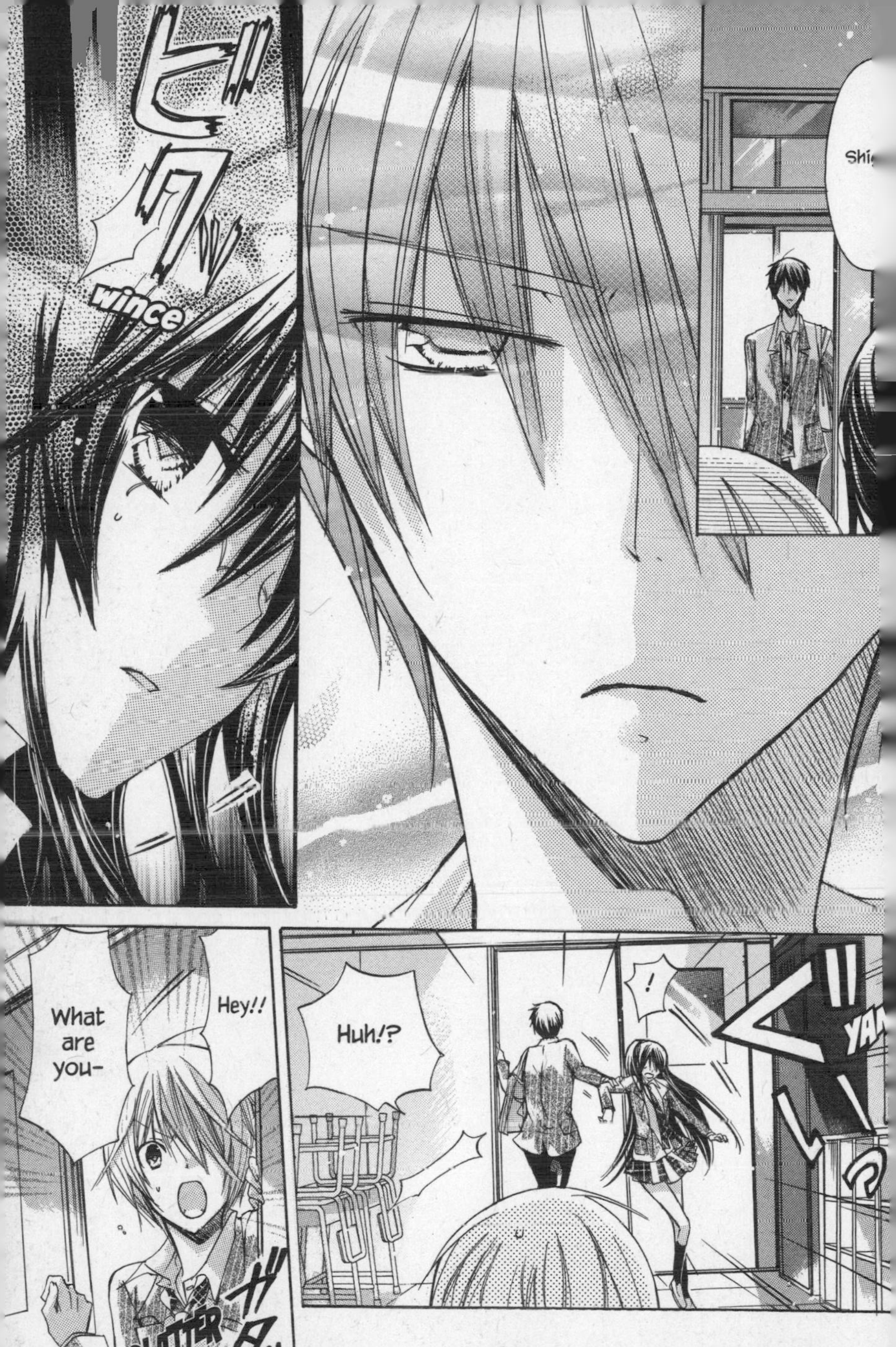
Shi
wince
!
YAM
Huh!?
Hey!!
What are you-
CLATTER

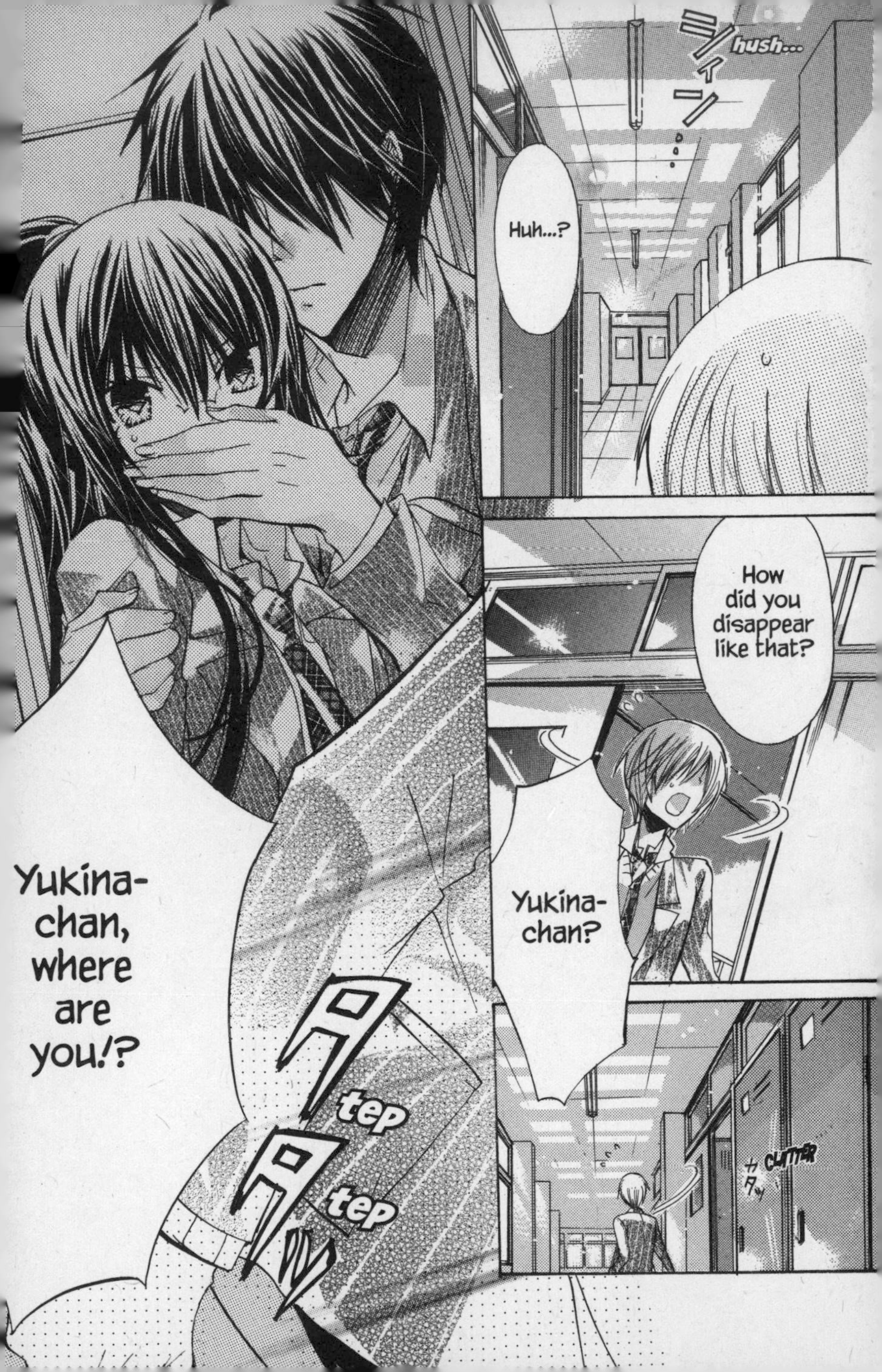
hush...
Huh...?
How did you disappear like that?
Yukina-chan?
CLUTTER
Yukina-chan, where are you!?
tep
tep

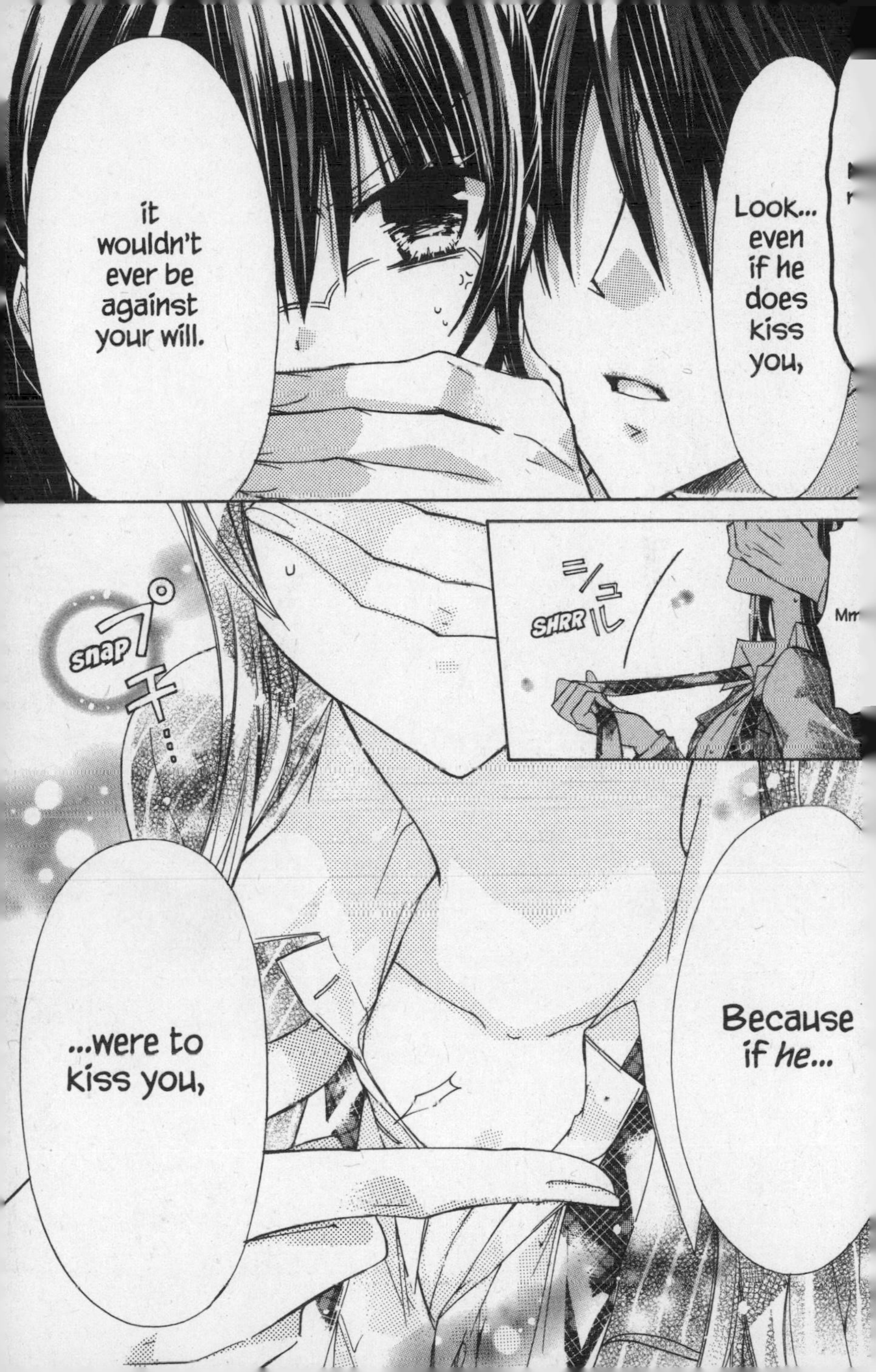
Look... even if he does kiss you,
it wouldn't ever be against your will.
Mrr
シュル
SHRR
プチ...
snap
Because if *he*...
...were to kiss you,

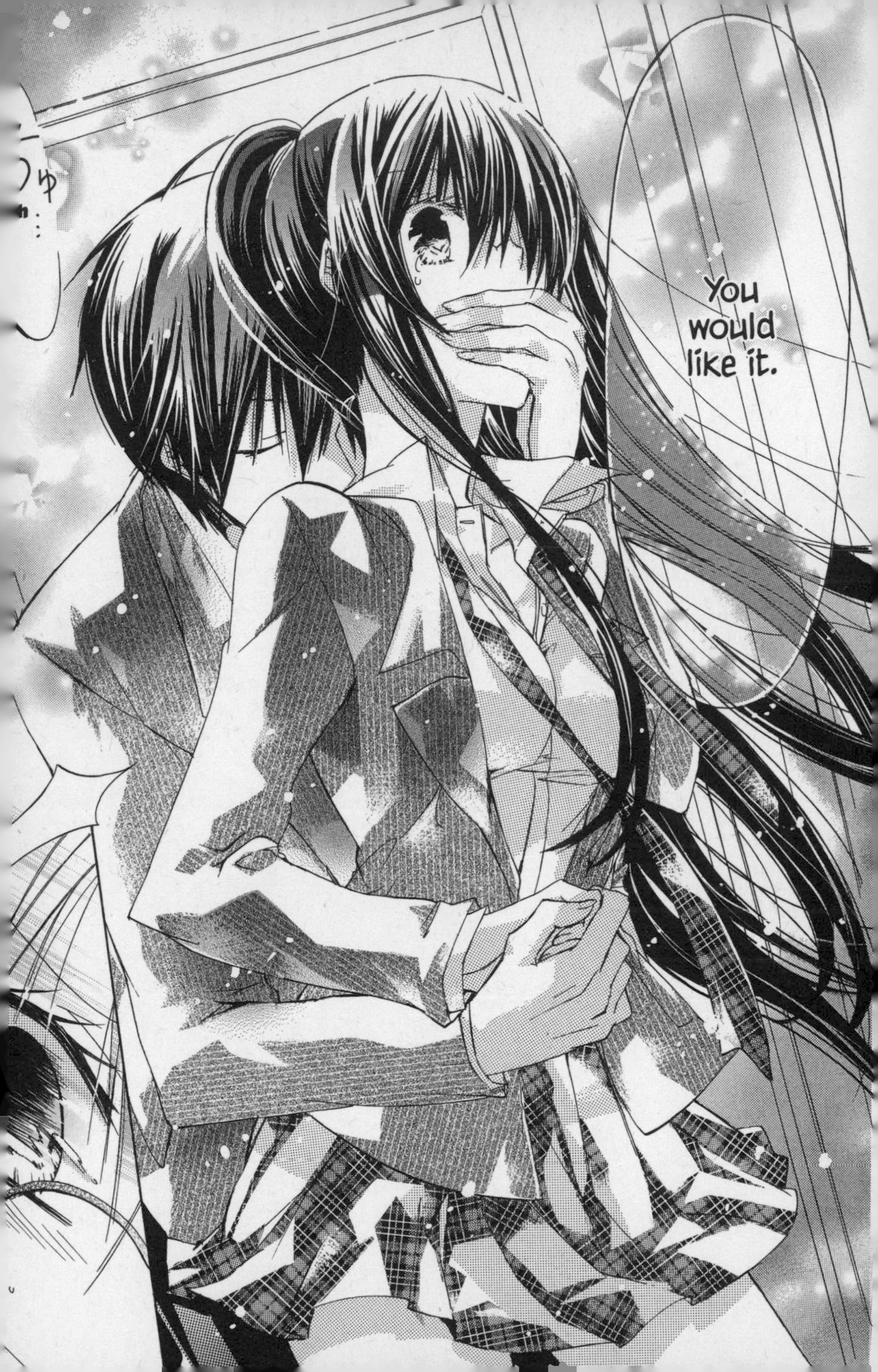
You would like it.

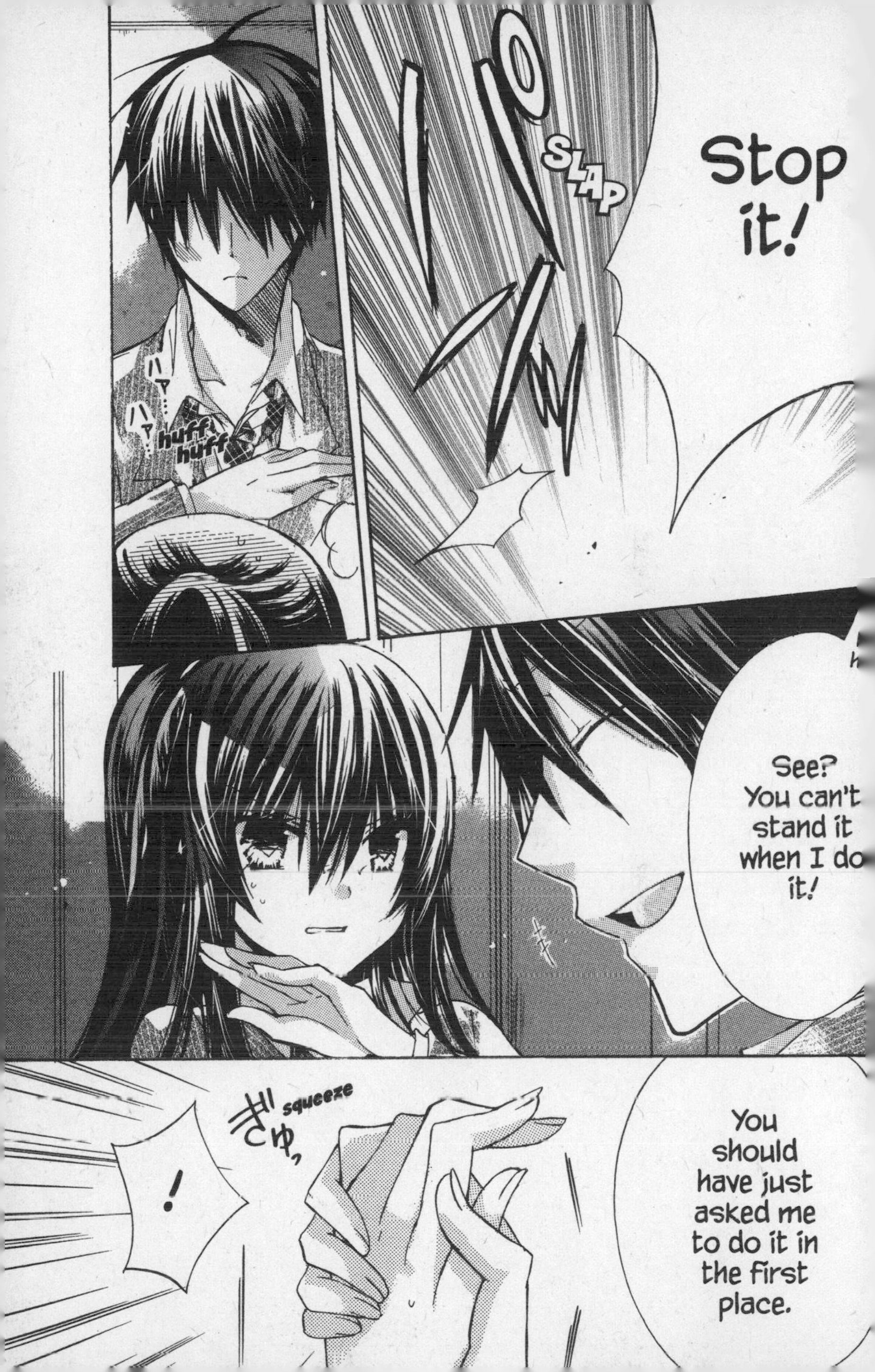
SLAP
Stop it!
ハァ… ハァ…
huff huff
See? You can't stand it when I do it!
You should have just asked me to do it in the first place.
!
ぎゅっ
squeeze

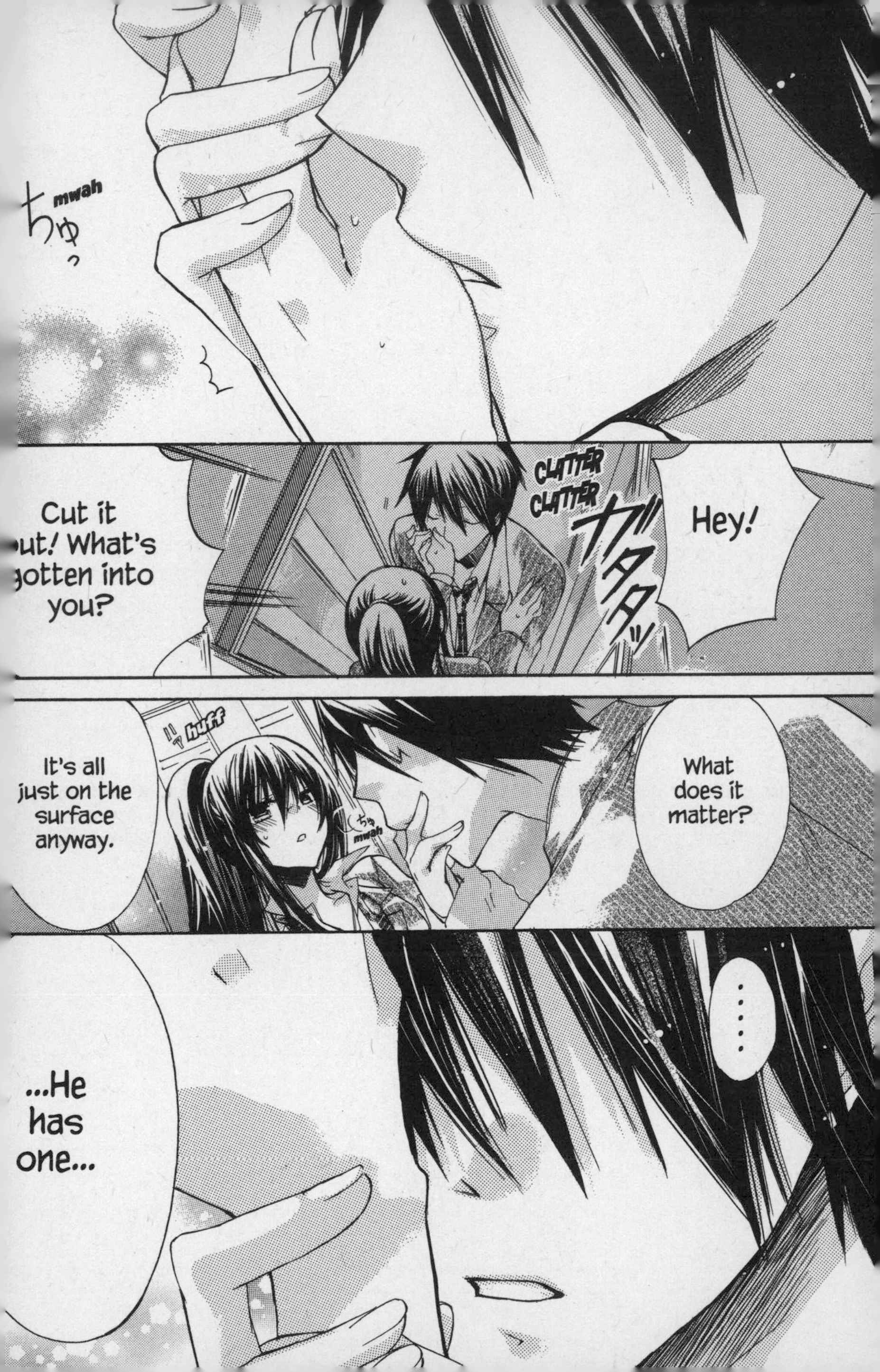
ちゅっ
mwah
Hey!
CLATTER CLATTER
ガダダッ
Cut it out! What's gotten into you?
What does it matter?
ハァ
huff
ちゅ
mwah
It's all just on the surface anyway.
......
...He has one...

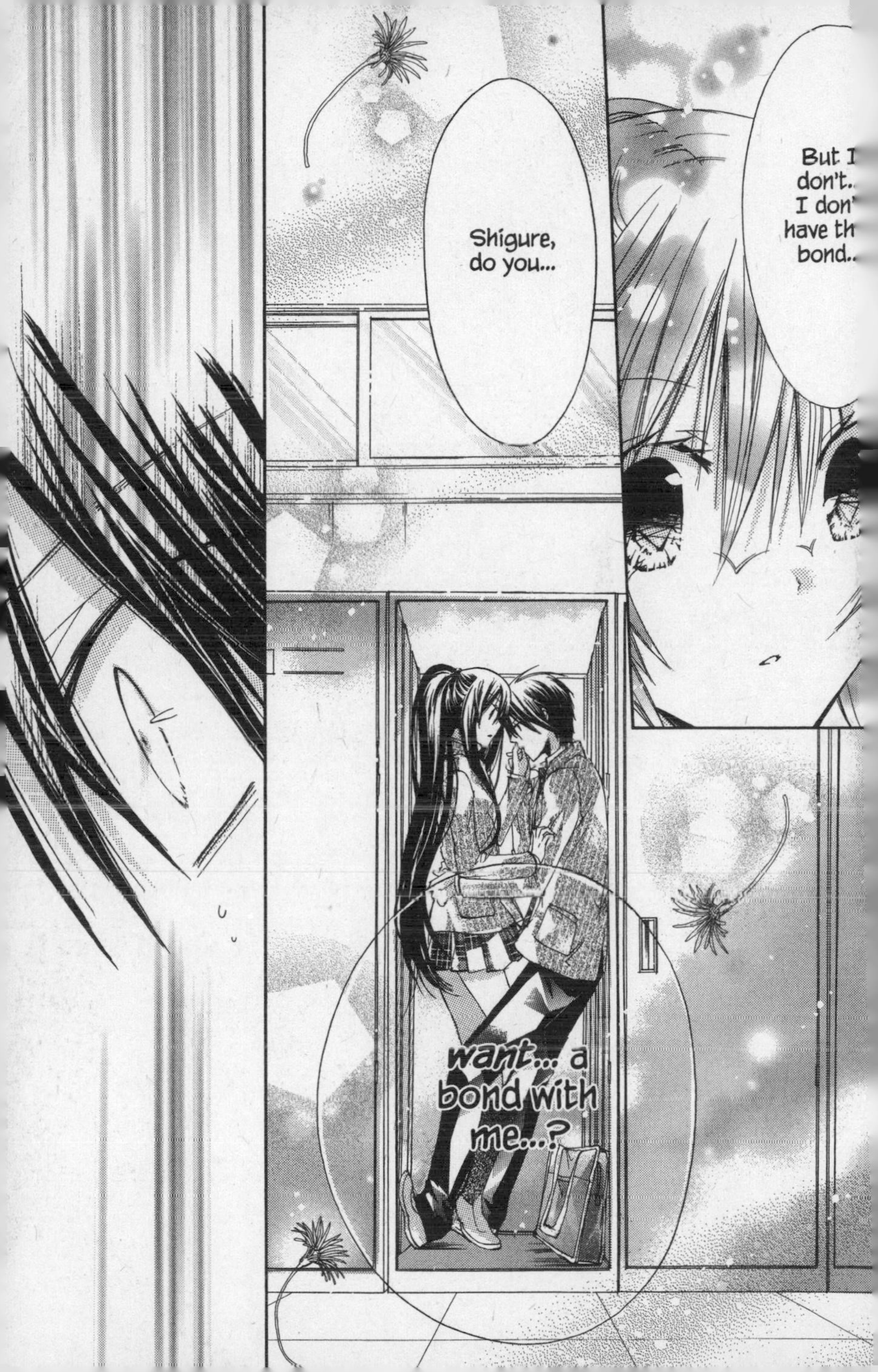
But I don't.. I don' have th bond..
Shigure, do you...
want... a bond with me...?

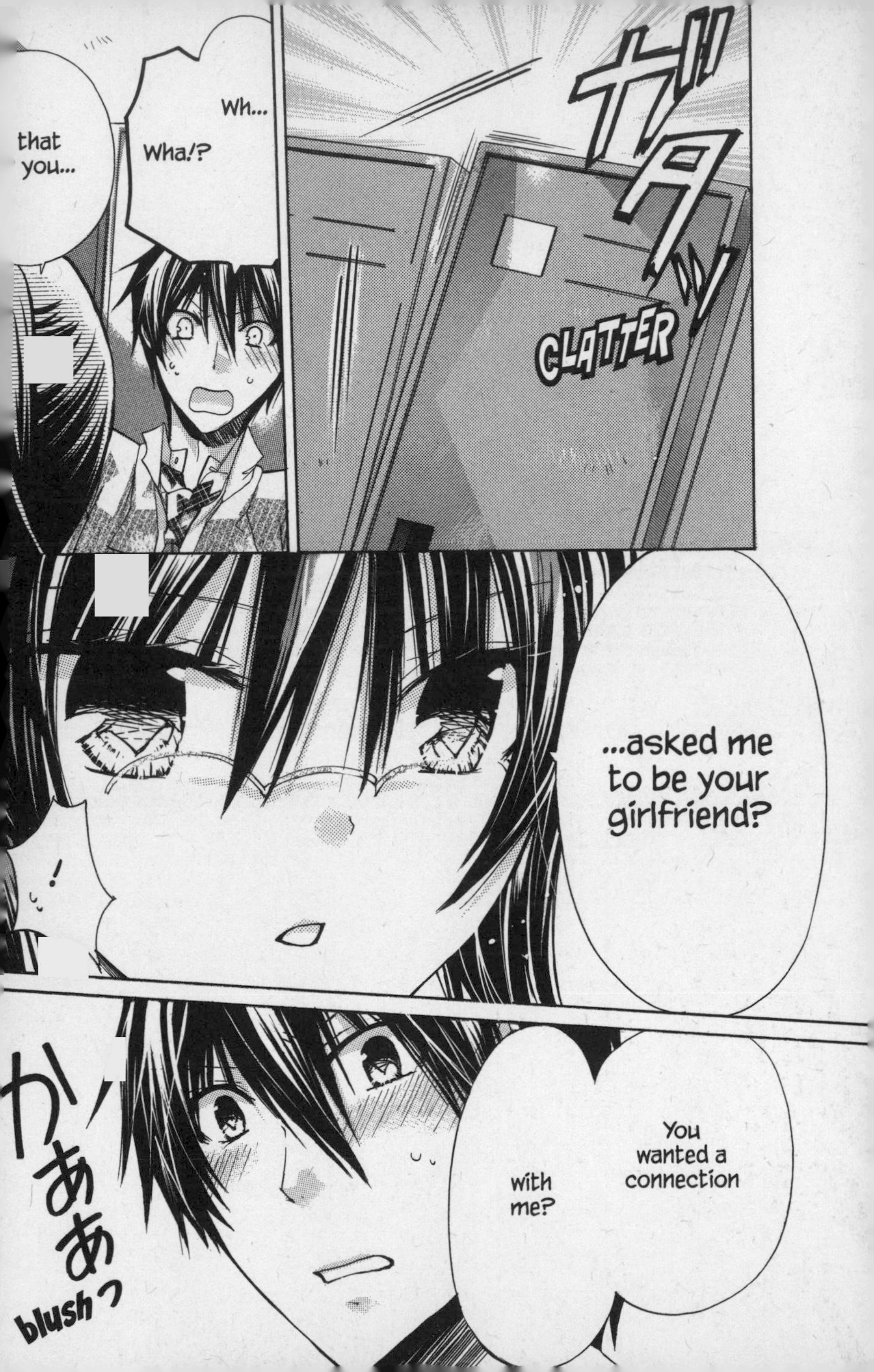
ガタッ
CLATTER
Wh... Wha!?
that you...
...asked me to be your girlfriend?
You wanted a connection with me?
かあぁっ
blush

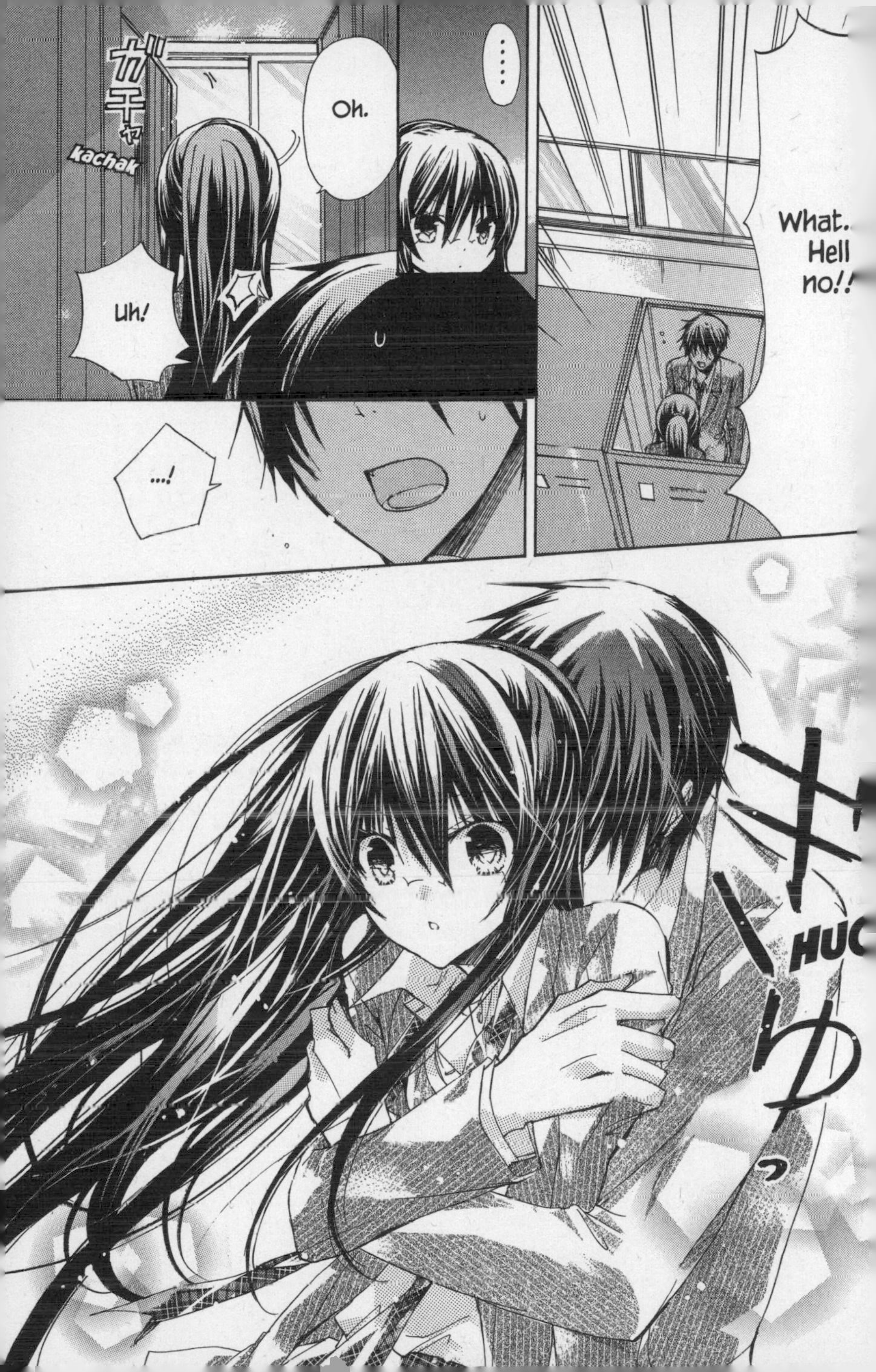
What..
Hell
no!!
......
Oh.
ガチャ
kachak
Uh!
...!
ギュッ
HUG

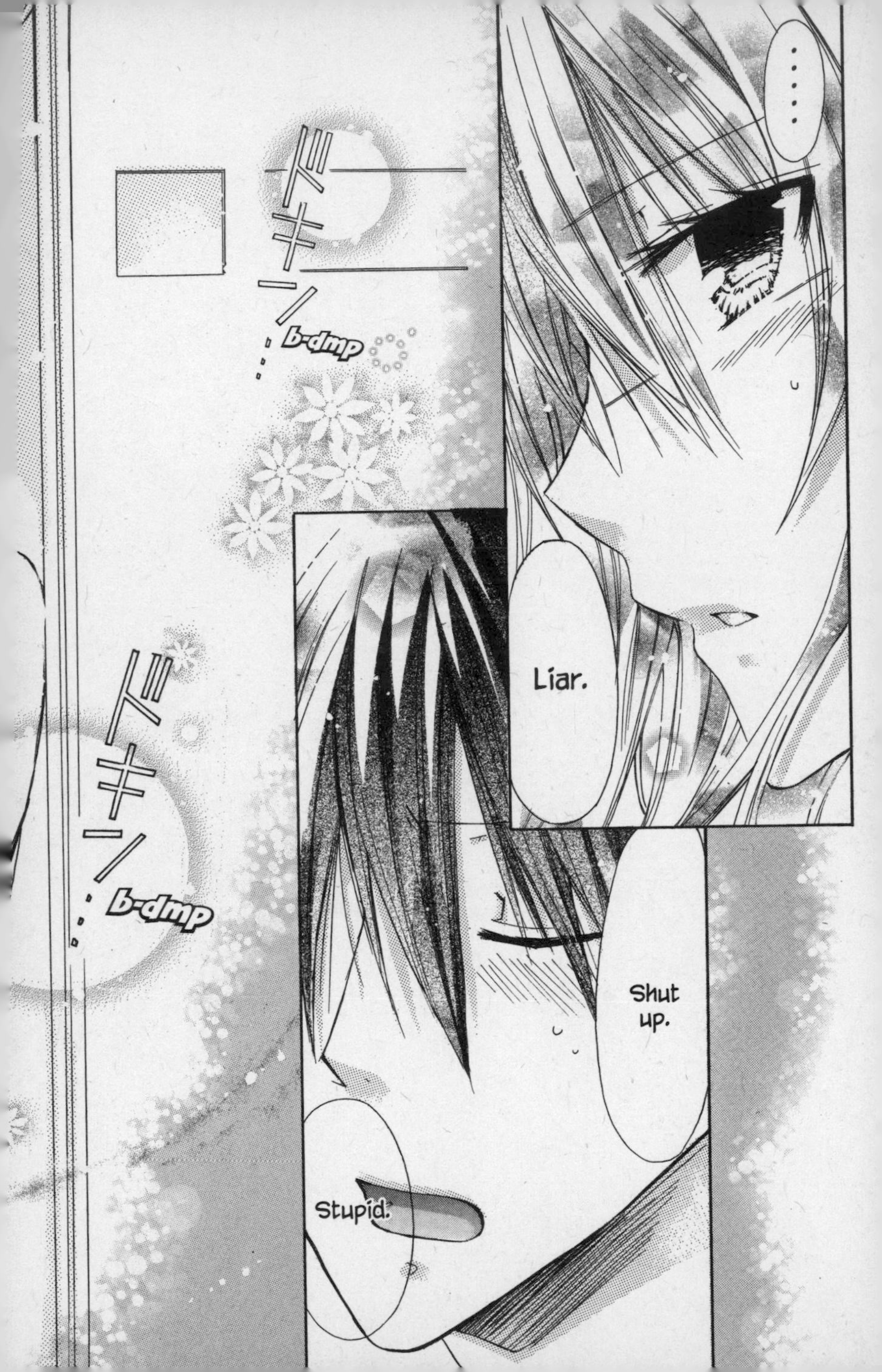
....
Liar.
Shut up.
Stupid.
b-dmp
b-dmp

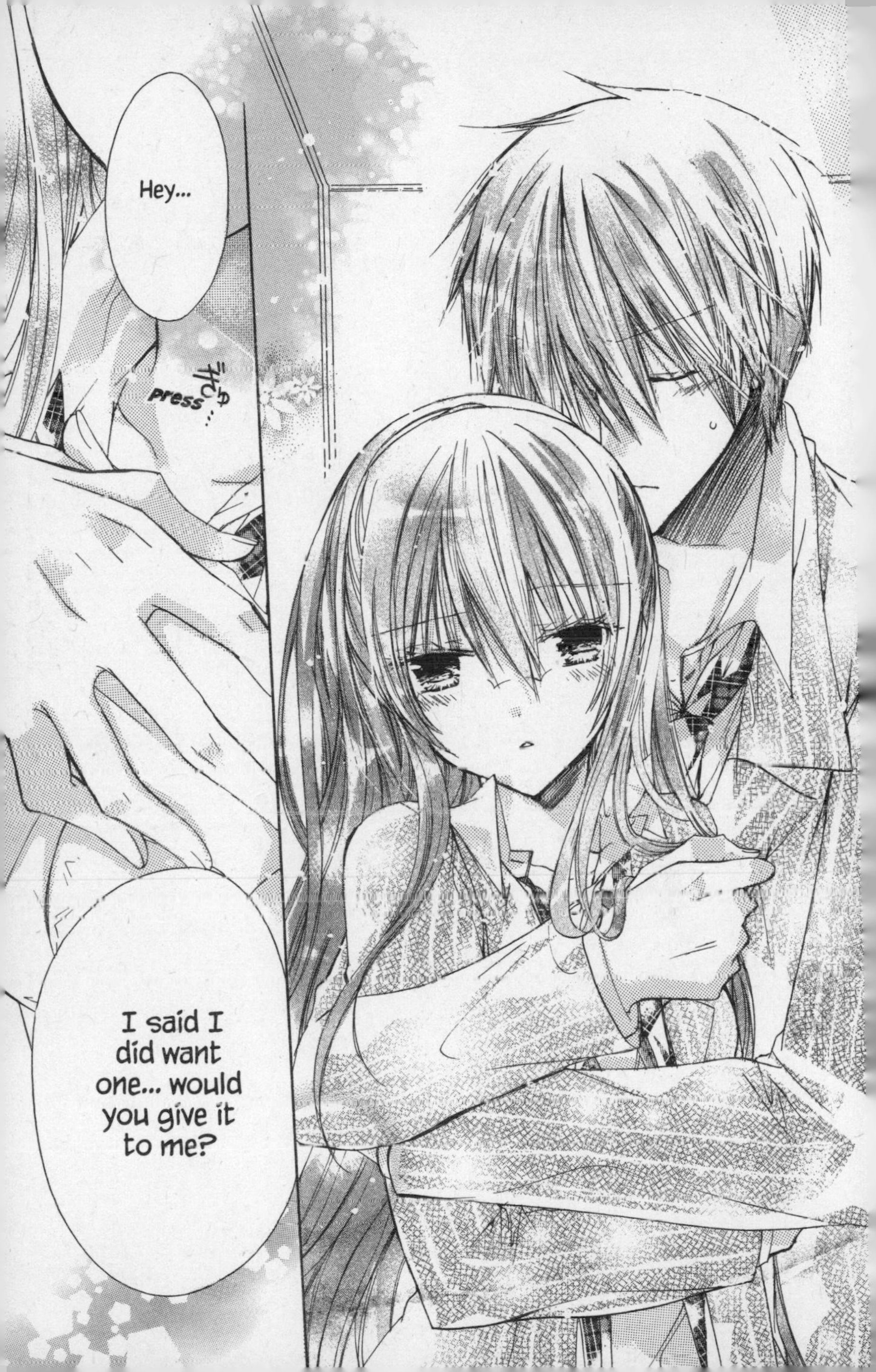
Hey...
press...
I said I did want one... would you give it to me?

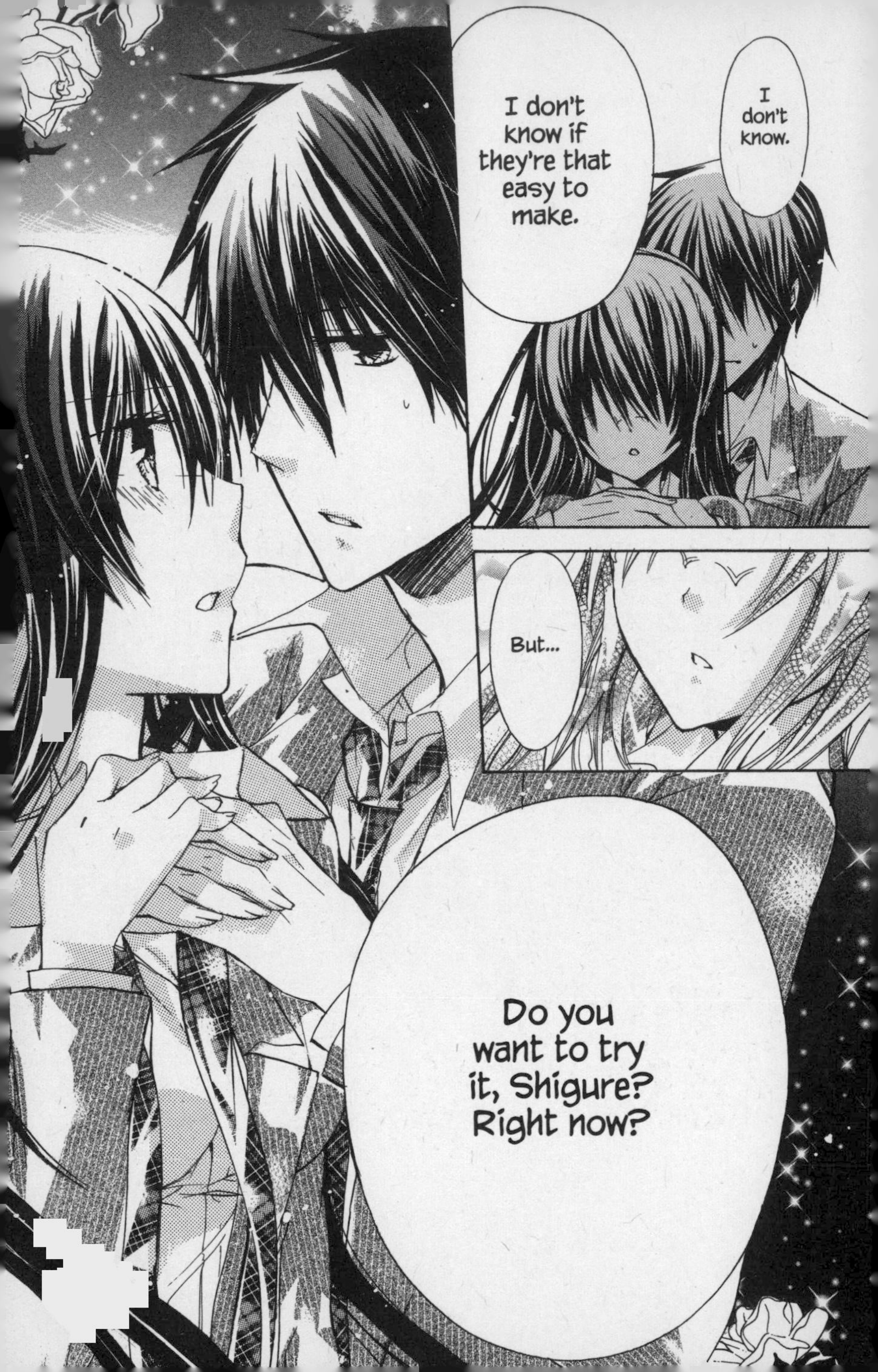
I don't know.
I don't know if they're that easy to make.
But...
Do you want to try it, Shigure? Right now?

Missions of Love

It is time for love.
Secret cell phone
novelist vs. the most
popular boy in school.
A mission of love for
absolute servitude.

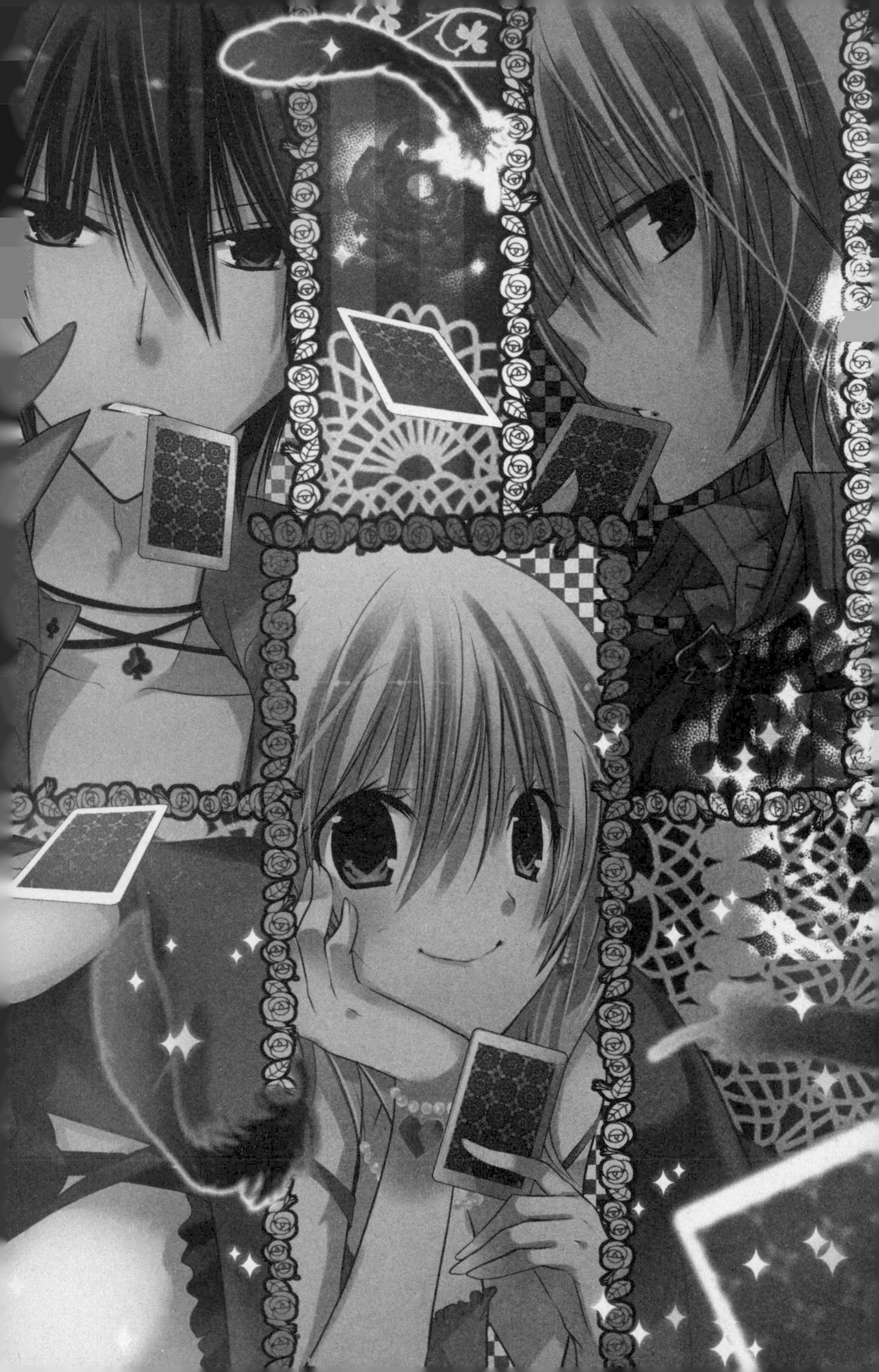

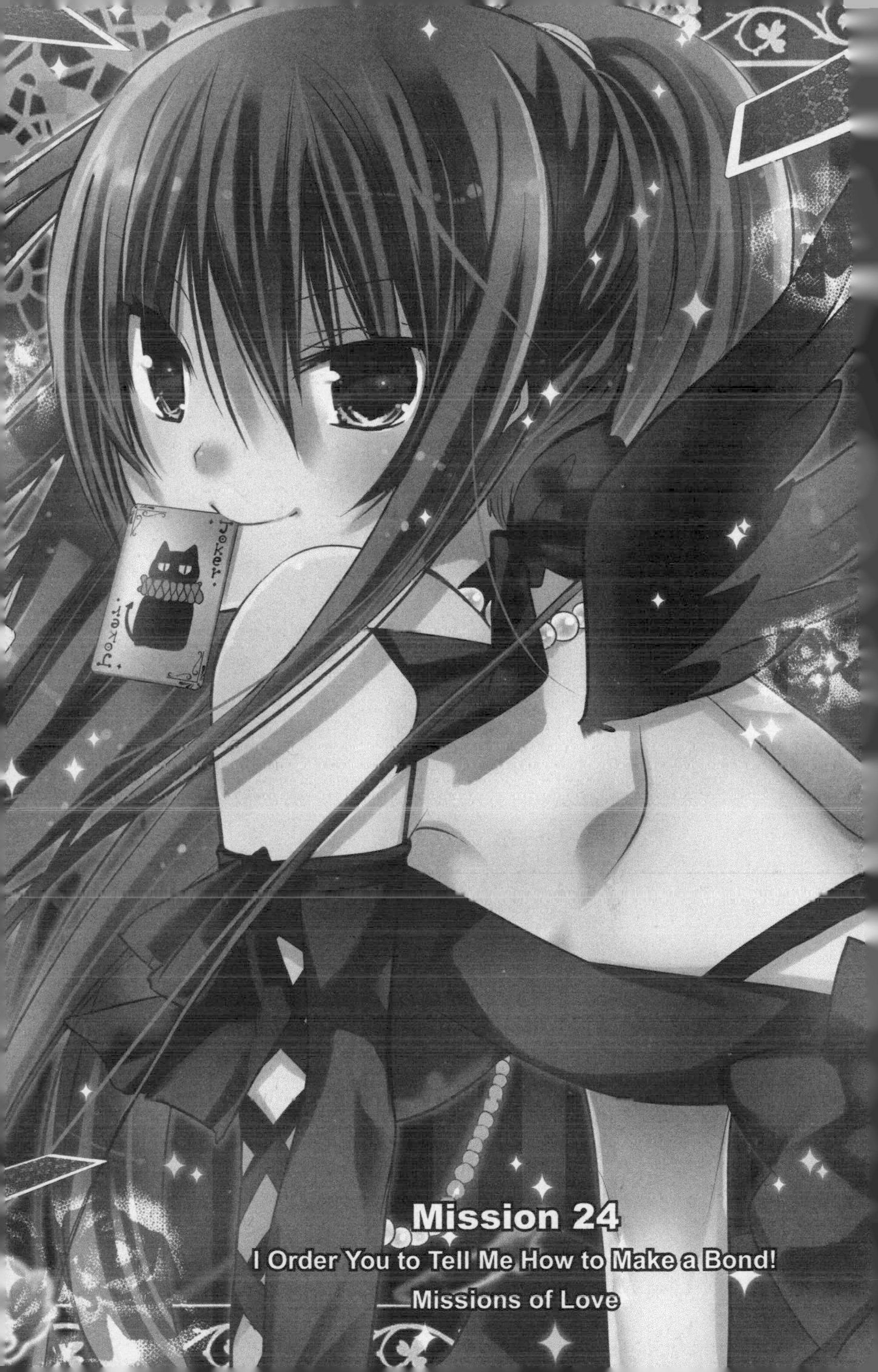
Joker
Joker

Mission 24

I Order You to Tell Me How to Make a Bond!

—Missions of Love

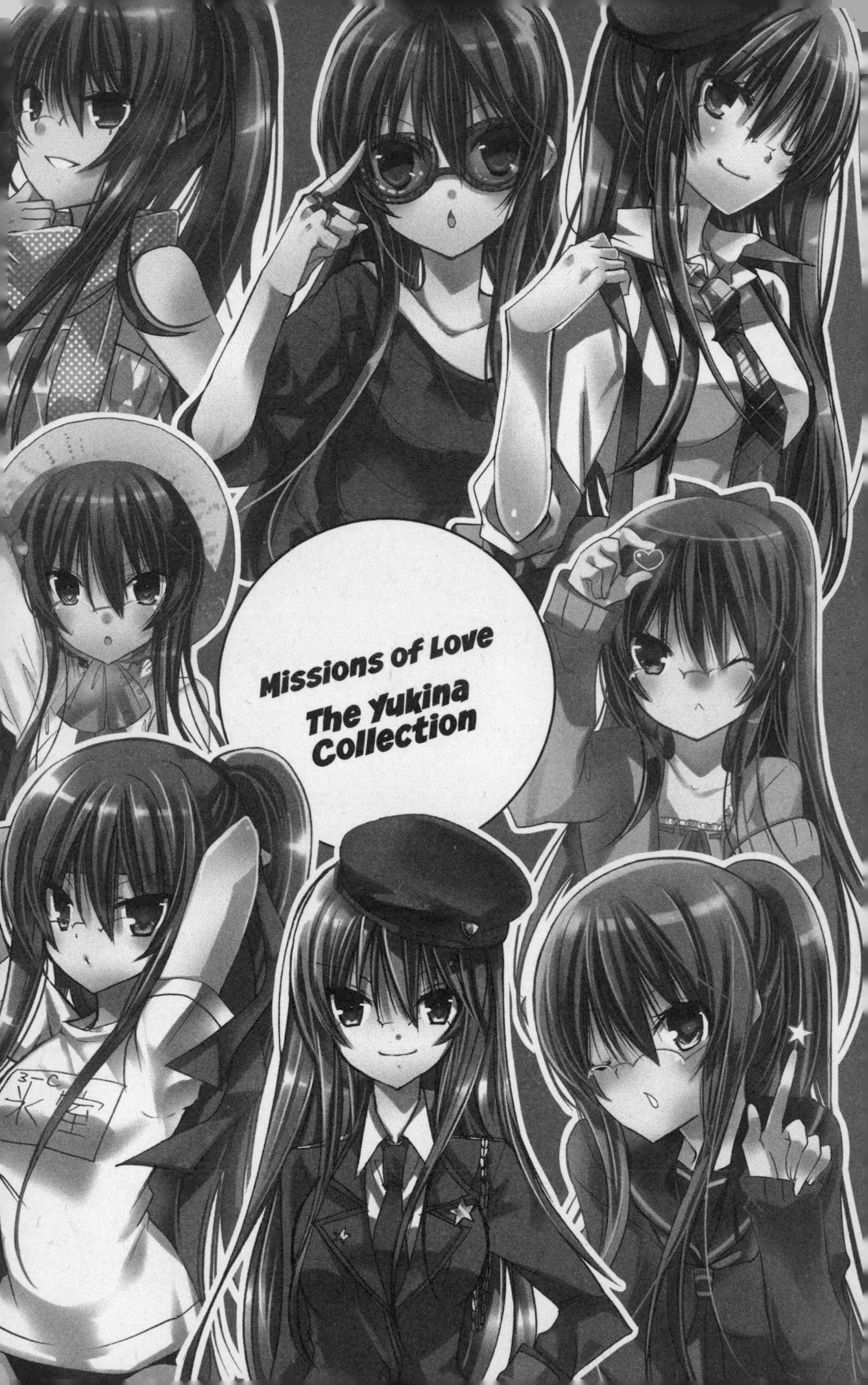
Missions of Love
The Yukina Collection
3-C

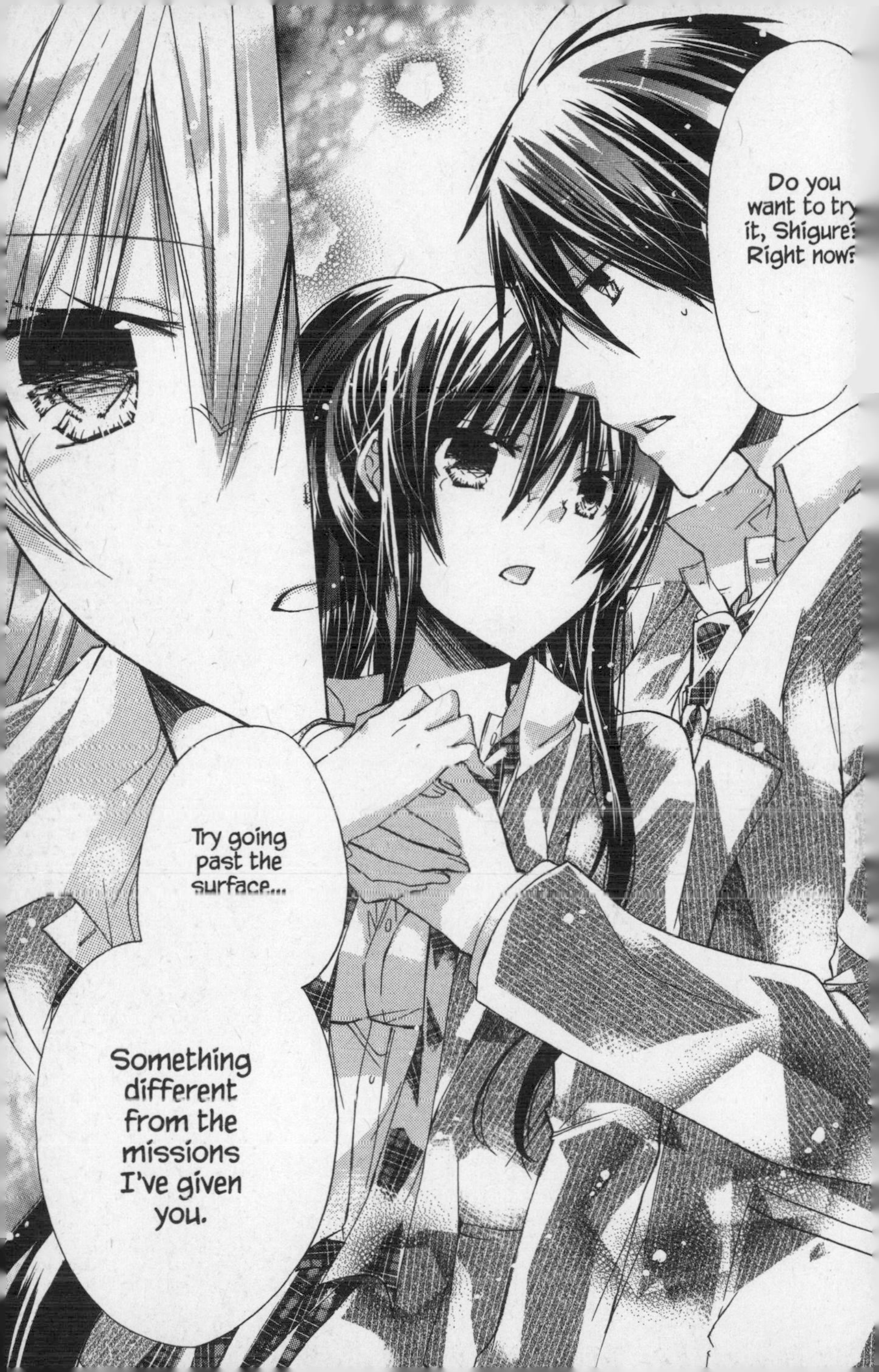
Do you want to try it, Shigure? Right now?
Try going past the surface...
Something different from the missions I've given you.

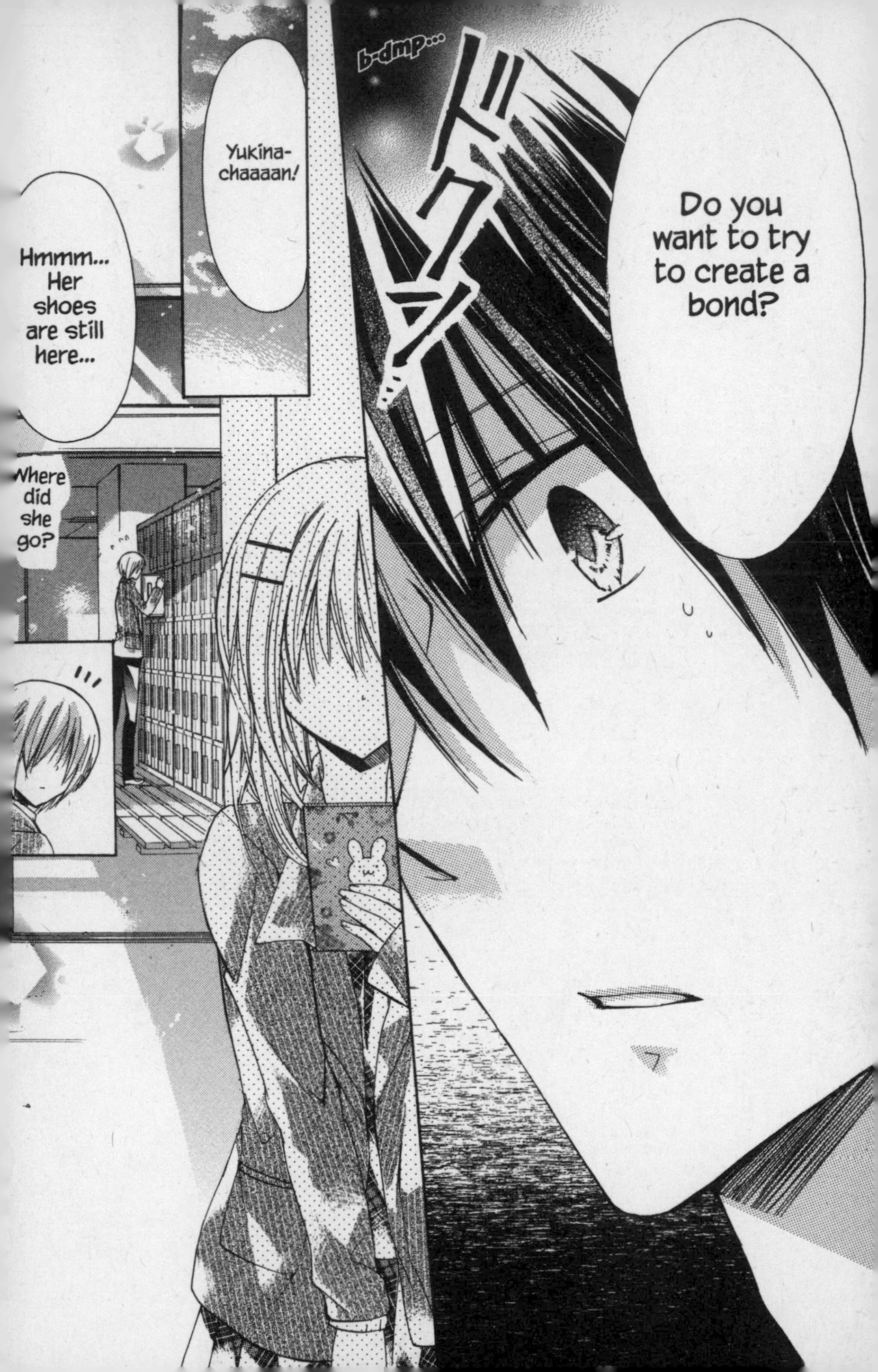
Do you want to try to create a bond?
b-dmp...
Yukina-chaaaan!
Hmmm... Her shoes are still here...
Where did she go?

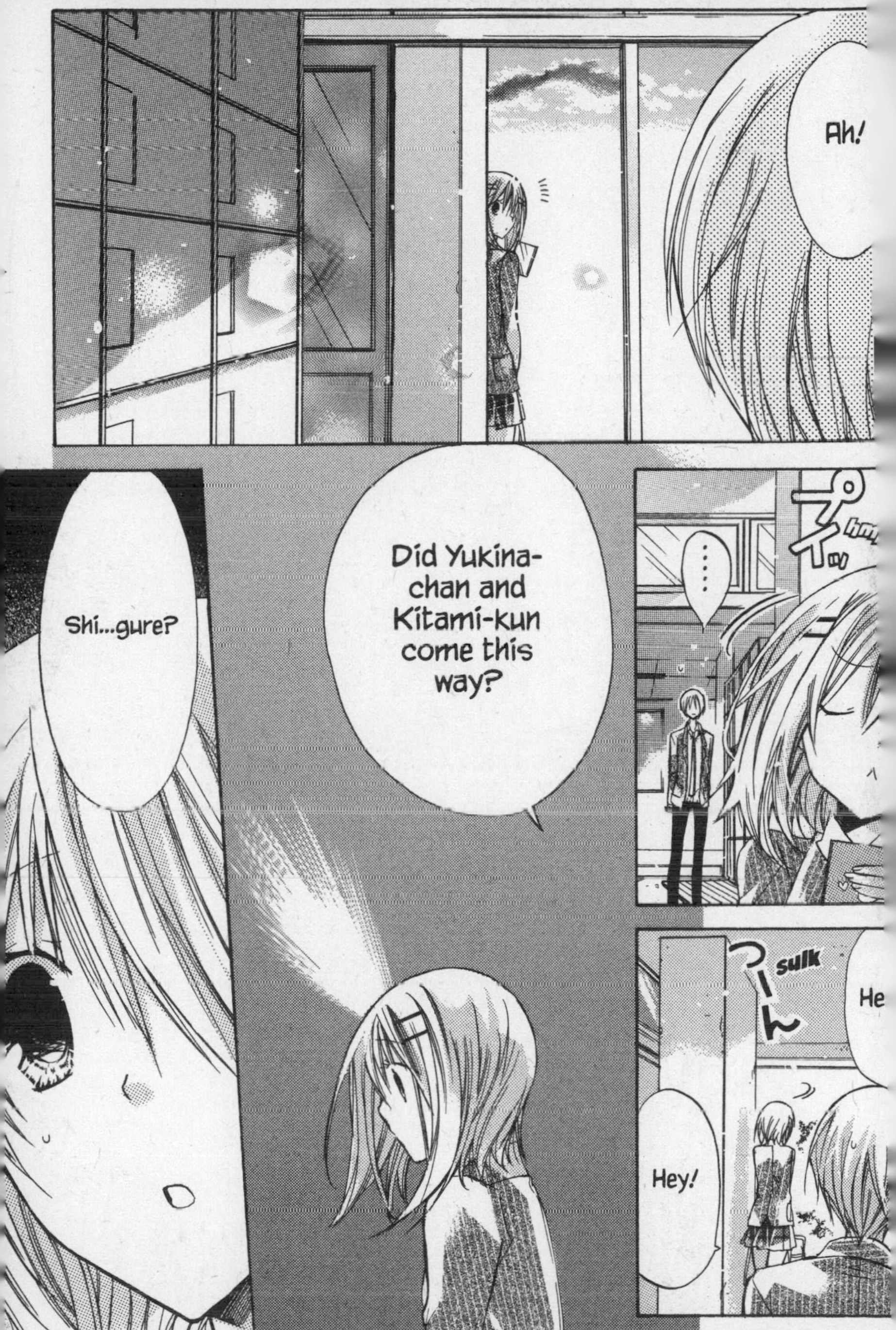
Ah!
.....
hmph
sulk
He
Hey!
Did Yukina-chan and Kitami-kun come this way?
Shi...gure?

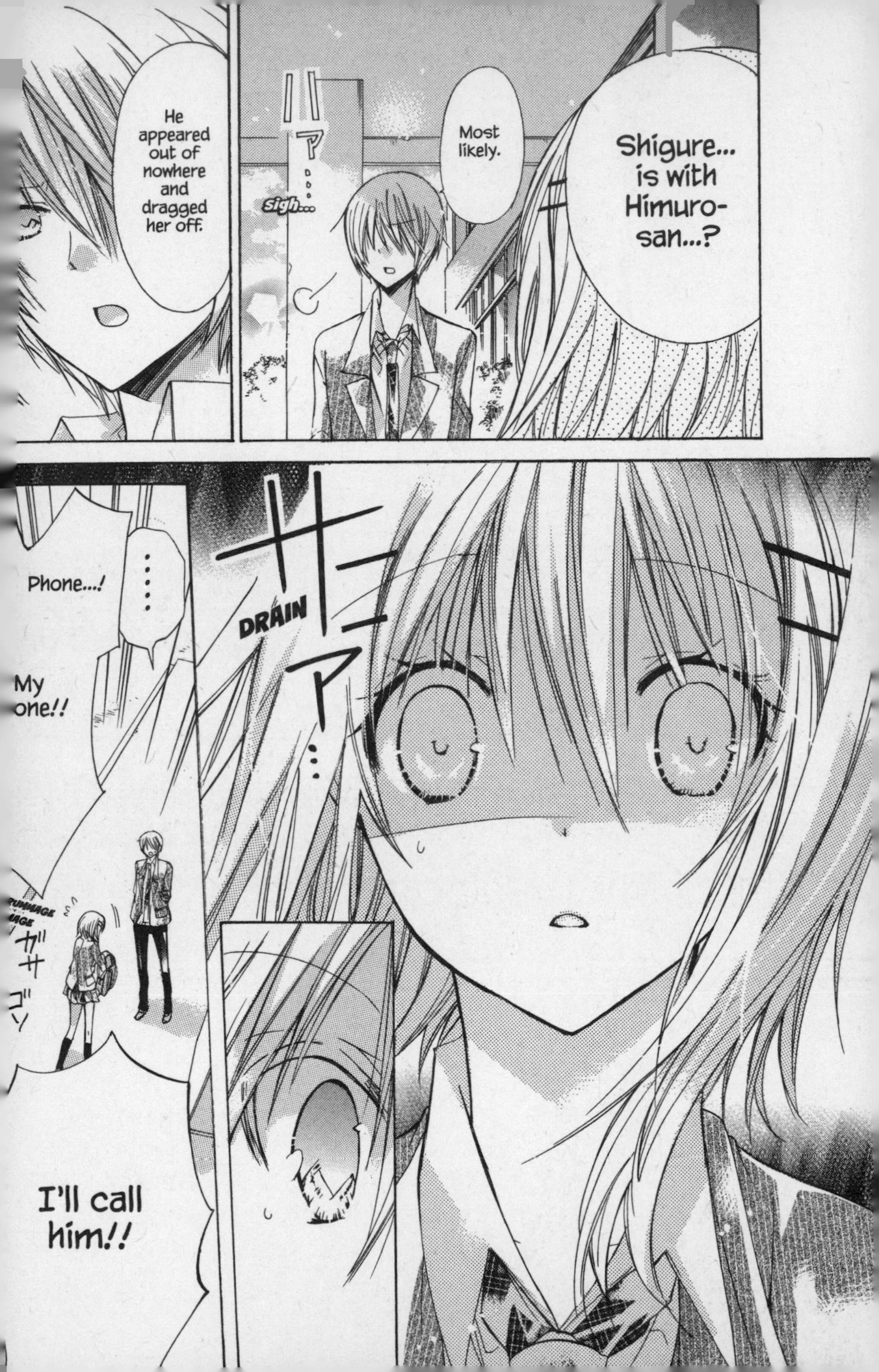

Shigure... is with Himuro-san...?
Most likely.
sigh...
He appeared out of nowhere and dragged her off.
DRAIN
......
Phone...!
My one!!
I'll call him!!

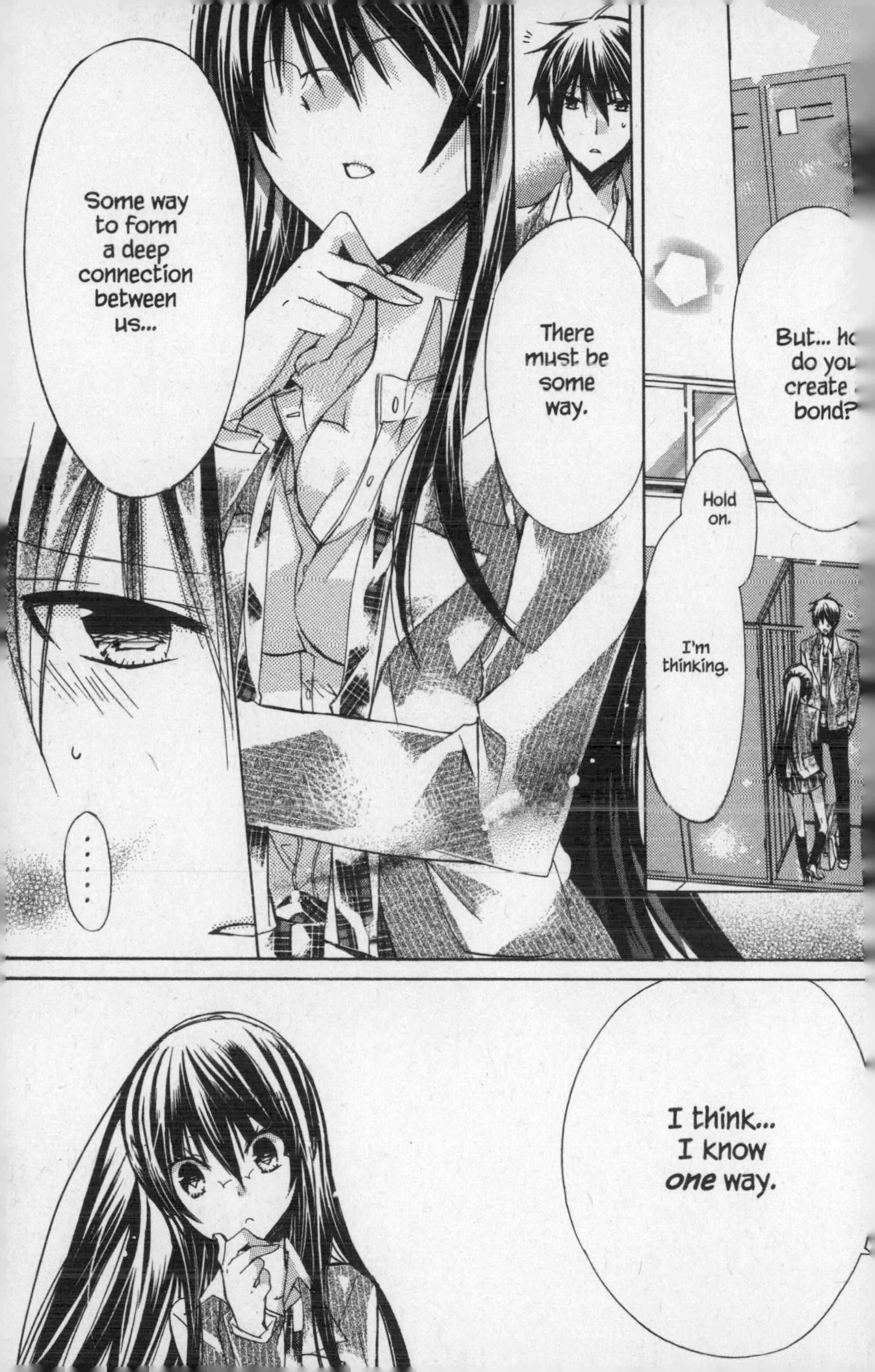
But... ho do you create bond?
Hold on.
I'm thinking.
There must be some way.
Some way to form a deep connection between us...
......
I think... I know *one* way.

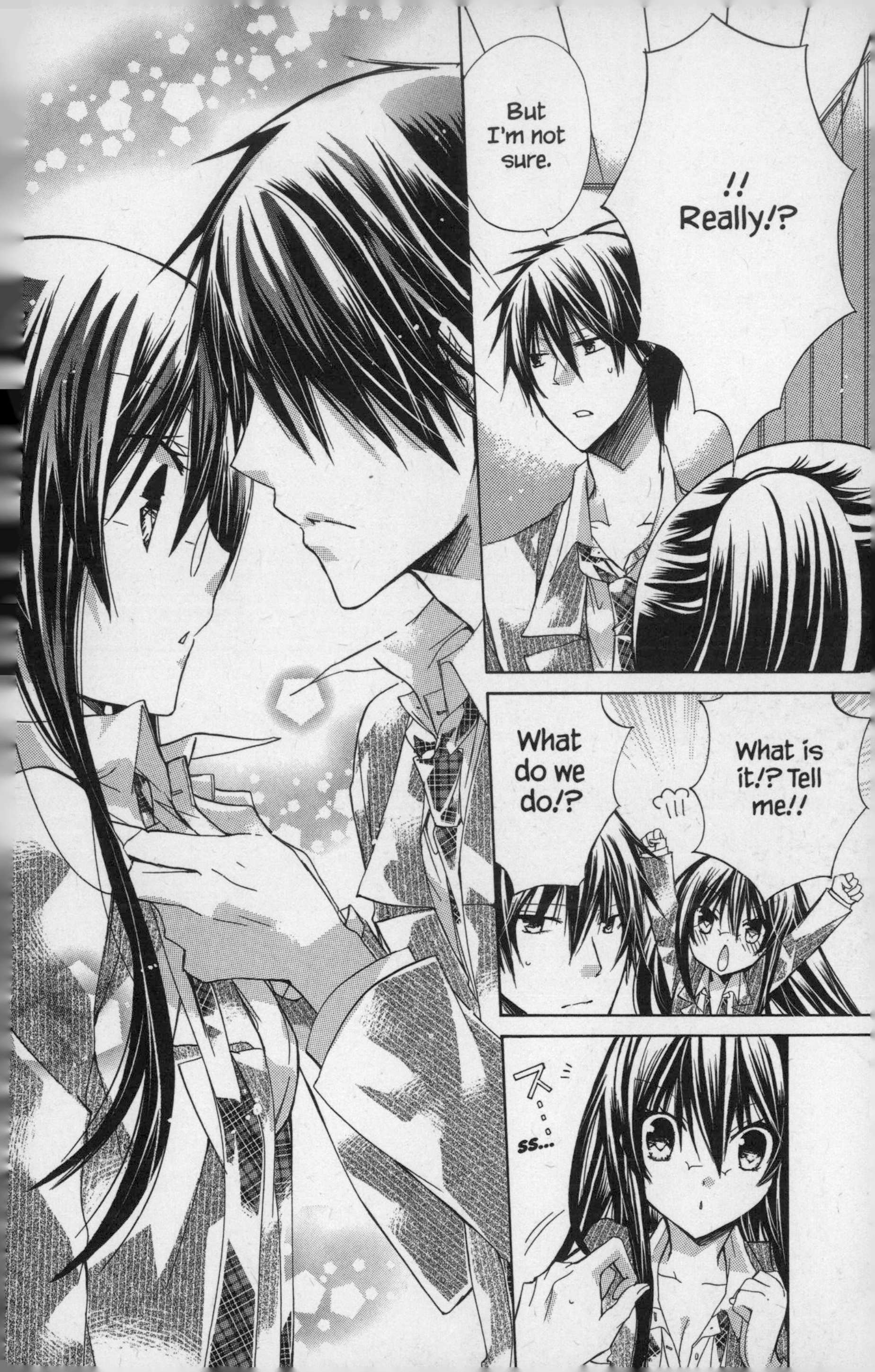
!! Really!?
But I'm not sure.
What is it!? Tell me!!
What do we do!?
ス
ss...

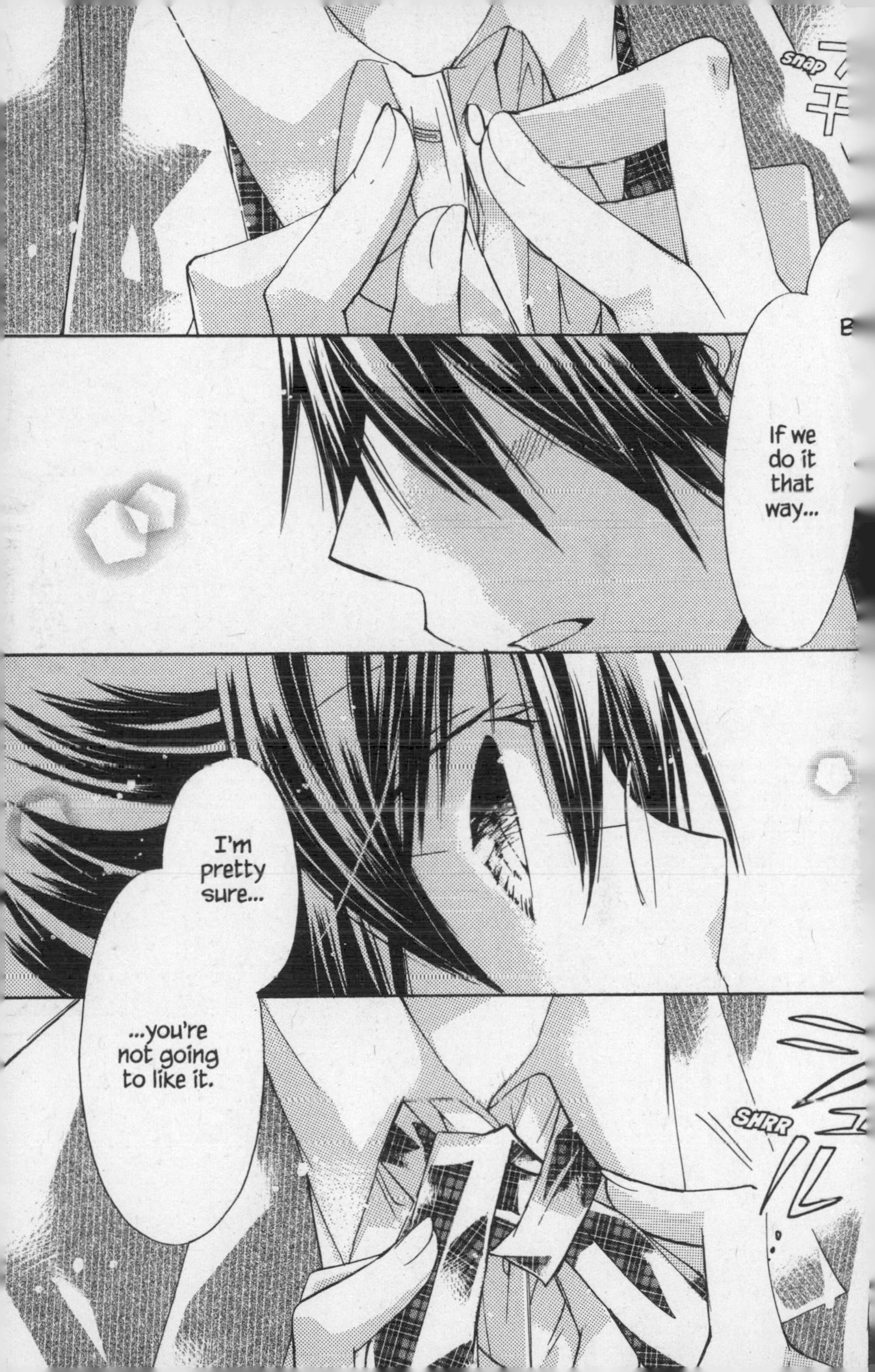
snap
If we do it that way...
I'm pretty sure...
...you're not going to like it.
SHRR

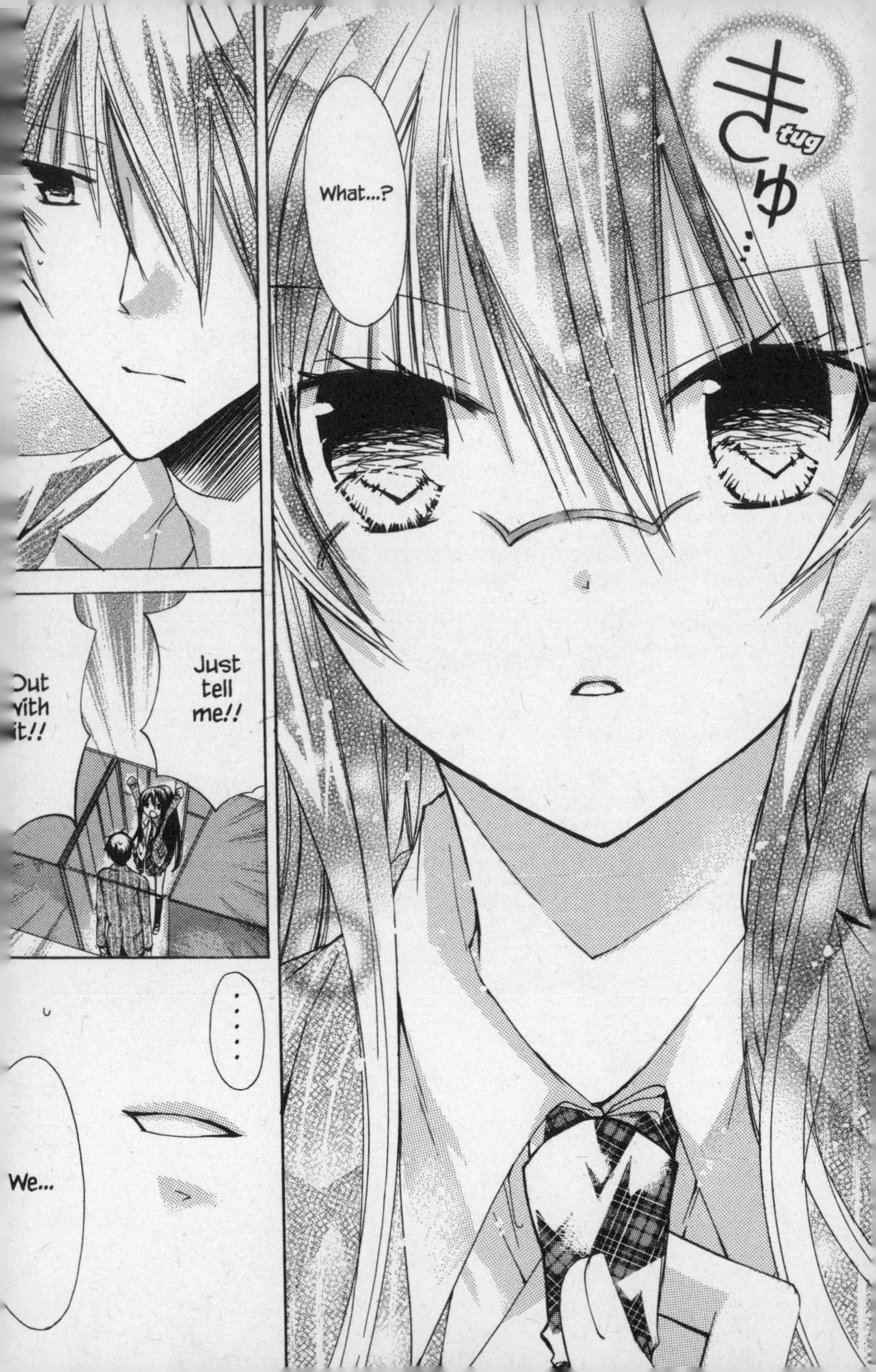
きゅ
tug
What...?
Just tell me!!
Out with it!!
.....
We...

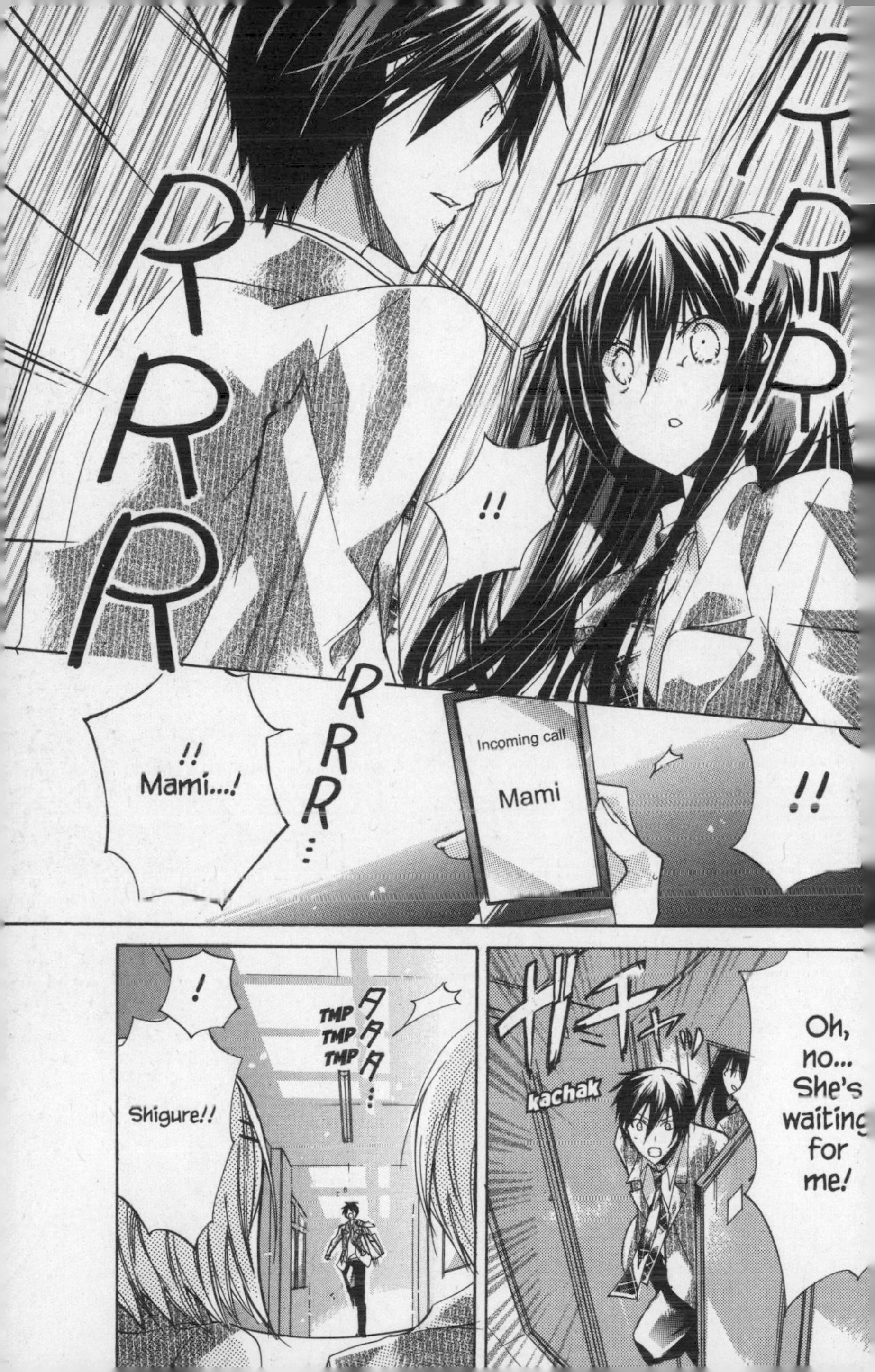
RRR
RRRR
!!
!!
Incoming call
Mami
RRR...
!!
Mami...!
Oh, no... She's waiting for me!
kachak
!
TMP
TMP
TMP
Shigure!!

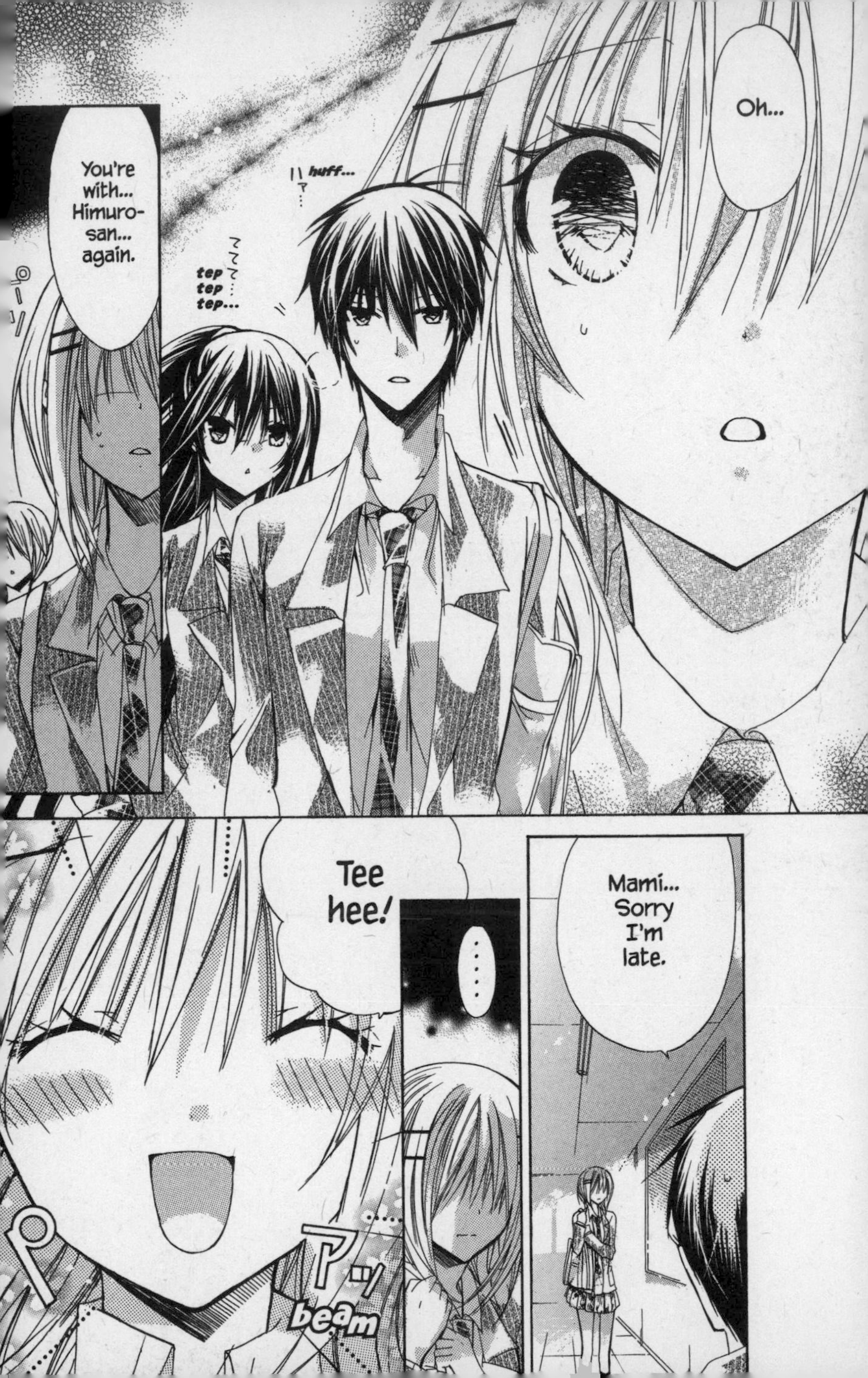

Oh...
huff...
tep
tep
tep...
You're with... Himuro-san... again.
Mami... Sorry I'm late.
......
Tee hee!
beam

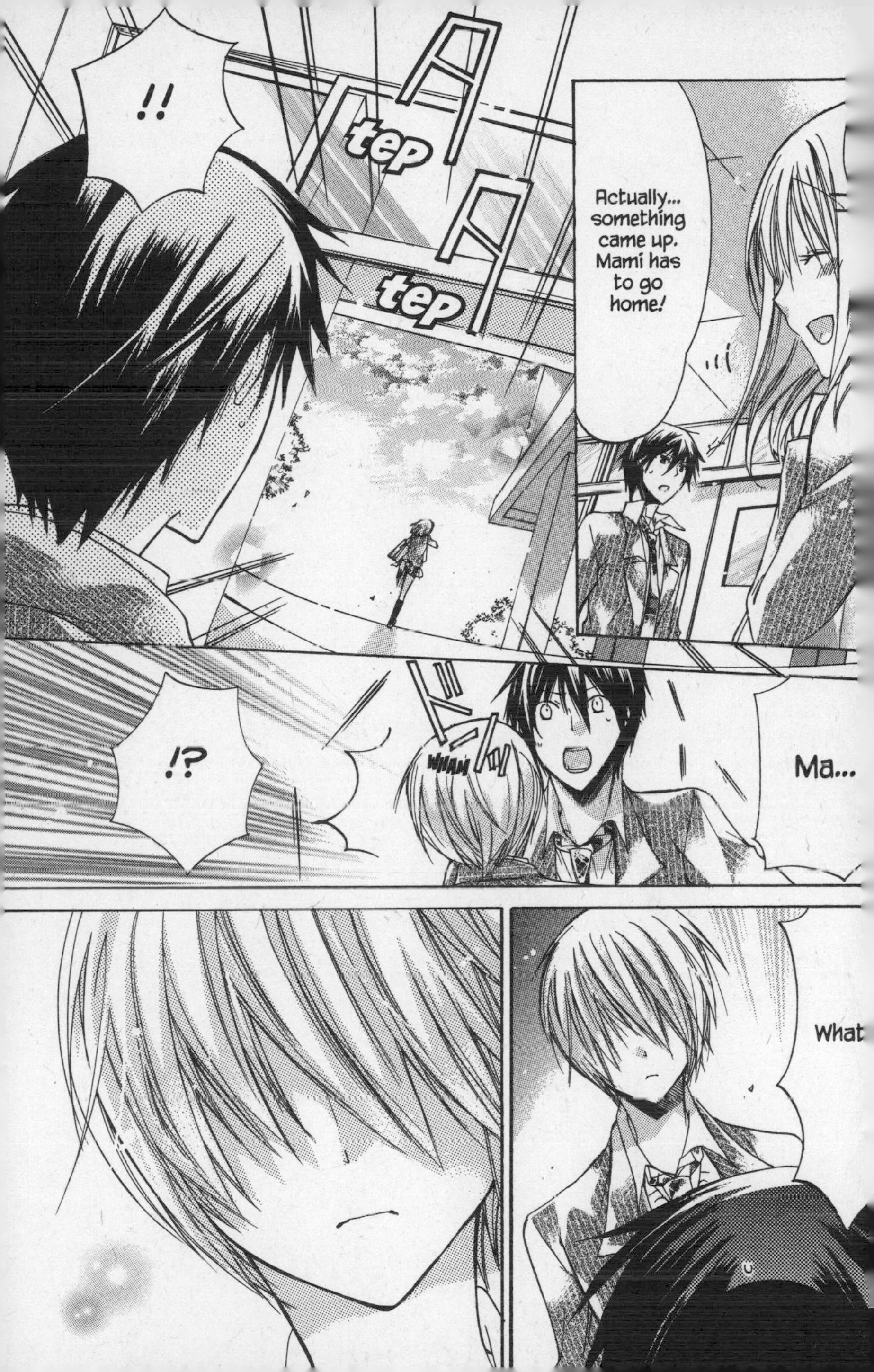
Actually... something came up. Mami has to go home!
tep
tep
!!
Ma...
WHAM
!?
What

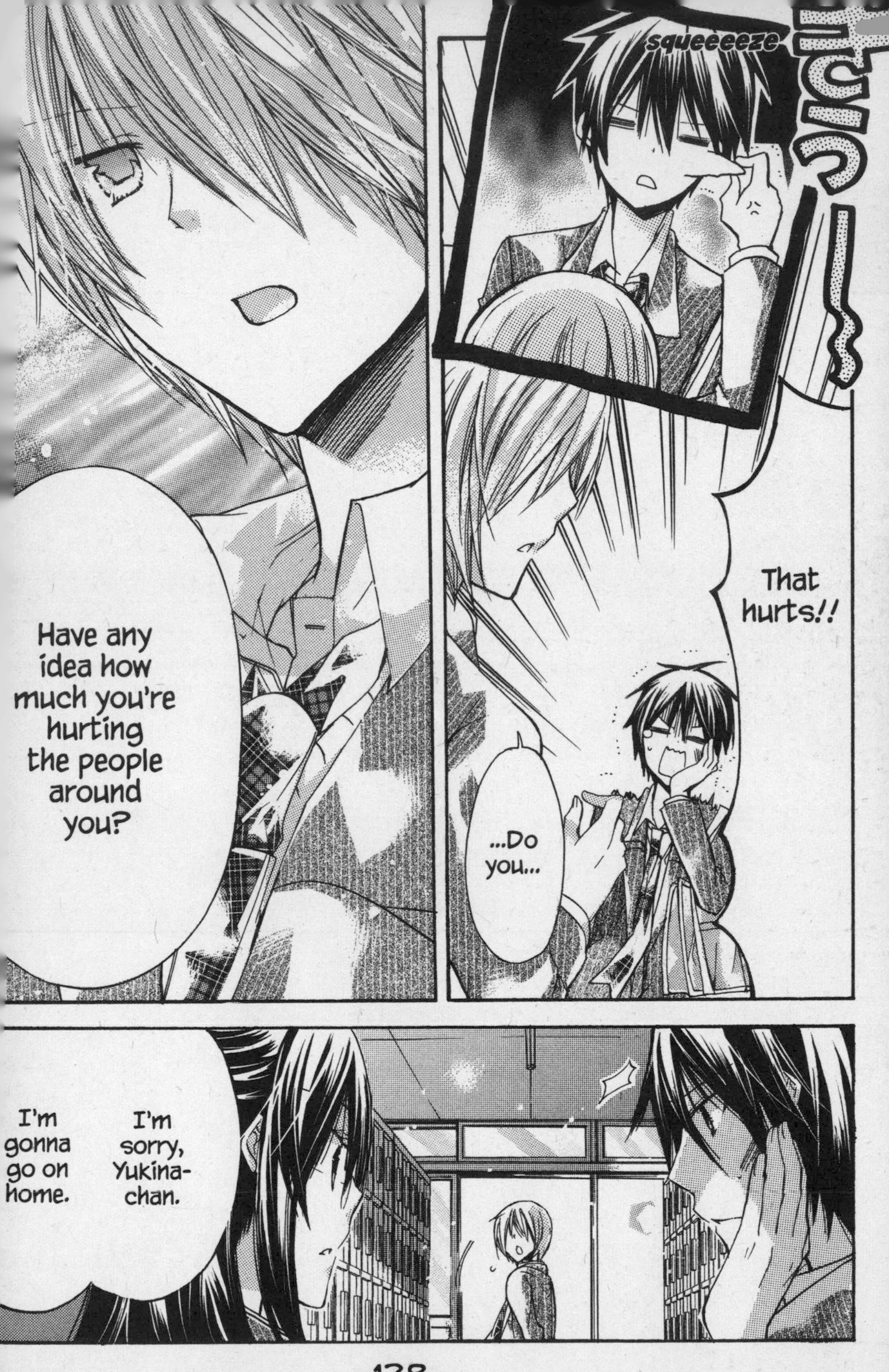
squeeeeeze
That hurts!!
...Do you...
Have any idea how much you're hurting the people around you?
I'm sorry, Yukina-chan.
I'm gonna go on home.

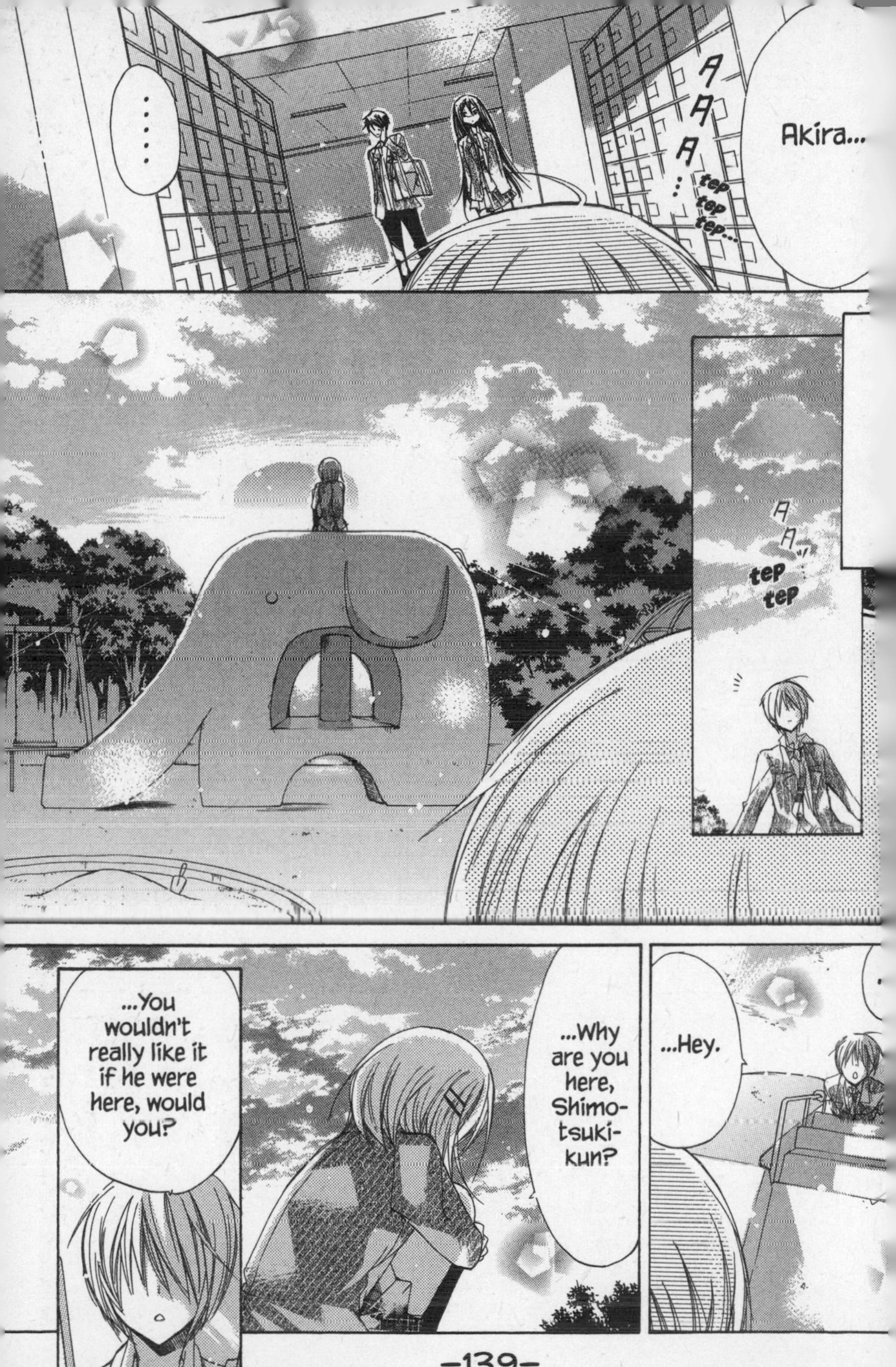
Akira...
AAA...
tep tep tep...
......
AA
tep tep
...Hey.
...Why are you here, Shimotsuki-kun?
...You wouldn't really like it if he were here, would you?

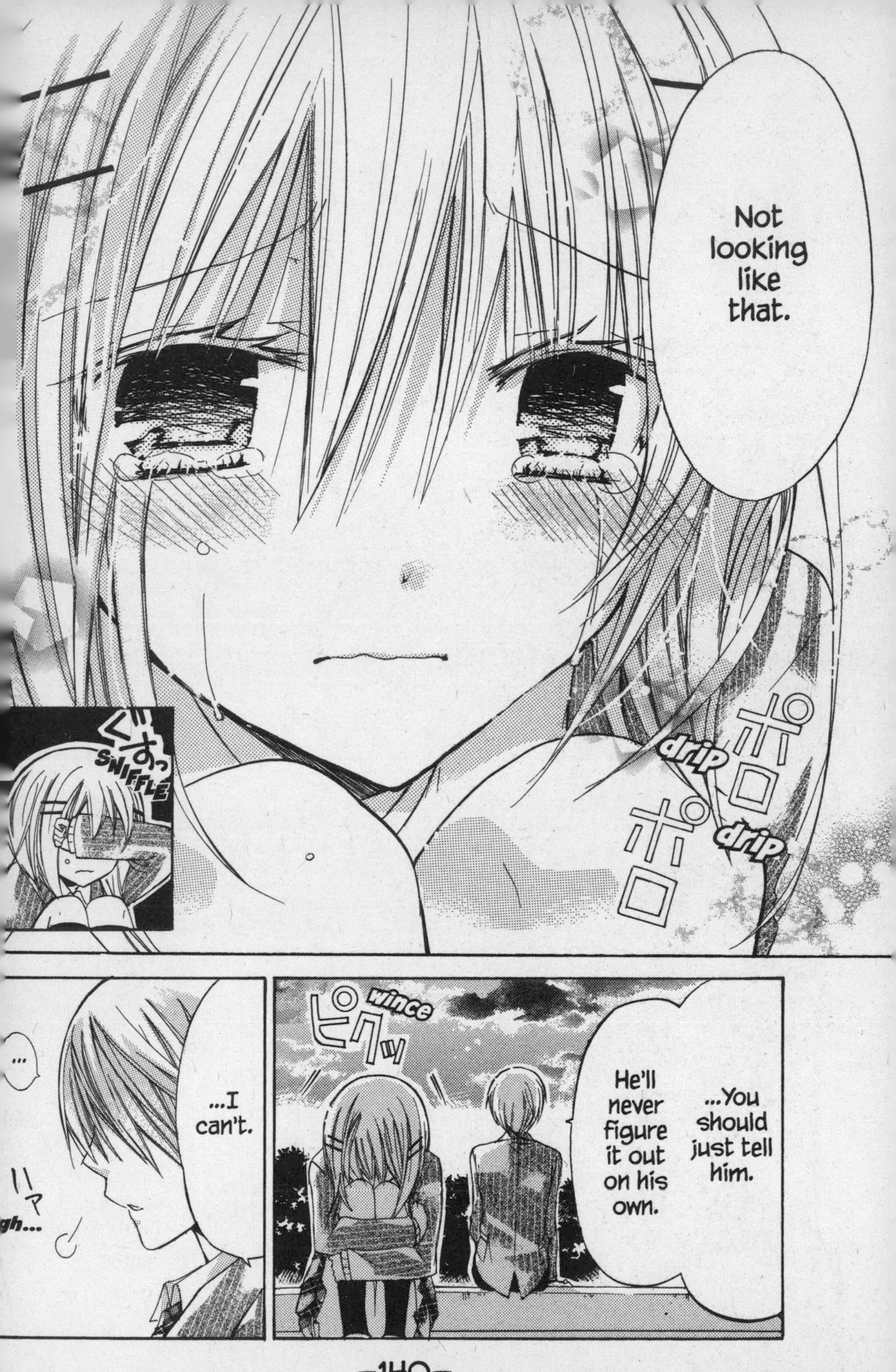
Not looking like that.
ポロポロ
drip
drip
ぐすっ
SNIFFLE
...You should just tell him.
He'll never figure it out on his own.
ピクッ
wince
...I can't.
...
ハァ
gh...

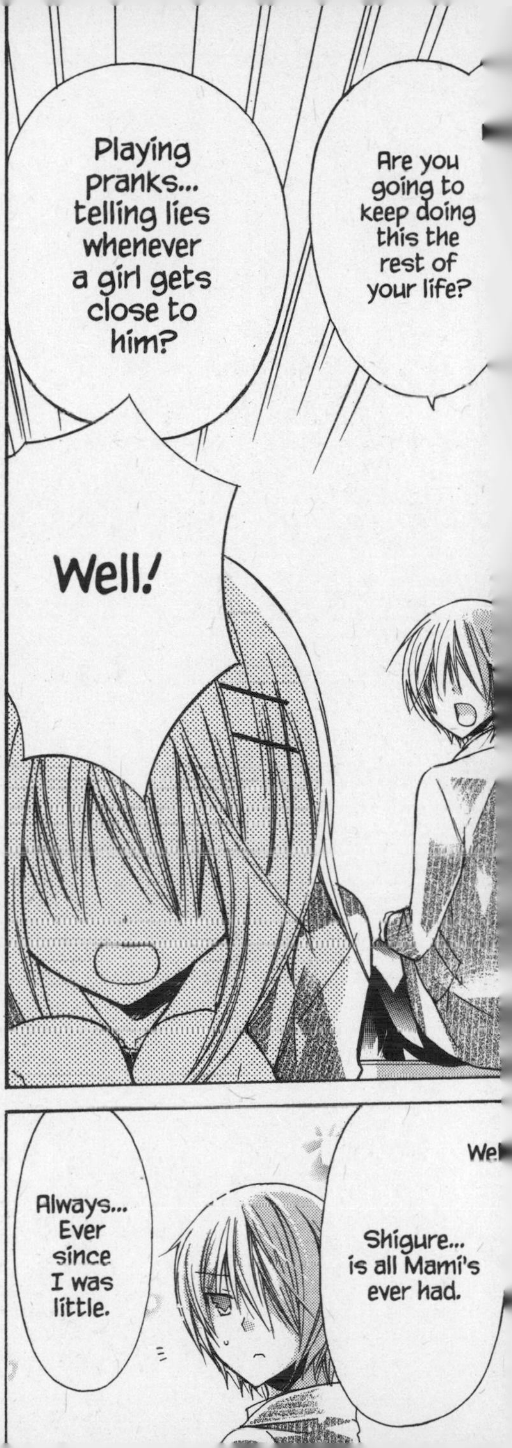
Are you going to keep doing this the rest of your life?
Playing pranks... telling lies whenever a girl gets close to him?
Well!
Wel
Shigure... is all Mami's ever had.
Always... Ever since I was little.

Snow Mami 3

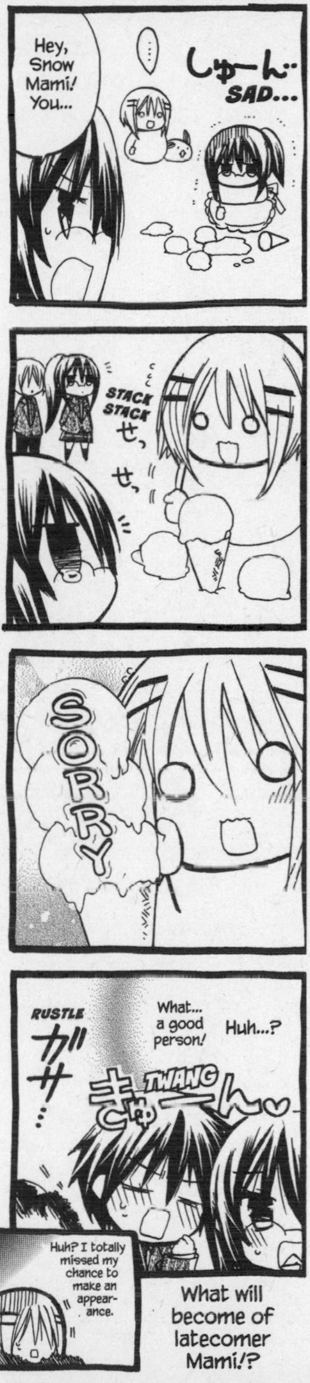
しゅーん‥
SAD...
...
Hey, Snow Mami! You...
STACK STACK
せっ せっ
SORRY
Huh...?
What... a good person!
RUSTLE
ガサ‥
きゅーん♡
TWANG
Huh? I totally missed my chance to make an appear-ance.
What will become of latecomer Mami!?

We were always together... because we're *friends.*
If I told him I like him...
...he would hate me... He would leave me.
ボロボロ
cry cry
Nnh...
Nnh...
Uwa-aa-aa-
wince
aa-aa-ah-hh!

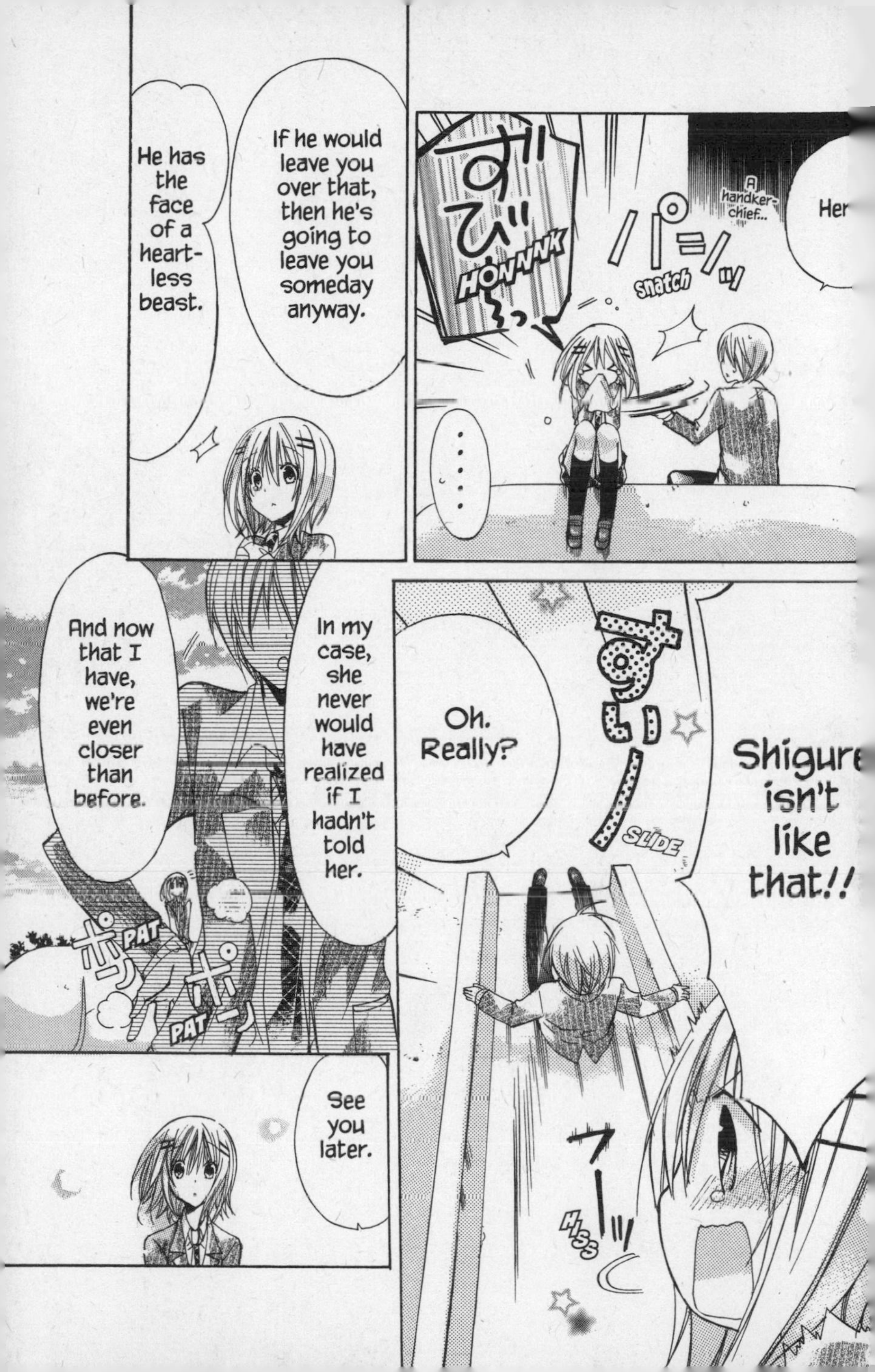
Her
A handker-chief...
SNATCH
HONNNK
.....
If he would leave you over that, then he's going to leave you someday anyway.
He has the face of a heart-less beast.
Shigure isn't like that!!
SLIDE
Oh. Really?
HISS
In my case, she never would have realized if I hadn't told her.
And now that I have, we're even closer than before.
PAT
PAT
See you later.

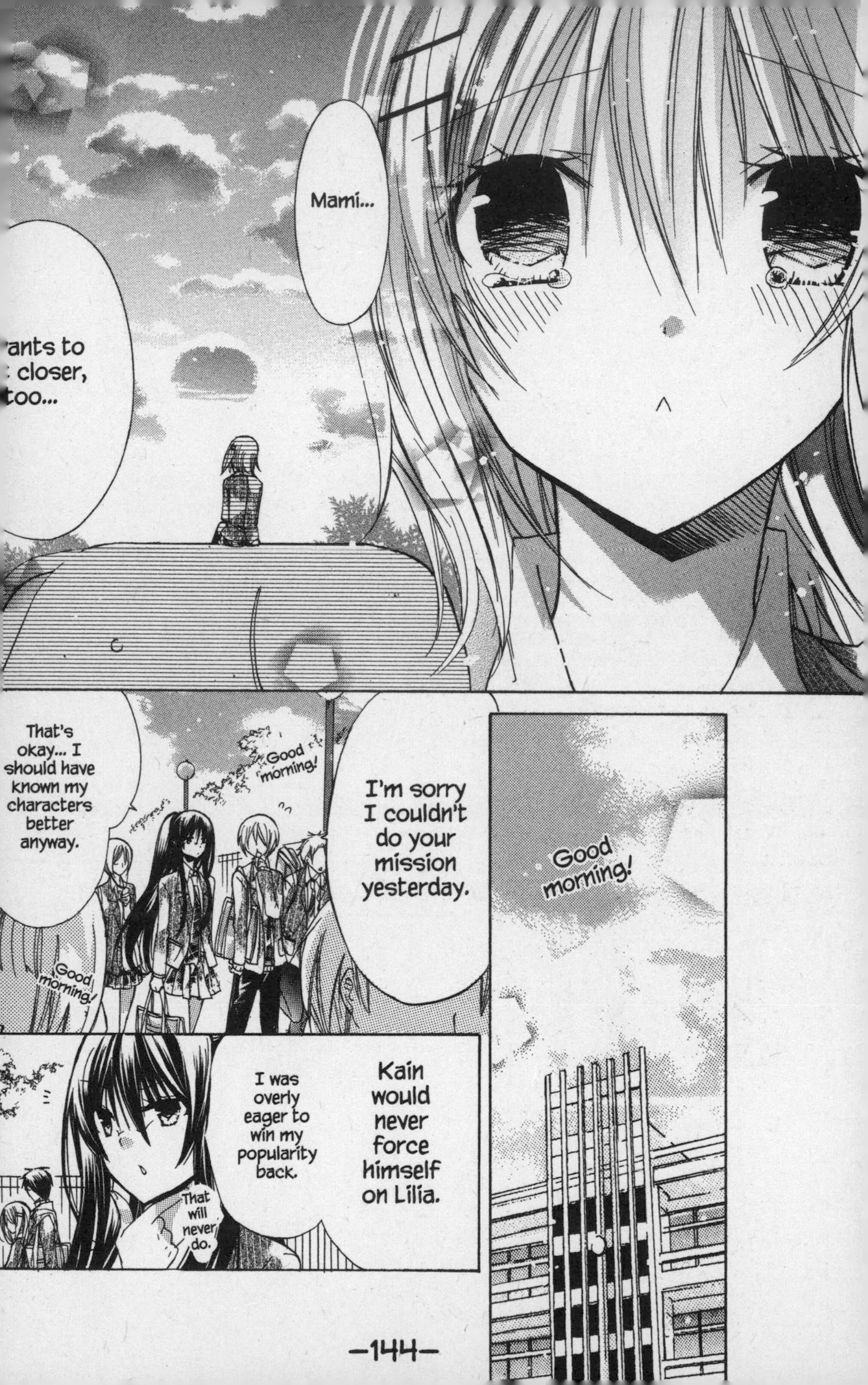
Mami...
ants to
closer,
too...
Good morning!
I'm sorry I couldn't do your mission yesterday.
Good morning!
That's okay... I should have known my characters better anyway.
Good morning!
Kain would never force himself on Lilia.
I was overly eager to win my popularity back.
That will never do.

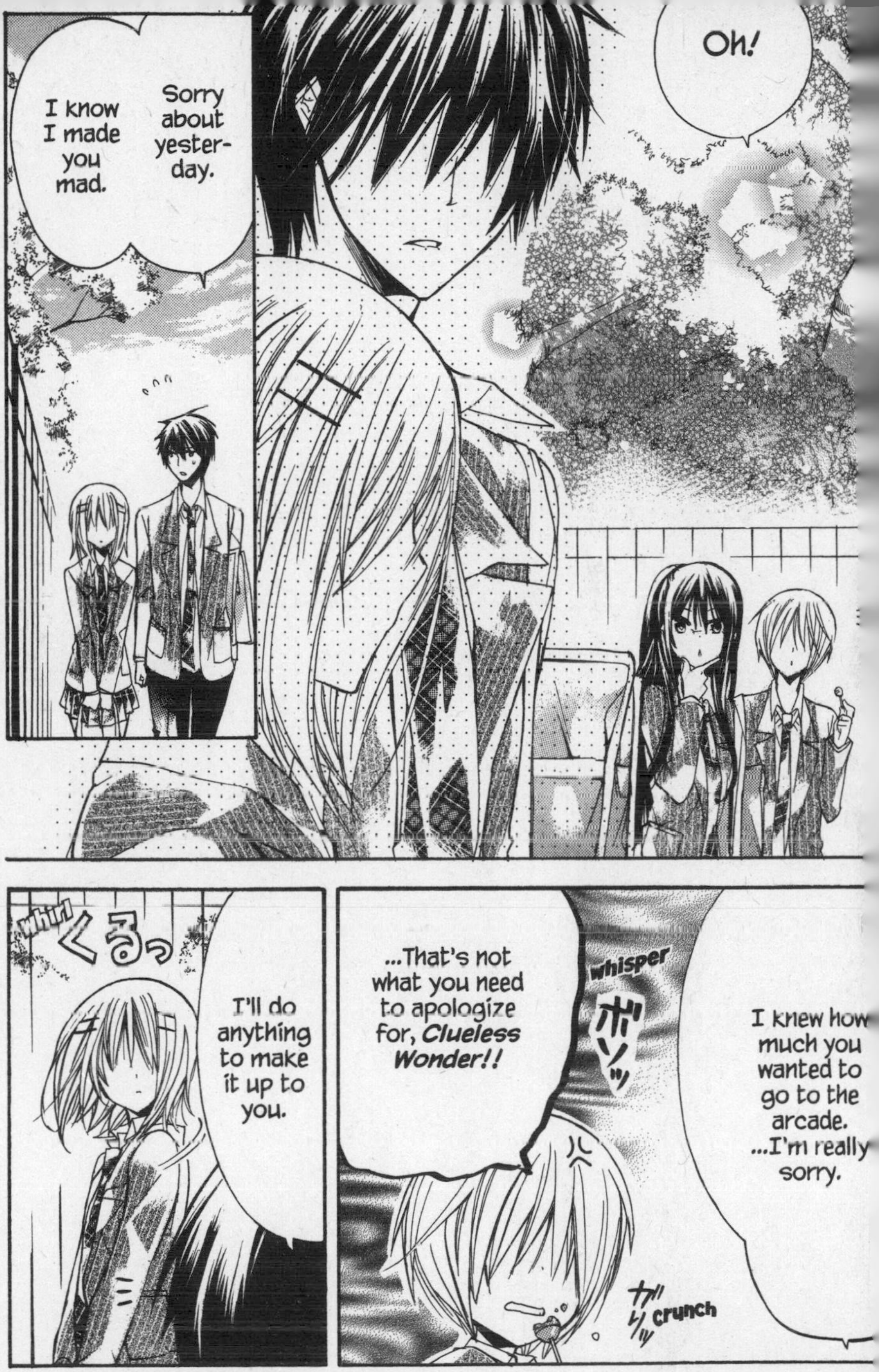
Oh!
Sorry about yesterday.
I know I made you mad.
I knew how much you wanted to go to the arcade. ...I'm really sorry.
whisper ボソッ
...That's not what you need to apologize for, *Clueless Wonder!!*
ガリッ crunch
whirl くるっ
I'll do anything to make it up to you.

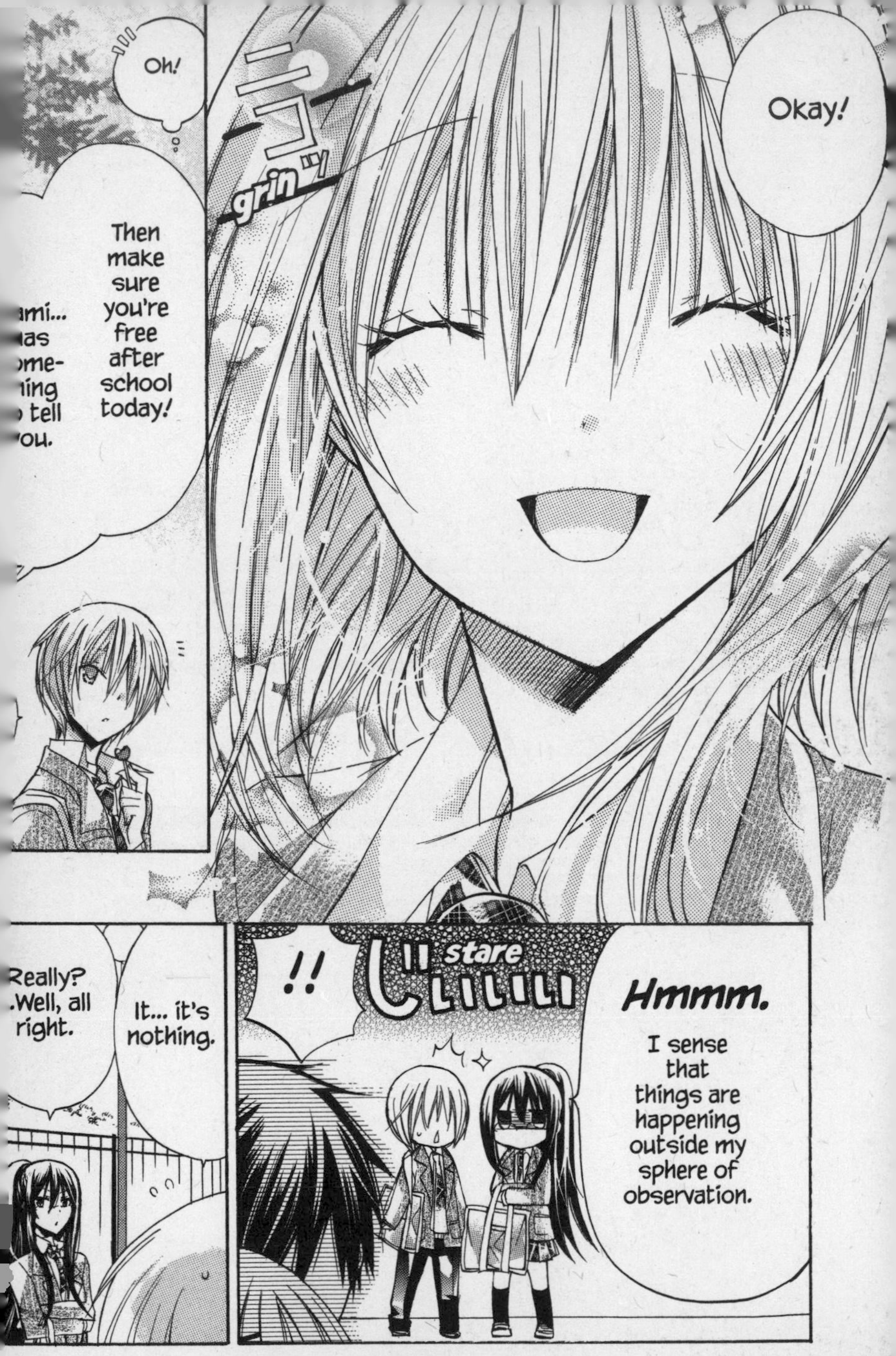

Okay!
ニコッ
grin
Oh!
Then make sure you're free after school today!
Hmmm.
I sense that things are happening outside my sphere of observation.
stare
!!
It... it's nothing.
Really? .Well, all right.

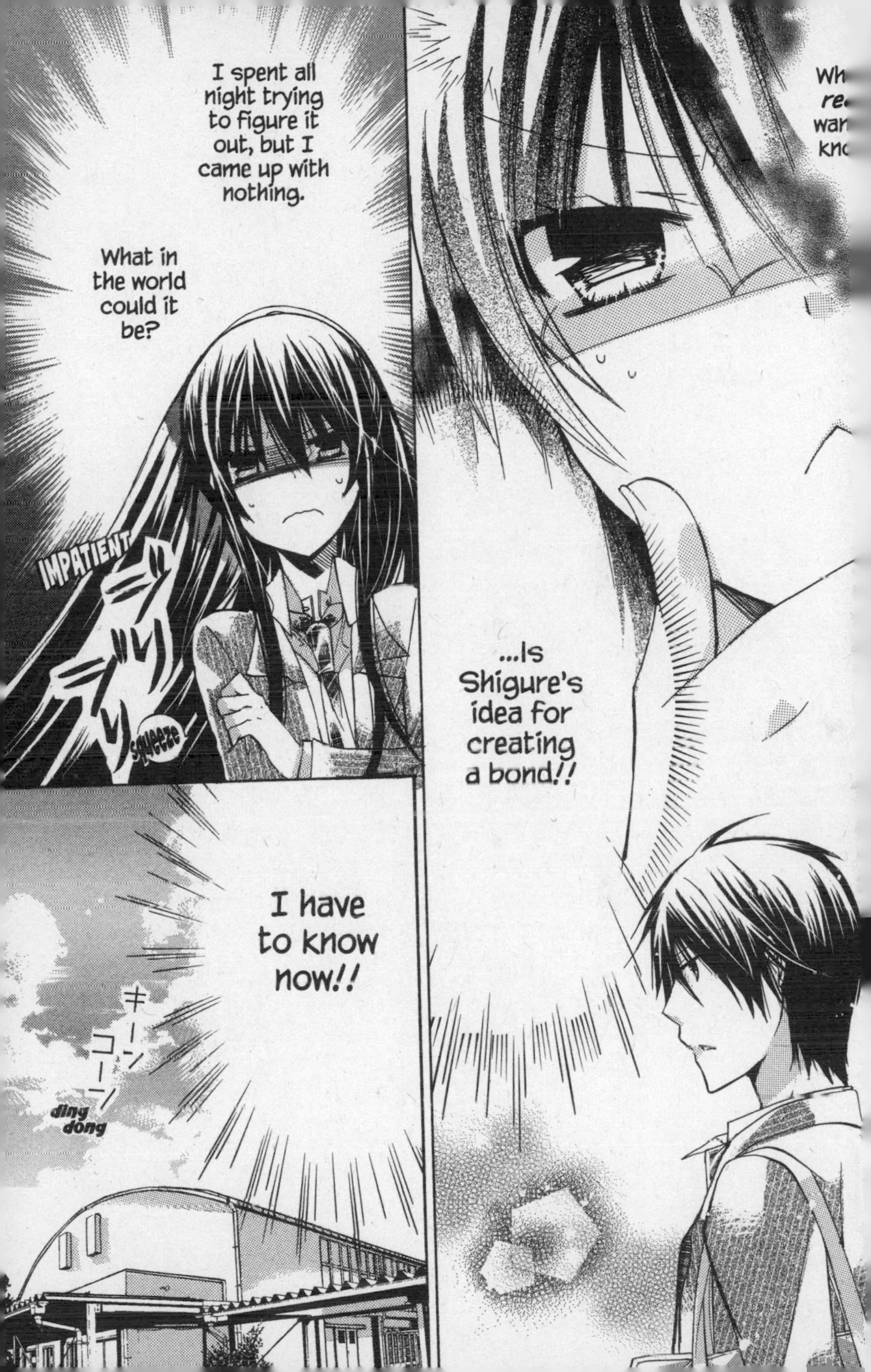
...Is Shigure's idea for creating a bond!!
I spent all night trying to figure it out, but I came up with nothing.
What in the world could it be?
IMPATIENT
squeeze
I have to know now!!
キーンコーンコーン
ding dong

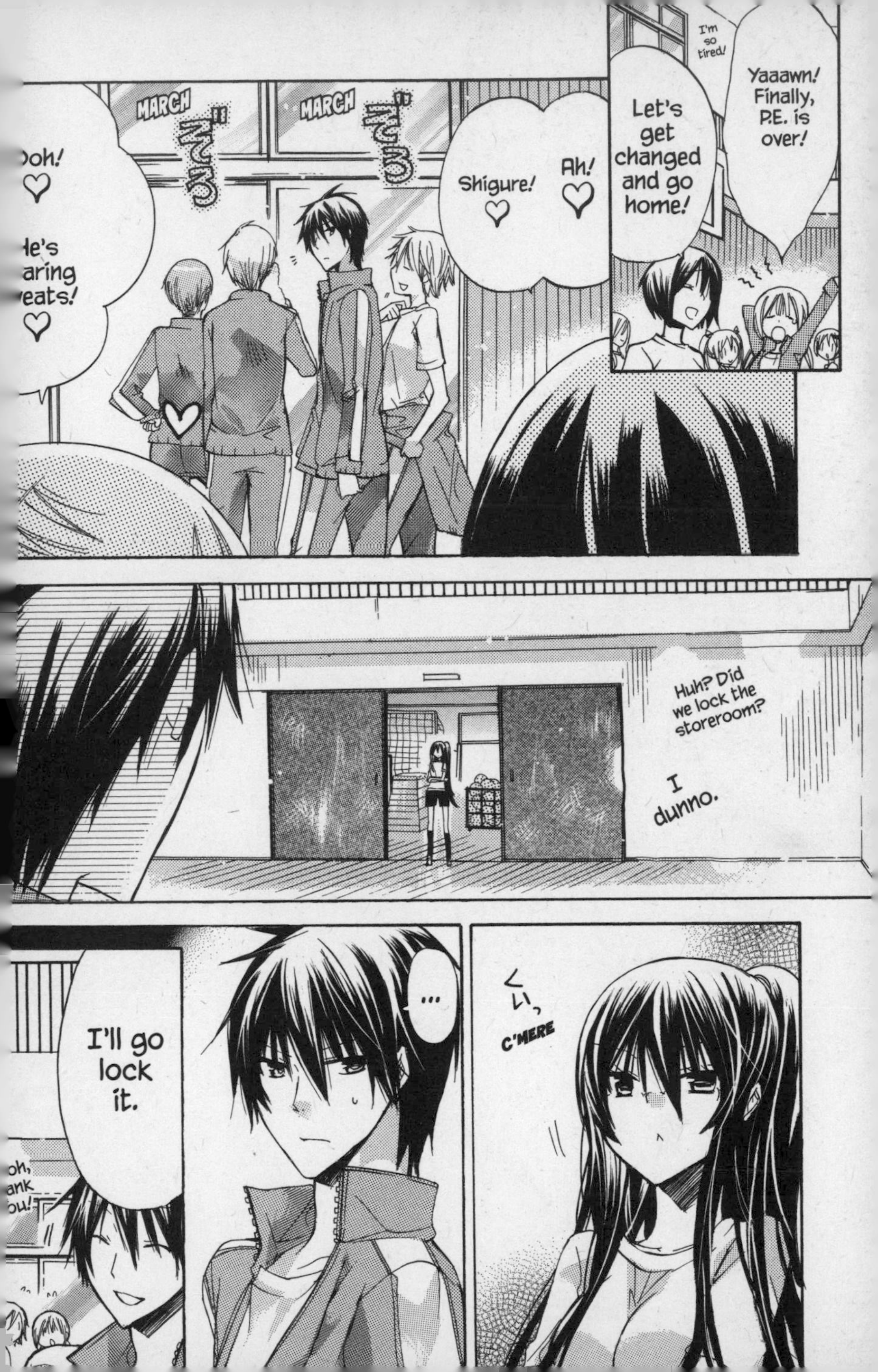
I'm so tired!
Yaaawn! Finally, P.E. is over!
Let's get changed and go home!
Ah! ♡
Shigure! ♡
ぞろ MARCH
ぞろ MARCH
oh! ♡
e's aring eats! ♡
Huh? Did we lock the storeroom?
I dunno.
くいっ C'MERE
...
I'll go lock it.
oh, ank ou!

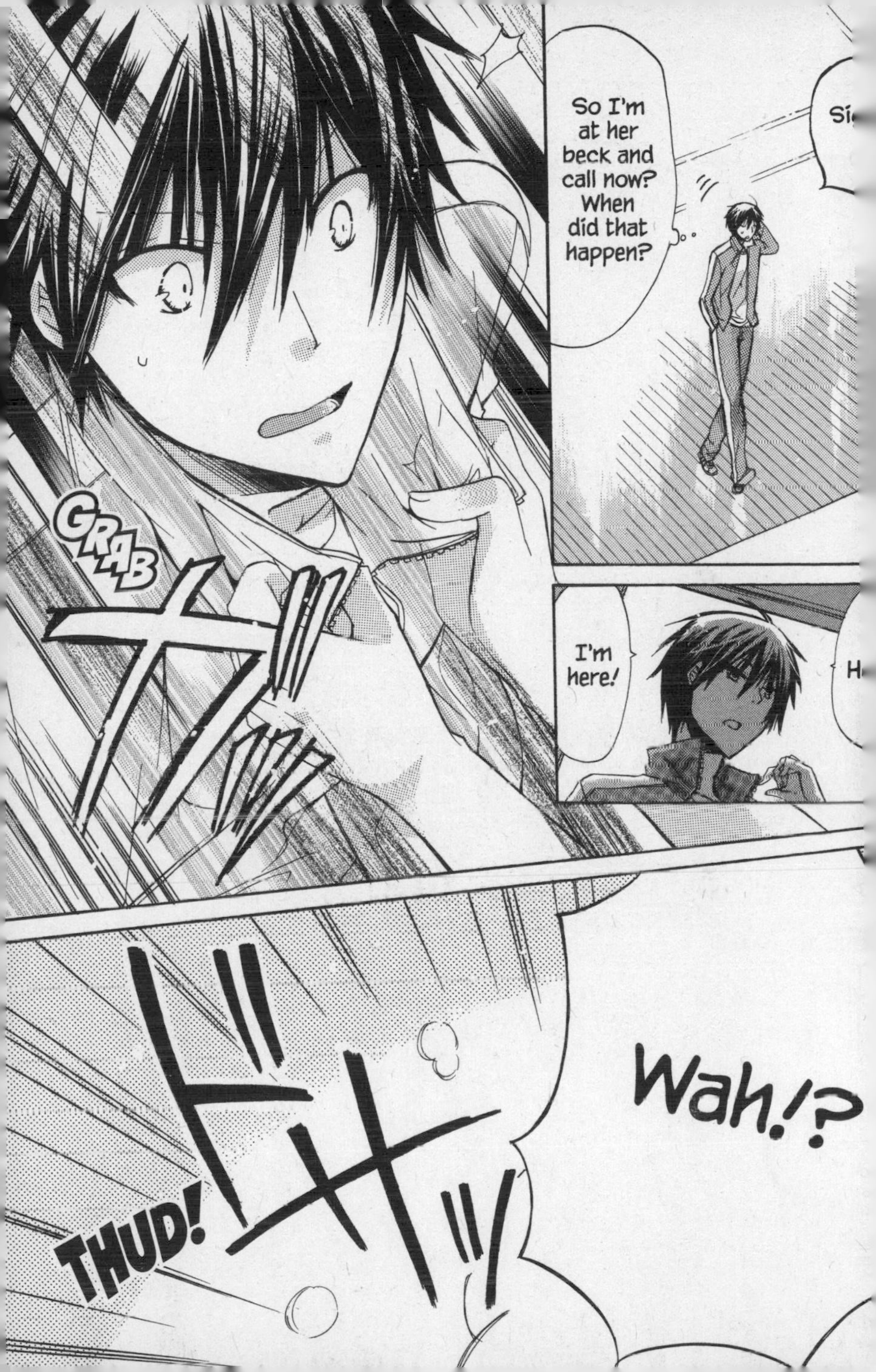
So I'm at her beck and call now? When did that happen?
I'm here!
GRAB
Wah!?
THUD!

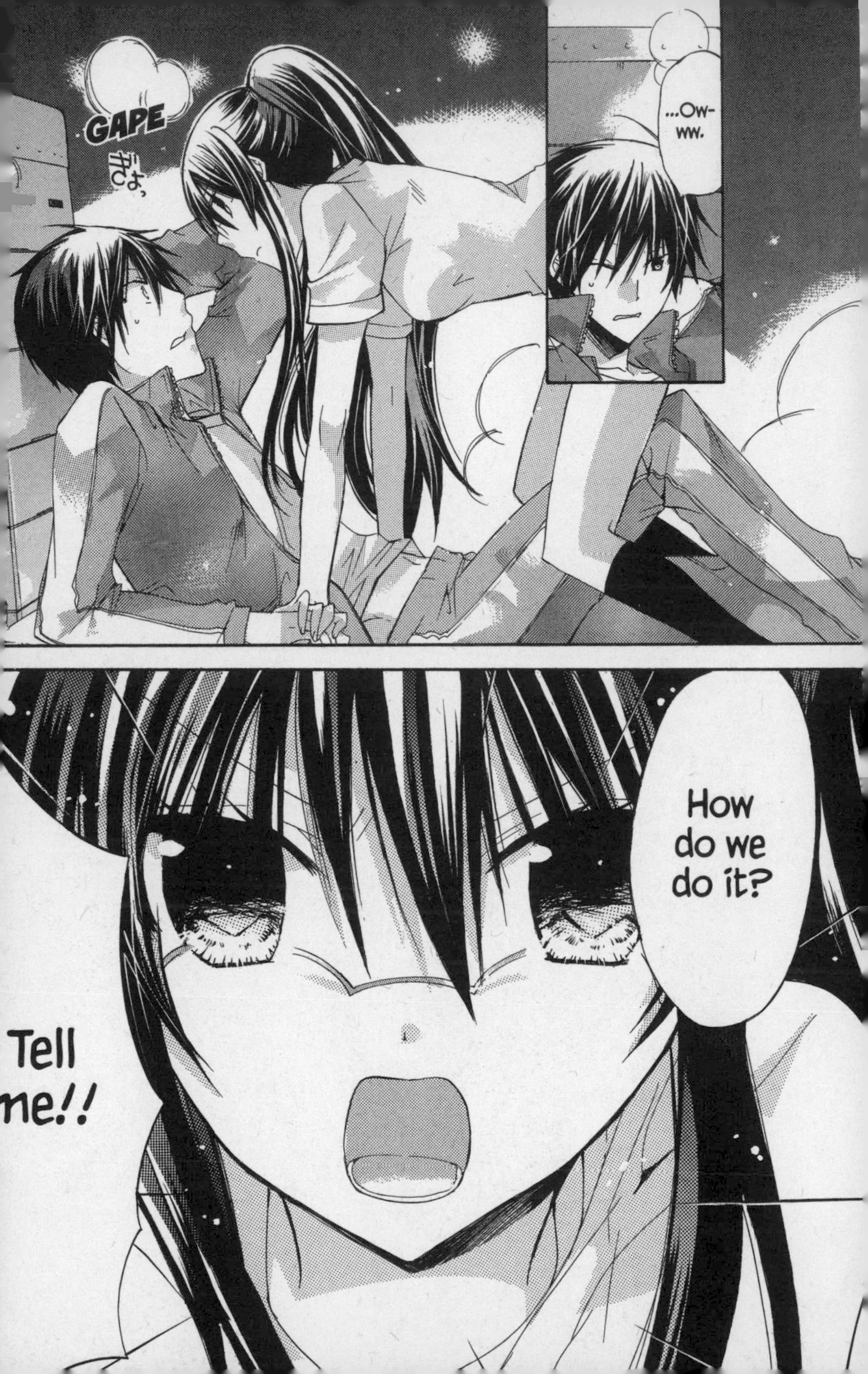
...Ow-ww.
GAPE
ぎょ,
How do we do it?
Tell me!!

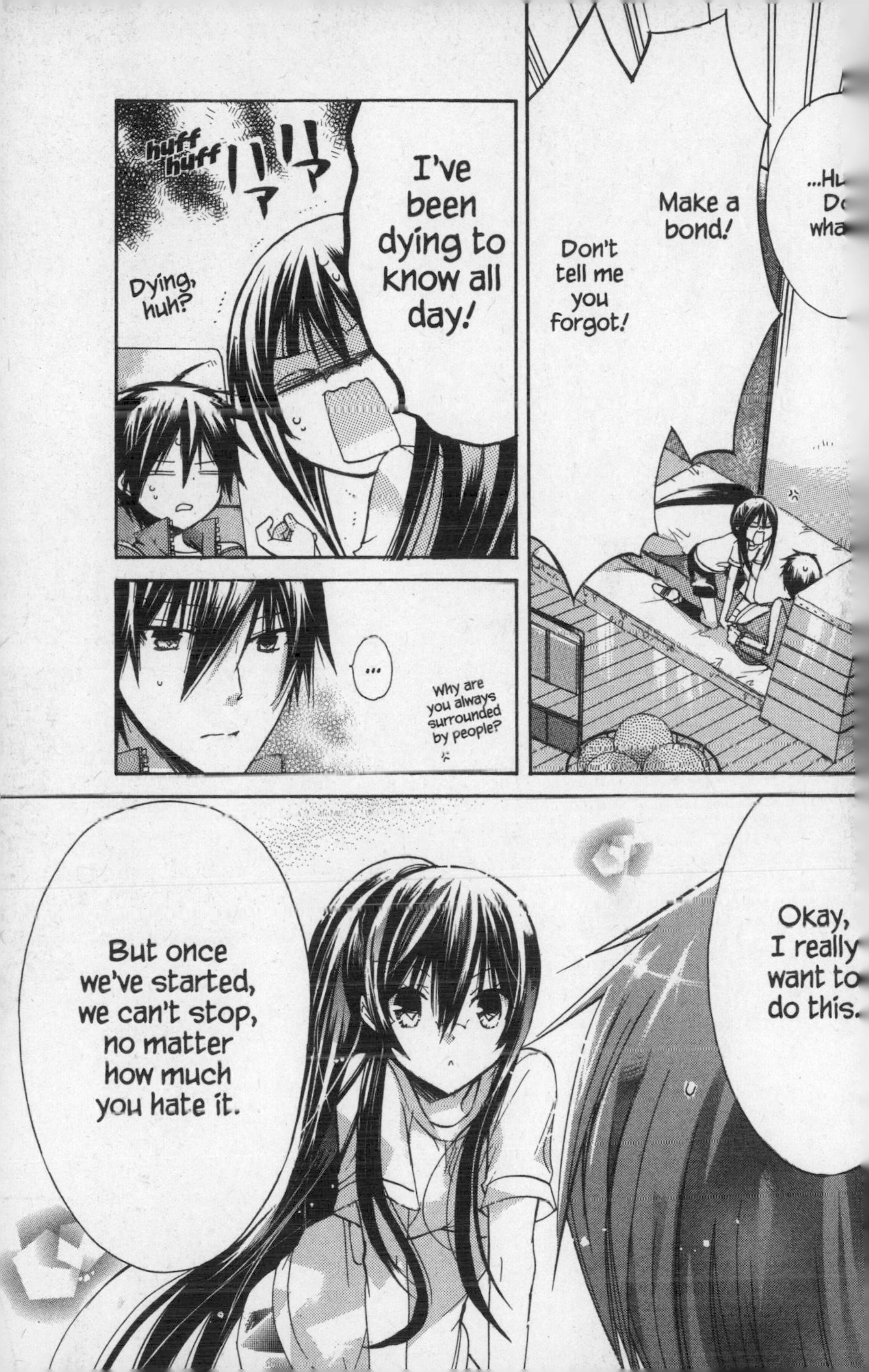

...Hu
Do
wha
Make a bond!
Don't tell me you forgot!
huff huff
I've been dying to know all day!
Dying, huh?
...
Why are you always surrounded by people?
Okay, I really want to do this.
But once we've started, we can't stop, no matter how much you hate it.

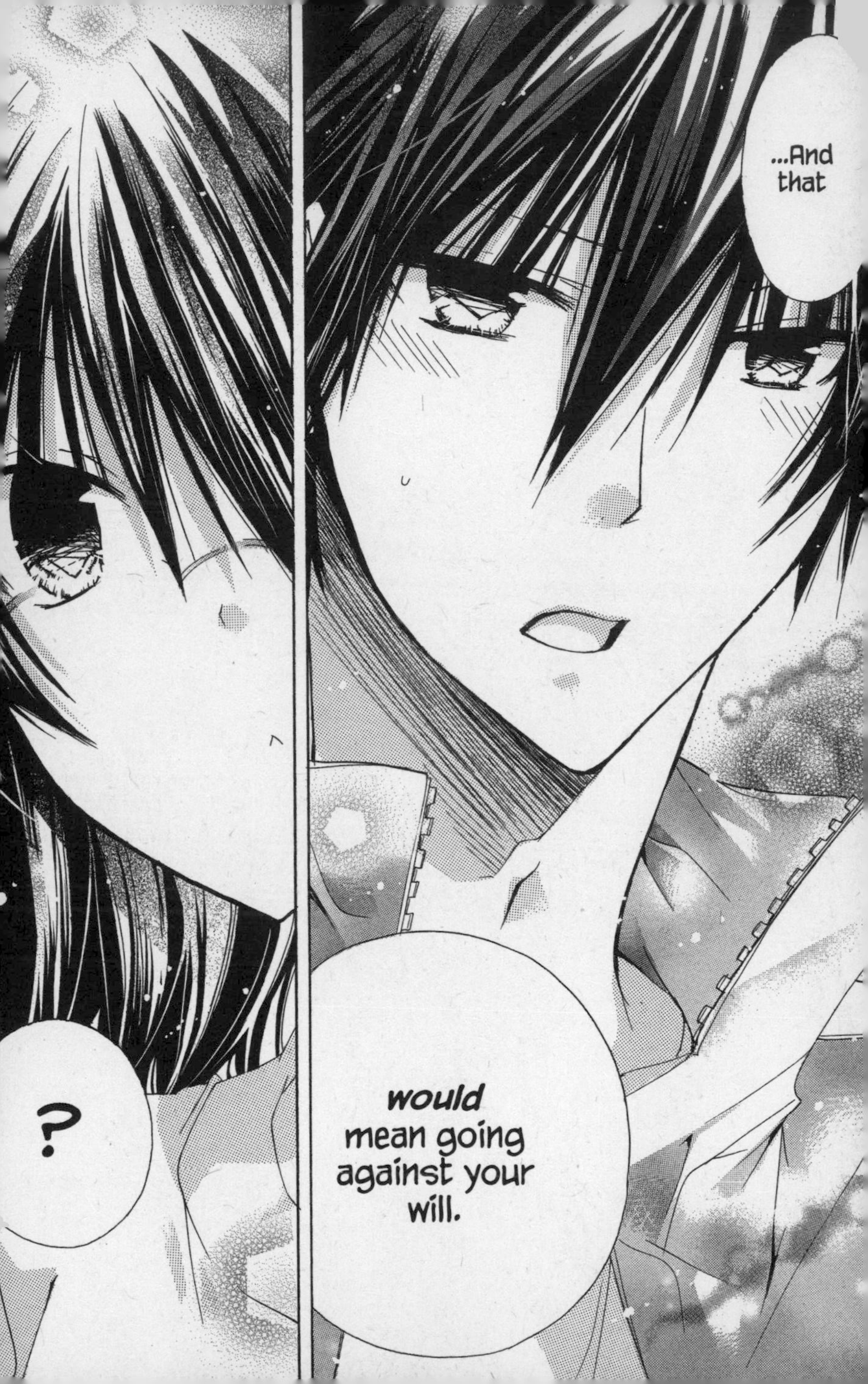
...And that
would mean going against your will.
?

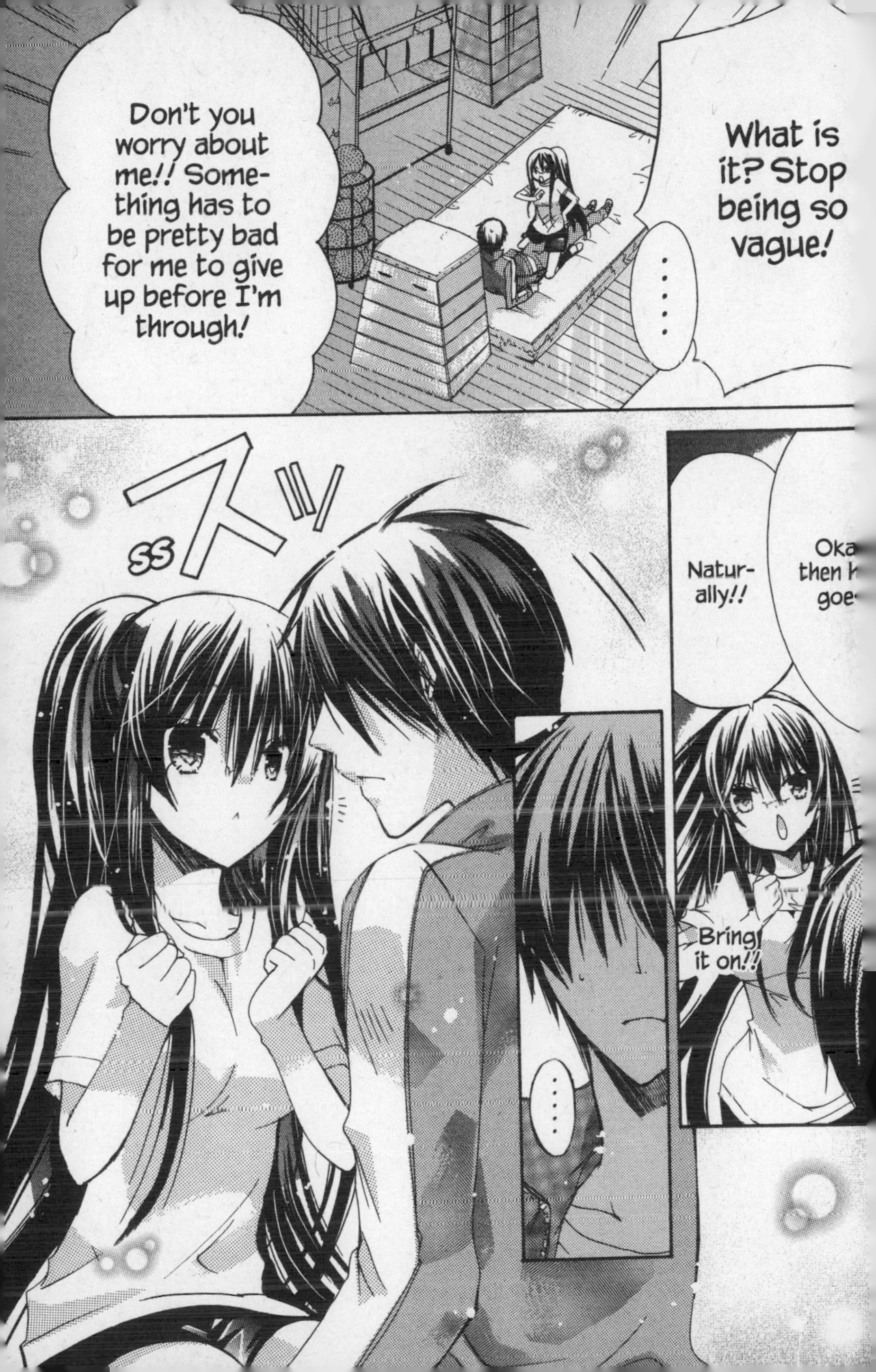

What is it? Stop being so vague!
.....
Don't you worry about me!! Something has to be pretty bad for me to give up before I'm through!
Oka then h goe
Naturally!!
Bring it on!!
.....
SS

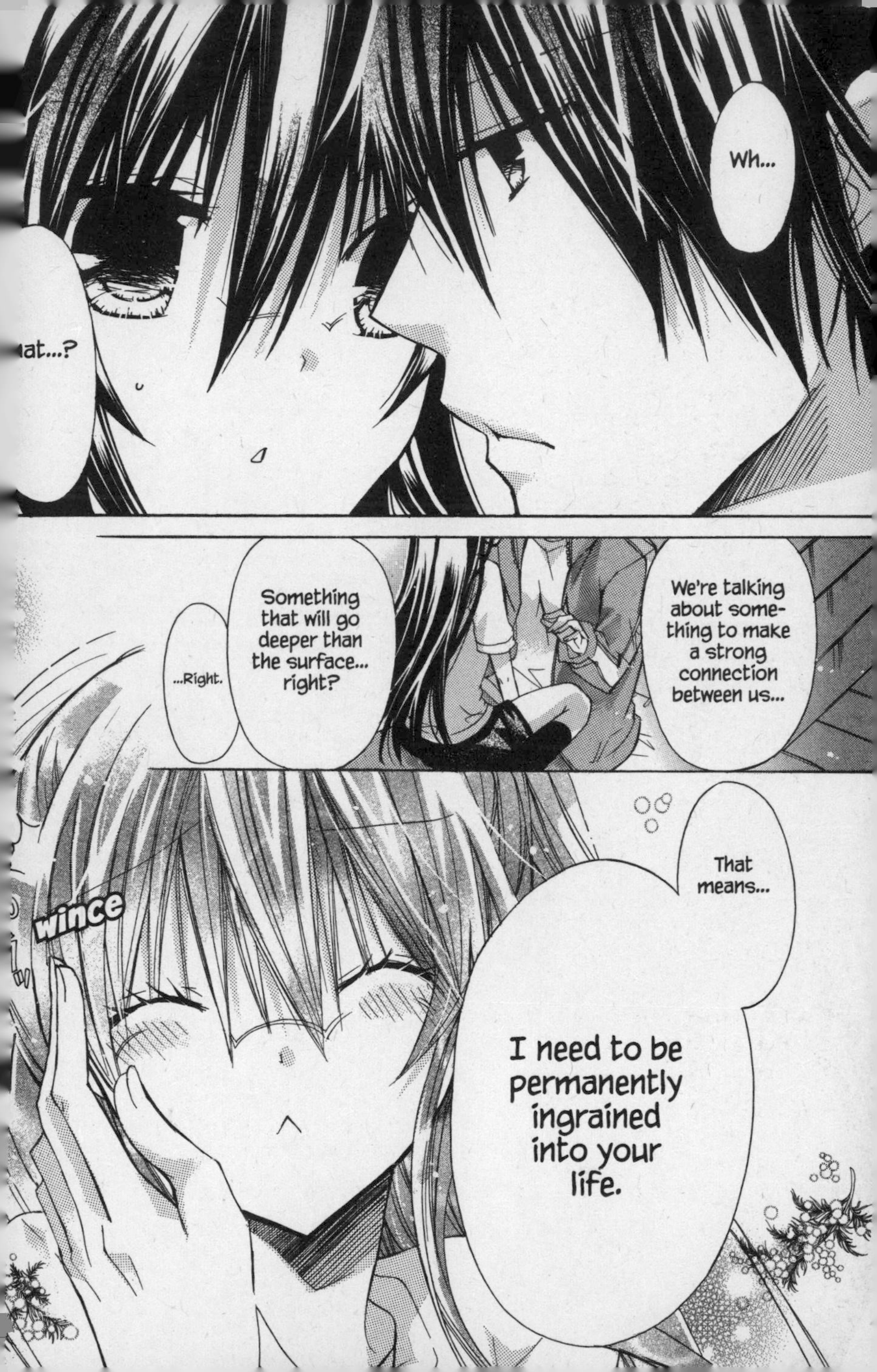
Wh...
at...?
We're talking about something to make a strong connection between us...
Something that will go deeper than the surface... right?
...Right.
That means...
I need to be permanently ingrained into your life.
wince

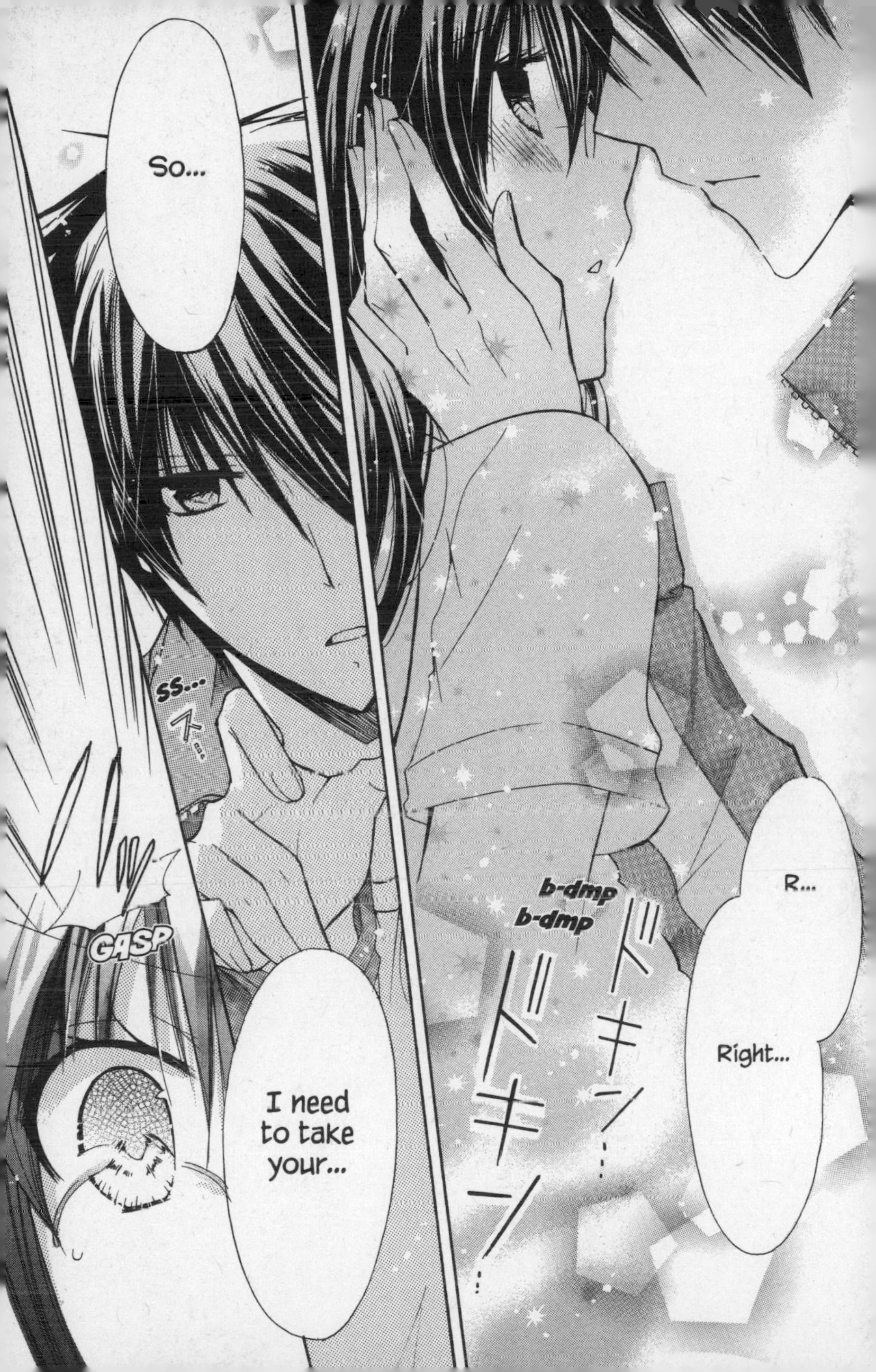
R...
b-dmp
b-dmp
ドキーン…
ドキーン…
Right...
So...
ss...
ス…
GASP
I need to take your...

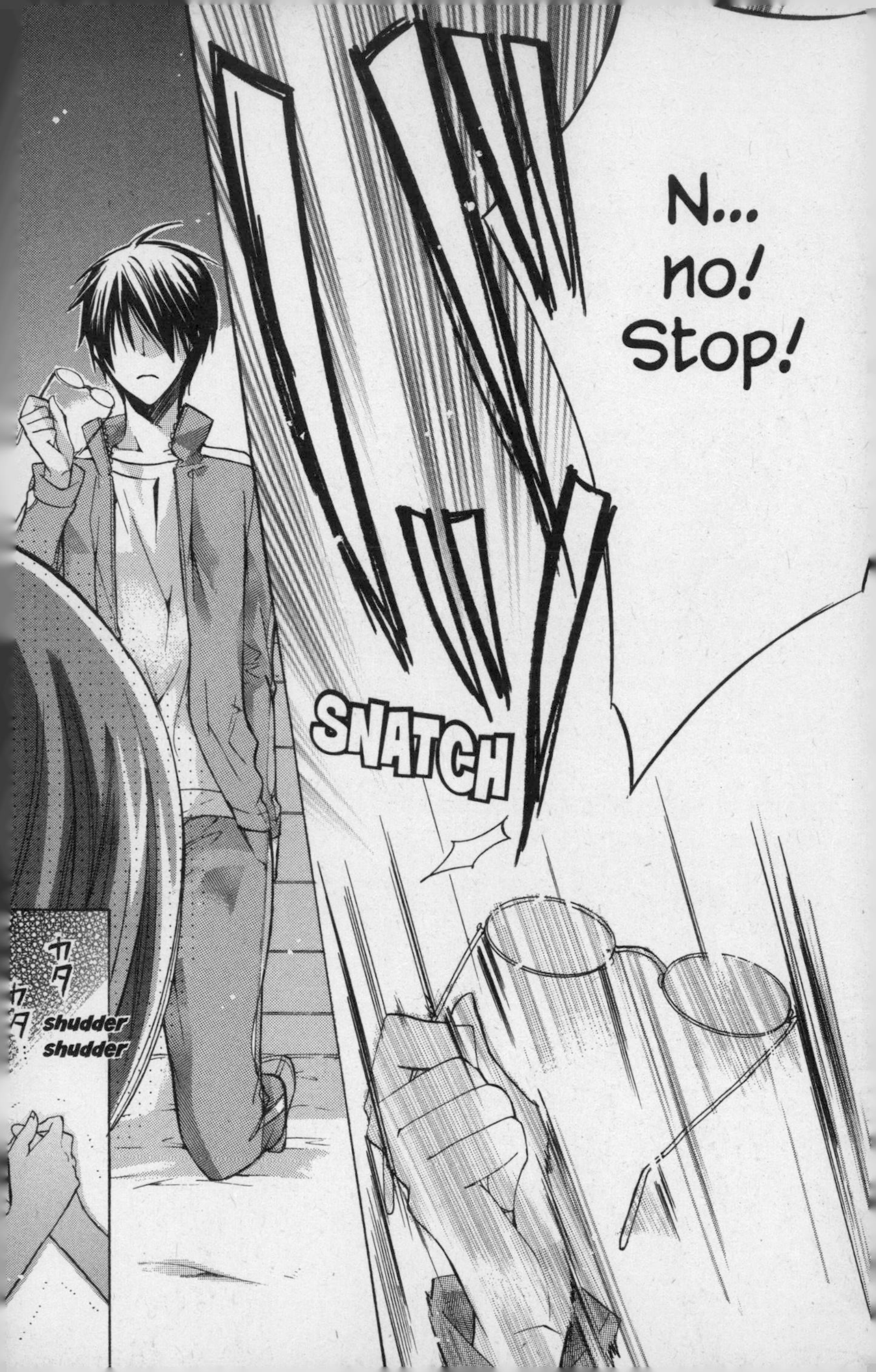
N...
no!
Stop!
SNATCH
カタカタ
shudder
shudder

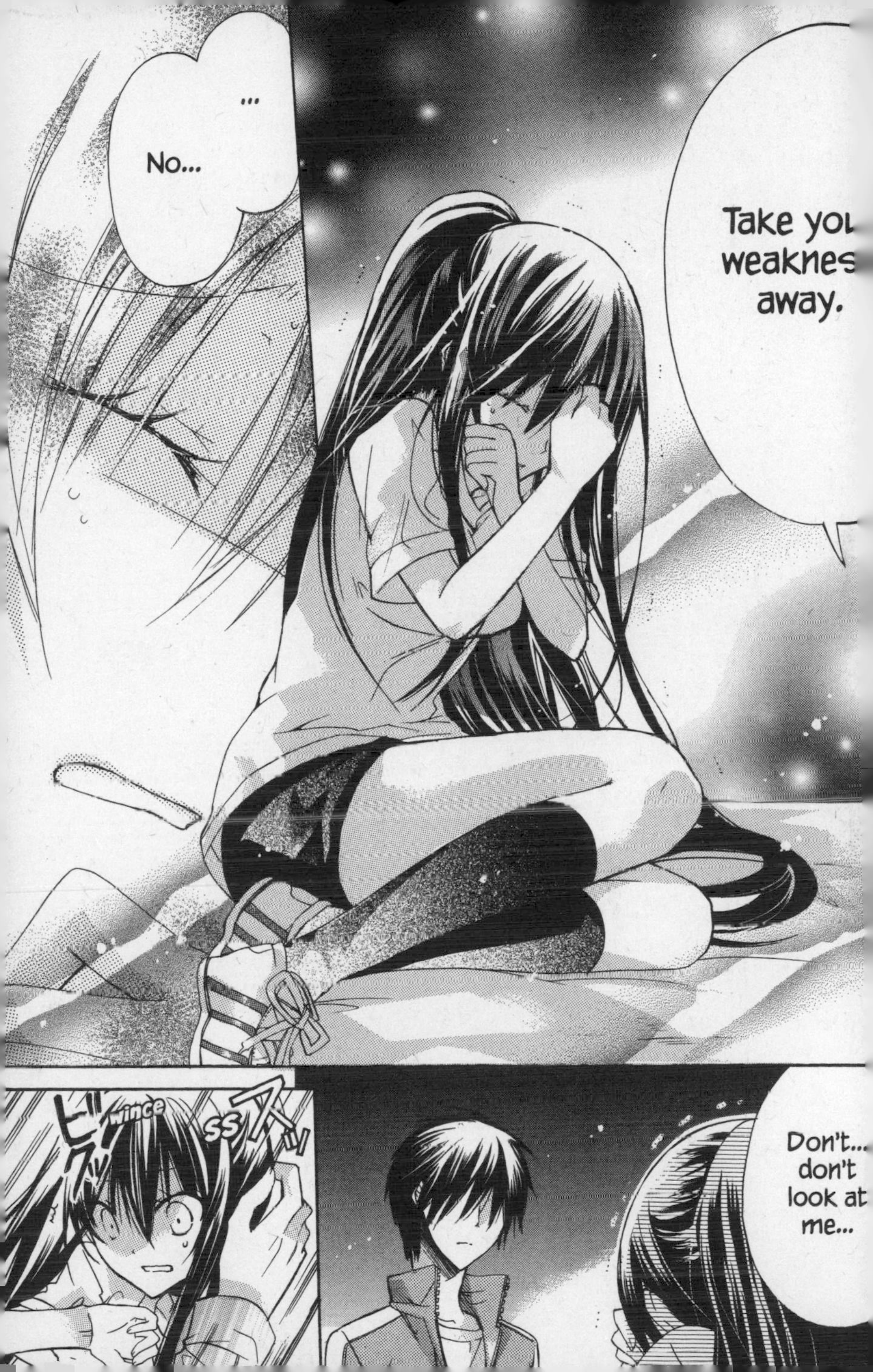
Take you weaknes away.
...
No...
Don't... don't look at me...
wince
SS

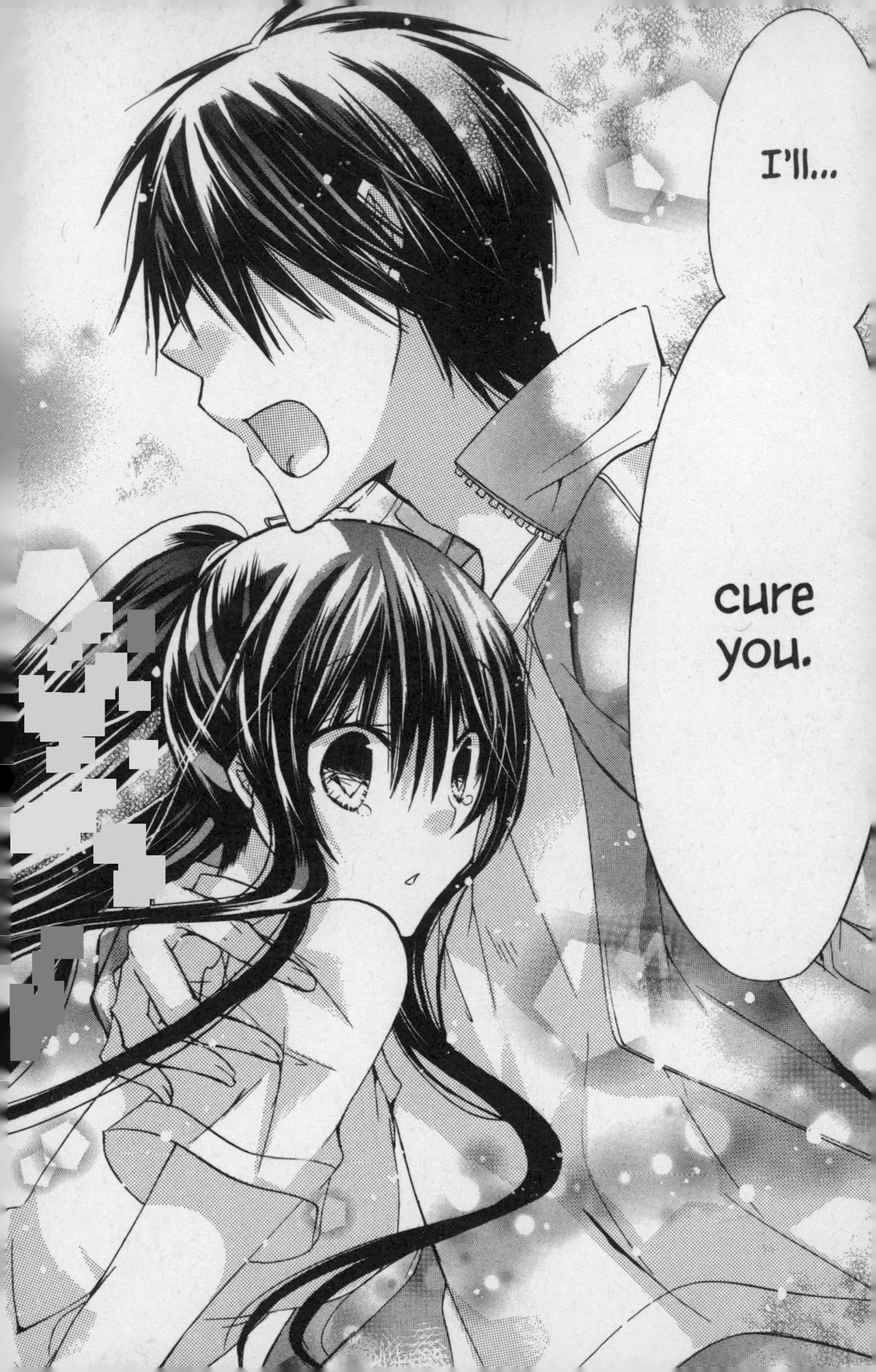
I'll...
cure you.

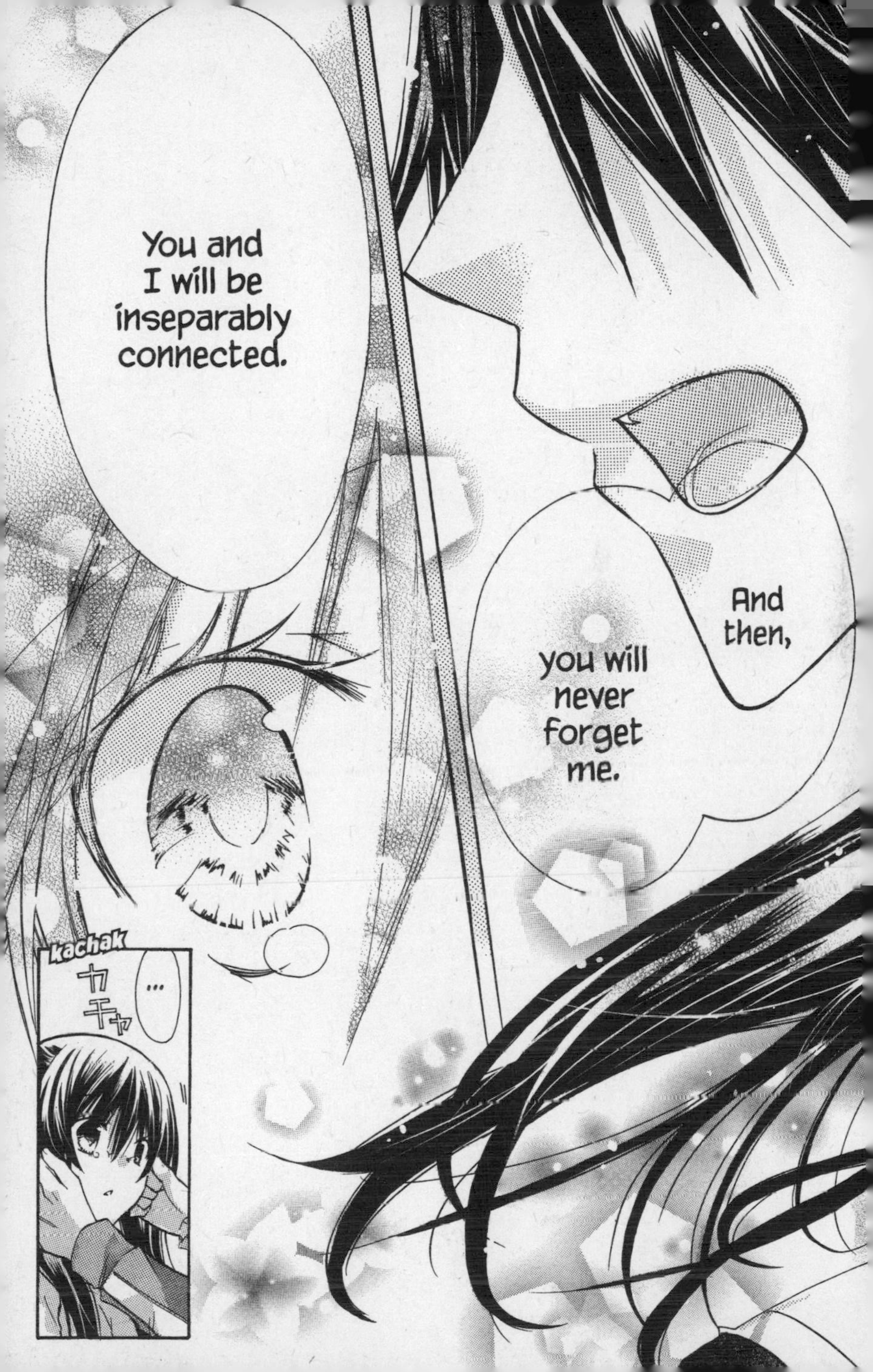
You and I will be inseparably connected.
And then, you will never forget me.
kachak
カチャ
...

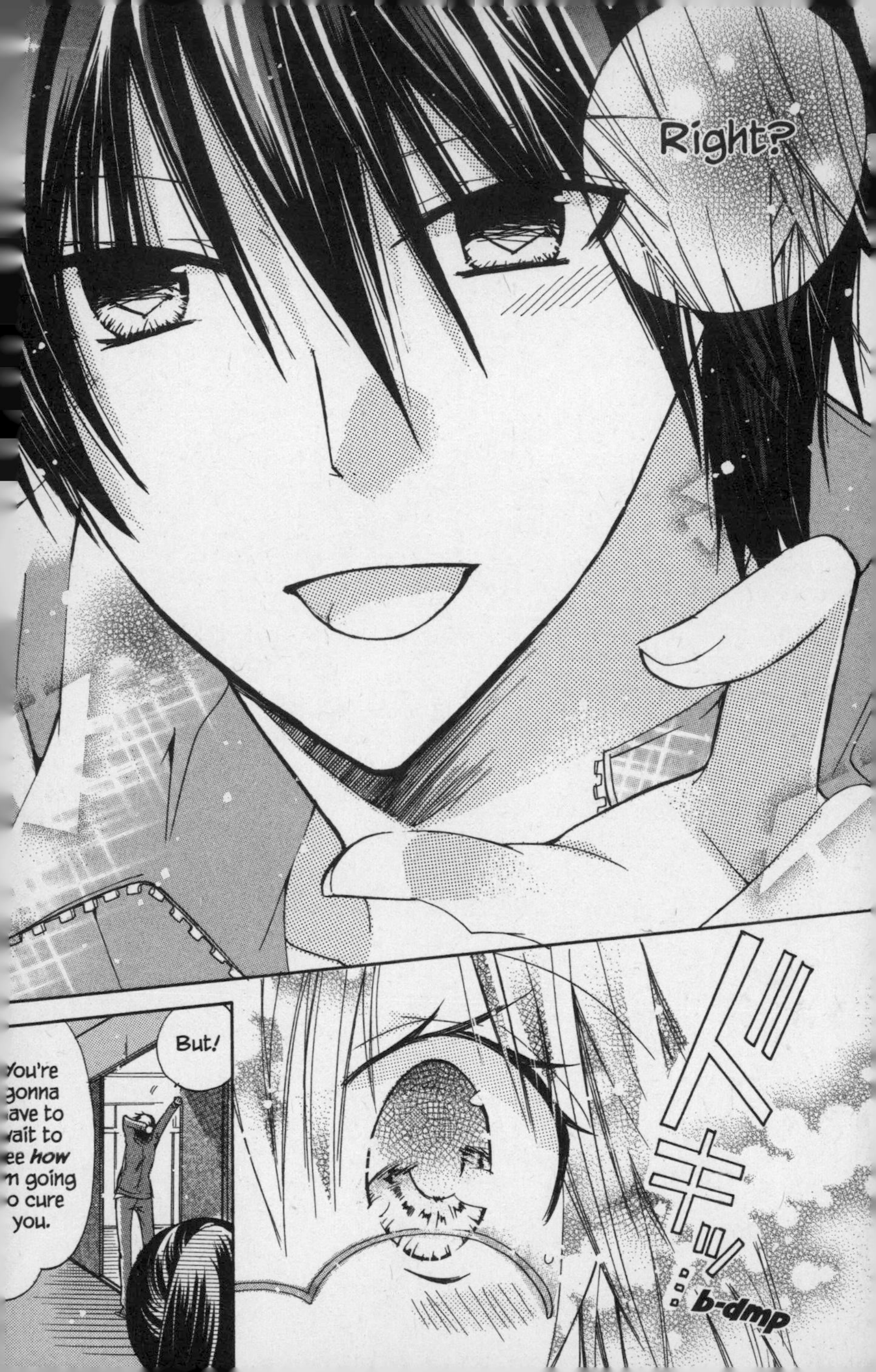
Right?
ドキッ
...b-dmp
But!
You're gonna ave to ait to ee *how* n going o cure you.

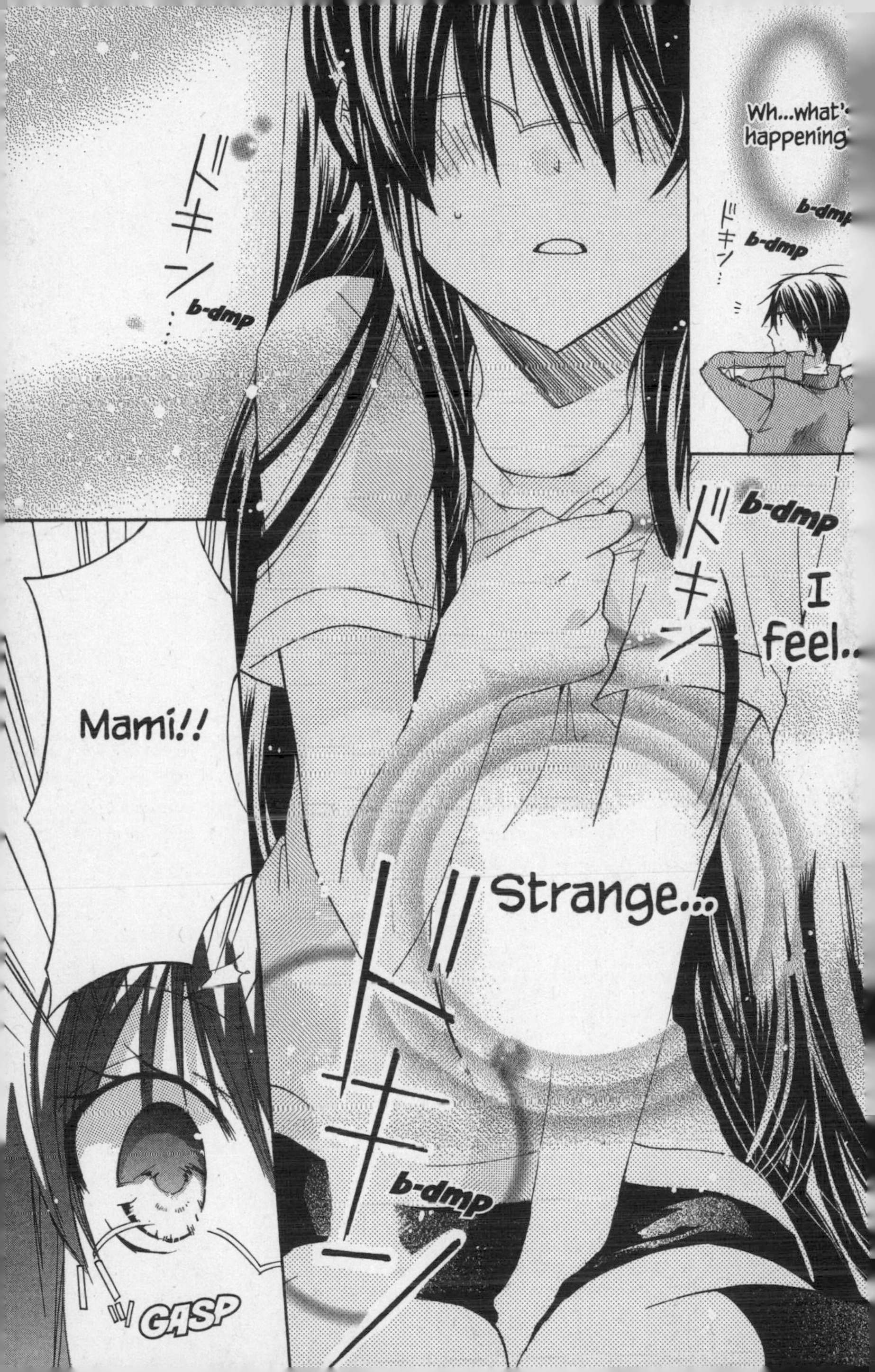
Wh...what'
happening
b-dmp
ドキン…
b-dmp
ドキン
b-dmp
I feel...
Strange...
ドキー
b-dmp
ドキン…
b-dmp
Mami!!
GASP

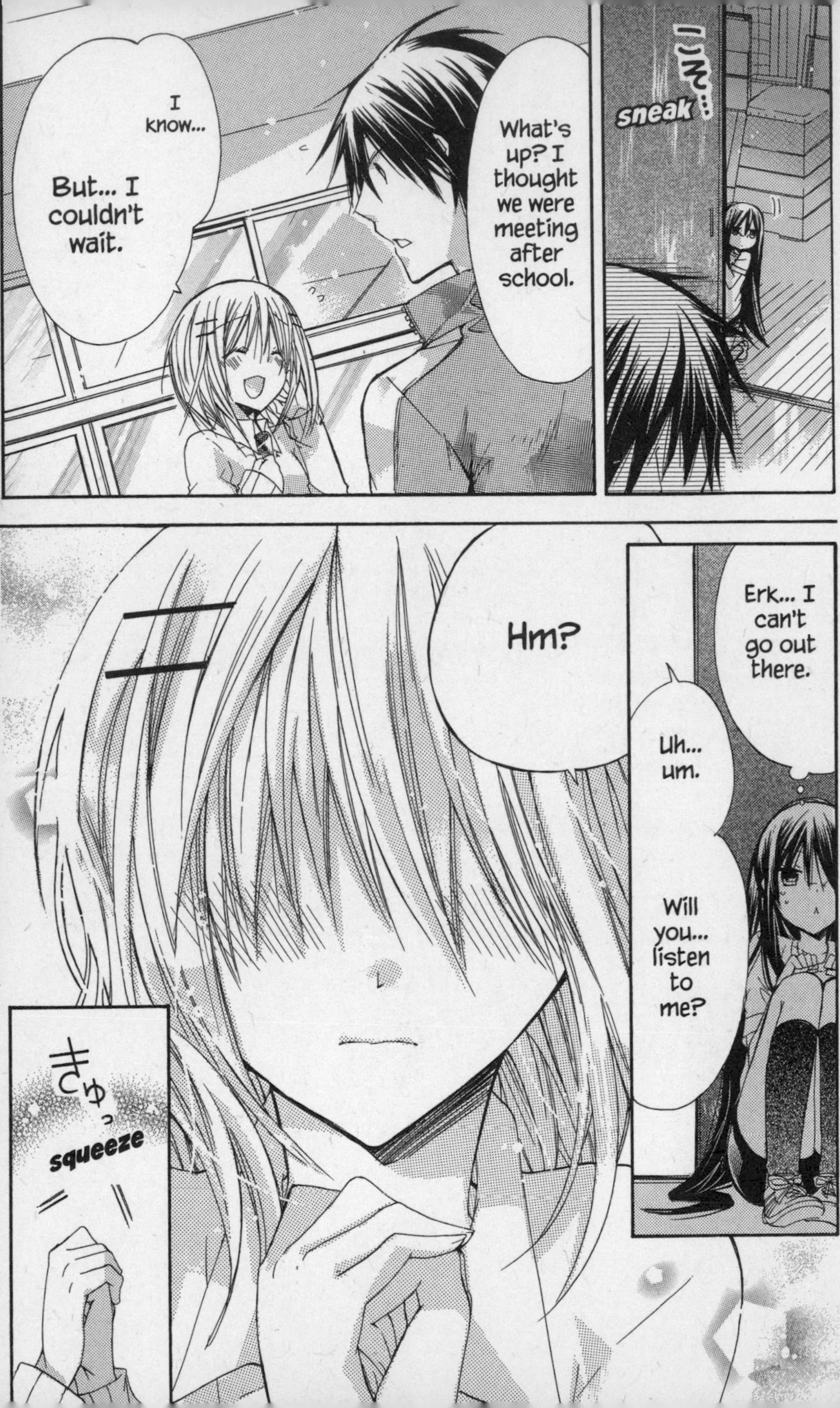
こそ…
sneak
What's up? I thought we were meeting after school.
I know...
But... I couldn't wait.
Erk... I can't go out there.
Hm?
Uh... um.
Will you... listen to me?
きゅっ
squeeze

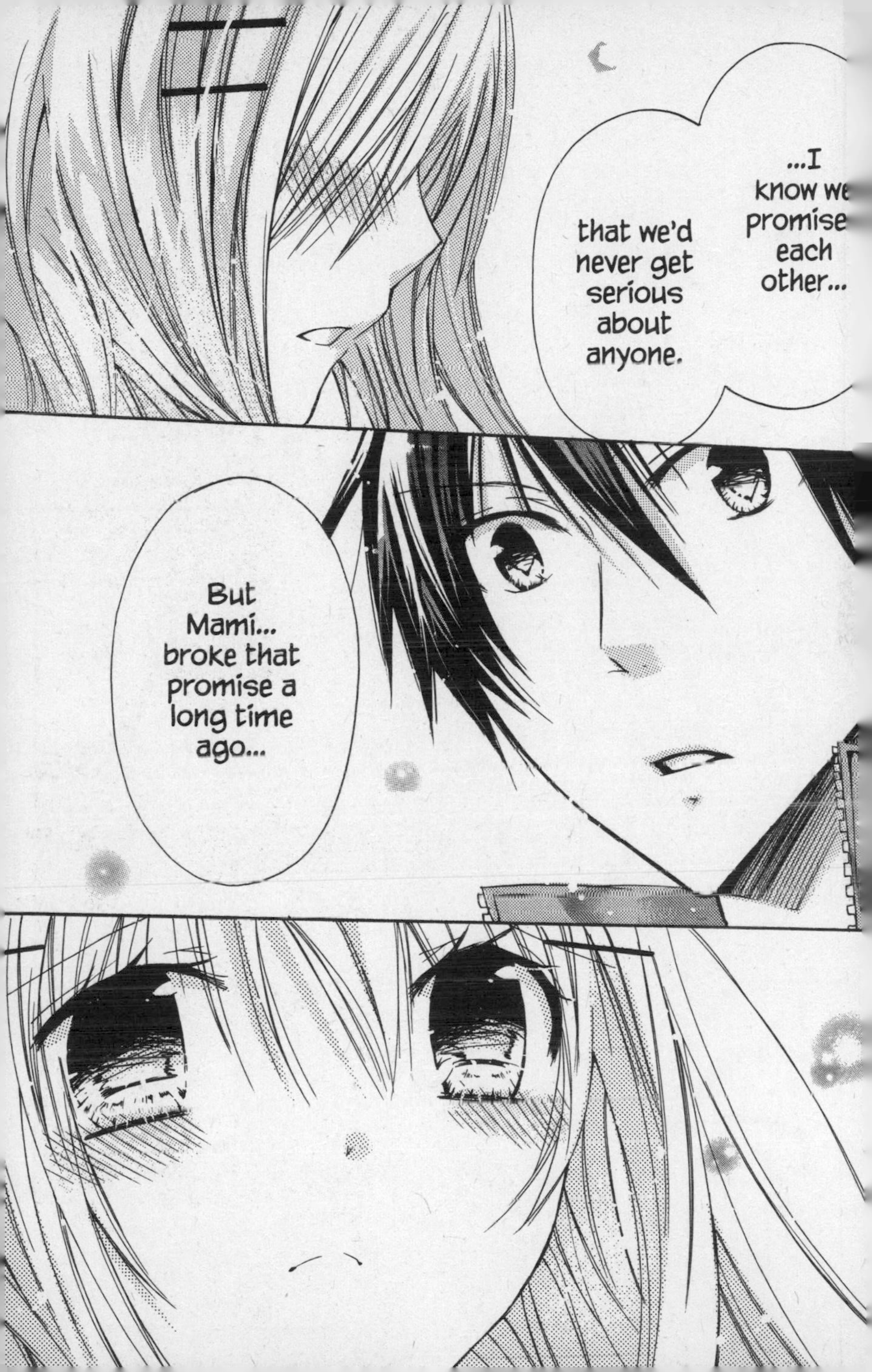
...I know we promise each other...
that we'd never get serious about anyone.
But Mami... broke that promise a long time ago...

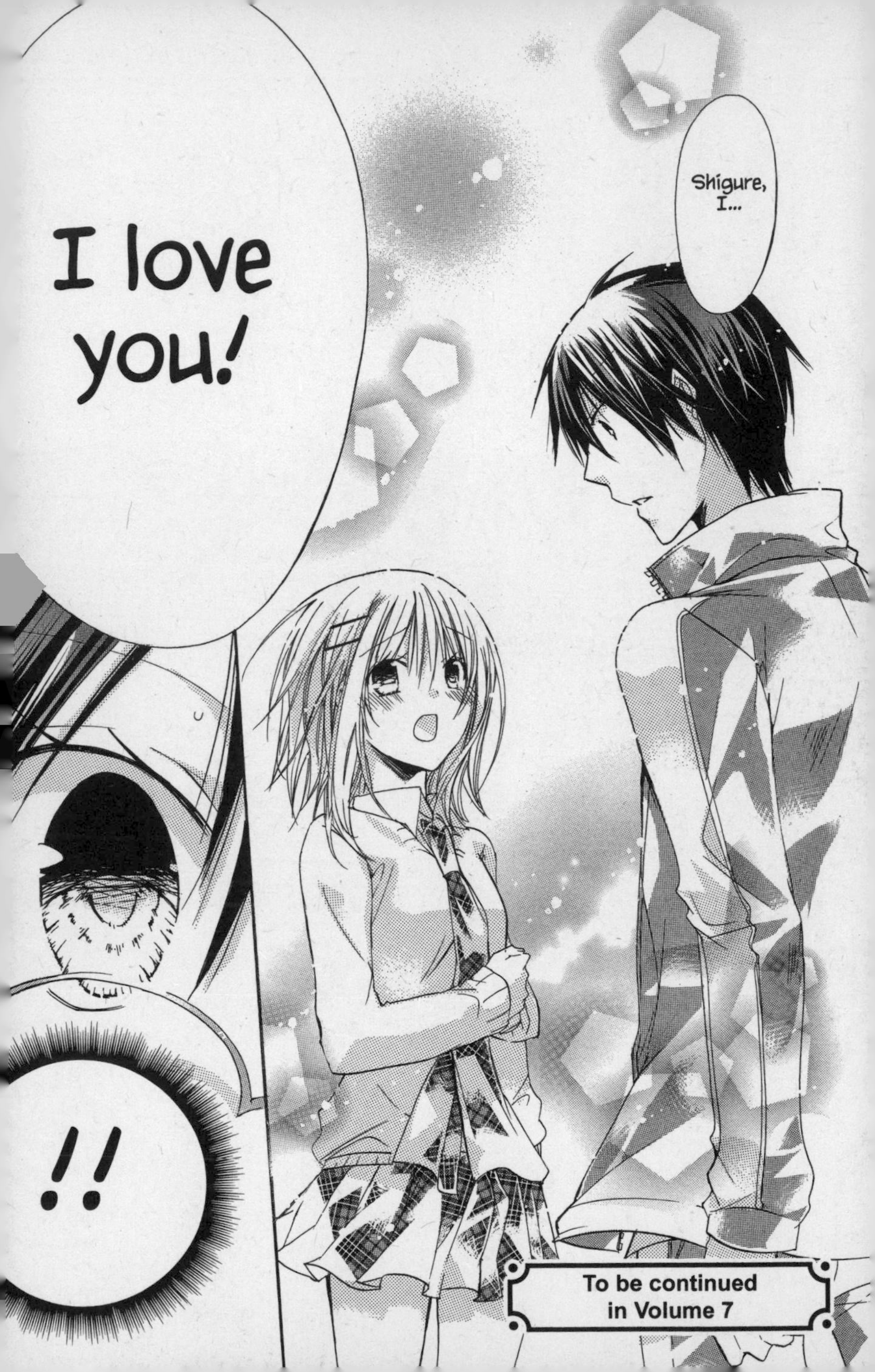
Shigure, I...
I love you!
!!
To be continued in Volume 7

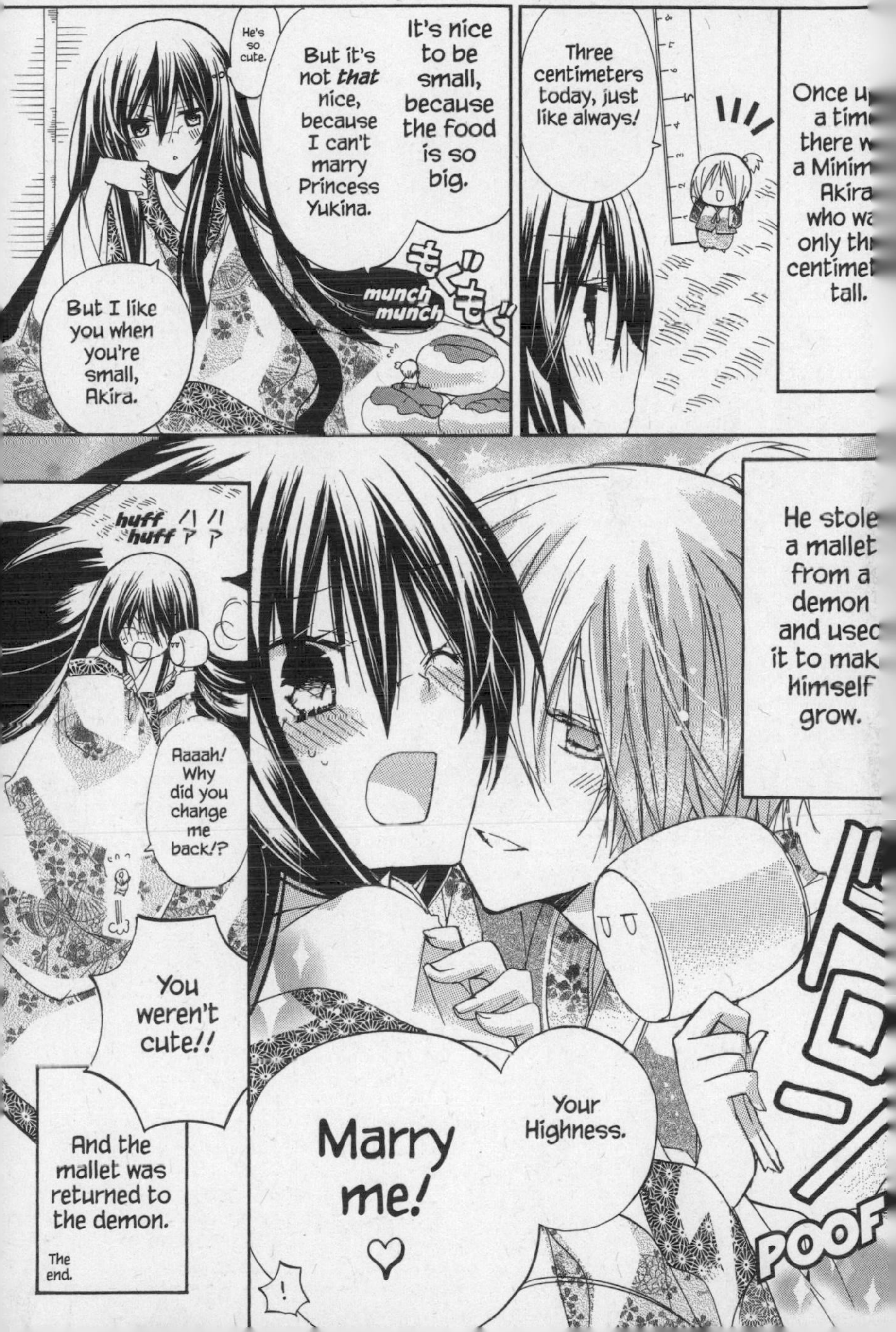
Once up a time there w a Minim Akira who wa only thr centimet tall.
Three centimeters today, just like always!
It's nice to be small, because the food is so big.
But it's not *that* nice, because I can't marry Princess Yukina.
He's so cute.
もぐもぐ
munch munch
But I like you when you're small, Akira.
He stole a mallet from a demon and usec it to mak himself grow.
POOF
Your Highness.
Marry me! ♡
!
huff huff
ハァ ハァ
Aaaah! Why did you change me back!?
You weren't cute!!
And the mallet was returned to the demon.
The end.

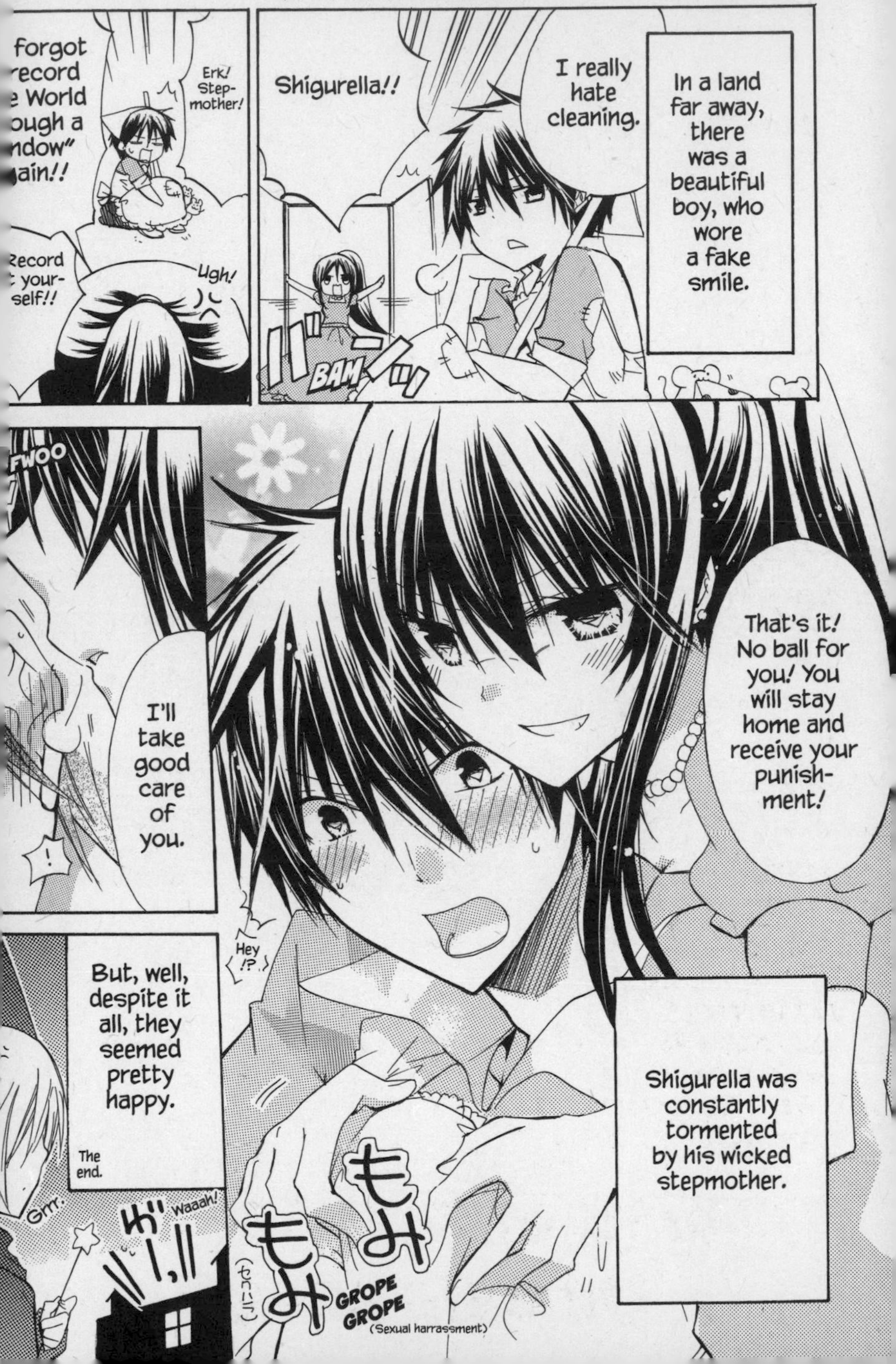
In a land far away, there was a beautiful boy, who wore a fake smile.
I really hate cleaning.
Shigurella!!
BAM
forgot
record
e World
ough a
ndow"
ain!!
Erk! Step-mother!
Record
t your-self!!
Ugh!
That's it! No ball for you! You will stay home and receive your punishment!
Hey !?
Shigurella was constantly tormented by his wicked stepmother.
もみもみ
(セクハラ)
GROPE GROPE
(Sexual harrassment)
FWOO
I'll take good care of you.
!
But, well, despite it all, they seemed pretty happy.
The end.
Waaah!
Grr.

I love you!

Shigure, I...

Shigure is shaken by Mami's confession.

He only had eyes

for me...

I can't do any of your missions anymore.

...If I start dating Mami,

"You and I will be inseparably connected." Was it all a lie? Shigure can think only of Mami, but Yukina...!?

A little more support for you.

...

I think I can spare

Missions of Love 7 On sale soon!!

thor: Ema Toyama
n May 23. Gemini.
od type B
but work: *Tenshi*
Tamago, winner of
n Annual Nakayoshi
wcomer Manga Award,
ecial Award, and
blished in the September
03 issue of *Nakayoshi*.
presentative Works:
ie Pop: Gokkun! Pūcho;
makore; *I Am Here!*
yama: Missions has
ually made it to volume
! I've been writing this
ies for two years, but I'm
finitely feeling the "time
s" thing. There are still a
of things I want to draw
this series; I hope I can
t through it all!

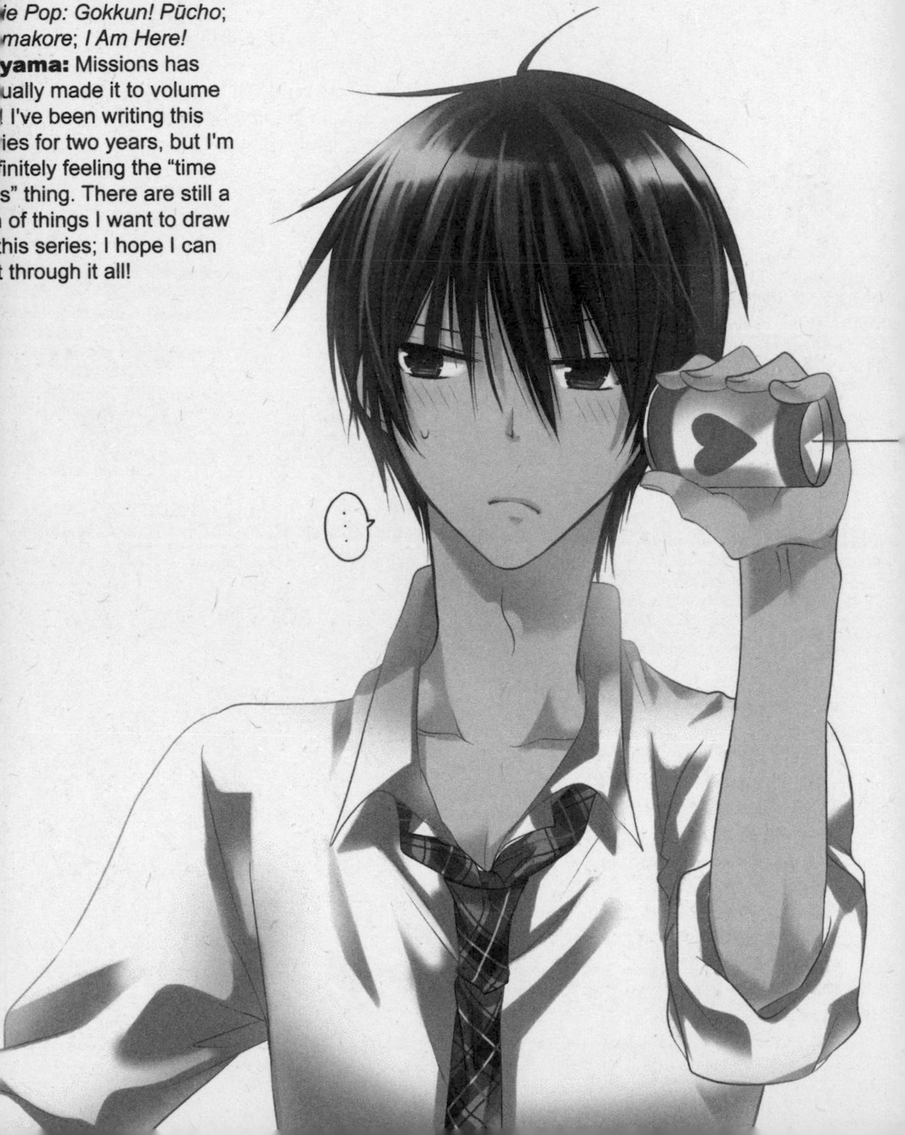

Translation Notes

Japanese is a tricky language for most Westerners, and translation is often more art th science. For your edification and reading pleasure, here are notes on some of the plac where we could have gone in a different direction with our translation of the work, or wh a Japanese cultural reference is used.

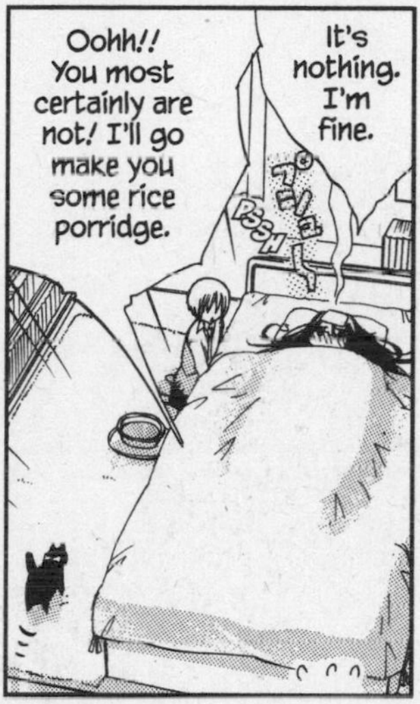
It's nothing. I'm fine.
Oohh!! You most certainly are not! I'll go make you some rice porridge.

Rice porridge, page 28
[28.4]
Rice porridge, or okayu, is a common dish served to people who are ill, because it is so easy to digest. It is made of mostly rice and water, possibly with some toppings, such as green onions or ginger, to add flavor.

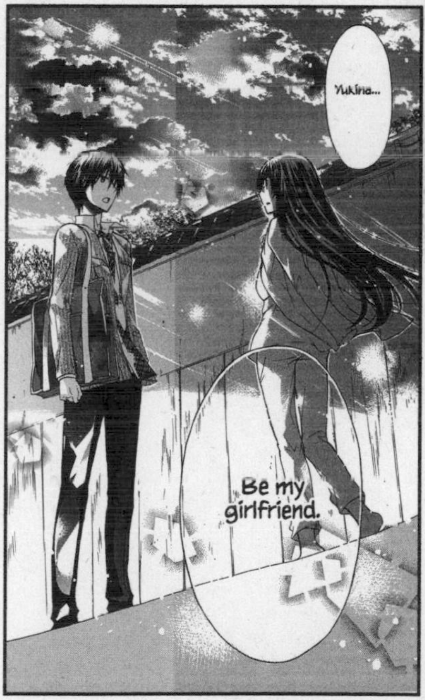
Yukina...
Be my girlfriend.

Be my girlfriend, page 82
[82.1]
A more literal translation of what Shigure said here would be, "Go out with me." That didn't seem to carry the same weight that Shigure seemed to be putting into this request, especially because in this case, he means it in the sense of, "Let's form a serious relationship," as opposed to, "Will you go out (on one date) with me?" He's saying, "Let's make this official," and so we the translators thought, "Be my girlfriend," would pack the punch that the situation called for.

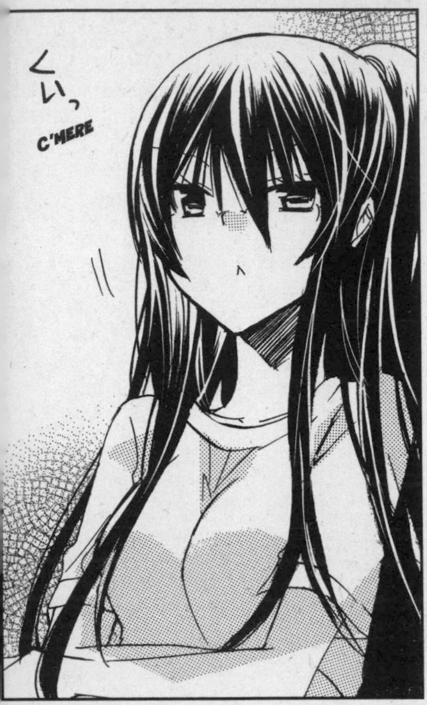
くい、
C'MERE

Beck and call, page 148

[148.4]

In Japanese, there is a phrase which roughly translates to "to use with the chin," which means "to boss people around." Here, Shigure is noticing that, not only is Yukina bossing him around, but she is literally doing it with her chin.

Vorld Masterpiece Theatre, page 166

166.1]

'he Japanese word used here for masterpiece" is a pun. Normally, ne Chinese characters used would ranslate to "famous work," but here, the haracters, though pronounced the same, nstead mean "confused/lost/disturbed vork." So a Japanese reader would now from first sight that this is more of "fractured" fairy tale—a silly version of ne original.

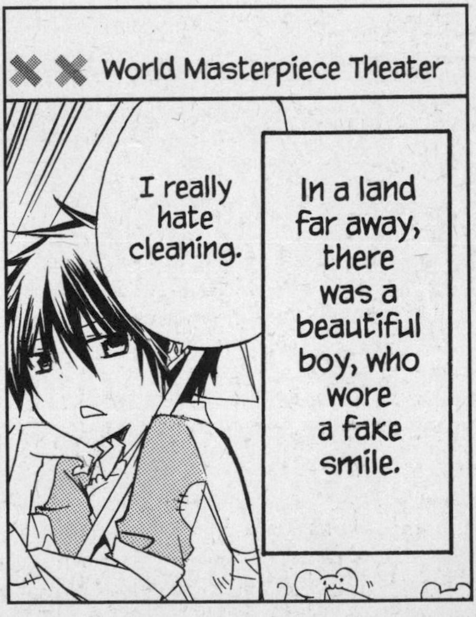
World Masterpiece Theater
In a land far away, there was a beautiful boy, who wore a fake smile.
I really hate cleaning.

SANKAREA

undying love

"I ONLY LIKE ZOMBIE GIRLS."

Chihiro has an unusual connection to zombie movies. He doesn't feel bad f
the survivors – he wants to comfort the undead girls they slaughter! When
his pet passes away, he brews a resurrection potion. He's discovered by
local heiress Sanka Rea, and she serves as his first test subject!

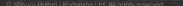

The Pretty Guardians
are back!

★

Kodansha Comics is proud to present
Sailor Moon with all new translations.

For more information, go to **www.kodanshacomics.com**

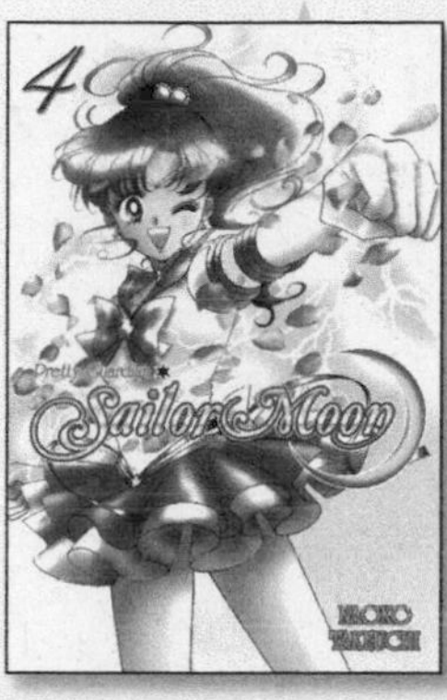
4
Pretty Guardian
Sailor Moon
NAOKO TAKEUCHI
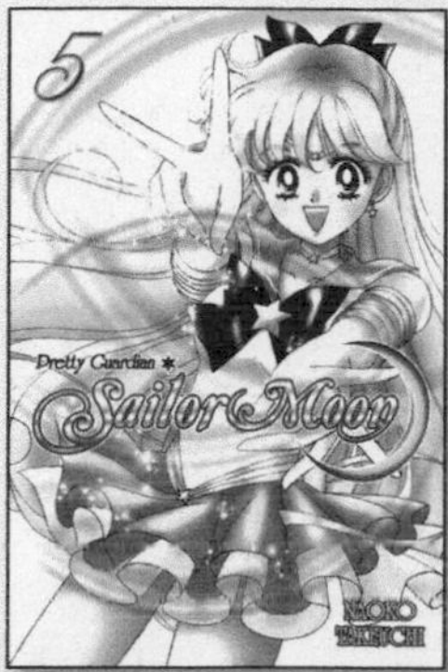
5
Pretty Guardian
Sailor Moon
NAOKO TAKEUCHI
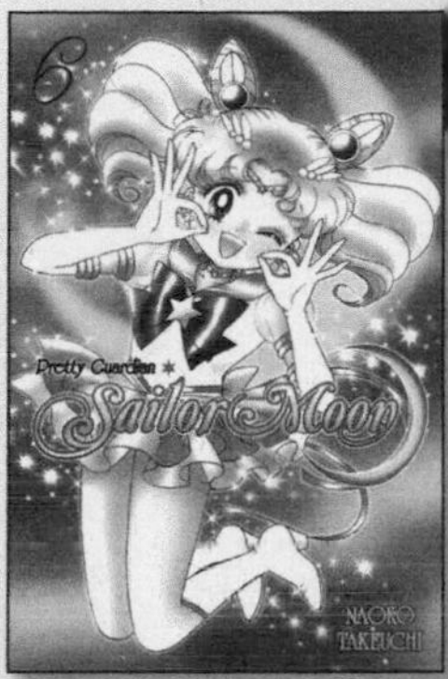
6
Pretty Guardian
Sailor Moon
NAOKO TAKEUCHI
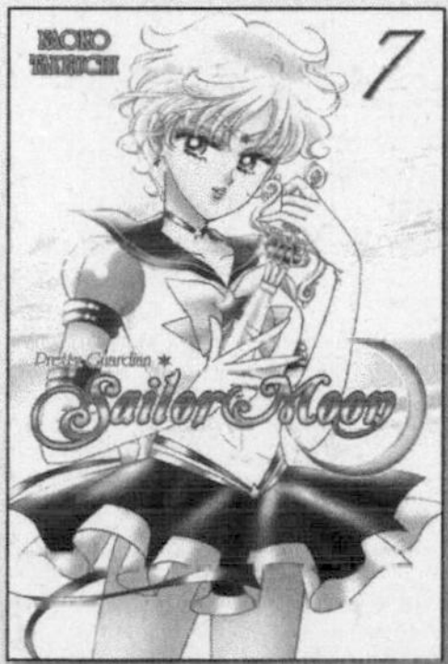
NAOKO TAKEUCHI
7
Pretty Guardian
Sailor Moon
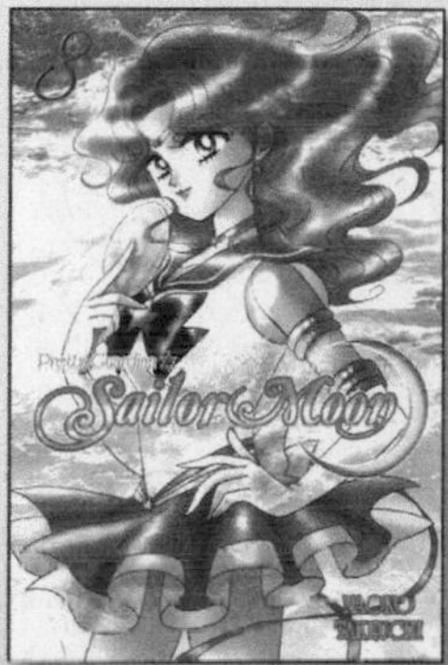
8
Pretty Guardian
Sailor Moon
NAOKO TAKEUCHI
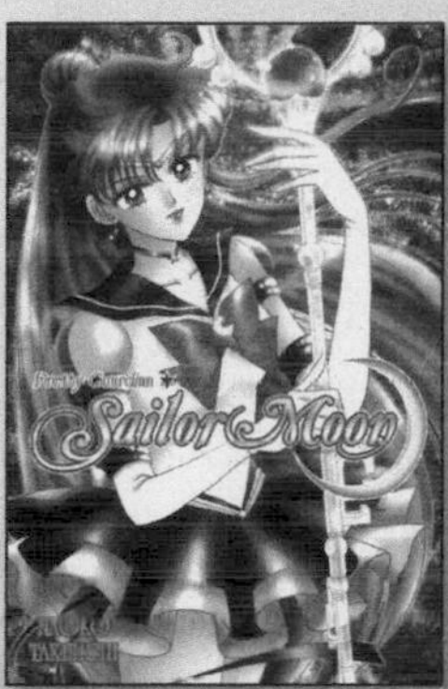
9
Pretty Guardian
Sailor Moon
NAOKO TAKEUCHI
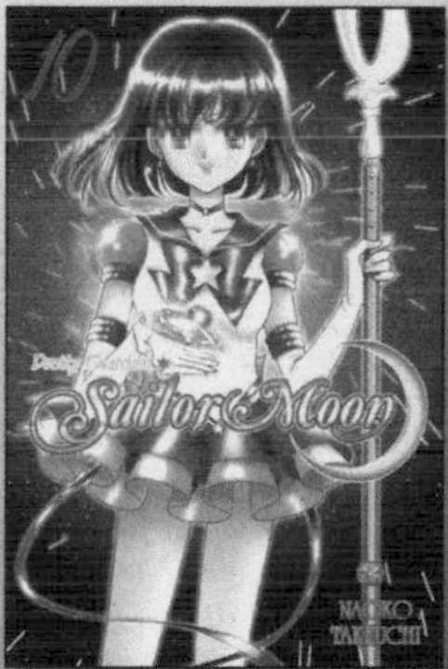
10
Pretty Guardian
Sailor Moon
NAOKO TAKEUCHI
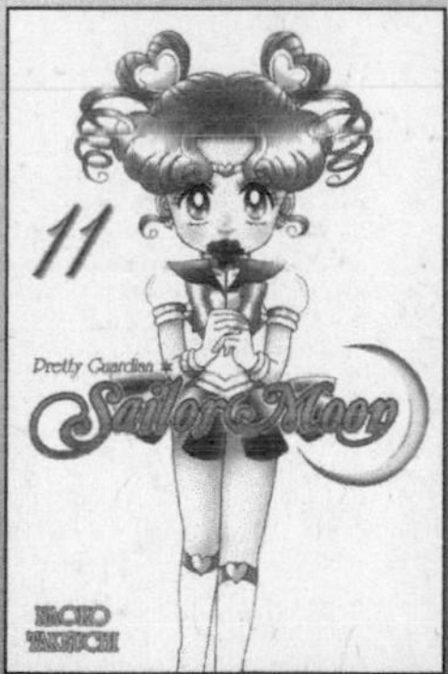
11
Pretty Guardian
Sailor Moon
NAOKO TAKEUCHI
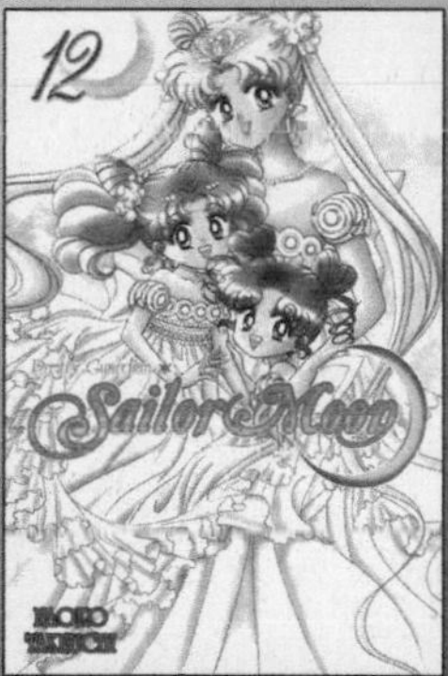
12
Pretty Guardian
Sailor Moon
NAOKO TAKEUCHI

KC
KODANSHA
COMICS

NO.6

A PERFECT LIFE IN A PERFECT CITY

r Shion, an elite student in the technologically sophisticated
ty No. 6, life is carefully choreographed. One fateful day, he
kes a misstep, sheltering a fugitive his age from a typhoon.
elping this boy throws Shion's life down a path to discovering
e appalling secrets behind the "perfection" of No. 6.

KC KODANSHA COMICS

A Kodansha Comics Trade Paperback Original.

Missions of Love volume 6 copyright © 2011 Ema Toyama
English translation copyright © 2014 Ema Toyama

All rights reserved.

Published in the United States by Kodansha Comics, an imprint of Kodansha USA Publishing, LLC, New York.

Publication rights for this English edition arranged through Kodansha Ltd., Tokyo.

First published in Japan in 2011 by Kodansha Ltd., Tokyo, as *Watashi ni xx shinasai!*, volume 6.

ISBN 978-1-61262-288-0

Printed in the United States of America.

www.kodanshacomics.com

9 8 7 6 5 4 3 2 1

Translator: Alethea Nibley and Athena Nibley
Lettering: Paige Pumphrey

Mission 0: Go Right to Left.

apanese manga is written and drawn from right to left, which ; opposite the way American graphic novels are composed. To reserve the original orientation of the art, and maintain the roper storytelling flow, this book has retained the right to left tructure. Please go to what would normally be the last page nd begin reading, right to left, top to bottom.

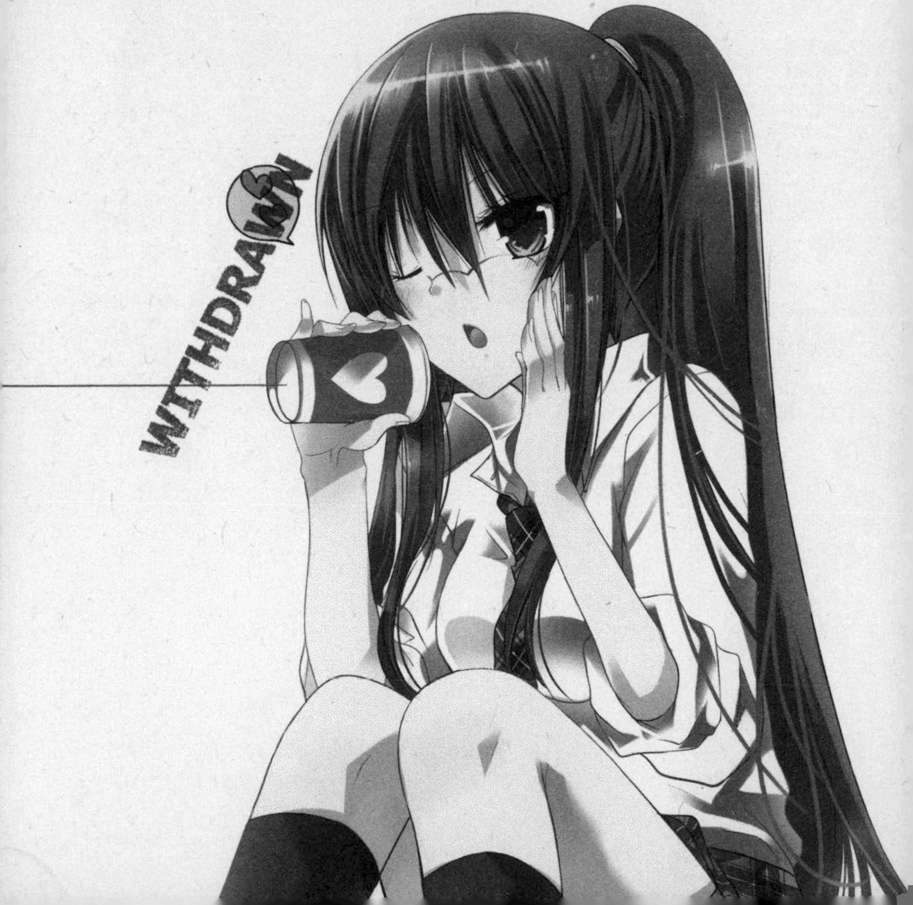